2056879

OCT 10 2012

The Oriental Obscene

D1570319

SYLVIA SHIN HUEY CHONG

The Oriental Obscene

Violence and Racial Fantasies in the Vietnam Era

DUKE UNIVERSITY PRESS *Durham and London 2012*

© 2012 Duke University Press

All rights reserved

Printed in the United States

of America on acid-free paper ∞

Designed by

Typeset in Quadraat by Keystone

Typesetting, Inc.

Library of Congress Cataloging-

in-Publication Data appear on

the last printed page of this book.

Contents

Illustrations

Notes on Terminology, Proper Names, and Film Titles

Since Asian American studies has criticized the term "oriental" as being racist, it may seem strange that I am resurrecting it for this study. My use of "oriental" rather than "Asian" is polemically motivated; I wish to rework Edward Said's notions of orientalism to apply to the American contexts and to distance the image of Asia and Asians produced in these texts from any strict reference to actual Asians and Asian nations. Also, following Lisa Lowe's practice in *Critical Terrains*, I do not capitalize the terms "oriental" and "orientalism" in order to emphasize the multiplicity and heterogeneity of objects and phenomena to which these terms refer.

I have written Chinese, Japanese, and Vietnamese surnames first and given names second to conform to the practice in these languages. The only exception is when such names have been partially Anglicized (e.g., Bruce Lee, Angela Mao). I use the last syllable of Vietnamese given names rather than the surname when referring to individuals (e.g., Ngo Dinh Diem is referred to as Diem or President Diem).

All film titles are followed by their year of release in parentheses at their first mention in each chapter. Names of characters in the films are followed by the actor's name in parentheses at their first mention. Films with multiple release titles are referred to by their most frequently used title, usually for U.S. release. Generally I transliterate Chinese titles into Mandarin using the *pinyin* Romanization system.

Acknowledgments

This book would not exist if I had not made that fateful switch from literary to film studies over ten years ago, in the Rhetoric Department at UC Berkeley. There I had the great fortune to work with brilliant scholars who were my professors and classmates. Above all, I need to acknowledge Linda Williams, who turned me onto film and constantly inspires me with her emotional strength and intellectual curiosity for strange topics. I also thank Anne Cheng, Colleen Lye, Carol Clover, and Kaja Silverman for being intellectual and professional role models, and my classmates who sustained me through many writing groups and seminars and are now scattered across the academic diaspora: Guo-Juin Hong, Scott Combs, Amy Corbin, Arne Lunde, Stuart Murray, Homay King, Masha Raskolnikov, Despina Kakoudaki, Nguyen Tan Hoang, Josephine Park, Jodi Kim, Steven Lee, and Marie Lo. I appreciate the dissertation seminar sponsored by the Department of Gender and Women's Studies and the Tangled Strands workshop sponsored by the Center for Race and Gender, both of which provided me with invaluable feedback during the early stages of this project.

Historical projects like this could not exist without the labor and resources of librarians and archivists. This project started with the excellent resources of the libraries at UC Berkeley, in particular the amazing film and video collection maintained by Gary Handman at the Media Resources Center and the Asian American studies resources collected by Wei-Chi Poon at the Ethnic Studies Library. The video store Le Video in San Francisco also supplied a vast collection of obscure martial arts films. I would also like to thank Barbara Hall, special collections librarian at the Margaret Herrick Library at the Academy of Motion Picture Arts and Sciences in Los Angeles, and the staff at both the Los Angeles and New York branches of the Museum of Television and Radio (now called the Paley Center for Media). At UCLA the Film and Television Archive and Judy Soo Hoo at the Asian American Studies Center also provided invaluable assistance. And the librarians at my home institution,

University of Virginia, especially the staff of the Robertson Media Center, have done mountains of work for this project, from scanning articles and chapters to acquiring obscure films and books.

The Society for Cinema and Media Studies and the Association for Asian American Studies have added so much to my professional life, and I must thank them for helping to create a sense of intellectual community for the two very fragmented, interdisciplinary fields to which I belong. The Asian Pacific American Caucus at SCMS has nurtured me since I was a graduate student, and I've been overjoyed to pay them back in official and unofficial ways. Thanks to my SCMS and AAAS colleagues: Eng-Beng Lim, Celine Parrenas-Shimizu, Jane Park, L. S. Kim, Sean Metzger, James Kim, Nitasha Sharma, Anita Mannur, Cathy Schlund-Vials, John Cheng, Julia Lee, Shilpa Dave, Camilla Fojas, Jeffrey Santa Ana, Glenn Man, Peter Feng, and Karen Tongson.

I am grateful to the Woodrow Wilson Career Enhancement Fellowship and the University of Virginia's Sesquicentennial Sabbatical Fellowship for helping me carve out crucial writing and research time. The Wilson fellowship also introduced me to a wonderful group of scholars I might not have otherwise met, especially Robert Lee and Naoko Shibusawa. The Futures of Asian America symposium organized by James Kim at Fordham helped me refine my introduction, and I thank Evelyn Hu-DeHart, Allan Punzalan Isaac, and Vijay Prashad for their feedback. At UVa the Arts and Sciences Research Support paid for some of the beautiful and painful images that accompany this book, and the Excellence in Diversity Fellowship funded other research materials.

I could not have survived these past few years without the laughter, teasing, and encouragement of my UVa friends across the university: Pensri Ho, Daisy Rodriguez, Sarah Wilcox Elliott, Amori Yee Mikami, Nancy Deutsch, Antonia Lolordo, Jennifer Tsien, Mark Ilsemann, Mrinalini Chakravorty, Marlon Ross, Susan Fraiman, Caroline Rody, Allison Booth, Andrea Press, Richard Handler, Geeta Patel, and Kath Weston. I also thank the following colleagues for reading and commenting on numerous drafts of this book: Lisa Woolfork, Victoria Olwell, Hector Amaya, Jen Petersen, Daniel Chavez, Rita Felski, Steve Arata, Siva Vaidhyanathan, Franny Nudelman, Eric Lott, Grace Hale, and Sandhya Shukla. The American Studies Program at UVa has been a welcoming and comfortable home, helping me to grow from a film theorist into a cultural historian. I have also learned so much from my graduate students Sarah Hagelin, Sarah Bishop, Swan Kim, and Shaun Cullen, and they have also helped me refine this book for a wider audience. Special thanks to Jean Franzino and Sarah Bishop for compiling the index. Jolie Sheffer and Michael

Lewis have helped me feel at home in the English Department and in Charlottesville. Madelyn Wessel gave invaluable advice on how to incorporate images into this book. My undergraduate students are a constant inspiration to me, in their activism, their enthusiasm, and their knowledge about this changing world; Huong Nguyen, Douglas Lee, and Navdeep Singh were the first, but they've been followed by many who continue to make me proud.

An earlier version of chapter 3 appeared as "Restaging the War: *The Deer Hunter* and the Primal Scene of Violence," *Cinema Journal* 44.2 (2005), 89–106.

I am honored to be working with the amazing professionals at Duke University Press and am lucky to have Ken Wissoker as my friend, mentor, and editor. This book has often felt like an unwanted and overdue baby, and Ken has been an intellectual and psychological midwife and helped see this project through, from conception to delivery.

Finally, I thank the Chong family—my parents, Ten and Lily, and my brother, Howard—for making me who I am today; my friends Alana Lee, who although not an academic anymore remains always an intellectual, and Alyssa Apsel, who understands academia well but maybe not this crazy humanities stuff; and my husband, Michael Puri, who contains multitudes from the air, the land, and the sea.

SPECTERS OF VIETNAM

Hello, Kuwait. Goodbye, Vietnam. Next month 16 years will have passed since Americans and their friends scrambled from rooftops into helicopters and left Saigon to Vietnam's victorious communists. The pain of that and so many other Vietnam memories—the dead children of My Lai, the shock of Tet '68, the coups and countercoups, the fraggings, the drugs, the invasion of Cambodia, the killing of American students at Kent State—somehow only increased as the years passed. When the U.S.-led forces raced across Kuwait and Iraq last week, however, they may have defeated not just the Iraqi army but also the more virulent of the ghosts from the Vietnam era: self-doubt, fear of power, divisiveness, a fundamental uncertainty about America's purpose in the world.

—Stanley W. Cloud, "The Home Front: Exorcising
an Old Demon," *Time*, 11 March 1991

What does it mean to view the present through the lens of the past? Even before it officially began, the Persian Gulf War of 1991 was seen as a second coming of the Vietnam War, both by those who welcomed it and those who dreaded its return. While the administration of President George Herbert Walker Bush tried to reassure an anxious public that this war would not become "another Vietnam," some sideline spectators saw the Persian Gulf War as an auspicious reincarnation of the Vietnam era, allowing the nation to right its historical wrongs. Uncannily echoing the publicity for the film *Rambo: First Blood Part II* (1985), the historian Robert Dallek exclaimed of the Persian Gulf War, "It's Vietnam revisited, Vietnam the movie, Part II, and this time it comes out right." On the verge of victory Bush claimed the role of national exorcist and psychoanalyst in banishing this unwelcome historical ghost. On 1 March 1991, two days after he announced the liberation of Kuwait at the end of this forty-two-day war, Bush proclaimed to a gathering of state legislators in Washington, "It's a proud day for America and, by God, we've kicked the Vietnam syndrome once and for all!" The following day, in a radio address to U.S. troops in the Persian Gulf, Bush repeated his triumphant claim in different words: "The specter of Vietnam has been buried forever in the desert sands of the Arabian Peninsula."[1]

Kicking the Vietnam Syndrome

The trope of describing the Vietnam War as a national trauma for the U.S. is omnipresent not only in popular and journalistic invocations but also throughout academic histories and cultural analyses. Modeled on an analogy of the nation to the individual subject, the "Vietnam syndrome" or the "specter of Vietnam" not only imagines the U.S. nation-state as wounded like the soldiers it sent to war, but also calls upon the discourses of forgiveness and redemption to heal the nation of its psychological malaise. In one of its earliest invocations, in the early 1980s, Philip L. Geyelin defined the Vietnam syndrome as composed of several disparate symptoms: policymakers' ambivalence toward the use of military force as an all-or-nothing option, legislators' anxious second-guessing of presidential diplomatic and military decisions, and the media's cynicism toward all actions of the government.[2] But in addition to these visible effects on public institutions, the Vietnam syndrome was also an affective disorder, coloring the mood of the nation, as seen in this reflection by one who had a hand in creating it, Richard Nixon: "Many of our leaders have shrunk from any use of power because they feared it would bring another disaster like the one in Vietnam. Thus did our Vietnam defeat tarnish our ideals, weaken our spirit, cripple our will, and turn us into a military giant and a diplomatic dwarf in a world in which the steadfast exercise of American power was needed more than ever before."[3] In Nixon's melodramatic language the emasculated leaders become metonymies of the nation-state, their tarnished ideals and crippled wills becoming ours through a contagion of weakness and passivity. Borrowing from both Nixon's first-person plural and Reagan's "war" on drugs, Bush Sr. recast the Vietnam syndrome as a national addiction to defeat and cynicism that only his strong leadership could kick on behalf of the nation, although more skeptical critics like June Jordan likened the spell of victory to a "hit [of] crack [that] doesn't last long."[4] To bury the specter of Vietnam is to reassert the wholeness and power of the nation in the face of a trauma that has paralyzed its legislative and military resolve.

However, embedded within these analogies is also a confusion of agency that undoes the stability attributed to this nation-subject. As Fred Turner asked in *Echoes of Combat: The Vietnam War in American Memory*, "Was Vietnam something Americans did? Or was it something that happened to them?"[5] Whether disembodied in the form of a ghost or a psychological ailment, the Vietnam War is transformed in these metaphors from an active endeavor to a passive suffering. The metaphor itself performs the cultural work attributed to its overcoming, burying the corpses—not only Americans of all races, but also Vietnamese, Cambodian, Laotian, Filipino, South Korean, and Thai— underlying the trauma of the Vietnam War, and replacing them with what Stanley Cloud of *Time* magazine describes as the other "ghosts" of Vietnam: "self-doubt, fear of power, divisiveness, a fundamental uncertainty about America's purpose in the world." Thus this initial transformation from activity to passivity stages its own reversal, allowing the Vietnam syndrome itself to be buried by the repetition of another war in the Persian Gulf.

Interestingly this national recovery takes place not on the analyst's couch but within the public sphere, through the images of the national media. Unlike the unconscious kernels of individual trauma that must be laboriously uncovered by the work of psychotherapy, the national trauma of Vietnam is glaringly manifest, present in the images of the Vietnam War produced not only by newspapers and television news but also by fictional films and other cultural narratives. When the journalist Stanley Cloud spoke of the "pain of . . . Vietnam memories," he located them not in the psychic contents of individual subjects, but in these visual objects of the national media: the iconic photojournalistic representations of My Lai, Tet '68, and Kent State, as well as the fictional dramatizations of fraggings (intentional friendly fire) and drug abuse found in popular films such as *Apocalypse Now* (1979). Susan Jeffords, Marita Sturken, Katherine Kinney, and many others have persuasively established the role of the visual mass media in constituting the collective memory of the Vietnam era—including not only the war, but the social and cultural movements shaped by their encounter with the war.[6] These images were not simply records of a historical past whose experience lay elsewhere. Because of their mass distribution in the public sphere, these images *were* the Vietnam War for many Americans, supplementing and shaping the memories even of those who served in the war.

On one level these images constitute a shared repertoire of visual memories that construct the U.S. as what Benedict Anderson calls an "imagined community," building a web of relations among the nation's citizens through the mediated experience of simultaneity and shared suffering.[7] On another level these images also complicate and perhaps subvert the notion of the imagined community by pointing to fragments of historical reality that are only incompletely digested by the process of national consumption and that subvert the centripetal forces of national consolidation. Their manifest appearance notwithstanding, these images point to a latency in the national imagined community, a psychic opacity that itself contributes to the traumatic effects associated with the Vietnam syndrome. What defines trauma is not simply the suffering of a violent shock, but the inability to fully comprehend that experience. If these images are symptoms of the Vietnam syndrome, it is not because they are evidence of tragic events, but because they depict scenarios that continue to elude our mastery, that refuse to be contained in historical narratives that close them off in a distant past.

In contrast to these messy, even obscene pictures of violence and civil disorder, the Persian Gulf War seemed to produce a series of clean, new images that directly rebutted the Vietnam syndrome. The dense, crowded greens of the Vietnam jungle and the black "pajama-clad" Vietnamese peasant-guerrillas gave way to the expansive pale deserts of Kuwait and the light, sand-colored uniforms of the professional armies of Iraq and the U.S. Based on a myth that images of wounded bodies turned the American public against the Vietnam War, the U.S. military took care to distance itself from the images of racialized violence that dominated perceptions of that war. In a double strategy of censorship (of images of bodily injury) and proliferation (of images of military technology) the military tried to avoid depicting racialized bodies in the Persian Gulf War altogether, substituting, in Margot Norris's words, the "hard" targets of weaponry, machinery, and buildings for the "soft" targets of Iraqi and Kuwaiti casualties.[8] In contrast to the images of Tet, My Lai, and Kent State, the most memorable symbol of the Persian Gulf War was reported to be the Patriot missile.[9] Despite the knowledge that this war was, like all wars, a violent event with significant casualties, especially on the Iraqi side, its visual representation was sanitized of such referents, leading Jean Baudrillard to ask, "Did the Gulf War take place?"[10]

Nonetheless the specter of Vietnam haunts one of the visual icons of the Persian Gulf War, belying these assertions of cleanliness and mastery. On the eve of victory in the Persian Gulf, both the New York Times and the Washington Post paired two photographs: a contemporary image taken by an anonymous Reuters photographer of U.S. marines landing by helicopter on a rooftop in Kuwait City to liberate the capital from Iraqi control, and an iconic image of the Vietnam War, Hubert Van Es's photograph of the fall of Saigon in 1975 (fig. 1). This historical photograph depicted what Stanley Cloud called "Americans and their friends scrambl[ing] from rooftops into helicopters and le[aving] Saigon to Vietnam's victorious communists." E. J. Dionne

1. Hubert Van Es's photograph of an evacuation by helicopter from the fall of Saigon, taken 29 April 1975. Source: Bettmann/CORBIS.

commented in the *Washington Post* that "there was no more powerful symbol of the transformation" of the Vietnam syndrome than the reversal between these two photographs.[11] These photographs thus became not only symptoms but the substance of this psychic transformation: the pain literally embodied by Van Es's photograph is answered not by an action, but by another photograph, one which quite literally restages the older image in order to resignify through it. As a reporter for the *New York Times* remarked, "There is an eerie similarity: military helicopters, rooftop landings in U.S. Embassy compounds, figures clambering through wide cargo doors. But the two images evoke a stunning difference in how two wars will be remembered: one helicopter brought in proud marines, the other carried out frightened evacuees." Saigon becomes Kuwait City, an evacuation becomes an arrival, fleeing families become liberating marines, and defeat becomes victory, all around the structuring figure of a military helicopter on the rooftop of a foreign building.[12] However, these inversions do not erase the previous image, which remains ghosted into the peripheral vision of the present.

However, even the Van Es photograph is far from historical bedrock for the Vietnam era. Contrary to popular memory, it does not depict "Americans being evacuated from U.S. Embassy compound in Saigon," as a caption in the *Chicago Tribune* asserted in 1975. Instead it shows the families of South

Vietnamese officials fleeing from the rooftop of an apartment building in downtown Saigon where CIA employees were housed.[13] From a distance, the camera paints a form of racial drag upon these bodies, allowing these South Vietnamese allies to be mistaken for American bodies, and thus framing the fall of Saigon as an American retreat from a foreign territory and the end of a war rather than a South Vietnamese exodus from a homeland and the beginnings of a diaspora. Van Es recounts that this misunderstanding became "a metaphor for all the misunderstanding that plagued the Vietnam War. Americans, whether conservative or liberal, often imposed their own ideas on that troubling war."[14] It is striking that, at this moment of triumph for U.S. militarism in 1991, Van Es's photograph would yet again be misunderstood in the service of symbolizing America's past historical trauma. The relationship between Van Es's image and the Reuters photograph of 1991 is not only one of inverted action, but of racial substitution, as U.S. marines triumph over the Vietnam syndrome in Kuwait by taking the place, not of fleeing Americans, but of South Vietnamese families soon to become postwar refugees in America, all against a background that erases both Kuwait and Iraq by incorporating them into the historical quagmire of Vietnam.

As a reminder that the disembodied specter of the Vietnam syndrome had a material and racial referent, some Vietnamese Americans spoke out during the Persian Gulf War against the reduction of their country of origin and themselves to mere historical ghosts. Pham Thanh, in a New York Times op-ed piece titled "My Two Countries, My Flesh and Blood," asserted against the dominant rhetoric employed by politicians and journalists, "Vietnam is not a myth, a metaphor, or a memory."[15] Similarly Andrew Lam wrote in the Nation that Vietnam "has become a vault filled with tragic metaphors for every American to use," and related the complaint of his uncle, a former pilot in the South Vietnamese Air Force, that "when Americans say 'Vietnam,' they don't mean Vietnam."[16] Thanh too is haunted by the ghosts of Vietnam—but not in the form of historical or national trauma. Rather he mourns the loss of his family during the Vietnam War: "My father was beaten to death by South Vietnamese soldiers as he demonstrated outside an American base against the bombing and shelling of our village. A few months later, my mother and grandmother were killed when a G.I. threw a grenade into our bomb shelter." Both Thanh and Lam—essentially children of the Vietnam War, although on different sides of the conflict—attempt to reinscribe in the American public sphere a memory of losses that the Vietnamese too incurred from the war, along with American complicity for those losses, all the while asserting their own claims on being part of the American nation. These dead and wounded

Vietnamese haunt the U.S. as well, casting an invisible racial phantasm into every image of the Vietnam War.

This visual palimpsest of the fall of Saigon beneath the liberation of Kuwait resists the conscious attempt to rewrite the memory of the Vietnam War through the Persian Gulf War, and ultimately shows how images cannot simply be reduced to narrative but retain the weight of their historical, material referents that lie within the field of perception but outside the grasp of conscious thought. As indexical media, photography and film are constructed not from the infinite play of linguistic signifiers, but depend quite directly on the material and historical substance of the world for their meaning. This is why, despite their propensity for commodification and mass reproduction, photography and film were heralded by Walter Benjamin as having the potential to isolate and reveal the "hidden details of familiar objects" which previously "floated along unnoticed in the broad stream of perception."[17] This optical unconscious, as Benjamin called it, opens indexical visual media to a materialist political critique that differs from the textual phantasmagoria that many scholars have associated with the linguistic turn in the humanities and the cultural turn in historiography. As Tom Gunning describes it, the optical unconscious erupts through photography and film as an "invasion of social history," as the camera records more than can be consciously or ideologically accounted for.[18] In my use of the term, the optical unconscious is not merely a negative unconscious in the sense of censorship (i.e., that which is excluded from the image); it is closer to what Foucault called a "positive unconscious," a set of structures, relations, and "rules of formation" that make possible the enunciation of desires and narratives.[19] Just as the individual unconscious may draw on the materials of everyday life to stage and structure its articulations of latent desire, the national unconscious makes use of these visual objects from film and photography—textual, but nonetheless material—as the conditions of possibility for articulating the political and social desires of its national subjects, and even the possibility of defining such desires as *national* to begin with.

The productivity of the optical unconscious is evident in the structural similarities between these two photographs of the Vietnam and Persian Gulf Wars. Although the Reuters photographer and the U.S. soldiers in Kuwait may not have intended to re-create Van Es's "Fall of Saigon," it is not pure coincidence that both photographs center on a similar scenario: the American military helicopter—a "Huey" or Bell UH-1 Iroquois in Vietnam, and an AH-64 Apache in Kuwait—performing a feat of technological mastery, ferrying the first or last U.S. occupants of a tiny piece of American territory embedded within a hostile foreign land.[20] The icon of the helicopter invokes not only the two historical endpoints marked by these photographs, but also a terrain of alternative scenarios, both fictional and nonfictional, from other periods: the "telecopter" surveillance of U.S.-domestic urban unrest in the early 1960s and in 1992, the failed helicopter rescue "Operation Eagle Claw" during the Iran hostage crisis, the Wagnerian helicopter raid of *Apocalypse Now*, and even the restaging of the fall of Saigon in the climax of *The Deer Hunter* (1978). Furthermore the sense of narrative opening or closure signified by these actions—the "fall" of Saigon, the "liberation" of Kuwait—invites journalists to commemorate these events for the home audience, and these photographers are not simply neutral bystanders at these events but are authorized witnesses acting in the service of the U.S. military. And of course there are those South Vietnamese bodies in the earlier photograph, who were never erased from the image but simply recast in a different drama, their symbolic incorporation into the American national body masking the historical expulsion of waves of Asians from the U.S. body politic. Similarly we may never know the race of the U.S. marines landing in Kuwait, but again the narrative draped over the Reuters photograph parallels the military uniforms on their bodies, both conscripting a multiracial army to stand in for a nation marked invisibly as white. Thus the repetition compulsion of this scenario in both photographs is a sign of the enduring political and military structures that have persisted during the historical interval between them, and which have been unwittingly captured along with the ostensible narratives that these images are supposed to illustrate. These material hidden details function like the detritus of everyday life in Freudian dream-work, producing an endless cycle of fantasies and narratives to make sense of their opacity.

In this book I propose to read the optical unconscious of the American imagined community as revealed through the myriad indexical visual representations of the Vietnam War from the late 1960s to the early 1980s. The Reuters and Van Es photographs provide one small example of the larger textual network that I investigate: not only newspaper photographs, but also television news, documentaries, and fictional films, all linked by shared scenarios imagining the Vietnam War. *Indexicality* will be a key concept in my analyses of these texts, but in a more capacious sense than the mere fact of a connection between indexical visual texts and the material reality they represent. Indexical texts not only contain the physical traces of people, places, and objects, but they also register the social and historical formations that bring such constellations of material reality together in the image.[21] In the case of nonfictional texts such as journalistic photographs, television newscasts, and documentary film indexicality includes not only the events and phenomena they purport to document, but also the situations that enabled such images to be produced in the first place: the presence of American journalists and cameras or the desire to reproduce on film first-person testimony of lost events. But fictional texts such as television dramas and narrative films are also indexical, even if their characters and plots are artificially constructed. The actors, directors, producers, and distribution companies are embodied agents whose personal histories—including their social positions, oeuvres of prior or future work, relations to other subjects, films, or contexts—are fleetingly captured by the moving images they help produce. Thus in my film analyses I attend to such elements from production and reception histories to augment more formalist reading techniques, but both methodologies are directed toward elucidating the content of the image that is ultimately framed and thus distributed.

In one sense these visual texts consciously represent the Vietnam era to its participants, converting direct experience into visual forms that can be widely disseminated, debated, and shared throughout the national community. But in another sense these visual texts also outline unconscious structures of relations that generate particular political desires in excess of direct experience. The path from Vietnam War to Vietnam syndrome traces an imaginary space of racial encounter between a multiracial American body politic and these racialized foreign bodies. In this imaginary space the emphasis is not on the discovery of authentic or realistic racial subject positions, but on imagined racial relations between the white, black, and Asian American personas interacting with these oriental bodies in extremis. Thus this book has two goals: a historiographic one that attempts to write a new history of the visual mass media of the Vietnam era that accounts for the visibility of Asian and Asian American bodies in these cultural texts, and also a theoretical one that draws upon psychoanalysis and film theory to provide new models for thinking about the relationship of cultural texts to racial and national politics.

In particular I am interested in one set of relations, which I term the "racial phantasmatic," building on the work of the French psychoanalyst Jean Laplanche. Racial phantasmatics describe imagined relations of identification, projection, transference, and countertransference between different racial subject positions, in ways that exceed the actual social relations between racialized subjects. The Vietnam era generates an especially fascinating set of imagined relations around the Vietnamese body-subject, which is situated within a nexus of relations involving Asian Americans, African Americans, Latino/as, Native Americans, and white Americans, as well as participating in the shaping of normative masculinity and femininity across racial lines. Even Asian Americans, a new political coalition and racial subject position that arose in the late 1960s, draw upon this racial phantasmatic to build their own imagined relations and similarities with a Vietnamese diaspora they have little contact with until the late 1970s, when significant numbers of Vietnamese begin migrating to the U.S. Thus the racial phantasmatic becomes a generative matrix for a Deleuzian politics—a becoming–Asian American, becoming-black, becoming-woman, becoming-nation—that takes place through the form of the indexical image. Drawing as well on Deleuze's film theory I will argue that the visual mass media—photography, television, film—articulate their own kinds of political thought through movement-images and time-images that exceed the meanings generated from existing ideological or narratological analyses, opening up spaces for productive crises of affect, ethics, and meaning.

There are many kinds of racial phantasmatics overlapping in American culture; Eric Lott's study of blackface minstrelsy and Philip Deloria's work on "playing Indian" describe other examples of this phenomenon.[22] But the specific racial phantasmatic I investigate is that of the "oriental obscene": a set of fantasies that reveal the relation between suffering and violation, activity and passivity, and victimhood and victory in the politics of the Vietnam War. Because of the enormous impact of the Vietnam War on U.S. social movements as well as the popular culture of the 1960s through the 1980s, the oriental obscene animates a variety of political narratives far beyond the war itself, from the political coalition building within the Asian American and black power movements and debates over internal colonialism and neo-colonialism in the Philippines and on Indian reservations, to changing foreign relations with China and Japan, the rise of neoconservative discourses of law and order, and the body politics of second-wave feminism in the 1970s and the men's movement of the 1980s. Thus the story of the oriental obscene is a narrative not simply of the Vietnam War, but also of the racialized and gendered subject positions that emerged and evolved during this period.

My periodization of the oriental obscene as spanning the years 1968 to 1985 traces a historical arc between a certain kind of collective memory of the Vietnam War, reified by films such as *Rambo: First Blood Part II* (1985), and the reputed source of that memory in the historical real of the Vietnam War. In a sense this book begins where it ends, following the story of the genesis of the Rambo narrative back to its purported roots in both the Tet Offensive and urban race riots of 1968. That the oriental obscene plays out equally in nonfiction genres such as documentary, photojournalism, and television news, and in fictional genres such as war films, martial arts films and television shows, and action cinema, reflects the situation of these scenarios in a space of psychic reality blurring the distinction between the historical real and collective fabulation. Thus what I term the Vietnam era is not bounded by the dates of the Vietnam War itself (of official U.S. involvement, 1964–73), but reflects the belated historical responses to the war in a variety of cultural contexts.[23]

Although this book is about the Vietnam War, I begin this introduction from the perspective of the Persian Gulf War because it offers a way to understand the continuing force of Vietnam on American collective memory. From the vantage point of the future we can reflect upon the potency of the past, and in particular upon the visual contents of collective memory and how they are structured and transformed. Both of the metaphors of Vietnam used by Bush Sr.—as "specter" and as "syndrome"—underscore the ability of the past to haunt the present in immaterial yet substantial ways. The visual media function as both the site and the substance of these hauntings, producing the images that come to symbolize our collective memories of the war, as well as occasioning the reappearance of these images in other locations—quoted in other texts, allegorized in other genres, and even projected onto other bodies. These images become even more haunting when we consider their referents: violated and mangled bodies, individual casualties signifying the mass violence of war. Images of the dead, displaced, and wounded become like ghosts themselves, disembodied yet visible, residing in an afterlife of reruns and quotations, all the while insistently drawing our attention backward through history. These are the literal phantasms that float through the racial phantasmatic of The Oriental Obscene.

Psychoanalyzing the Imagined Community

What might it mean to traumatize a nation? To borrow this diagnosis from psychology might seem to impose an unnatural unity upon the unruly collective known as the U.S. nation. It is the same unity summoned by Bush Sr. in his declaration "We've kicked the Vietnam syndrome," projecting a present-tense semblance of national consensus regarding the Persian Gulf War by tying it to a seemingly shared historical past. However, it is in this move from subject to nation that psychoanalytic theory provides the insight lacking in popular psychological tropes often invoked in American cultural studies. If the personification of the nation as a patient on the cultural critic's couch is to be more than mere poetic analogy, it must take into account the way poststructuralist psychoanalysis has fundamentally challenged the coherence of the subject. To analogize the nation as subject is not necessarily to adopt the organic unities of the body politic or the universalities of the Jungian collective unconscious or the "myth and symbol" school of American studies.[24] Far from lending wholeness to the concept of nation, the individual subject in psychoanalysis is fundamentally split and lacking, whether in terms of the inaccessibility of the unconscious in Freud, the castration symbolized by the entrance into language in Lacan, the "Copernican" decentering of human agency in Laplanche, or the foundational foreclosures of sexuality and race expounded upon by Judith Butler, Anne Cheng, and others.[25] The modern nation, like the modern subject, must be understood as fundamentally split, historically and socially contingent, and incapable of complete self-presence or self-awareness. The nation becomes a "subject" in my analysis only insofar as it is a fictive field within which the scenarios of the oriental obscene circulate and take on meaning.

One useful place to begin the psychoanalysis of the nation is to interrogate Anderson's definition of the nation as an "imagined political community" that lives on primarily in the minds of its members: "It is imagined because the members of even the smallest nation will never know most of their fellow-members, meet them, or even hear of them, yet in the minds of each lives the image of their communion."[26] The inadequacies of Anderson's concept of the imagination have already been noted by many commentators, especially his collapse of "imagining" with "thinking" in the broadest sense, to the exclusion of the visual realm—an understandable association, if we consider his main focus to be forms of print capitalism such as the novel and the newspaper.[27] However, if we factor in visual culture, and in particular the indexical visual media that are the subject of this book, we enter a realm wherein images precede conscious thought, in many cases providing the materials for further ideological or intellectual elaboration, much like image rebuses of Freud's dream-work.[28] This optical unconscious underlying Anderson's imagined community might be more precisely linked to what Marita Sturken has called "cultural memory" and Lauren Berlant has called "national fantasy" —a space where public images and ideas circulate consciously and unconsciously through private psyches such that the national and individual, the collective and the local begin to blur into one another in a mutually constitutive yet contentious relationship.[29]

Furthermore the optical unconscious, like the individual unconscious, does not function like the ego to guarantee the illusion of a coherent, active self, but rather becomes a repository for forms of otherness that interrupt this illusion. The theoretical framework of *The Oriental Obscene* draws mainly on the work of Laplanche and Deleuze to build a psychoanalytic theory of social trauma that precisely resists the dominance of ego-centric psychology. Laplanche's key concepts of primal scene, trauma, belatedness (*Nachträgligh-keit*), and the phantasmatic—terms I discuss in detail throughout the book—all share at their core a conception of the subject as a site of passivity rather than as an agent who acts masterfully on the external world. Laplanche's definition of the unconscious reveals the essential disruption of the self by otherness, evidenced by the fact that he calls the unconscious, following Freud, "das Andere, the other-thing in us," an "internal foreign body" that is itself the trace of the influence of another form of otherness, "der Andere," the other *person* against whom the self emerges as a subject.[30] As a result the radical alterity that lies at the heart of the subject for Laplanche is not only an existential but also a social reality, embedding the subject within a social order that he or she cannot transcend. By employing Laplanche I challenge the misconception of psychoanalysis as a purely bourgeois discourse of liberal individuality, designed only to normalize and discipline the unruly subject into an existing social order. In fact this model of disrupted agency shows the difficulty of maintaining ideological structures such as the self and the nation in the face of the otherness and other subjects who might resist such subjugation. Despite a set of shared images, an optical unconscious ultimately undoes the nation-building project associated with the print cultures of the Andersonian imagined community, interrupting the assertion of a national "we" through the visualization of various alterities: the internal foreignness of racial difference and political dissent, the external foreignness of international warfare, and even the interruption of the present moment by the traumatic historical past.

This difference between Laplanchian psychoanalysis and more popular psychological understandings becomes even more apparent in Laplanche's definition of the phantasmatic, over and against notions of fantasy as mere wish fulfillment or daydream.[31] Even critiques of the "myth and symbol" school utilized this impoverished definition of fantasy, thus falling into a hermeneutics of suspicion by which one uncovers the false consciousness of national mythology only to find another fantasy that better describes the desires of the hegemonic state.[32] But this meaning of fantasy overemphasizes the agency of the desiring subject, whether an individual or a collectivity such as the nation. In contrast Laplanche asserts that such presentations of fantasies effect a "reversal of passivity into activity through which an auto-centered or re-centered subject claims to be at the origin of what, primarily, he has submitted to."[33] The fantasy of fantasy, then, is not simply the content of the particular wish fulfillment (e.g., "I desire the frontier as a virgin bride waiting to be taken"), but is ultimately the fantasy of the subject *as agent*, reversing the passivity of historical traumas (Indian wars, class conflict, economic crisis) into a narrative of mastery. The difference between fantasy and the phantasmatic is thus similar to that drawn by Louis Althusser between false consciousness and ideology or by Judith Butler between performance and performativity; in each case the former term denotes a narrower realm of consciously driven and directed activity, whereas the latter decenters the subject within larger systems of desire, interpellation, or norms.[34] Throughout *The Oriental Obscene* I deploy the term "phantasmatic" in order to emphasize this contrast from ordinary fantasy as well as to invoke the sense of haunting and death conveyed by its root, "phantasm," even as I sometimes use these terms interchangeably in order to highlight the slippage between them.

It is in this spirit of decentering the nation-subject that I also include Deleuze in my larger psychoanalytic framework. Deleuze has been lauded by many theorists as antipsychoanalytical, especially in resisting the binary and normalizing forces associated with Freud.[35] But Deleuze is also interested in the passive, masochistic subject as a counterpoint to the centripetal force of the Oedipal, neurotic ego. It is Deleuze who reminds us in *Anti-Oedipus*, coauthored with the anti-authoritarian psychoanalyst Félix Guattari, of the essentially social nature of fantasy and thus of fantasy analysis: "Fantasy is never individual—it is *group fantasy*."[36] Writing this text in the wake of May 1968, Deleuze and Guattari link a classic Freudian fantasy, "A Child Is Being Beaten" (which is also central to Laplanche's revision of Freud and is discussed further in my chapter 3), to the larger contemporary social landscape of repression and desire, and ultimately to the Vietnam War, riffing off the American documentary *Hearts and Minds* (1974): "If there is a *mise en scène* [in "A Child Is Being Beaten"], it is directed by a social desiring-machine whose product should not be considered abstractly, separating the girl's and the boy's cases, as if each were a little ego taking up its own business with daddy and mommy. . . . It is a whole chorus, a montage: back in the village after a raid in Vietnam, in the presence of their weeping sisters, the filthy Marines are beaten by their instructor, on whose knees the mommy is seated, and they have orgasms for having been so evil, for having tortured so well. It's so bad, but also so good!"[37] Deleuze and Guattari do not discard the terms of psychoanalysis altogether; rather they turn their analysis away from the individuating and normalizing aims of healing and reintegrating the ego and toward the critique of psychoanalysis itself as a symptom of the repressive systems of capitalism and state power. "Daddy-mommy-me," the classic Oedipal triangle that Deleuze and Guattari deride here, not only participates in its privatized familial dramas but also replicates the power structures that underlie the military unit and the nation at war. We might think of the oriental obscene as a similar group fantasy, but with race taking the place of gender and kinship. Not only do phantasmatic, racial categories such as black, white, and oriental reflect the imaginary relations of individuals to their real conditions of racial difference in the U.S., but the identifications, projections, and transferences across racial categories provide the conditions of possibility that underlie the political identifications, projections, and transferences that emerge in the public sphere.

I also draw from Deleuze's film theory, the two *Cinema* books which outline a phenomenological theory of film in opposition to the psychoanalytic and semiotic approaches of French film theorists such as Christian Metz and Jean-Louis Baudry. Although Deleuze's *Cinema* books are often read separately from his more explicitly political work, they also participate in the larger project of decentering of the individual bourgeois subject and outlining new political possibilities. Following Deleuze's own cues in situating these books against the backdrop of the Second World War, I deploy his theories of the breakdown of the movement-image into the time-image as an indirect form of trauma theory complementary to Laplanche's work on trauma. The historical traumas of global warfare are inflected in cinematic thought, not only in direct representation (i.e., films *about* war), but also in the impact on film's formal structures (frame, shot, montage), including its presentation of movement and agency in general. It is here that the indexicality of the optical unconscious reemerges, in excess to the manifest, narrative content of photography and film. Just as the Second World War registered in Italian neorealist and French New Wave cinema as a new breed of characters and narratives in search of new ways to interact with the devastated social and physical landscapes left behind by the war, the Vietnam War produces crises of the paradigmatic Hollywood action cinema that manifest not only in film narratives but also in the techniques used to portray action and plot. The explosion of violence in American visual media after Vietnam is not simply a straightforward representation of historical reality within this cultural superstructure; it also raises important questions about what it means to see, display, and ultimately understand the violence of war.

Most important, Deleuze's film formalism merges with the play of the Laplanchian phantasmatic to free this study from the refrain of stereotype analysis that paralyzes many discussions of race in mass media. Despite the frequency of images of Asian violence in this study, the oriental obscene does not refer to a stereotype of Asians as violent, which then must be refuted on the grounds of verisimilitude, or of the political economy of representation. The tragedy of the stereotype, as Homi Bhabha argued, is that it "impedes the circulation and articulation of the signifier of 'race' as anything other than its *fixity* as racism."[38] Under this Laplanchian and Deleuzian framework the oriental obscene foregrounds exactly this circulation and articulation of race through visual mass media. It is not the product of any one author's or audience's fantasies or desires regarding the Vietnam War, but rather constitutes a phantasmatic space of imagined racial relations from which the various meanings of the Vietnam War emerge and are contested. If the Vietnam War is a national primal scene rather than an American Dream, the aim of this book is not to heal the nation of this trauma, exorcising its ghosts through an act of recuperative, truth-telling historiography. If anything, this national trauma proves to be extraordinarily productive, enabling the formation of both progressive and reactionary political alliances in the wake of the Vietnam War that persist even today. Like the constitutive melancholia that supports ego formation, the trauma of the Vietnam War both aids and undermines the formation of national identity. To paraphrase Freud, *the shadow of Vietnam fell upon the nation*, a war that was both loved and lost—loved precisely because it was lost, and lost but forever preserved in the form of the nation itself.[39]

American Orientalism

My resurrection of the term "oriental" over "Asian" or "Asian American" is in some ways a throwback to an earlier regime of racist representation, now referred to as "orientalism" and criticized for its distortion of Asian peoples and cultures. This project is inspired by Said's foundational definition of orientalism as "a Western style for dominating, structuring, and having authority over the Orient," in which I interpret "style" as referring to a visual formalism that exceeds the content analysis used in most critiques of racial stereotypes.[40] In contrast with Said's many critics, I take seriously the Foucauldian roots of his concept of orientalism, treating it as a discursive formation with material roots in the history of colonialism.[41] While Said's work has focused on academic disciplines and artistic genres that provided epistemological and rhetorical support for structures of European domination over Africa and Asia, my project extends Said's analysis of literary tropes—"figures of speech, setting, narrative devices, historical and social circumstances"—to include the visual, extralinguistic aspects of film and television that also shape the meaning of the moving image.[42] Visual media such as film and television, far from "reinforc[ing] the stereotypes by which the Orient is viewed" by "forc[ing] information into more and more standardized mold[s]," as Said maintained, in fact make orientalism more diffuse, broadening his notion of "latent orientalism" to include a visual unconscious in which the mnemonic traces of historicized power relations are deposited in all aspects of visual form and structure.[43] Throughout my analyses I emphasize visual style as a way of moving away from the racial indexicality of many forms of stereotype analysis, which assume an uncomplicated mapping of racial meaning onto bodily difference. If there is a difference between orientalism and racialization, it is that orientalism's psychic terrain reveals conflicted forms that do not easily translate into the clear social categorizations that mobilize racial hierarchies. Orientalism comments as much upon fantasies of the normative self as upon the construction of racial others.

By invoking this phantasmatic construction of the "orient" rather than a veridical discourse about Asia, I also intend to focus on the mutability of concepts of racial difference as they are put into play in what Michael Omi and Howard Winant have called "racial formations," or historically contingent deployments of racial categories in specific sociopolitical contexts.[44] In the phantasmatic, racial formations such as "oriental," "black," and "white" always appear as provisional positions rather than stable signifiers with clear referents to an outside reality or racial essence. In using the terms "imagined" and "phantasmatic" I am not arguing for a postmodern phantasmagoria in which race does not exist. Nevertheless I am less interested in the actual positioning of these racial categories in social reality than in the imagined relationships between them. One way to conceptualize this approach is as a psychoanalytic version of what Claire Jean Kim calls "racial triangulation": each racial formation is not hermetically sealed into its own history, nor are they all arranged into a single racial chain of being.[45] Instead triangulation entails a consideration of all the combinatory relationships that might be engaged in any imagined scenario of social being. Racial triangulation complements the nondyadic nature of Laplanchian psychoanalysis, which refuses to reduce scenarios into binary oppositions: self/other, occidental/oriental, active/passive. While my central concern is to uncover the meanings placed onto orientalness (my preferred term for phantasmatic Asian racial difference), this project requires forays into the phantasmatic meanings mapped onto whiteness, blackness, and other racial formations as well.

Although I began by invoking Said's orientalism, the specific history of

American encounters with Asia, particularly through war and immigration, produces a different form of orientalism than the totalizing system of radical difference between the Christian West and Muslim East that Said reads in European colonialist memoirs and comparative religion and history. Lisa Lowe begins her own critique of British and French orientalisms by arguing for "a conception of orientalism as heterogeneous and contradictory."[46] She continues, "The Orient as Other is a literary trope that may reflect a range of national issues; at one time the race for colonies, at others class conflicts and workers' revolts, changes in sexual roles during a time of rapid urbanization and industrialization, or postcolonial crises of national identity."[47] As the presence of Asians in America indicates, a crucial part of American orientalism is its reconfiguration of American national identity, character, and subjectivity. Mae Ngai summarizes the contribution of Asian American studies to the study of orientalism as "reframing the question of distance and the location of the subject. . . . If [Said's notion of] oriental difference relied on distance, that difference was altered, but not eliminated, by the mass immigration of Chinese to the American West in the mid-nineteenth century."[48]

The American oriental was and continues to be represented not only by the foreigners in Asia, but also the "foreigner-within," the Asians in America who apparently cannot be assimilated within the American mainstream. As a unique internal other whose racial formation brings together issues of domestic racial order with American colonialism, the Asian American poses interesting questions for the American body politic, especially during periods of social crisis. The idea of the foreigner-within persists even in the late twentieth century, after the repeal of the immigration laws of the late nineteenth century and early twentieth that singled out Asians for exclusion and restriction. As Lowe explains in Immigrant Acts, "In the period from World War II onward, 'Asia' has emerged as a particularly complicated 'double front' of threat and encroachment for the United States: on the one hand, Asian states have become prominent as external rivals in overseas imperial war and in the global economy, and on the other, Asian immigrants are still a necessary racialized labor force within the domestic national economy."[49] The importance of Asian immigrants in the formation of a particularly American orientalism is also emphasized by Henry Yu, who claims, "If there was a unique feature of American Orientalism in the 1920s that distinguished it from earlier American and European versions, it was the connection of Orientals at home with those in the Orient."[50] Echoing Lowe's "double front," David Palumbo-Liu describes a "double movement" in which American orientalism copes with the oriental other both inside and outside its borders, using a psycho-analytic model which constructs the American nation as a form of bodily *imago*, by "imagining a set of possible modes of *introjecting* Asians into Amer-ica, and *projecting* onto East Asia a set of possible rearticulations of 'western presence.' "[51] This model points to a psychoanalytic understanding of other-ness within orientalism that goes beyond a prosaic concept of difference, exclusion, or rejection—an otherness which, although radically different from the self, is also constitutive of the self.

In the second half of the twentieth century the trajectory of U.S. military and political relations with the Far East replaced immigration to become the main influence on American orientalism. The events which Said called "our recent Japanese, Korean, and Indochinese adventures" not only generated a large quantity of images for the American culture industry, but also sparked changes in Asian immigration to the U.S.[52] David Desser has called this historical period America's "encounter with Asia": "veritable encounters with Asian cultures and societies that offered sometimes different, troubling, chal-lenging, or intriguing (usually all at the same time) alternatives to American culture and values."[53] The violence of these encounters is readily apparent in their largely military nature: the Pacific theater of the Second World War, the American occupation of Japan, the status of communist China in the cold war, and military actions in Korea and Vietnam, which some continue to call "conflicts" rather than "wars."[54] These encounters facilitated the introduc-tion of cultural forms which produced the oriental obscene. For instance, martial arts, mainly in the form of Japanese karate, first entered America with U.S. soldiers stationed in Japan and Okinawa during the occupation of Japan after the Second World War. The Vietnam War instigated the development of televisual and filmic representations of explicit violence in a quantity and with an immediacy lacking in previous newsreel coverage of the Second World War and the Korean War. Thus, like Asian immigration, these wars were not simply encounters with the orient as a foreign entity; they also brought the orient home to the U.S. through popular culture, television, and film.

The political collectivity known today as "Asian America" came into be-ing during the Vietnam era, in response to the issues raised by American orientalism: racism against Asian immigrants and their descendants that marked them as unassimilable and essentially foreign, and the effects of American neocolonialist militarism abroad that associated Asians in America with larger Asian diasporic communities. Led in large part by middle-class, college-educated Chinese, Japanese, Korean, and Filipino Americans who

were born and raised in the U.S., the Asian American movement was influenced by the New Left and the broader antiwar movement as well as by African
Americans in both the civil rights and black power movements.[55] The Asian
American movement attempted to build panethnic coalitions among previously separate Asian ethnic groups by mobilizing a shared history of discrimination and racial violence. Its first large-scale activities took place in
1968 and 1969, as students at San Francisco State University and the University
of California, Berkeley, protested institutional racism and lack of community
self-determination in higher education. These strikes led to the formation of
the first Asian American studies and ethnic studies programs in the country,
and also coincided with the activities of the burgeoning Chicano and American Indian movements.

Additionally, as I discuss in greater detail in chapter 2, Asian American
activists participated in antiwar protests and draft resistance mobilizations,
since the war against North Vietnam made this history of anti-Asian violence
especially visible. The historian Sucheng Chan recalled her own moment of
consciousness raising during the Vietnam War: "With the help of the television evening news, an increasing number of Asian American college and high
school students realized with a shock that the 'enemy' whom American soldiers were maiming and killing had faces like their own."[56] Given the symbolic importance of the Vietnamese in the formation of an Asian American
identity, it is notable that Vietnamese Americans themselves were absent from
this panethnic coalition, since the overwhelming majority of Vietnamese
Americans did not immigrate until after the end of the war in 1975. The
Vietnamese were no less phantasmatic to Asian Americans than they were to
whites and African Americans, existing mainly as media images in the public
sphere. But Asian Americans themselves were a fragile and small imagined
community, having little or no voice in the mainstream press and nearly as
spectral as the Vietnamese. In the Vietnam era Asian Americans were "missing," as Deleuze might say, not because they did not exist per se, but because
they were "always several peoples, an infinity of peoples, who remained to be
united, or should not be united."[57]

The phantasmatic status of Vietnam and of Asian America in general is
complicated but by no means eradicated by the growth of the Asian American
population as a result of the Immigration and Nationality Act of 1965 and the
eventual mass immigration of Vietnamese to the U.S. after the Vietnam War.
Much has been written about the extraordinary character of Asian immigration after 1965, focusing on how the changes made to immigration law

replaced restrictive quotas based on national origins with a system of preferences that favored skilled, middle-class workers—and partially contributing to the phenomenon of the "model minority."[58] Describing the Asian immigrant after 1965 as the return of the repressed of American neocolonialism in Asia, Lowe argues that these immigrants, a large number of whom come from Vietnam, Cambodia, Laos, Taiwan, the Philippines, and South Korea, "embod[y] the displacement from Asian societies in the aftermath of war and colonialism to a United States with whose sense of national identity the immigrants are in contradiction precisely because of that history. . . . These immigrants retain precisely the memories of imperialism that the U.S. nation seeks to forget."[59] Asian immigrants' bodies are corporeal memento mori of such acts of violence, even if they themselves are not the refugees of war and colonialism. Importantly, though, the material effects of Asian immigration after 1965 are not felt significantly until after the Vietnam era. Even before these Asian bodies migrate to the U.S., images of Asians, both fictional and nonfictional, enter into American visual culture and anticipate the arrival of their bodily referents. It is difficult to say which of these bodies are real and which are phantasmatic, for even though the later bodies mingle in the flesh within the American body politic, they seem belated afterimages of the earlier bodies whose images were burned onto American retinas.

In short the "oriental" in the oriental obscene refers not to Vietnamese Americans or other Asian Americans in particular, but rather to this phantasmatic, visual presence that dominates the American cultural imaginary in the absence of an Asian American political collectivity that can speak for itself. Asian American identity—a still nascent formation in the Vietnam era—defines itself dialectically against the American national body as well as against the Vietnamese bodies affected by the war. Hence my focus on the oriental is less about recuperating an authentic Asian American subject at the moment of its origin and more about exploring the imagined set of relations that create not only orientalness but also particular forms of whiteness, blackness, and other positions in the racial networks that mark the Vietnam era in the U.S. Revisiting my earlier statement that the *shadow of Vietnam fell upon the nation*, we might understand this melancholic formation as referring not only to the war, but also to the racialized otherness of the Vietnamese nation helping to constitute an American nation that refuses to acknowledge the Asian subjects that it itself incorporated previously. Thus the oriental obscene ultimately speaks not only to the trauma of the imagined oriental body, but also to that oriental body as the index of trauma within the national body.

The Obscenity of Violence

And so when thirty years from now our brothers go down the street without a leg, without an arm, or a face, and small boys ask why, we will be able to say "Vietnam" and not mean a desert, not a filthy obscene memory, but mean instead where America finally turned and where soldiers like us helped it in the turning.

—John Kerry and Vietnam Veterans Against the War, quoted in Tom Buckley, "Reports of Its Death Have Been Greatly Exaggerated," New York Times, 25 April 1971

Violence is a key element of the scenarios of the oriental obscene. Violence not only directs attention to these images in a crowded visual field, in a sense *demanding* to be seen, but it also solicits a visceral and affective response that complicates the intellectual or cognitive reception of the image. Thus the oriental obscene is an *obscene* scenario, featuring a dialectic of transgressive visibility and invisibility that pushes its images to the forefront of the national consciousness. As described by John Kerry in his testimony to the Senate Foreign Relations Committee as part of a weeklong Vietnam Veterans Against the War (VVAW) protest nicknamed "Dewey Canyon III," the memory of the Vietnam War is not only traumatic but "filthy obscene," encapsulated in the maimed bodies of American veterans. Previously censored or hidden by the mainstream news media, these bodies now literally demanded to be seen, as many disabled veterans participated in Dewey Canyon and other events sponsored by Vietnam Veterans Against the War, displaying their wounds as a form of protest against the violence of the war. Interestingly although the obscenity of such images is obviously heightened by expectations that the normative American body be whole, healthy, and self-sufficient, it is not the American body but the bodies of its foreign others—the Vietnamese—that form the bulk of obscenely violated bodies in the Vietnam era. Like the misidentified bodies in Van Es's photograph of the fall of Saigon, the Vietnamese of war coverage and Hollywood war films stand in for the suffering of American soldiers and citizens as a result of the war, their extremely visible bodily violation taking the place of invisible violence done to American bodies and psyches. Even the antiwar movement fetishized the violence done to Vietnamese bodies, at times using them to dramatically illustrate the moral quandaries presented by the use of napalm or aerial bombing.

Images of the Vietnam War and its antiwar movement were not the only sources of violence in the visual media in this era. In the news media images of the civil rights movement, the Kennedy assassination, the murders of Martin Luther King Jr. and Robert Kennedy, and urban race riots were often as

violent as those from the war itself. The loosening of censorship over Hollywood films also unleashed a flood of fictional violence in various genres, such
as the crime film, horror and science fiction, the western, and the martial arts
film. Arthur Schlesinger Jr., a liberal historian and Kennedy speechwriter,
lamented in 1968 what seemed to be the exceptionally violent character of
contemporary American life, excoriating in particular the development in film
and television of "a pornography of violence far more demoralizing than the
pornography of sex which still seizes the primary attention of the guardians
of civic virtue."[60] For Schlesinger and other critics of "televiolence" in the
1960s and 1970s the representation of violence in the visual media was clearly
tied to the increasing violence taking place in the world: crime, war, assassination, riots. These images helped contribute to the sense of an American nation under siege, traumatized by the visual repetition of already traumatic violence.

But these images did not only capture an index of physical violence taking
place throughout the U.S. and the world. They also symbolized an epistemic
violence taking place within the American body politic, as its citizens engaged
in various social and political movements that would alter the symbolic identity of the nation: the civil rights movement, second-wave feminism, gay and
lesbian rights, black power, Chicano power, and the Asian American and
American Indian movements. Maurice Isserman and Michael Kazin even
named this era the "Civil War of the 1960s," evoking the conflict that also tore
the nation apart over issues of race and sovereignty.[61] This epistemological
chaos within the terrain of national identity parallels the civil unrest caused by
the realignment of social relations, even if such rearrangements of power
were not as permanent or far-reaching as the utopian desires that accompanied them. Images of violated and violating bodies seemed to mirror the
transgressive movements of American subjects from their "proper" places
throughout the social body. Writing in this same period, Raymond Williams
commented in *Keywords* that the various meanings of the word "violence" as
physical assault, social disorder, and vehement affect constantly overlap, such
that the term even does "violence" to itself, by being "wrenched from its
meaning or significance."[62] In this last sense the demands of formerly mar-
ginalized or silent subjects did violence to the normative conception of the
American citizen as a white, heterosexual, middle-class male, even if these
subjects were not themselves agents of violence.

Obscenity law provides an important hermeneutic and historical context to
the reception of violence in the Vietnam era. As I have argued elsewhere, the
rhetoric surrounding the legal redefinition of sexual pornography in the

1960s impacted the emerging debates on the role of violence in American film and television and framed the transition of film censorship from the regime of the Production Code to the age-based restrictions of the Motion Picture Association of America (MPAA) ratings system.[63] Following a speculative etymology of the term itself, I assert that obscenity simultaneously invokes the violation of the body's boundaries (*caenum*, or filth) and the display of that violation (*scaena*, or scene), showing a mutual imbrication of physicality and visuality.[64] Both the anxiety over sexual obscenity and violent obscenity centered on a shared debate over the status of the body as object—as physical object and as object of spectacle. John Kerry's fear of the "filthy obscene memory" of Vietnam centered on the excessive visibility of wounded bodies, "without a leg, without an arm, or a face," whose presence threatens to obliterate other ways of memorializing the Vietnam War era.

But if sexual obscenity foregrounded the gendering of the body and becomes an important terrain for second-wave feminism, violent obscenity in the 1970s highlighted the racialization of the body, particularly as documentary representations of violence in the news media exerted pressure on systems of realism in fictional visual media. In 1968, against the backdrop of the Tet Offensive, Jack Valenti, president of the MPAA (and a former assistant to LBJ), defended the new ratings system and its more lenient orientation toward film violence: "For the first time in the history of this country, people are exposed to instant coverage of a war in progress. When so many movie critics complain about violence on film, I don't think they realize the impact of 30 minutes on the Huntley-Brinkley newscast—and that's real violence."[65] Because of the informal censorship of American casualties in the news media, the "real violence" of the Vietnam War entered American living rooms through the guise of the Asian rather than the white American body. The Asian body served as an economical condensation of the overdetermined meanings assigned to violence in the Vietnam era. The image of a South Vietnamese general executing a Viet Cong spy on national television, or of the dead bodies of Vietnamese women and children in the My Lai massacre, seemed to convey the violence of the Vietnam War better than any written report of body counts or troop movements. Even the iconic photograph of the fall of Saigon, which does not depict an act of violence directly, comes to symbolize the loss of the Vietnam War and the totality of individual losses as a result of that war.

But journalists of the era also connected the racialized violence of the Vietnam War with another, domestic crisis: the unruliness of the black body in both civil rights protests and urban race riots, which itself draws on a long tradition of disciplining and violating the black body in U.S. history. Thus when the phantasmatic oriental body emerges from the Vietnam era, it is already embedded in a preexisting black/white binary in American culture. Nonetheless the oriental obscene reveals new possibilities of relations with and between these black and white subject positions. Both the participants and the critics of black rebellion and white counterculture made elaborate analogies between these movements and the Vietnam War, showing the political flexibility of this cross-racial identification. Even as law enforcement agencies were casting urban black ghettos as mini-Vietnams that called for the deployment of military manpower and weaponry, figures as disparate as Muhammad Ali and the Weather Underground claimed allegiance with the Viet Cong. Yet as the structure of the oriental obscene makes clear, these contradictory narratives are not unrelated, but express the vicissitudes of the fantasy of violence and violation enabled by the foreign otherness of the Asian body. These various iterations of the Asian body, real and imagined, are celebrated, pitied, reviled, and mourned as part of fantasies that reimagine the American body politic in relation to the Asian body.

In a different vein the martial arts films of the "kung fu craze" of the 1970s, which began just as the Vietnam War was ending, also seemed to reveal the mysterious potential of the Asian body to commit as well as to absorb fantastic forms of violence. Although ethnic enclaves such as Chinatowns and Little Tokyos had been importing martial arts films for diasporic Asian audiences for many decades, the martial arts trend of the 1970s is marked by the lack of participation of Asian Americans, as American film distributors imported films directly from overseas studios and targeted them to non–Asian American audiences. Overtly these images of Chinese kung fu and Japanese karate seem to have little to do with the concerns of the Vietnam War. But, as David Desser speculates, "surely it is not coincidental that interest in the Asian martial arts increased with continued, ongoing and intense exposure to Asia."[66] Indeed during the representational lull between 1974 and 1978, when the Vietnam War largely disappeared from Hollywood as well as the news media, the most prevalent and striking images of Asian bodies came from martial arts films imported from Asia. Although used primarily in fictional texts, martial arts also introduced a different form of realism to the staging of violence, offering more direct points of contact between clashing bodies on screen. The transmission of Asian martial arts into American culture is itself a symptom of the history of U.S. militarism, as American soldiers stationed in East and Southeast Asia took up the martial arts as a sport and hobby, and eventually even the U.S. military adopted martial arts as part of its own training. Ironically Asian martial arts are also linked with pacifism in the 1970s, as the philosophies behind these practices meld with a countercultural orientalism that also celebrated Zen Buddhism, tai chi, and yoga as oppositional to Western modernity. In this dialectical binary between militarism and pacifism the Asian martial arts enter the oriental obscene as both an extension of and a response to the enigma of Vietnamese guerrilla warfare, offering American culture a way to master the violence of the Vietnam era even as it continues to propagate that violence in a different visual form. These contradictions come to a head in the figure of Bruce Lee, whose death in 1973 and posthumous fame challenges the fantasy of using violence to overcome violence.

As a result the oriental obscene is dispersed across multiple genres. Beyond the literal restaging of the Vietnam War in war films, the oriental obscene also structures the individualized combat of the martial arts film, both in traditional forms such as the Hong Kong import *Five Fingers of Death* (1972) and in the hybrid American, Hong Kong, and Japanese genres in which martial arts are crossed with the Western, blaxploitation, or crime thrillers—the television show *Kung Fu* (1972–75) and the films *Cleopatra Jones* (1973) and *Street Fighter* (1974), respectively. Using the martial arts, the oriental obscene refigures violence not only as a setting for the loss of control, as it was in the Vietnam War and urban race riots, but also as a site of mastery over physical pain. As an allegory for Vietnam, martial arts explain the fantastic power attributed to the bodies of Viet Cong guerrillas and other Third World soldiers, and also offers the opportunity for others to embody this power by performing its racialized movements. The fictional Vietnam veterans portrayed by Sylvester Stallone and Chuck Norris in the early 1980s are not descended solely from the American soldiers seen in Vietnam War footage and war films, but are also the product of the Asian martial arts. These reactionary heroes may emerge during a period that fetishizes and celebrates white male working-class masculinity, but they are essentially orientalized heroes, not only full of the violence of the Vietnam War in their (fictionalized) personal histories, but also remade into hard bodies through the intervention of Asian martial arts.

Part of what made the oriental obscene *obscene* was the way it revealed the otherness of the racialized, oriental body through the violence done to it or through it. Its way of suffering violence and of dying revealed the utter alterity of the body, as an object alienated from and rejected by other living subjects. Just as anxieties over sexual obscenity tied visual representations to real-world effects, the oriental obscene also linked the real and the represented, showing the real effects of the violation of the body through fictionalized forms, and later the styles of real combat within staged violence. Whether in the form of documentary images such as news footage of the "Saigon Execution" or in hyperstylized fictional films like *The Deer Hunter*, the violence of the oriental obscene staged a form of realism that *forced* one to look at violence rather than hiding that violence behind the veil of obscurity, inscrutability, or unrepresentability. Simultaneously the oriental obscene brought the Asian body itself into the spotlight in the 1960s, a body that usually faded into the background of American visual culture. Ironically it is within the visual style of the oriental obscene that the Asian body again fades from view, subsumed into the body of the white Vietnam veteran in the early 1980s just as the racial formation of Asian Americans gains political traction.

The Topography of *The Oriental Obscene*

Mirroring the complex temporalities of the psychic structures it describes, the organization of *The Oriental Obscene* is not strictly chronological, nor does it trace a linear, causal narrative between texts and reception. I have imagined the chapters as representing interlocking stages of a larger racial phantasmatic, along the lines of the phases in Freud's infamous case study of beating fantasies, "A Child Is Being Beaten": my father is beating the other child; my father is beating me; a child is being beaten, and I am looking on (these stages are discussed at length in chapter 3). Each individual stage of the larger fantasy of the oriental obscene has its own narrative logic—the nation is being beaten, is invaded, is invading, is triumphant—but the meaning of that narrative and the subject positions it provides do not make sense until we look at the fantasy as a whole, seeing how the stages are structurally related. Also the stages are not developmental, in the sense that one stage must end before giving way to the next stage in an orderly temporal progression. Instead all the stages coexist simultaneously, varying to the extent that certain narratives become manifest at certain moments in time, while others may become latent without disappearing. Each version of the oriental obscene that arises always implicates all the others within this racial phantasmatic. Borrowing from Laplanche's theatrical metaphor for fantasy: the actors may change, the props may move around, but the scenario remains the same. In essence this book is structured like the optical unconscious it attempts to map.

Befitting such a structure, *The Oriental Obscene* begins where it ends, that is from a memory of 1968 from the perspective of the late 1980s, mediated through the television screen and derived from the original author of the text that caps off the end of this study: David Morrell, "the man who created

Rambo." Chapter 1, "Bringing the War Home: Spectacles of Violence and Rebellion in the American 1968," treats the year 1968 as a primal scene for the oriental obscene. Just as the Freudian primal scene is more than a simple recounting of an infant's memory of parental sex, Morrell's reminiscences, which link the Vietnam War to domestic racial violence and the antiwar counterculture, as well as his novel, *First Blood* (1971), show 1968 to be more than a historical point of origin for the violence of the Vietnam era. In fact this first chapter does not even deal with the Vietnam War as such, but rather concentrates on the nascent genre of television news and its framing of the civil rights movement of the 1950s and early 1960s, urban race riots of the late 1960s, and antiwar protests of the late 1960s and early 1970s, all of which are echoed in Morrell's tale of a Vietnam veteran's traumatic return to the U.S. Thus even before the war supposedly burst into American living rooms, it is already a continuation of preexisting narratives intertwining race, violence, and visuality, and this continuity is affirmed by allegorical deployments of "Vietnam" as descriptors for the Detroit riot (1967) and the Days of Rage in Chicago (1969). This chapter also introduces Laplanche's theories of the primal scene, primal fantasies, and *Nachträglichkeit* (belatedness), reworking them from their intrapsychic origins into components of a theory of socio-historical trauma. The primal scene in particular provides a model for television viewing as a conduit for the optical unconscious of the Vietnam era to enter into the imagined space of the nation. If 1968 is the point of origin of anything, it is not the source of a unique form of racial violence, but the beginning of a particular scenario of violation and victimization linking black and white subjects to an imagined Vietnamese other.

The Vietnam War proper enters this study in chapter 2, "Reporting the War: Ethical Crises of Action in the Movement-Image of Vietnam." Here I introduce Deleuze's theory of the movement-image as the foundation of narrative cinema and link the formal crisis faced by this visual style with the historical crisis of war (for Deleuze and European cinema the crisis was the Second World War, but for American visual culture and the oriental obscene it is the Vietnam War). In a continuation of trauma theory developed in the previous chapter, I use Deleuze to think through how the violence taking place in the real is not simply converted symbolically into images and narratives of violence, but also ends up doing violence to the form of the image—in this case the ability of film to organize images into coherent sequences of organic movements and events. This chapter also continues the previous chapter's focus on the news media, but this time concentrating solely on the Vietnamese who were mere absent presences in chapter 1. I look at the ruptures that occur between photojournalism (still images) and television news (moving images) of the same iconic events: the "Saigon Execution" of 1968, the My Lai Massacre (occurring in 1968 but reported in 1969), and the "Napalm Girl" of 1972. Because of the unsuccessful conversion of these events into movement-images, they are enigmatic signifiers that only obliquely support the antiwar narratives into which they are thrust. But despite the extreme abjection of the Vietnamese depicted as subjects and objects of violence, they serve as the inspiration for a remarkable political poesis: the emergence of an Asian American movement—a Deleuzian becoming—constructed through a phantasmatic relationship with the Vietnamese in these images. Together chapters 1 and 2 delineate a spectrum of political possibilities derived from phantasmatic identifications with Vietnamese suffering, from a variety of racial positions.

As we move from nonfictional, documentary images to Hollywood narrative films, the fantasy of empathetically viewing violence done to the Vietnamese slowly becomes a fantasy of suffering that violence in the place of that racial other. In chapter 3, "Restaging the War: Fantasizing Defeat in Hollywood's Vietnam," the images and narratives outlined in the first two chapters return as the setting for masochistic film pleasures as American soldiers are stripped, maimed, drugged, shot at, and cut apart by Vietnamese aggressors. In the first wave of films to directly represent the Vietnam War after its conclusion—*The Boys in Company C*, *Coming Home*, *Go Tell the Spartans*, and *Apocalypse Now*, all released in 1978—Vietnam is the site of American rather than Vietnamese trauma. I return to Laplanche's theories of fantasy, and in particular his reworkings of masochism and Freud's beating fantasies, to understand the movement of racial subjects between roles in the scenario of the oriental obscene. Although these filmic narratives seem to be less progressive than the political movements born from the documentary images of the war, it is possible to recover a critical history even from such crude ideological fantasies. By attending to the material conditions of production behind these films—especially their use of neocolonial film locations such as Thailand and the Philippines and their deployment of Asian bodies as backdrop, including refugees from the Vietnam War—we can see the return of the repressed of the war coming back to haunt the narcissistic disavowals of Hollywood's Vietnam. Just as the iconic news images of the Vietnam War resist full incorporation into an antiwar narrative, these films ultimately fail to support the recuperation of American moral legitimacy that their narratives outline.

The second half of *The Oriental Obscene* recapitulates the early history of the

Vietnam era covered by the first half, but through a very different fantasy: that of war and violence as the occasion for the practice of mastery over both the self and the other. The particular inflection of this fantasy through the oriental obscene takes place through Asian martial arts, which become a cultural phenomenon in the early 1970s with the importation of Chinese and Japanese martial arts and kung fu films. In chapter 4, "Kung Fu Fighting: Pacifying and Mastering the Martial Body," I link the popularity of Asian martial arts as a sport in the U.S. to the history of American militarism in the Pacific Rim since the Second World War, preparing for the introduction of the martial arts film genre into American popular culture in 1972, in the midst of the Vietnam War. The American film Billy Jack and television series Kung Fu, along with the American reception of Asian films such as Deep Thrust and The Street Fighter, reveal, on the one hand, a seemingly apolitical and pacifist rhetoric of improving the individual body, and on the other hand, the use of violence to challenge the state or existing social structure. This dialectic provides a way for the American body politic to transform its passive suffering of violence in the Vietnam War into its opposite fantasy, an active form of self-mastery. In particular I examine the ways that white counterculture, black power, and the feminist movement utilize the orientalized violence of martial arts for different kinds of critique against the state.

But the intertwining of martial arts with the violence of the Vietnam War restrains the fantasy of control within these visions of mastery. Even as the martial arts film choreographs a repertoire of fantastic movements—iron skin, flying kicks, piercing fists—that grants the subject power over the physical world, the ultimate limit of that power lies in the physicality of that embodied subject, and the terminus of all violence, in death and the return of that subject to the material world. In chapter 5, "Being Bruce Lee: Death and the Limits of the Movement-Image of Martial Arts," I focus on the macabre rise of the most famous of the martial arts stars of this era, the Asian and then Asian American Bruce Lee, after his sudden death in 1973 a month before the American premier of his top-grossing film, Enter the Dragon. Returning to the Deleuzian critique of the movement-image introduced in chapter 2, I show how Lee's death provides a limit-case to the ability of the martial arts to function as a fantasy of complete bodily mastery and thus to compensate for the violence of the Vietnam War. But death is not entirely unproductive, and in the case of Lee's commodified, celebrity persona the loss of his living referent opens up further possibilities of political becoming, as the detritus of his filmic existence is cut up and recombined into utopian time-images such as the posthumous Game of Death (1978), an unwieldy but playful text no longer beholden to organic, lived time or historical fidelity. Resurrected by Asian American and African American filmmakers and fans in later films such as *They Call Me Bruce* and *The Last Dragon* as a hero against racial violence, this dead Lee embodies the ambivalence between activity and passivity that also marks the struggle between oppressive racialization and empowering racial identification.

These vicissitudes of the oriental obscene culminate in the condensation of the martial artist and the Vietnam veteran in the Vietnam action stars of the 1980s, Chuck Norris and Sylvester Stallone, whose film series *Missing in Action* and *Rambo*, respectively, mark the end of the Vietnam era as such and the emergence of a new period of Asian and Asian American racialization, triggered by the ascendancy of an Asian American body politic from the immigration and politicization of the previous decades and by the replacement of the Vietnam War with the trade war with Japan. In my conclusion, "Returning to 'Nam: The Vietnam Veteran's Orientalized Body," I point to a constellation of texts from the mid-1980s from both mainstream American commercial film and the growing body of independent Asian American theater and cinema that resituate the trauma of Vietnam as the reconfiguration of the racial composition of the American body politic. While Norris's and Stallone's Vietnam veterans merge the fantasies of mastery and suffering from previous iterations of the oriental obscene, they also reframe those racialized roles within the politics of failed white masculinity that mark the Reagan years, and this failure is echoed in the Hollywood films *The Year of the Dragon* and *The Karate Kid*, which separate the "bad" violence of the Vietnam era from the "good" violence necessary to bring Asian American subjects into the national fold. In contrast to the Asian American phantasmatic identification with the Vietnamese in antiwar protests, now a distinction is being drawn—by both Asian Americans and other Americans—between Asians and Asian Americans, allowing for political inclusion within the nation at the cost of forgoing a transnational political imaginary that animated "third worldist" movements of the 1970s. Nonetheless this distinction is fragile, as Asian American works of the early 1980s such as Frank Chin's play *The Year of the Dragon*, Wayne Wang's feature film *Chan Is Missing*, and Renee Tajima-Pena's and Christine Choy's documentary *Who Killed Vincent Chin?* reveal the continuing slippages between foreign enemy and assimilated immigrant transferred from war to economics.

Chapter 1

BRINGING THE WAR HOME

Spectacles of Violence and Rebellion

in the American 1968

The people of America are deeply concerned about violence. *They have seen* a President struck down by an assassin's bullet, and then seen the assassin himself slain while in police custody. *They have seen* other assassinations of national figures, and none more devastating than the killings earlier this year, first of a major leader of the civil rights movement, and then of the brother of the dead President.

Americans have seen smoke and flames rising over the skylines of their cities as civil disorder has spread across their land—holocausts of rioting, looting, firebombing, and death—a pattern of disorder and destruction repeated in city after city.

Americans have seen students disrupt classes, seize buildings and destroy property at institutions of learning. *They have seen* young people confronting police at the Pentagon and at draft induction centers across the country. *They have seen* them heckling, vilifying and even physically abusing public officials. *They have heard them* shouting obscenities and the strident rhetoric of revolution.

Americans have also come to know the fear of violent crime. *They know* that robberies and assaults have increased sharply in the last few years. *They know* that a small fraction of all such crimes is solved.

For many Americans this is the sum and substance of violence.

But many Americans see additional kinds of violence. They see the violence of overseas war. At home, *they see* the violence of terrorist murders of civil rights workers, of four little black girls bombed to death in a Sunday school class, the violence of police dogs, fire hoses and cattle prods; *others see* "violence" in discrimination and deprivation, disease, hunger, and rats. *They see* the violence of capital punishment, of slaughter on the highways, of movies, of radio and television programs, of some professional sports.

In the minds of some Americans all these different sorts of violence overlap.

—National Commission on the Causes and
Prevention of Violence, *Progress Report*, 1969

In the wake of Robert Kennedy's assassination in June 1968 President Lyndon B. Johnson formed one of the final commissions of his administration, the National Commission on the Causes and Prevention of Violence, to be chaired by Milton S. Eisenhower.[1] The introduction to the commission's *Progress Report*, released in January 1969, provides an interesting conflation of forms of violence. Speaking from the point of view of the imagined community, this introduction interpellates the nation into being through the pronoun "they," casting this national subject as the addressee of these acts. Each repeated citation reveals a stunning repetition compulsion, wherein assassinations and revolutions are not singular events linked to proper names and specific dates but rather generic instances in a series full of imitations and variations. The categories of violence also mirror and blur into one another, as the body of the slain leader becomes like the burning city, each a symbol of the nation whose boundaries are threatened by dissolution. Violence also extends to the disruption of social roles, as the examples of rioting and student unrest suggest a populace out of control, its members refusing to stay in their proper places. The U.S. that emerges as "home" in this report appears to be a land in the process of disintegration, witnessing the "terrorist murders of civil rights workers" within its boundaries and "overseas war" without.

But in seeking a diagnosis of the plague of violence breaking out in the American body politic, the Eisenhower Commission targeted not only acts of violence such as war, riots, and crime, but also the representation of violence in television and film. In this wide-ranging description of American violence there is a constant emphasis on sight rather than experience: "Americans have seen." The repetition of this phrase at the beginning of nearly every sentence, in comparison to the rare instances of the verbs "know" and "hear" and the complete absence of "experienced," "felt," or "survived," suggests the primacy not of lived experience but of the consumption of visual media, and in particular of television news. Calling television a "technology of memory," Marita Sturken argues that the cultural memory of the Vietnam War era necessarily exceeds the bounds of immediate experience and official historical discourse, residing instead in a range of cultural products such as fictional dramas, television images, and public memorials that "entangle" with personal memory and historical fact.[2] If, as the Eisenhower Commission's report concludes, "in the minds of some Americans all these different sorts of violence overlap" into one single scenario, then television might be the literal screen on which these screen memories collide.

Screen Memories of 1968

If the televisual apparatus embodies the nation's memory, what do we make of a memory of a memory—that is, a memory of watching television? Long before John Rambo became a household name symbolizing Sylvester Stallone's muscle-bound body and the American military's will to power, he was simply a character in the debut novel of a newly minted American literature professor named David Morrell. Morrell loosely based his novel, First Blood (1972), on the traumatized Vietnam veterans beginning to filter back to the U.S. in the late 1960s and trickling into the classes he taught as a graduate student at Penn State. In a later essay, "The Man Who Created Rambo," Morrell traces the genesis of Rambo back to what might be called a televisual primal scene. He recounts seeing the images that inspired First Blood juxtaposed on the CBS Evening News one "sultry August evening" in 1968:

> The first showed a fire fight in Vietnam. Sweaty American soldiers crouched in the jungle, shooting bursts from M-16s to repel an enemy attack. Incoming bullets kicked up dirt and shredded leaves. Medics scrambled to assist the wounded. An officer barked coordinates into a two-way radio, demanding air support. The fatigue, determination and fear on the faces of the soldiers were dismayingly vivid.
>
> The second story showed a different sort of battle. That steamy summer, the inner cities of America had erupted into violence. In nightmarish images, National Guardsmen snapped bayonets onto M-16s and stalked the rubble of burning streets, dodging rocks, wary of snipers among devastated vehicles and gutted buildings.
>
> Each news story, distressing enough on its own, became doubly so when paired with the other. It occurred to me that if I'd turned down the sound, if I hadn't heard each story's reporter explain what I was watching, I might have thought that both film clips were two aspects of a single horror. A fire fight outside Saigon, a riot within it. A riot within an American city, a fire fight outside it. Vietnam and America.
>
> What if I wrote a book in which the Vietnam war literally came home to

America? There hadn't been a war on American soil since 1865. With America splitting apart because of Vietnam, maybe it was time to write a novel that dramatized the philosophical division in our society, that shoved the brutality of war right under our nose.[3]

A quick review of CBS *Nightly News* broadcasts from 1968 shows that the images Morrell recalls could not have appeared in a single news broadcast that year: the riots of the "long, hot summer" reached their height in 1967, whereas images of fighting in Vietnam did not escalate until after 1968.[4] Yet the importance of his recollection lies not in its ostensible truth value, but in the explanatory value accorded to this origin story and its particular condensation of images.

Morrell's origin story for Rambo is a phantasmatic screen memory that provides a condensation of the many images that formed his and many other people's conception of the 1960s. In this anecdote, as well as throughout the novel *First Blood*, Morrell references many of the iconic events of the Vietnam era, such as the Tet Offensive and the string of urban riots stretching across the country, from Watts to Newark. Morrell's phrase "America splitting up because of Vietnam" invokes not only these events alone, but also the accelerating intensity of antiwar protests in the late 1960s, most visibly represented by the "Battle of Chicago" at the 1968 Democratic National Convention. Like many commentators, Morrell conflates the urban riots with the civil rights movement of the 1950s and early 1960s, describing the urban rebellions as "Civil Rights riots [that] had begun and were destroying several of America's inner cities."[5] The most brutal scenes of the Vietnam War itself, except for those of the Tet Offensive, had not been broadcast or published at the time Morrell locates his anecdote; scenes of the My Lai massacre appeared in 1969 and the napalmed young girl in 1971. Morrell's purported night of television news watching encompasses a decade or more of images, connected through links both visible and invisible.

Morrell's recollections reveal a fascinating and phantasmatic triangulation between traumatized white war veterans, black urban rioters, and oriental guerrillas, all mediated through the screen memory of television news. In each news story the white soldier or policeman is besieged by the violence of the racial other, although in Morrell's recounting these racial others are invisible, represented only by the proxy of their respective home spaces, Vietnam and the inner city. The absent presence of these two racial others also morphs the spaces of Vietnam and America into distorted mirror images of one another, connecting the late capitalist landscape of "devastated vehicles and gutted buildings" with the primitivist, premodern "jungle" of "dirt and shredded leaves." With the soundtrack removed the images merge into a dreamscape, allowing all three racialized characters to condense eventually into the figure of Rambo.

It is not coincidental that Morrell imagines the origin of First Blood in 1968. Like many other artists and writers, he posits 1968 retroactively as a phantasmatic point of rupture between an America that used to be, before the Vietnam War, and the America that it will become, after this violent encounter with the oriental obscene. In this chapter I consider what it means to posit the American 1968 as a historical and representational origin of the Vietnam era, and in particular how 1968 functions as a primal scene in the nation's visual unconscious from which other texts will emerge. I flesh out the concept of the primal scene—one of the privileged sites of fantasy in Laplanchian psychoanalysis—in relation to the televisual apparatus in order to understand the link between this phantasmatic cultural imaginary and the historical reality it purports to represent and mediate. The primal scene, like many other forms of traumatic memory, is characterized by a complicated temporality designated by the term Nachträglichkeit, often translated into English as "belatedness" or "afterwardness," which takes on new meanings in the context of the temporal lag between historical events and their cinematic, photographic, and televisual representations. If mass media images of violence can only be understood nachträglich—after the fact, belatedly—then what sorts of condensations or structural relations can be found latent in the image, even upon its initial reception?

The racial condensations and triangulations dealt with in this chapter— between white, black, and oriental—also form the basic constellation of substitutions that are considered, in various permutations, throughout the rest of the book. As First Blood shows, the oriental obscene underlies the racial interactions that structure its narrative, even while the oriental remains missing, appearing only in the black and white figures that stand in for it. Morrell's primal scene sets up the Vietnam War as the primary scenario through which other American civil disorders, such as civil rights protests, urban race riots, and antiwar protests, are to be understood, even while the actual war remains off-screen. The next chapter looks closely at the Vietnam War itself; this chapter explores the links between these other scenes of violence that frame by analogy the meaning of the Vietnam War for Americans. What does it mean to link black rioters or white protesters with Vietnamese guerrillas? How is black and oriental racial difference to be understood with respect to whiteness, as well as to each other? What is politically at stake in each of these connections? If Morrell frames *First Blood* as an illustration of what might happen if "the Vietnam war literally came home to America," we might reframe what Rambo brings home of the war as not simply violence but also the oriental obscene, premised on a cross-racial identification in a shared scenario of violence.

The American 1968 as Primal Scene

Morrell's account of the genesis of *First Blood* is also a phantasmatic origin story for the American 1968 as the starting point of the Vietnam era.[6] Although the various strands of events in this origin story can obviously be traced even further back—in the civil rights movement to the murder of Emmett Till or Montgomery bus boycotts in 1955, in the Vietnam War to the Gulf of Tonkin Resolution of 1964—they condense into a particularly visible public scene around 1968, made possible by the simultaneous growth in television news in the late 1960s.[7] Sasha Torres argues that television news first established its authority and prominence by its coverage of the civil rights movement in the 1950s, positing itself as a "national medium" capable of forging a "national consensus" on what seemed to be problems isolated in the South.[8] Part of the power of television news over the print media was its monopoly on realism, especially in representing seemingly unmediated spectacles of black suffering for the white (i.e., national) gaze. In the late 1960s the Vietnam War began to take the place of the civil rights movement as the content in this equation between the news apparatus and the body politic, with equally abject spectacles of oriental suffering. Newscasts' oft-noted desire for authenticity, objectivity, and immediacy were well aligned with the growth of cinéma vérité styles that privileged mobile, hand-held cameras and synchronous, live sound, especially when representing exotic images of foreign warfare. According to Daniel Hallin, "television news came of age on the eve of Vietnam," being both ideologically and technologically primed to convey the war.[9] Morrell's *First Blood* becomes a savvy index of media consumption, situating Morrell as a member of a larger imagined community of television viewers consuming the "living-room wars" for the first time. That Morrell singles out this year as the moment for this novel to emerge from his imagination suggests that 1968 functions as a kind of primal scene: an imagined point of origin from which other fantasies of violence will emerge.

It is remarkable how much the American 1968 could be considered itself a television event, marked by images from a violent public sphere invading the privacy of the home. From the characterization of the Vietnam War as a

"living-room war" and the proximity to press conferences of the assassinations of Martin Luther King Jr. and Robert Kennedy, to the riots that accompanied the Republican and Democratic National Conventions, television was
a necessary and structurally significant element of the events of 1968. Television retrospectives such as the CBS News Special "The Making of the President: 1968" (1969) and the CBS documentary *Nineteen Sixty-Eight: A Look for New
Meanings* (1978) often elide the difference between historically embedded
perspectives of the visual media and the transcendental perspective of a
historical imagination.[10] In *Nineteen Sixty-Eight* the voice-over narration by the
correspondent Harry Reasoner begins, "A whole year can pass through the
mind's eye in just a few seconds, but the mind can also seize on a moment in
time." Optical effects such as fast and slow motion, still frames, blurred
transitions, double exposures, and swish-pans literalize the movements of
the mind's eye through the images of history: images of King and Kennedy
before their deaths, Johnson's exit from the presidential race, and the violent
antiwar protests at the Democratic National Convention (fig. 2). Yet the images are obliquely rather than directly representative of these events, especially in the case of King's and Kennedy's assassinations. These events are
missing from the visual record, and in place of an image of death we are given
indexical images of their living moments, an uncanny substitution that only
moving images can achieve. The effect is that of a melancholic reanimation as
well as a compulsive repetition, framing 1968 as a phantasmatic space and
time in which King and Kennedy live again, only to die repeatedly in each re-
viewing of the year. The key to this documentary, and all similar media
documentaries, is that one is never merely "watching 1968" but also always
"watching oneself watching 1968," or reliving one's past engagement with
the media apparatus.

To help us understand this relationship between viewing and experience
and their role in constituting a sense of historical memory, I turn to the
psychoanalytic concept of the primal scene. In Freud the primal scene typi-
cally refers to an infantile memory of having witnessed one's parents having
sexual intercourse.[11] Laplanche treats the primal scene as part of the larger
category of primal fantasies (*Urphantasie*), which he posits as an archetypal
structure that underlies "the phantasy life of every individual."[12] What is
intriguing about the primal scene is not its truth value as a record of a real
event, but rather the way it theorizes the act of witnessing and a subject's
relationship to his or her own history. Freud's own warnings against accepting the primal scene as pure fact reveal a shift from the content of memory
to the act of remembering itself. As Laplanche and Pontalis describe in

2. Representing 1968: the camera eye moves through the collective memory of the assassinations of Martin Luther King Jr. and Robert Kennedy, President Johnson's announcement not to seek reelection, and the antiwar protests at the Democratic National Convention. Frame enlargements from *Nineteen Sixty-Eight: A Look for New Meanings.*

The Language of Psycho-analysis, the primal scene and primal fantasies necessarily imply the concept of an origin and its role in constituting a narrative for the formation of a subject: "If we consider the themes which can be recognized in primal phantasies (primal scene, castration, seduction), the striking thing is that they have one trait in common: they are all related to the origins. Like collective myths, they claim to provide a representation of and a 'solution' to whatever constitutes a major enigma for the child. Whatever appears to the subject as a reality of such a type as to require an explanation or 'theory,' these phantasies dramatise into the primal moment or original point of departure of a history."[13] It is significant that the "solutions" to the enigmas of birth, sexual difference, and the emergence of sexuality take the form of a dramatization rather than a causal narrative; elsewhere Laplanche and Pontalis emphasize the "scenic" and "visual" nature of such fantasies.[14] These primal fantasies do not explain the enigmas of origin, even in the allegorical language of mythology; instead they provide a storehouse for unassimilated memories and experiences that do not become significant until *nachträglich*, afterward.

The concept of Nachträglichkeit is also an important part of the primal scene and of primal fantasies in general.[15] The form of temporality implied by the term (and its adjectival form, nachträglich) offers a model for the relationship between texts and the history they purport to represent, one that is neither strictly deterministic nor wholly retroactive. Freud uses the term to refer to the convoluted causality and temporality associated with traumatic memory: "eine Erinnerung verdrängt wird, die nur nachträglich zum Trauma geworden ist" ("a memory which becomes a trauma only after the event").[16] This describes a situation in which an earlier, repressed scene of memory fails to cause a trauma until it is activated by a second scene which may seem to have little do to with the first. Because of the time delay between the original scene and the onset of symptoms, as well as the necessity of the second scene as the conscious trigger, the causality between the primal scene and the trauma is indirect and the direction of their temporality is confused. Laplanche argues that this apparent confusion of temporality and causality is productive and should be maintained in its ambiguity rather than resolved into a clear, linear narrative. He glosses Freud's use of nachträglich: "Here is the heart of the argument: we try to track down the trauma, but the traumatic memory was only secondarily traumatic: we never manage to fix the traumatic event historically. This fact might be illustrated by the image of a Heisenberg-like 'relation of indeterminacy': in situating the trauma, one cannot appreciate its traumatic effect, and vice versa."[17] Applied to the primal scene of 1968,

Nachträglichkeit requires that we complicate the causality between historical referents and the texts that represent them, and that we also investigate the nature of the temporality between referents and signifiers. Cathy Caruth has argued that this temporal gap is precisely what "permit[s] *history* to arise where *immediate understanding* may not."[18] Rather than trying to fix the events of 1968 into a singular narrative of the Vietnam era, we should examine the temporal disorder that characterizes the emergence of texts and memories about the Vietnam era.

We can see the dynamics of the primal scene and Nachträglichkeit playing out in one of the most iconic phrases of the American 1968: the "living-room war." Popularized by Michael Arlen in the *New Yorker* in the late 1960s, the phrase has been popularly misinterpreted as a statement about the immediacy of the Vietnam War to the American public as compared to previous wars, a televisual form of "bringing the war home" that helped sway public opinion against the war. In fact Arlen was far from celebrating the power of television to make the war real. The essay that brings us this famous phrase also contains a telling critique of way the Vietnam War arrives in the living room:

> They look at Vietnam, it seems, as a child kneeling in the corridor, his eye to the keyhole, looks at two grownups arguing in a locked room—the aperture of the keyhole small; the figures shadowy, mostly out of sight; the voices indistinct, isolated threats without meaning; isolated glimpses, part of an elbow, a man's jacket (who is the man?), a part of a face, a woman's face. Ah, she is crying. One sees the tears. (The voices continue indistinctly.) One counts the tears. Two tears. Three tears. Two bombing raids. Four seek-and-destroy missions. Six administration pronouncements. Such a fine-looking woman. One searches in vain for the other grownup, but, ah, the keyhole is so small, he is somehow never in the line of sight. Look! There is General Ky. Look! There are some planes returning safely to the *Ticonderoga*.[19]

Arlen's scenario of a child peering through a keyhole stages the television viewing of the Vietnam War along the lines of a sexual primal scene. Like the enigma of adult sexuality presented to a child, the Vietnam War appears as an indistinct, puzzling spectacle, but a spectacle nonetheless that fascinates with its "figures shadowy" and "isolated glimpses." The hazards of war are not made more real for the American public, as Arlen argues, but are in fact "diminished, in part, by the physical size of the television screen, which, for all the industry's advances, still shows one a picture of men three inches tall shooting at other men three inches tall, and trivialized, or at least tamed, by the enveloping cozy alarums of the household."[20]

However, the secret that the living-room primal scene seems to hide is not the question of personal origins—Where do babies come from?—but the origins of a highly public war whose causes, actions, and goals cannot be completely pieced together from the available information. The Nachträglich-keit of television here has two facets: it is delayed from the event by the processing and transfer of film footage, but it is also delayed in the sense that its viewers are "as a child," watching the event prematurely, before its full meaning for the child (and the nation) can mature. The child in Arlen's analogy is forced to make meaning of the spectacle not only because of its low definition—"shadowy" figures and "indistinct" voices viewed through a "small" aperture—but also because of his historical immaturity with regard to the full meaning of the scenario before him. In this developmental narrative Arlen seems to imply that the war acts like a catalyst which, belatedly, inaugu-rates an "adult" sensibility toward violence in the Vietnam era, much like the primal scene inaugurates adult sexuality through its premature implantation of images in the child's psyche. But the paradoxical juxtaposition of the infantilizing televisual apparatus, with its keyhole aperture and three-inch men, and the obscene violence of bombing raids and search-and-destroy missions, seems to show that this purported American innocence is itself a fiction, constructed through the hindsight narrative of the American 1968 as a historical rupture point.

Whether television news actually helped to foster active participation in the debates over the Vietnam War is not known. The myth of the heroic press certainly arose in this era, but others have argued for the press as a follower rather than a leader in public opinion.[21] Certainly there were many debates in the 1960s about the dangers of television watching producing a generation of passive consumer subjects.[22] However, from the viewpoint of the primal scene, I contend that there remains a deeper level of existential passivity beneath the passivity of consumption, one which marks the American subject as "thrown," in a Heideggerian sense, into a world not of his making, and sit-uated within a symbolic and ideological structure that exceeds him. Laplanche reminds us that the primal scene is not simply a tale of voyeurism, but also contains a story about the passivity of viewing: "Impotent in his crib, [the child] is Ulysses tied to the mast or Tantalus, on whom is imposed the spectacle of parental intercourse."[23] In an era of media saturation the fact that events such as the Vietnam War are widely available as media representations may itself be taken as a form of violence on the viewer. As Laplanche states, "Even the *letting-see* . . . is always in a sense a *making-see*, an exhibition."[24]

What exactly is the child and the nation being *made to see*? A nation under attack by another, as in the Tet Offensive and nightly assessments of American body counts? Or a nation attacking itself, as in the assassination of antiwar figures like King and Kennedy and in the battles between police and protesters and rioters? In the documentary *Nineteen Sixty-Eight* and the Eisenhower Commission's *Progress Report*, even the time between these events disappears as they overlap and merge through filmic montage into a single nightmarish scenario, one that condenses their meanings as well. As the primal scene helps us to understand, it does not matter whether these scenes of violence are actually causally related. What matters is that they are understood together, and thus are *seen* together on the televisual screen of cultural memory. Following Freud, we might conceive of the American 1968 as a memory rather than an event, and one that becomes traumatic only long after the fact of its occurrence.

The Wars on the Home Front: White Antiwar Protest

A curious slogan, "Bring the war home." Curious too, the particular slant Ted Gold gave it in a talk with an old Columbia comrade he met in the West End Bar on Broadway not long before he died. As things stood, Ted Gold said, the Vietnam war was an abstraction; liberals could afford to sit back and let it happen on the other side of the world. "We've got to turn New York into Saigon," he said.

—Todd Gitlin, *The Sixties: Years of Hope, Days of Rage*

[Captain Trautman to Sheriff Teasle:] Now you talk about fighting him [Rambo] one-to-one, yet you imply there's something diseased about a man who kills for a living. Christ, you haven't fooled me, you're as military as he is, and that's how this mess got started. I hope you do get a one-to-one fight with him. It'll be the last surprise of your life. Because he's something special these days. He's an expert at his business. We forced him into it over there, and now he's bringing it all back home.

—David Morrell, *First Blood*

Whereas *First Blood* is a phantasmatic staging of what would happen if Vietnam came home to America, there were yet more manifestations of this desire to be found within American society.[25] As we investigate this novel that seeks to narrativize the confused, televisual memory of the American 1968, it is worth separating out the individual historical scenarios that make up this complex primal scene, beginning with the antiwar movement, the originator of the slogan "Bring the war home." If the distance of the Vietnam War made its violence abstract and invisible, many antiwar activists aimed precisely to make that violence concrete and visible, even at the cost of threatening the tranquility of peacetime that they wished to preserve by ending the war. The disruptions caused by antiwar protests were sometimes themselves experienced as another theater of the war, and even viewed by pro-war advocates as the front line of the cold war's larger struggle against communist agitation. Nonetheless there were clear differences between the nature of the war brought home by the antiwar movement and the war depicted in Morrell's novel, as well as arguments about what "Vietnam" meant as a modifier to that war. The antiwar movement invented its own notion of the Vietnam War in the act of bringing it home to the U.S., even as it sought to unearth hidden truths about that war through the act of protest. Morrell's phantasmatic war draws on the American 1968 by overlaying the violence of Vietnam upon the violence that accompanied antiwar protest, thus producing a projection of a projection that further distances the Vietnam War even as it seeks to embody it in the character of Rambo. This interplay between historical fact and its belated fictionalization begins to bring out the contours of the wounded American national identity that arises from the structuration of 1968 as a primal scene.

The novel First Blood (1972) follows Rambo, a former Green Beret and recent prisoner of war in Vietnam, as he drifts through the small town of Madison, Kentucky. Madison's sheriff, Wilfred Teasle, arrests him, but he soon escapes from jail and embarks on a killing spree that results in his own death when he is shot by police. Like its later film version (1982), the novel contains a mix of countercultural and mainstream symbols and ideologies. One early reviewer called the book "carnography," mimicking the media discourse on the pornography of violence, and described Morrell's work as a "meat novel" equivalent to the "meat movie, the kind in which we pay to see meat fly off someone's head as he is shotgunned."[26] Yet there is a vague sympathy with the counterculture and antiestablishment politics of the 1960s hidden beneath the blatant celebration of violence for violence's sake, one that directly invokes the antiwar movement. Sheriff Teasle and the judge sentencing him at first mistake Rambo for a young, antiwar hippie because of his long hair and scruffy looks. "I see kids on the TV demonstrating and rioting and all," Judge Dobzyn teases Rambo, "and what I have to know, doesn't that hair get itchy down the back of your neck?"[27] Morrell reports that a direct inspiration for the jailhouse confrontation between Rambo and Teasle is a news article about "a group of hitchhiking hippies [who] had been picked up by the local police, stripped, hosed and shaved."[28] But Rambo's military training quickly breaks with his hippie appearance, as he subsequently hunts down and ruthlessly kills each of Teasle's deputies during a long chase through the woods—a plot detail left out of the film version for the sake of creating a more sympathetic antihero.

But as the antiwar movement itself would prove, violence and antiwar sentiments were not mutually exclusive, and Rambo's violence is offered as an indirect critique of the violence of the war. Capt. Sam Trautman, the man who headed the military school where Rambo received his training, refutes Teasle's attempts to pathologize Rambo as a psychotic killing machine by drawing parallels between Rambo and Teasle's law enforcement role. When Teasle objects to Trautman's analogy, claiming, "I don't kill for a living," Trautman disdainfully replies, "Of course not. You tolerate a system that lets others do it for you. And when they come back from the war, you can't stand the smell of death on them."[29] Rambo's death drive is thus framed as the return of the repressed at the heart of the institutionalized violence usually reserved for the authority of the state. The hypocrisy of the state is made clear in the way it disavows its warriors after their use value is exhausted. Rambo's violence is partly a protest against this system and anticipates the critiques made by antiwar veterans later in the decade about the lack of social services designed to help these veterans transition back into nonviolent civilian life. "We forced him into it over there," Trautman continues, "and now he's bringing it all back home"—a phrase echoing the famous antiwar slogan, "bring the war home."[30]

This ambivalence toward violence is also found in other debates during the Vietnam era, most notably the internal struggle between antiwar groups over the efficacy of violent rather than peaceful protest. The antiwar movement was never a homogeneous campaign driven by a single organization or a unified set of principles, and the liberal and radical branches of the movement differed greatly on whether the ultimate goal of its actions was to simply end the war or to effect a larger transformation of American society. One event that brought these tensions into spectacular conflict was the protest at the Democratic National Convention in Chicago in August 1968, in which over 12,000 policemen, 6,000 National Guardsmen, and 6,000 regular army troops violently attacked approximately 10,000 antiwar protesters, resulting in over 1,000 injured and 662 arrested over the course of the weeklong convention.[31] Although the protests were marred by the conflicting goals of the numerous antiwar groups that took part, including the anarchy-inclined Yippies, the moderate pacifist National Mobilization to End the War in Vietnam (Mobe), and the New Left group Students for a Democratic Society (SDS), any non-violent intentions on the part of these organizers were undermined at the start by the refusal of Mayor Richard J. Daley to grant protesters permits that would have let them lawfully congregate and march in Grant Park, near the site of the convention. The tension at these protests was further heightened by the orders given to the Illinois National Guard to used armed force to defend themselves and city property, echoing Daley's own "shoot to kill" orders to Chicago policemen during the riots in April 1968 following King's assassination.[32] The resulting violence from both sides was shocking but not unanticipated, as police used tear gas and nightsticks to subdue a raucous and chaotic crowd which was itself armed with rocks, bricks, and bottles.

What made the protests even more spectacular was the presence of over 6,000 newsmen in Chicago, drawn by the convention itself but also awaiting the inevitable clashes between protesters and police. One director, Haskell Wexler, filmed the last scenes of his fictional homage to cinéma vérité, *Medium Cool* (1969), at the protests and the convention: "We all knew for months beforehand that there would be clashes. . . . What surprised us was their extent. For my film I'd planned to hire extras and dress them up as Chicago policemen, but in the end Mayor Richard Daley provided us with all the extras we needed."[33] These scenes, which feature the actress Verna Bloom wandering around Grant Park during the daytime in the midst of the actual chaos, show some of the actions that were not featured prominently in the television or print news coverage of the protests. There are images of reporters and their interactions with the protesters, the police, and the National Guard. Protesters scream almost jubilantly, "The whole world is watching!," as an ABC cameraman films them, revealing the importance of televisuality to the protest's rhetorical tactics. Without direct access to the channels of power inside the convention hall, antiwar protesters must relay their message to these politicians through the proxy of a national audience. But in the next several shots we see a press photographer stripped of his camera, and then an NBC camera car retreating behind a line of policemen and Guardsmen, and the crowd's exuberance turns into despair at the loss of television's gaze: "NBC, come back! Stay with us!" (fig. 3). Still the press was a thin shield against the onslaught of police brutality, as newsmen and their cameras and microphones also found themselves at the receiving end of the violence. Over sixty journalists were injured in the Chicago protests, at times producing startling images of policemen charging directly toward cameras, thus giving the lie to the supposed disembodiment of the apparatus.[34] To illustrate this violence the CBS *Evening News* broadcast of 27 August showed its cameraman Delos Hall

3. An NBC camera car at the protests outside the Democratic National Convention in Chicago in 1968. Frame enlargement from *Medium Cool.*

from both sides of the camera: first filming images of his own assault, and then narrating that assault as an interview subject. This reversal of roles directly implicated the visual mass media as not only recorders of historical events but also participants in that same history. CBS's description of the protests a few days later ironically applies as much to their own journalists as to the protesters on screen: "Many of the over 300 injured were attacked as they stood quietly, watching the waves of police charge the protesters in the street."[35]

Although a large part of the antiwar movement contested the war from the perspective of loyal American citizens, one of the tactics of the more militant groups was to embrace an active identification with the North Vietnamese and the National Liberation Front (also known pejoratively as "Viet Cong"), as a way of indicating their estrangement from not only the culture of war but from traditional American values. Jerry Rubin, a leader of the Yippies at the Chicago protests, equated liberation from the constraints of American society—what he described as "Detroit, Newark, campus disruptions, every-one smoking pot, people learning to speak out and be different"—with "be-com[ing] Vietcong."[36] A group of protesters enacted their own symbolic warfare in Grant Park, screaming "Take the hill!" and occupying a large equestrian statue of the Civil War general John Logan with the red and blue flags of the Viet Cong.[37] Even the Mobe leader Rennie Davis, a moderate in comparison with Rubin, declared to a crowd at the end of convention week,

"Don't vote. . . . Join us in the streets of America. . . . Build a National Liberation Front for America."[38] Among the most fervent interpreters of the slogan "Bring the war home" was the radical group known as the Weather Underground, which split from the SDS the spring after the Chicago riots. One of the Weather Underground's first public actions was the Days of Rage in Chicago in October 1969, which were planned as a response to police violence that accompanied the Democratic National Convention and timed to coincide with the trial of the Chicago Eight.[39] As one Weatherman, the Japanese American activist Shin'ya Ono, remarked of his participation in the Days of Rage, "The abstract phrase 'international solidarity' began to have a real meaning. We began to feel the Vietnamese in ourselves."[40] But despite these gestures of solidarity, the antiwar movement never fully came to terms with the racial dimensions of the Vietnam War. Its largely white members borrowed the racial otherness of the Vietnamese as a symbol of their rejection of American society but could not shed its own orientalist assumptions. Jeremy Varon notes that the Weathermen's advocacy of violence was fueled by a triangulated identification with both Vietnamese guerrillas and militant blacks such as the Black Panthers, which was "a volatile and often vexed effort of members of the white middle class to confront and somehow renounce their structural privilege."[41] As it was for Jerry Rubin, "becoming Viet Cong" for the Weather Underground was first and foremost about redefining whiteness and its privileges.

Although such overtly violent tactics alienated more pacifist partners in the antiwar coalition, this type of revolutionary rhetoric was echoed even by other moderate groups in performative acts of violence, such as guerrilla theater troupes, die-ins, and draft card burnings. Radical Catholic pacifists such as the Catonsville Nine raided draft boards and burned thousands of draft cards with homemade napalm, turning the weapons of war against the war itself.[42] The Vietnam Veterans against the War staged some of the most publicized acts of performative violence, such as Operation RAW (Rapid American Withdrawal), in which VVAW members marched from New Jersey to Pennsylvania in September 1970 and staged "search-and-destroy" missions throughout the small towns they passed through, including taking and torturing prisoners, seizing property, and shooting civilian bystanders.[43] Each of these acts of performative violence was intended to dramatize the violence of Vietnam for an uninformed or apathetic American public, although that same public was often repulsed by the tactics of the movement even as it came to agree with its antiwar positions.[44] If the antiwar movement succeeded in bringing the war home, it did so at the price of being seen as part of the war.

Unlike the antiwar protesters who deliberately utilized violence as a rhetorical strategy, it is unclear whether Rambo brings the violence of the war home as a conscious protest or because he is physically and psychically unable to leave the war behind. Rambo illustrates the overdetermined political meanings assigned to the Vietnam vet during the later years of the war, caught in a tug of war between those who claim the vets as patriotic heroes and those who deride them as crazed killers.[45] On his deathbed Rambo gives himself conflicting reasons for why he escalated his feud with Teasle to such excessive ends. At first he sides with a libertarian ethos that vaguely recalls New Left antiestablishment views: "To live his way, he had been determined to fight anyone who interfered . . . in a way he had fought for a principle." But he also admits a secret and uncontrollable pleasure in committing violence: "He had enjoyed the fight too much, enjoyed too much the risk and the excitement. Perhaps the war had conditioned him."[46] In one sense Rambo dramatizes the accusations of both antiwar pacifists and anti–media violence alarmists, who feared that the prevalence of violence would anesthetize people from its moral horrors. But there is also an element of unconscious trauma that structures his violent outburst, making him an early symbol of the Vietnam War's victimization of its combat soldiers. The theme of posttraumatic stress disorder, although not yet having been named, was certainly on Morrell's mind, as he claimed to have based Rambo's psychological profile on the figure of Audie Murphy, a famous veteran of the Second World War who reportedly suffered from shell shock.[47] Rambo explodes with violence in Teasle's jail not merely because of indignation over the officers' rough treatment, but because the jailhouse abuse belatedly recalls an episode of torture he experienced in Vietnam. Upon entering the cold, cramped jail cell, he alludes to the tortures the novel has yet to describe, and this experience gives way to a chapter-long flashback to Vietnam. When one of Teasle's officers approaches Rambo to shave his beard, a flash of light triggers a violent reaction: "Rambo watched the long blade flash in the lights, and remembered the enemy officer slicing his chest, and that was the end. He broke, grabbing the razor and standing, pushing them away."[48] It is at this point that the violence of the novel commences in earnest, with Rambo slicing the officer across the stomach and watching his guts spill out. The victim quickly becomes the victimizer, and Rambo regresses into guerrilla warfare in the rural jungles of Kentucky.

If *First Blood* highlights Rambo's ability to go native and assimilate to the tactics used by the Vietnamese enemy, it is important to note that his assimilation is involuntary and traumatic rather than calculated and deliberate, marked by the experience of being a victim rather than an agent of violence.

His experiences as a prisoner of war in Vietnam are set apart from the rest of the novel as the only chronological deviation from an otherwise linear plot. Tortured, starved, and forced to do heavy manual labor, he survives his ordeal because, ironically, his training as a Green Beret had primed him for pain and physical depravation: "There was not much they could do to him that his instructors had not already put him through."[49] Although Vietnamese barbarity is presented as the polar opposite of American civilization, it also ends up mirroring the modern discipline and elite training that represents the technological advancement of that civilization. When Rambo escapes his captors and finds his way back to South Vietnam, he hides for days while evading what he thinks are enemy soldiers but turn out to be Americans who almost mistake him for an enemy as well. In the heterotopic space of the jungle identities become confused, and Rambo becomes alternately the Vietnamese evading the Americans and the American evading the Vietnamese. Far from being a playful role reversal, his experiences in the POW camp and the jungle become the traumatic kernel that sparks Rambo's violent and excessive rage in the jail cell. His sudden flashback, sparked by the flash of a razor in the light, invokes a complex set of identificatory postures, in which he is forced back into the position of being the victim of an oriental violence and then rejects that position by occupying the role of an orientalized aggressor. Teasle's own backstory, as a decorated veteran of the Korean War, only furthers the oriental backdrop to this confrontation, as he and Rambo chase each other over the Kentucky hillside as if each were back in his respective Asian war zone.

The multiplicity of ways Morrell's fictional narrative and the antiwar movement's historical activities brought the Vietnam War home ultimately converge in the oriental obscene, as this invisible fantasy begins to manifest itself in the structure of the primal scene of 1968. Although the element of unconscious trauma seems to separate Rambo from the protesters at the Chicago Democratic National Convention, they both return to the absent but crucial figure of the Viet Cong as a source of their respective forms of violence. While members of the Yippies and the Weather Underground may have viewed the Viet Cong as a politically utopian symbol that allowed them to transcend their own Americanness and whiteness, Rambo reveals the nightmarish side of this fantasy that binds Vietnam and America together. But orientalness is not the only form of racial otherness that structures this fantasy. Perhaps even more primary within American culture is the black/white binary, which itself comes into the national consciousness around 1968. It is not simply America at large that Morrell opposes to Vietnam in his televisual memory of 1968, but an America of racial conflict, its inner cities a euphemism for black urban ghettos. While some commentators compare the black urban riots of the 1960s to the Vietnam War as a way of disciplining black bodies, some blacks themselves adopt the analogy to Vietnam as a utopian gesture of resistance against white supremacy, but with a crucial difference from their white radical counterparts. Both these tactics of allegorizing blackness through oriental-ness continue to play upon the figure of the Viet Cong as an absent presence in the phantasmatic scenarios each constructs out of the visual materials of historical representations. They continue to bring the war home for their own political agendas while at the same time revealing how the meanings of the Vietnam War exceed the bounds of their narratives.

The Other Living-Room War: Urban Black Rebellion

The U.S. film industry is far from adopting or likely to adopt an "anything goes" creed. The screen is well behind political demonstrators in bawdy language, and well behind the newspapers and magazines in subject-matter. . . . Perhaps sometimes there is the further point of realism: who will it offend, in what number, and at what costs? These doubts stop films dealing with the two unpopular wars of the moment, Vietnam and Ghetto.

—Robert J. Landry, "Many Themes Nix for Pix: 'Anything Goes'
Only Semi-True," *Variety*, 17 January 1968

[Sheriff Teasle to Rambo:] Listen, I don't get it. That rig of yours, the clothes and hair and all. Didn't you know when you came back down the main street out there you'd stand out like some black man?

—David Morrell, *First Blood*

Perhaps even more than antiwar protests, the racial violence that swept through American cities in the late 1960s in the form of urban rebellions was consid-ered by contemporary observers to be a form of war brewing within American borders.[50] By one estimate there were 397 instances of black riots between 1964 and 1971, 130 of which took place in the week following King's assassina-tion in April 1968.[51] As *Variety* termed it, "Vietnam and Ghetto" were two sides of the violent primal scene of 1968 from which *First Blood* and other Vietnam texts emerged. This sentiment was echoed at the convention for the National Association of Broadcasters, where a panel of news experts declared, "The coverage of racial incidents is the touchiest issue in broadcast news today, with reportage of Vietnam running a close second in explosiveness."[52] Like Vietnam, "Ghetto" was a living-room war that played out on American television screens, showing miniaturized versions of segregated American inner cities as foreign as Saigon to most white, middle-class, suburban viewers.[53] As Morrell described it, the aftermath of the riots saw damaged American cityscapes reminiscent of South Vietnamese cities, with smoke-filled ruins, sidewalk debris, and the strong presence of military troops. Even the liberal sociologist Todd Gitlin, then a member of the SDS, remarked of the riots in 1967, "The Vietnam war seemed to be coming home."[54] Nonetheless, despite their location in the heart of the nation, in some cases only miles from the living rooms such scenes had invaded, the urban rebellions and black riots of the 1960s were depicted as distant spectacles, reflecting the foreignness of the Vietnam War they purportedly mirrored. However, the scenario of black rioting was not simply a visual template for inflicting violence upon the nation, but also conjured the "racial incidents" of the civil rights movement as a way of identifying with victimhood. In his role as a southern sheriff, Teasle interpellates Rambo into the subject position of blackness. It is telling that in *First Blood*, despite the absence of black characters, blackness appears only when Rambo is arrested and mistreated by the police, in the form of a momentarily mistaken identity. Racialized policing connects both the first half of the novel, when Rambo is unjustly harassed by police, and the second half, when he becomes a murderer and harasser himself. Likewise in the conflation of the civil rights movement with the urban riots of the 1960s the other living-room war makes use of black racial otherness to stage both the act of violation and the suffering of that violence, resulting in an intimacy with violence not found in the purely foreign scenario of the Vietnam War.

One major difference between the race riots of the 1960s and those that occurred before 1960 was the racial makeup of the rioters. Incidents such as the Rock Springs, Wyoming, massacre in 1885, the race riot in Chicago during the "Red Summer" of 1919, and the Zoot Suit riots in Los Angeles in 1943 were characterized by the participation of large numbers of whites in mass violence against racial minorities, in these cases Chinese, blacks, and Mexicans, respectively.[55] In contrast the riots of the 1960s mostly took place in black neighborhoods and were directed at private and civic property as proxies for white power and white capital. A majority of the riots in the 1960s also took place outside of the South, the region previously stigmatized as a site of overt racial violence in news coverage of the early civil rights movement. All of the cities stricken by rioting had hidden histories of decades of employment and housing discrimination, coupled with poor police–community relations, that produced conditions of segregation and economic disparity to rival that of the more explicitly policed Jim Crow South.[56] The riots of the 1960s were responses to these hidden forms of racism deeply embedded in institutions, as opposed to the overt, personalized racial prejudice made visible by the civil rights movement. This explains why, for many African Americans and some white liberals, the riots were viewed more as revolts or rebellions that forcibly drew attention to previously invisible problems, while at the same time taking a small measure of revenge against the institutions that seemed to be the cause of these problems.[57]

However, these differences between the riots of the 1960s and the civil rights movement also meant that their media images relied on very different configurations of race and violence. The civil rights movement used non-violence not only as a moral ideology but as a rhetorical tactic. Acts of nonviolent civil disobedience such as sit-ins and marches were used to draw out and make explicit the violence of the racist state. If coverage of news events such as the desegregation of Central High School in Little Rock, Arkansas, in 1957 and the civil rights demonstrations in Birmingham and Selma, Alabama, in 1963 and 1965 gave television news a newfound sense of moral legitimacy and social relevance, as Sasha Torres and J. Fred MacDonald have argued, it did so by focusing overwhelmingly on the iconography of passive, victimized black bodies.[58] For example, at Little Rock, one of the most iconic events of the civil rights movement, President Dwight D. Eisenhower called upon federal troops to protect nine black students from white citizen mobs, local law enforcement, and even the Arkansas National Guard. Like the eye of a storm, the students of the Little Rock Nine carried themselves in these images with dignity and grace, barely responding to the chaos of the protests surrounding them. But some of the most striking spectacles of this incident are not of the students, but of the jeering whites surrounding them, their faces and bodies distorted with anger. The bayonets of the 101st Airborne that appear in these images were used not in the defense of but rather against white subjects, as soldiers formed a barricade between the Little Rock Nine and white protesters and in some cases pointed their weapons at these white bodies (fig. 4). Although the black teenagers were the cause and the focus of the racial conflict at Central High, many of the confrontations caught on film were white-on-white, and were even interpreted as a variation of the North-on-South conflict of the Civil War.[59]

Despite the drama of the Little Rock protests, events from the early 1960s brought even more shocking images of what the Eisenhower Commission called "the violence of police dogs, fire hoses, and cattle prods," this time directly striking at black bodies. The march known as "Blood Sunday," which

4. Soldiers of the 101st Airborne disperse white protestors while escorting the Little Rock Nine, the first black students to attend Central High School in Little Rock, Arkansas, 25–26 September 1957. Frame enlargements from "Fighting Back, 1957–1962," *Eyes on the Prize I: America's Civil Rights Years (1954–1965).*

took place on 7 March 1965 in Selma, provides some of the starkest examples of the suffering black body offered up as sacrificial lamb to both southern policemen and national television and news cameras. With barely any provocation or warning, Selma's Sheriff Jim Clark and his men attacked peaceful black marchers with billy clubs and tear gas, all of which was captured by ABC news cameras (fig. 5). Torres has chronicled how strategists in the Southern Christian Leadership Conference actually courted police violence at Selma and elsewhere and actively sought the presence of the visual media to capture these confrontations, manipulating these images of black victimization to garner more publicity and support for the movement, particularly outside the South.[60] However, the power of these images relied upon the complete visual passivity of the black bodies before the cameras, allowing sympathetic white viewers to imagine themselves as saviors of these bodies and spurring them into active participation in civil rights activities. These images worked for the civil rights movement only insofar as white viewers disidentified with the oppressive whiteness seen on screen, aligning themselves instead with the benevolent whiteness of the camera and the press.

But the same tactics that succeeded for the civil rights movement in the South—boycotts, sit-ins, demonstrations, intervention of federal law, and appeals to white morality—were inapplicable to the black riots that took place elsewhere. Mainstream commentators almost uniformly condemned the violence of the riots as meaningless and deviant criminal activity. The sociologist Robert Fogelson attributes this "riff-raff theory" of the riots to a widely held conviction that "no matter how grave the grievances there are no legitimate grounds for violent protest, a conviction shared by most Americans which reflects the nation's traditional confidence in orderly social change."[61] In this sense these black urban rebellions suffered from the same backlash in public opinion that afflicted the antiwar movement, as viewers responded more negatively to the violence of the protests than to the violence they protested. Yet the use of power by the police was never itself designated as a form of violence, since its deadly force is sanctioned by the legitimacy and authority of the state—an ironic exclusion, considering that the visual presence of police and other military troops is what gives the riots an atmosphere of war in the news media. By stepping outside of a tradition of orderly protest, the rioters become aligned with the Vietnamese as terrorists whose violence challenges the sovereignty of the state as if it were an act of war. Accordingly the analogy between Vietnam and Ghetto is not just a statement about the similarity of racialized violence, but also a way of delegitimizing the protests embodied in the riots by associating them with the chaotic violence of war.

5. Police officers under Sheriff Jim Clark of Selma, Alabama, attack black protestors on the Edmund Pettus Bridge, 7 March 1965, as cameras from ABC *Evening News* film the violence. Frame enlargement from "Bridge to Freedom," *Eyes on the Prize I: America's Civil Rights Years (1954–1965)*.

Television and photojournalism visually reinforced the interpretation of the riots as criminal activity rather than black protest, often by positioning the camera at the point of view of police. The National Advisory Commission on Civil Disorders (also known as the Kerner Commission, after its chairman, Governor Otto Kerner of Illinois), convened in the wake of the Detroit and Newark riots in the summer of 1967, noted that news media "tended to emphasize law enforcement activities, thereby overshadowing underlying grievances and tensions. Television coverage tended to give the impression that the riots were confrontations between Negroes and whites [rather] than responses by Negroes to underlying slum problems."[62] Studies of print journalism found a similar bias toward the perspective of authority figures invested in putting down the riots rather than that of members of the community sympathetic to the riots, thus continuing patterns of black invisibility in the white press.[63] For instance, both *Newsweek*'s print coverage and NBC's television footage of the riots in Detroit in July 1967 portray blacks as criminals, either caught in the act of looting or rock throwing or being arrested or subdued by white law enforcement (fig. 6).[64] Ironically, although these particular images were meant to signify the physical threat posed by black rioters, they actually depict blacks as the objects of state violence as they are injured and rounded up.

6. Photographs of National Guardsmen and injured rioters during the riots in Detroit in 1967. From *Newsweek*, 7 August 1967.

News cameras also replicate the perspective of white law enforcement, shooting from behind police lines and from "telecopters," news helicopters that mimic military-style aerial reconnaissance from the front lines of Vietnam. As Paul Virilio notes in *War and Cinema*, wartime aerial observation produces both a perceptual and an epistemological shift, as visual technologies change the goal of war from destruction to representation: "Since the battlefield has always been a field of perception, the war machine appears to the military commander as an instrument of representation, comparable to the painter's palette and brush."[65] From such an aerial vantage point black bodies lose their significance as human subjects and become "information," extended features of a wild landscape that is itself racialized as other.[66] Such positioning differed starkly from news coverage of the larger, mostly white antiwar protests I described earlier, in which news cameras freely mingled among protesters as a sympathetic presence and, in the case of Chicago, were even attacked by police. In the black riots, however, rioters perceived the white press as being aligned with white authority, and sometimes even attacked the reporters and cameramen.[67] Such hostility reflected the estrangement of these segregated black communities from their local press, which had basically ignored these communities prior to (and sometimes after) the riots. As Fred Rheinstein, an NBC producer, observed, "None of us in the news business had any real contacts in the black community. We did not know how to cover the situation any more than the police knew how to control it."[68]

The visual presence of federal troops and the National Guard further elevated the sense of siege described in news coverage of the riots, as their dark green uniforms, helmets, military-grade weaponry, and even tanks contrasted with the lighter uniforms and pistols worn by local police, producing the images described by Morrell that tied the riots to combat in Vietnam. However, this escalation of state violence beyond the capabilities of local police belies the easy characterization of the riots as ordinary crime. As James Button notes, "The Detroit riots thus marked a significant turning point in federal policy toward local law enforcement since this severe upheaval clearly demonstrated to federal officials the inability of local and state forces to contain disorders."[69] State-based National Guard troops, which were usually the first supplemental forces to be called into riots, were overwhelmingly white and middle class, especially during the Vietnam era, when those with the financial means or social connections to avoid the draft considered the National Guard a safer alternative.[70] Their presence, in contrast to the predominantly black residents of these segregated ghettos, also heightened the racial contrast between those policing and those policed, lending credence to the idea of a race war. For instance, the Detroit riot featured images of white Guardsmen patrolling empty streets in formation, with bayonets strapped to their rifles and pointing ominously at the camera, creating the sense of a military occupation that extends to the homes of the people who are watching it (fig. 7). Although the orderly formation of these Guardsmen may suggest the restoration of law and order, there is an ominous tone to such footage, particularly as the streetscape behind them, full of familiar icons such as movie theater marquees and storefronts, remains eerily devoid of activity and residents. Such footage reconfigures the relationship between viewers and racial spectacle made familiar in civil rights coverage; instead of inciting protective sympathy for black victims of racism, here whites in their suburban homes become the victims of the riots, menaced by black urban subjects who remain unseen, off-camera. As one reporter remarked of Detroit, "It was as though the Viet Cong had infiltrated the riot-blackened streets."[71] These images from Detroit mirror images from the Vietnam War by aligning black rioters with Vietnamese terrorists, both invisible yet omnipresent, threatening except when subdued by overt force.

The presence of federal troops in some of the larger riots such as those in Detroit complicated the clear racial division between the police and the policed, since such troops were over 20 percent black and were often better

7. The Michigan National Guardsmen on patrol during the
Detroit riots in 1967. Frame enlargement from "Two Societies,"
Eyes on the Prize II: America at the Racial Crossroads (1965–1985).

received by black communities and demonstrably less racist in their treatment
of black rioters.[72] Many blacks, particularly those who served in the early years
of the Vietnam War, perceived the military as an institution of racial progress,
given that it had integrated more fully than other civilian institutions and
became a potential means of upward mobility.[73] In response to the Detroit riot
President Johnson made use of these associations by employing two army
units with symbolic ties to the civil rights movement: the 101st Airborne,
which had escorted the Little Rock Nine in 1957, and the 82nd Airborne,
which in 1962 defended James Meredith, the first black student to enter the
University of Mississippi.[74] However, the very presence of black soldiers in the
riots highlighted the contradictions of American race relations, with integrated troops being used to put down racial violence in segregated cities.
Ironically the Detroit riot itself was indirectly started by black Vietnam veterans, as the precipitating incident that enraged the community was a police
raid on an after-hours drinking establishment hosting a party for two black
veterans and another man who was about to be sent to Vietnam.[75] As one
black officer stationed in Saigon declared shortly after the riots following
King's assassination, "We're building to a black and white civil war and black
troops—look at the high percentages of black troops in the elite units—black
troops will be used to zap black civilians."[76] As a result some black soldiers categorically rejected riot duty, In August 1968 over sixty black soldiers

8. A black soldier on riot duty in Detroit in 1967. Frame enlargement from "Two Societies," *Eyes on the Prize II: America at the Racial Crossroads* (1965–1985).

stationed at Fort Hood refused to be deployed to the upcoming Democratic National Convention in Chicago, claiming that they "felt they were carrying the white man's burden."[77]

Even those black soldiers who consented to be sent to black riots became overdetermined symbols of the uneven progress of black rights, held up by the mainstream media as signs of racial progress even as they stood amid explosions of racial tensions. As an African American and an American soldier, the black soldier working on riot duty was at once insider and outsider: his racial identity pointed to potentially divided loyalties, while his military service in Vietnam seemed to give him the unique authority to judge the exceptional violence of the riots. The news media seized upon this conflation of roles, producing numerous stories highlighting black soldiers and veterans, comparing Vietnam and Detroit in terms of safety.[78] In an archival clip from the "Two Societies" episode of *Eyes on the Prize II* (1990), a television crew asks one black soldier in the midst of the Detroit riot, "Could you tell us how it feels to have to come from one zone of combat in a foreign land to one in your own land?" He answers, "It's not a good feeling, not one I'm kinda proud of. But it's a job, it's a duty. It has to be done" (fig. 8). Another black soldier, shown in the documentary *1967 Detroit Riots: A Community Speaks* (2003), attempts to resolve this contradiction with the language of racial uplift: "Why doesn't someone go into the army, they could shoot better overseas, for their country? Instead of standing over there shooting at each other, why don't they go over there and fight?" These docile black soldiers are presented to refute the idea that the riots represent a unified black voice of protest; the second soldier even offers military service in Vietnam as a solution to the riots, channeling naturalized black aggression into avenues of state-sanctioned violence. However, such reports did little to mitigate black grievances; the coverage of the riots may even have contributed to the growth of militant black nationalism by highlighting the continued repression and disciplining of black bodies. In a survey of black soldiers in 1971 Wallace Terry found that "83 per cent of the blacks believe that America is in for more race violence than has shattered the nation in the last decade, and most of these, 45 per cent, believe that they would join renewed rioting."[79]

The visual analogy of the ghetto as Vietnam in the mainstream visual media produced a sense of whiteness under siege, which is reinforced by the site of reception for these images: the living room as a private and domestic space that is diametrically opposed to and under the threat of invasion by the public and chaotic space of the ghetto or Vietnam. But the construction of whiteness here is itself premised on two forms of cross-racial identification with blackness. For one, the threat purportedly posed by the racial other is actually embodied in these images by white law enforcement who wield obvious symbols of violence against black bodies in neighborhoods that have become essentially black reservations. Outwardly directed white aggression is projected onto the racial other and then reflected back as a threat against the self. Furthermore the victimized blacks within the image are transformed into victimized white subjects off-camera, who experience the viewing of such violence as a violation of their own personal sense of safety. Mike Davis argues that, despite the fact that "most of the carnage is self-contained within ethnic or class boundaries . . . white middle-class imagination . . . magnifies the perceived threat through a demonological lens."[80] As the *Wall Street Journal* reported in the midst of the riots in the summer of 1967, there appeared to be "an indiscriminate hardening of anti-Negro sentiment among whites" that threatened public support for both civil rights legislation and War on Poverty programs.[81] It is as if the nation can support civil rights only if it sees itself as mobilizing on behalf of a helpless other; the minute that other presents itself as capable of inflicting as well as suffering violence, sympathy is withdrawn.

But despite these ambivalent meanings of threat and violence laid onto the black body, it remains a powerful symbol of victimhood. Linda Williams has cast this ambivalence as a dialectic between a Tom and an anti-Tom tradition in American racial representations, vacillating between the melodrama of the beaten slave body in *Uncle Tom's Cabin* and the menacing black rapist in *Birth of a Nation*.[82] While Morell may have staged *First Blood* with the threatening black rioter in mind, the martyred bodies of civil rights protesters also exert their force on this narrative. Rambo may borrow the ferocity of his attacks from the images of Viet Cong and black rioters, but he derives the righteous indignation of his victimization from the civil rights movement. Sheriff Teasle, his tormentor, is cut from the mold of Bull Connor or Jim Clark, the bigoted police chiefs of the Birmingham and Selma protests, and Rambo's tortures follow the script of these same protests, as he is thrown into jail for no reason and taunts Teasle's deputies to call him "boy."[83] But after Rambo escapes by killing Teasle's men, the narrative flips from the Tom to the anti-Tom side of this dialectic, as Teasle follows the lead of city officials during the black riots by calling for backup from the National Guard.[84] The figure of Rambo combines both these scenarios of racialized violence, starting out as the innocent victim of police brutality and ending as a cop killer and fugitive from the law. Yet this troubled identification with blackness persists mainly when the novel remains in the civilized spaces of the town and the jail. Once the town gives way to the jungle, Rambo's main preoccupation returns to the oriental "they" who populate his flashbacks and mediate his relationship with bodily violence and with death.

Despite Morrell's condensation of the two televised scenes of racialized violence in Vietnam and America, there remains a crucial difference that prevents the two racial others, oriental and black, from collapsing entirely into one another, and that is the association of blackness with "home," America, and the oriental with the *unheimlich*, Vietnam ostensibly, but really a no-place of the imagination that most closely resembles Said's Orient. The distance between the orient and America suggested by this imaginary geography has been translated into a symbolic difference that cannot be spanned. In *First Blood*, as in countless other texts of the Vietnam era, that oriental racial difference comes to signify the most radical of alterities—that of death, or nonbeing—even as black racial difference is aligned with forms of violence more intimately familiar to American culture: the everyday violence of racial discrimination and segregation. Paradoxically, though, the difference between the imagined positions of the oriental and the black within American culture is also the difference that allows for further metaphorical substitution. One of these identifications, found in the living-room war and its ghetto other, cast orientals and blacks as common enemies of white America. But another form of identification, one anxiously disavowed within the previous scenario, brought Vietnam and black America into a metaphorical alliance against white oppression. Seizing upon this metaphor as a political tactic, black revolutionaries embraced the accusations of conservative white commentators and reframed the riots as an active continuation of the Vietnam War, and black rioters as inheritors of the Viet Cong's style of guerrilla warfare.

"No Vietnamese Ever Called Me Nigger": Black Antiwar Protest

If the examples of Third-World courage provided a major lesson for this generation's Black awareness, the obscene spectacle of U.S. "intervention" in Vietnam offers a negative reinforcement of that same lesson in the transparent connection of its racism and its imperialism. "If they do that to them, what would they do to us," the thought occurred. One attitude, then, toward the Vietnamese revolutionaries among resistant Black people is "No Vietnamese ever called me nigger!" A more radical reaction is "We are all in the same boat." The most radical response has been "We are allies."

—Clyde Taylor, "Black Consciousness in the Vietnam Years," *Vietnam and Black America*

The analogy between the Vietnam War and African Americans was not simply the product of a white racist projection; it was also a politically potent form of identification that some black radicals actively embraced toward counter-hegemonic ends. To consider this last permutation of the American 1968, we must consider the antiwar movement and black protest—by which I mean both the civil rights movement and its more radical successor, black power—not as separate phenomena, but as linked political movements, overlapping in the black antiwar movement. In most histories of the antiwar movement the participation of black activists and organizations is overshadowed or even eclipsed by the larger presence of white-dominated organizations such as the SDS, VVAW, and the National Mobilization to End War in Vietnam. However, black organizations, and in particular radical groups such as the Southern Non-Violence Coordinating Committee (SNCC) and the Black Panther Party (BPP), were very influential in introducing a critique of the Vietnam War premised upon an anti-imperialist and anticolonialist stance. The introduction of an active black-Vietnamese link in this context worked against the marginalization of black grievances in the mainstream news coverage of the black riots of the 1960s, and instead drew upon a rich strain of African American orientalism and Third World internationalism that inspired other radical groups, including the Weather Underground and the Asian American movement.

The difference between this black embrace of the Vietnam-ghetto analogy and the mainstream white version outlined in the previous section is not a difference of authenticity, since black activists also worked within the bounds of the phantasmatic to identify with an imagined Vietnamese ally and employ an orientalist geography to map the potential relations between Vietnam and black America. As captured in one of the slogans of the black antiwar movement, "No Vietnamese ever called me nigger," this version of black-oriental identifications was premised as much on the absence of a relation as on actual alliances between the two groups. But in the absence of an actual social relation between blacks and Vietnamese in the U.S., there arose a rich symbolic relation based on the perceived shared experience of oppression and imperialism that triangulated blacks and Vietnamese in relation to white America. For many blacks who opposed the Vietnam War there was a sense of visceral identification with the Vietnamese that went beyond mere altruism or sympathy. The violence against the Vietnamese was felt to be a direct extension of the violence against blacks in the U.S., with both forms of violence betraying the same vein of racism in American society.

Perhaps the popular figure who drew the most attention to the idea of a black-Vietnamese alliance was the former heavyweight boxing champion Muhammad Ali, who fought his induction into the army for the Vietnam War. His high-profile case also brought to light the glaring inequities of the draft, especially its disproportionate toll on the poor and working class, and on blacks in particular. Ali himself was a victim of Project 100,000, a misguided program introduced by Secretary of Defense Robert McNamara in 1966 that sought to mesh the goals of the War on Poverty and the Vietnam War by using military service as a way to help train undereducated, underprivileged males.[85] Ali had originally failed the Armed Forces Qualifying Test in 1964, making him ineligible for service, but after Project 100,000 lowered the minimum score he and eventually over 100,000 other black men were drafted under these new standards.[86] Upon being notified of his new draft status in February 1966, Ali declared his opposition to the war and uttered his infamous quote, "I don't have no personal quarrel with those Vietcong."[87] In subsequent interviews addressing black audiences Ali elaborated on his statement, calling the Vietnamese "Asian brothers" who "never lynched you, never called you nigger, never put dogs on you, never shot your leaders." Elsewhere he challenged blacks to consider the fight for their own freedom in the U.S. as their primary duty: "Why should they ask me and other so-called Negroes to put on a uniform and go 10,000 miles from home and drop bombs on brown people in Viet Nam while so-called Negro people in Louisville are treated like dogs and denied simple human rights?"[88] Although Ali was most strongly influenced in his opposition to the Vietnam War by his Black Muslim beliefs, it is notable that he drew upon the language of solidarity with the Vietnamese in order to describe his refusal to fight in a war against them. He even reportedly proclaimed on a Louisville radio show, "I am an Asiatic black man."[89]

Ali's case eventually became a rallying point for the black antiwar movement. He was praised by both Martin Luther King Jr. and Stokely Carmichael—two figures on opposite sides of the political spectrum in black politics—as a symbol of the multiple forms of institutional racism of the Vietnam War.[90] Ali's comments also echoed similar statements made by organizations such as SNCC and the BPP, which both proclaimed varying levels of solidarity with the North Vietnamese and the National Liberation Front. SNCC was one of the first major civil rights organizations to come out against the Vietnam War. Their "Statement on Vietnam" in 1966 drew an analogy between the murder of Samuel Younge, a twenty-one-year-old black navy veteran shot to death while attempting to use a white restroom in Tuskegee, Alabama, and the "the murder of people in Vietnam."[91] The BPP went a step further, publicly pledging their own "troops" to the National Liberation Front in the war against their "common enemy . . . the American imperialist who is the leader of international bourgeois domination."[92] In an essay published in 1968, "The Black Man's Stake in Vietnam," Eldridge Cleaver, the BPP's minister of information, outlined black America's role in the anticolonialist struggles taking place outside the U.S.: "If the nations of Asia, Latin America, and Africa are strong and free, the black man in America will be safe and secure and free to live in dignity and self-respect."[93] Cleaver's sentiments invoke the symbolic Afro-Asian alliances imagined but never fully realized by the Bandung Conference in Indonesia in 1955.[94] These statements and symbolic gestures contributed to the dream of an international Third World coalition that united American activists with their counterparts in the decolonizing countries of Africa, Asia, and Latin America—specifically Vietnam and Cuba, the latter having captivated black intellectuals since Castro's visit to Harlem in 1950.[95] While the tactics of SNCC and the BPP have their roots in a rich tradition of black internationalism reaching back to C. L. R. James and W. E. B. Du Bois, their application to a black–Vietnamese alliance rather than a pan-African or diasporic black consciousness derives more from what Bill Mullen calls "Afro-Orientalism," a body of black thought that has specifically looked to Asia—from Gandhi's India to Mao's China—as an inspiration for black liberation politics.[96]

The large numbers of blacks in the U.S. military would seem to belie these black antiwar sentiments; although only 10 percent of the general population at the time was black, they constituted an estimated 20 percent of the combat troops in Vietnam and over 25 percent of the paratroopers and front-line supervisors. Yet the presence of these black soldiers also contributed greatly to the GI resistance movement, antiwar protests by active military personnel. These protests differed from those engaged in by antiwar veterans groups such as the VVAW because they revealed significant sources of dissent from within the military apparatus itself, directly challenging its ability to efficiently wage war. Significantly the first widely publicized group of military resisters, the Fort Hood Three in 1966, was composed of a multiracial group of soldiers: David Samos, a Lithuanian Italian American; Dennis Mora, a Puerto Rican; and James Johnson, an African American.[97] Around the time of the Detroit riots of 1967 two Black Muslims, William Harvey and George Daniels, led a protest at Camp Pendleton to question why they were contributing to a "genocide toward the colored people of earth."[98] These instances suggest that the experience of military service actually fostered antiwar sentiments as well as a sense of black militancy, rather than simply indoctrinating black soldiers into its cold war agenda.[99]

The documentary *No Vietnamese Ever Called Me Nigger* (1968), directed by David Loeb Weiss, a founding member of the Socialist Workers Party, illustrates these various strands of black antiwar thought, particularly the central role that military service played in awakening black consciousness. *No Vietnamese Ever Called Me Nigger* was frequently screened in antiwar GI coffeehouses along with documentaries on leading black nationalists and groups such as the Yippies, providing a form of political education for soldiers in training.[100] The film is structured by the very paradox of the black antiwar movement: its intertwining of pacifism and militarism, focusing on the Vietnam War less as an issue unto itself than a stepping stone to a larger critique of American society. Scenes from the 1,500-strong Harlem contingent of the Spring Mobilization to End the War, which took place on 15 April 1967, are intercut with a conversation filmed in May 1968 between three black veterans recently returned from Vietnam. The Spring Mobilization was conceived of as a "means of joining the whole antiwar movement in an action comparable to the 1963 March on Washington," and involved simultaneous marches in San Francisco and New York City in order to dramatize the *national* scope and ideological range of the antiwar movement.[101] In the New York march, which traveled from Central Park to the United Nations building, black leaders such as King and Harry Belafonte were seen marching arm-in-arm with white antiwar activists such as Benjamin Spock and Monsignor Charles Owen Rice, and white protesters bore signs featuring the peace symbol and slogans such as

"Stop the Bombing."[102] But the images of the adjacent march in *No Vietnamese*, from Harlem down to Central Park East to join the main march, form a striking counterpoint. The Harlem contingent was almost exclusively black, and in the first scene of the documentary dedicated to the march, a white man who lives in Harlem tries to join the black marchers but is turned away with the comment, "Don't you respect the right of black people to organize their own march?" The signs carried by the Harlem marchers also explicitly linked race with the war: "No Vietnamese Ever Called Me Nigger," "Black Men Should Fight White Racism, Not Vietnamese Freedom Fighters," and "They Are Our Brothers Whom We Fight" (fig. 9). In addition to such printed slogans, the black marchers in the documentary shout, "The enemy is whitey, not the Viet Cong!," "Black power!," and "Hell no, we won't go!" Such elements frame the black antiwar movement as distinct from rather than derivative of the mainstream antiwar movement, using the abuses of the Vietnam War to stage a larger critique of white racism and gesture toward a Third World internationalism that aligns American blacks with the Vietnamese as brothers in a common struggle.

The most powerful statements of *No Vietnamese* come from the filmed conversation between three black veterans—Dalton James, Akmed Lorence, and Preston Lay Jr.—that begins and ends the documentary. These veterans describe at length the racism they experienced both in Vietnam and the U.S., their difficulty finding jobs in the U.S. commensurate with their training in the military, and above all the gradual dawning of their racial consciousness through such experiences. Their discussion, filmed after the violent escalation of the war after the Tet Offensive and the disillusionment over King's assassination, reflects the growing dominance of the black power rhetoric used by Carmichael and the BPP. Lorence insists:

> I'm pretty angry, angry about the whole mess. Not only black veterans, but angry about the way black people have been treated on the whole. Everyone knows what's going on, and still yet, there are people who insist that nothing has gone bad and things are going for the better. . . . I have been made even more angry by going to Vietnam and having to contribute, and seeing black youth dying in Vietnam. And still yet, coming back, and no one wants to listen to us, no one wants to hear what we have to say, and no one wants to do anything for us. We're still being treated as subhumans.

Arguing against black military service as racial uplift, Lorence expresses deep disappointment at the futility of his "contribution." Not only has his experience in Vietnam done nothing to further the cause of civil rights, but it

9. Placards from the Harlem contingent of the New York City march of the Spring Mobilization to End the War, 15 April 1967. Frame enlargements from *No Vietnamese Ever Called Me Nigger*.

provides little personal value to Lorence in shielding him from racism. As he later exclaims, "If this country ever decides to exterminate black people, I am sure they are not going to exclude me because I've been in Vietnam."

One of the other black veterans, James, also narrates his progression from compliant soldier to potential militant. James's quiet demeanor—he has a soft, sometimes stuttering voice and a boyish face—contrasts with the bitterness that increasingly creeps into his words. He tells of being trained in aircraft maintenance before going to Vietnam, but being forced into menial jobs fixing trucks and killing rats once there. Once he returns home he faces the same discrimination; the only job he can get is packing lightbulbs in a factory, and he is even denied service in a store while wearing his uniform. These experiences harden him, and as the conversation continues he renounces his uniform as a way of repudiating white American institutions altogether: "Four little girls died in a Sunday school. The man who laid the charge was a white National Guardsman. Yet the white people in this damn United States have the nerve to get shaken up when I say I will use my skills to fight for a revolt for four hundred years of racism. That's a bunch of bull. Because I will be out in the damn streets and I won't be wearing a fatigue uniform and boots of some damn armed force." As a veteran turned militant, James embodies the violence of the U.S. war machine turned upon itself, as he threatens to "use [his] skills" to fight against rather than for his country. Juxtaposing the Sunday school bombing in Birmingham in 1963 with the rioting and rebellion in 1968, James also demonstrates the transition from the philosophy of nonviolence associated with King and the Southern Christian Leadership Conference to the militancy of black power advocated by Carmichael and the BPP and increasingly taken up by black veterans. Unlike the white violence in Birmingham, which was an attack on blacks for the purpose of maintaining Jim Crow segregation, black power is framed as the reactive, justified violence of self-defense, belatedly appearing after years of assault. James's critique of American hypocrisy over violence echoes Carmichael's own statements defining black power:

> The only time I hear people talk about nonviolence is when black people move to defend themselves against white people. Black people cut themselves every night in the ghetto—don't anybody talk about nonviolence. Lyndon Baines Johnson is busy bombing the hell of out Vietnam—don't nobody talk about nonviolence. White people beat up black people every day—don't nobody talk about nonviolence. But as soon as black people start to move, the double standard comes into being.[103]

The genealogy between Carmichael and James's newfound language of rebellion is further reinforced by James's final statement in the documentary. Immediately after James declares, "The days of Steppin' Fetchit are dead. The days of the blackface, big, wide-eyed, gin-drinking black man are dead. Now we have what is called black consciousness," we see a shot of Carmichael accompanying black marchers shouting "Hell, no, we won't go!," an image which also appeared near the beginning of the film. It is as if veterans such as James are being positioned to fulfill Carmichael's prophecies of black power rebellion.

Black radicals such as Carmichael did in fact attempt belatedly to claim the black urban riots of the 1960s as part of this program of revolutionary change. Days after the Detroit riot in 1967, Carmichael, who had traveled to Cuba to attend a conference of the Organization of Latin American Solidarity, released the following statement to the American mainstream press: "We must internationalize our struggle and, if we are going to turn into reality the words of Che to create two, three and more Vietnams, we must recognize that Detroit and New York are also Vietnam. . . . We must join all the other struggles and this means convert ourselves into brothers and when the revolution triumphs we will have developed a new concept of humanity."[104] After the Newark riots a month later Carmichael even boasted of having helped "prepar[e] groups of urban guerrillas for our defense in the cities."[105] By invoking the Marxist revolutionary Che Guevara, who had promoted the proliferation of "many Vietnams," or attacks on American military and political power, Carmichael raised the specter of communist incursions into the heart of American cities in the form of racial violence.[106] His analogy of Detroit as Vietnam and black rioters as urban guerrillas anticipated the utopian visions of Sam Greenlee's novel, *The Spook Who Sat by the Door* (1969), whose protagonist is a black CIA agent trained in counterinsurgency methods who turns against the government by using his methods to arm and organize black youth in urban ghettos.[107] Like Carmichael and the BPP, Greenlee imagines the endless political possibilities that arise out of converting the *lumpenproletariat* into a black guerrilla movement that converts American civil disorder into true revolution. Yet Carmichael was more like the Detroit-based black nationalists Milton and Richard Henry than Greenlee's protagonist. The Henrys sent telegrams to the White House and Governor Romney during the Detroit riots, threatening continued violence if these officials did not accede to their demands, and yet the Henrys simultaneously denied having any control over the rioting.[108] Rather than a well-oiled guerrilla army, the mass of black rioters proved to be a headless soldier unable to follow the demands of its black radical leaders.

Such visions of armed black rebellion held more powerful sway over white law enforcement, who were mobilized by fear to shut down all forms of black militancy, regardless of their actual ties to acts of violence. In fact one of the main reasons that such a black revolution did not arise out of the riots was the strength of state-sanctioned violence, such as the FBI's COINTELPRO (Counter Intelligence Program), which wiped out the ranks of black and white revolutionaries alike. Through a program of propaganda, surveillance, informants, and police harassment, COINTELPRO succeeded against black revolutionary groups such as the BPP where the U.S. military had failed in Vietnam, fomenting violence and dissension within the group, and possibly even conspiring in the deaths of several Panthers.[109] But even without the help of historical hindsight, we can see how the visual and narrative structure of mainstream news coverage itself works to contain this revolutionary impulse. The flip side of the positive identification of blacks with Vietnamese freedom fighters is an act of negative identification, akin to police profiling, that likens blacks to feared but unseen Viet Cong terrorists. Rather than viewing black revolutionaries' links with Vietnam as a utopian attempt at Third World solidarity, the mainstream news raises the specter of American cities regressing into a Third World state of destitution. Yet even with the visual dominance of one version of this scenario, both sides of this black–Vietnamese identification remain in play. Although television footage concentrates on the viewpoint of white law enforcement and reinforces this version of the scenario, the heroics of the guerrilla fighter, whether Vietnamese or black, flowers offscreen, in the imaginative realm of speculative fiction and political rhetoric.

By considering different scenes as part of a single primal scene—Vietnam, Detroit, Selma, and others—I have tried to show the complexity of the act of identification with respect to racial identity: how what seems like a singular act of identification, with a particular subject position in the scenario, simultaneously implicates an entire nexus of identifications that cross racial lines. Like layers of memory superimposed on one another, these different scenes provide further visual density to the primal scene of 1968, complicating the singular interpretations that specific historical actors have promoted. Even hegemonic and counterhegemonic interpretations of the same scenario bleed into one another, since they depend on fragile distinctions between different forms of relations that are easily inverted. To call these images of the American 1968 a primal scene is not to posit them as a stable origin story for the violence of the Vietnam era that follows, but rather to open the question of *why* we return to these particular national memories, as opposed to other historical configurations, to explain the peculiarities of American race relations. What is this repetition compulsion that animates the 1960s and 1970s as not only a site of origin, but of trauma? Tellingly, in the novel First Blood, Rambo does not go on to refight the Vietnam War in Vietnam proper, as he does in the film sequel Rambo: First Blood II (1985), but dies after an orgy of violence against Sheriff Teasle and the southern town that wronged him. The horror that Morrell pictures is not of an America becoming Vietnam, but of an America that is already Vietnam, where small-town abuse of police power consumes both the police and the white subjects they purport to protect. This may be the most perverse version of bringing the war home.

Chapter 2

REPORTING THE WAR

Ethical Crises of Action in the

Movement-Image of Vietnam

During the latter half of the fifteen-year American involvement in Viet Nam, the media became the primary battlefield. Illusory events reported by the press as well as real events within the press corps were more decisive than the clash of arms or the contention of ideologies. For the first time in modern history, the outcome of a war was determined not on the battlefield but on the printed page and, above all, on the television screen.

—Robert Elegant, former correspondent for the
Los Angeles Times, "How to Lose a War"

Ever since the Vietnam War, U.S. military journals have been stuffed with antimedia cant designed to prove that the press—not the Pentagon, not the U.S. government, not the nature of revolutionary struggle, not, as Dean Rusk once put it, "the tenacity" of the North Vietnamese—lost the war.

—Marvin Kalb, former diplomatic correspondent
for CBS and NBC, "A View from the Press"

In a tenacious and widespread myth, it was the press and not the military that lost the war in Vietnam, by focusing solely on negative images that distorted the war, aided the enemy, and sapped the nation of its will to fight. In such arguments the press is presented as a kind of negative propaganda machine, automatically taking up an oppositional stance to the state and antagonizing it with every article, photograph, and news broadcast filed from Vietnam. Despite numerous scholarly and journalistic rebuttals of this "oppositional press," showing the constant collusion between press and state, this extension of the Vietnam syndrome continues to occasion self-reflexive denunciations and vindications from within the media industry each time a new military conflict occurs.[1] In one infamous example, on the eve of U.S. involvement in El Salvador, Robert Elegant accused his profession of seeking "by graphic and unremitting distortion the victory of the enemies of the correspondents' own side," and thus threatening the lives of "the peoples of the non-Communist world," prompting the CBS News reporter Morley Safer to defend the importance of a free press and to compare Elegant to Joseph Goebbels and "a Soviet department of agitation and propaganda."[2] Yet both defenders and detractors of the Vietnam-era press share a common, unquestioned assumption: that the depiction of violent actions is inherently antiwar. This belief was held not only by conservatives and military officials eager to limit press coverage of war, but also by many members of the antiwar movement, who desired even more explicit and extensive coverage of the violence of war than the press was providing. This was the basis of the conceit of "bringing the war home": to reduce the distance between America and Vietnam by narrating, depicting, analogizing, and performing the violence of war in the spaces of the home front, and in the process elicit shock, disgust, or even sympathy from American citizens toward ending the war.

The Pictures That Lost the War

While print journalists were certainly included in this pilloried oppositional press, some of the most vilified (or valorized) targets were visual journalists: still photographers and television cameramen and correspondents who produced the images that framed the Vietnam War for the home-front audience. Even the celebrated newspaperman David Halberstam deferred to these visual journalists, recently eulogizing those who had died while covering the war: "We who were print people and who dealt only in words and not images always knew that the photographers were the brave ones, and in that war, which began in an era of still, black-and-white photography and ended in one of color videotape beamed by satellite to television stations all over the world, they held a special place in our esteem."[3] Three images stand out as particularly exalted icons of the war: "Saigon Execution" (1968), photographed by Eddie Adams and NBC and ABC television news crews; the My Lai massacre (1968), photographed by Ronald Haeberle and published in 1969; and the burning of the "Napalm Girl," Phan Thi Kim Phuc (1972), photographed by Nick Ut and NBC and ITN news crews. This Vietnam triptych has been hyperbolically described as the "decisive photographs" that "changed history," and they stand out as some of the most reproduced images of the war.[4] But many also assume that they are antiwar images, particularly given historical hindsight that invests these images with the power of having moved public opinion against the war.

These three images have certainly been used in many contexts to summarize the Vietnam War. But they are far from representative of the bulk of images produced by visual journalism of the war, the "familiar catalogue" of generic images that Marita Sturken describes as commonplaces of Vietnam War documentaries: "the view from above as American bombs fall endlessly on forested landscapes, the pleading faces of Vietnamese villagers, American soldiers laden with equipment walking through burned-out villages, GIs running away from the rotating blades of a helicopter."[5] In contrast this triptych of iconic images is distinguished by their foregrounding of race and violence, not only as poetic allusion but as their unavoidable content. While the Vietnamese often functioned as an absent presence allegorizing the violence of the antiwar movement and of black rebellion, they are all too present in these particular images. Here, as Susan Moeller observed, "Americans stand offstage. These pictures are about the Vietnamese"—a striking fact, given the overwhelmingly American-centric perspective of both journalists and historians toward the Vietnam War.[6] Strictly speaking, Americans are not absent in these photographs; they are present offstage, in the form of the photographers taking the photos (even Ut, who is Vietnamese, was employed during the war by the Associated Press and eventually immigrated to the U.S.), as well as serving as the privileged audience for these photographs. Vietnamese bodies may dominate the content of these iconic images, but it is Americans whom the camera's gaze addresses.

It is important that race and violence be considered together in these three iconic images that form the core of this chapter, for the race of their subjects is what allows the violence of these images to be shown, while violence helps to bring race into visibility. This conjunction epitomizes the oriental obscene, which finds its most clear articulation in these images of violated and violating Asians. In a way these photographs are the continuation of a larger tradition of racial sentimentalism or melodrama, in which the spectacle of the suffering racial other is staged for the moral uplift of a middle-class, white, and often female audience.[7] The privileges of whiteness disallow similar images of violence on American bodies to enter the public sphere, and at the same time ignore nonviolent images of Asian bodies, whether in fictional or nonfictional form.[8] Hence these images represent one way in which oriental bodies enter America—not as physical immigrants per se, but as psychic entities intruding into the American imagined community. By the time of the Vietnam War a small but significant population of Asians existed in America, and two significant events that reshaped that community take place at the same time as the war: the formation of a political coalition of Asian Americans that cuts across different Asian ethnicities and communities, and the growth and diversification of Asians in America as a result of the reforms of the Immigration and Naturalization Act of 1965. The convergence of these historical developments is not coincidental, since these immigration reforms arose from the same cold war politics that produced the Vietnam War, and the racial consciousness of Asian American identity politics derived much force from the antiwar movement. Like a dream whose repetition marks a hidden site of repression, these images of the oriental obscene mark America's traumatic incorporation and assimilation of its oriental other at the exact moment of its rebirth in American political life as Asian America.

Even as we deal with images of actual Asians rather than oriental allegories or metaphors, these images remain part of a phantasmatic matrix; that is, they take part in various imagined encounters and relations that cannot be reduced to their factual content. The shuttling of Americans to the outside of the frame of these iconic images necessitates different forms of phantasmatic identification and transference, which make sense of the suffering within the frame by relating it to other, more familiar contexts: sentimentalism, humanism, an antiwar critique, or even the pragmatics of war. But even Asian Americans employ similar strategies of imagined relations to structure their identification with these images, drawing upon imagined genealogies and constructed sympathies with the Vietnamese that help to form the very notion of Asian American identity. In other words, the Vietnamese depicted in these images are no less "other" to Asian Americans than to other American subjects. This complicates the critique of appropriation or misrepresentation often leveled at images of racialized subjects produced for the gaze of hegemonic audiences. Who is to say which identifications are proper and real? This is not meant to collapse the obvious differences in Asian Americans' and other Americans' power relations and psychic investments in these images of the oriental obscene. Nonetheless both racial subject positions enter into equally phantasmatic relationships with these images in the act of looking.

In the previous chapter I posed the trauma of the Vietnam War in the language of psychoanalysis; in this chapter I turn to Gilles Deleuze's film theory in order to analyze trauma from the perspective of the phenomenology of visual form, which allows me to pose a different question about the ethics of looking. Whereas the concepts of the primal scene and Nachträglichkeit foreground questions about temporality and experience in order to critique the causal relations being asserted between different scenarios—war, anti-war protest, urban riots—Deleuze's phenomenology forces us to consider the assumptions that collapse visual representation with visual experience, witnessing violence rather than consuming a visual text representing violence. American moving images have relied upon what Deleuze calls the "movement-image" or "action-image," depictions of bodies and objects moving through space, as a basic building block of representation.[9] But the movement-image also imposes a narrative of mastery that asserts the possibility of control over those bodies and objects. What happens when the movement-image breaks down, dissolving the temporal narrative within the image that allows us to assign both causality and ethical responsibility? The assumptions behind the movement-image underlie both the myth and the critique of the oppositional press: that looking at violence implies an ethical stance toward violence, which is itself premised upon the possibility of acting upon that stance.

Deleuze has located one source of trauma in the Second World War, which shatters the mastery implied by the movement-image by creating intolerable conditions for human existence that cannot simply be translated back into movement as such:

> The fact is that, in Europe, the post-war period has greatly increased the situations which we no longer know how to describe. These were "any spaces whatever," deserted but inhabited, disused warehouses, waste ground, cities in the course of demolition or reconstruction. And in these any-spaces-whatever a new race of characters was stirring, kind of mutant: they saw rather than acted, they were seers. . . . Situations could be extremes, or, on the contrary, those of everyday banality, or both at once: what tends to collapse, or at least to lose its position, is the sensory-motor schema which constituted the action-image of the old cinema.[10]

This break between the movement-image and the time-image, which Deleuze calls the "crisis of the action image," functions like a trauma theory, mapping an aesthetic crisis over the representation of movement onto a historical crisis that itself calls into question the function of the sensory-motor schema.[11] As a result what seem to be mere aesthetic or formalist changes in the vocabulary of the image can portend larger cultural or sociopolitical movements that are only belatedly translated into direct representation. The "Saigon Execution," the My Lai massacre, and the burning of the "Napalm Girl" are images that raise questions not only about the ethics of war, but also about the ethics of representing, broadcasting, and consuming images of war.

Following Deleuze, I locate the trauma of the Vietnam War in the question of visual form rather than the representational content of these three iconic images of the war. There is ample evidence of trauma in the content of these photographs alone—execution, massacre, bombings. However, these iconic images also underscore a formal dialectic between stillness and movement that leads to questions about ethical action and paralysis. This dialectic comes up both in the interplay between still and moving images of the same event and in the debates about what, if anything, one should *do* in response to these images. This visual style characterizes the coverage of the Vietnam War more than any previous military action. As Moeller notes, "Instead of careful compositions isolating decisive moments of combat, [these photographs] appeared simply to arrest randomly selected scenes. . . . The new photographs looked like freeze-frames from a film."[12] Both still photography and moving images of the Vietnam War converge toward a visual style that allows for the perception of movement across space and time and the fixed stare of arrested vision, both the movement-image and its implicit crisis. Thus even when I am dealing with still photographs of these three iconic events I treat them as movement-images in a larger sense, as stylized tableaux vivants that gesture toward the continuation of movement outside their frame. In arguing that these images provoke an American "crisis of the action-image," I am not claiming that movement literally ceases in these iconic images of Vietnam. Rather the situations they present resist being integrated into any narratives, whether those of heroic war or of antiwar resistance, and thus resist being converted from images into action. How does one look at an execution, a massacre, a war atrocity? And how does one even begin to react to them, to respond to these situations with another action? These images in fact paralyze their viewers, casting them—both the photographers and the media audience —fundamentally as seers rather than actors, bound in a passivity that forces them to bear witness without the solid promise of intervention or resolution. If one of the purposes of narrative is to create the semblance of agency and causality, then these images fail to be narrativized because the spectacles of violence that they portray deeply destabilize the notion of action and responsibility. They restage the passivity of the primal scene as the impossibility of responding to the Vietnam War except as phantasmatic trauma, always belated even at the moment of first encounter.

Death Mummified: "Saigon Execution" (1968)

On 1 February 1968, in the midst of the Tet Offensive, Brig. Gen. Nguyen Ngoc Loan of the South Vietnamese Army executed an unnamed Viet Cong suspect on the streets of Saigon before a crowd of astonished press photographers and television cameramen, including Eddie Adams of the Associated Press, Vo Suu and Vo Huynh of NBC News, and an unnamed South Vietnamese camera-man for ABC (fig. 10).[13] This "shot seen round the world" became instant history; a mere five days after the image was taken, *Variety* magazine compared it to the flag raising at Iwo Jima, and the following year, 1969, the Pulitzer committee awarded Adams the prize for Spot News Photography.[14] Although it was not the first violent image to emerge from Vietnam—Malcolm Browne photographed Buddhist monks setting themselves on fire in 1963, images of former South Vietnam president Ngo Dinh Diem's corpse appeared in Ameri-can papers soon after his assassination in November 1963, and Dickey Chap-elle and Akimoto Keiichi photographed executions for obscure and non-American publications in 1961 and 1965—these other images did not capture the public's imagination in the same way.[15] However, General Loan's execu-tion of a Viet Cong was widely represented, appearing not only on countless prominent newspaper front pages, but also broadcast on NBC's *Huntley-Brinkley Report* and the ABC *Evening News*. Subsequent iconization of this image by historians, journalists, and filmmakers only confirmed the judgments of media commentators that arose during the picture's first impact.

Despite its iconicity, "Saigon Execution," as the Pulitzer committee called Adams's photo, was a strange symbol for the Vietnam War. Although it is inexorably linked with the Tet Offensive, the photograph reflects very little of the greater significance attributed to Tet. It does not show Americans to be losing the war, as Walter Cronkite later suggested, nor does it portray the Viet Cong attacking Americans, as the attack on the U.S. Embassy in Saigon during Tet displayed. Instead it depicts in close-up an act of violence between two Vietnamese combatants, allowing the American public to stare at a death it was unwilling to view of its own soldiers.[16] Paradoxically, although the racial otherness of the figures in this scenario seemed to allow Americans to distance themselves from this event, the ubiquity of the image brought this execution closer to home, opening up a larger contemplation of the meaning of death in discourses of war. "Saigon Execution" is an extraordinary example of "death mummified," a phrase which, following André Bazin, describes the capture of an elusive, singular event that might otherwise fade into the pas-sage of time.[17] But this image is "mummified" in more ways than one; not

only does it fix this event into the form of a reproducible object, as Bazin notes, but it also represents the paralysis of its viewers, both its photographer and the viewers at home, who are visually fixated by a horrific event they can neither stop nor completely comprehend. "Saigon Execution" thus becomes the instigator for a Deleuzian crisis of action and reaction, in which American audiences struggle not only with the ethics of war, of which acts are permissible and which are intolerable, but also the with ethics of viewing war, of reacting as witnesses to such actions.

As I noted earlier, Deleuze associates this crisis with the breakdown of the movement-image. In a phenomenological sense the movement-image maps time indirectly, by tracking bodies and objects as they move through space.[18] This allows cinema to approximate ordinary visual perception, or a "sensory-motor schema," which Gregory Flaxman glosses as "a neural network that 'affectively' contains the image-flux: the images procured are recognizable, capable of being linked to other images along a methodical, and ultimately normative, chain."[19] As a result the movement-image is tied to narrative, causality, and linear time in a way that mimics the syntax of written language: "Just as perception relates movement to 'bodies' (nouns), that is to rigid objects which will serve as moving bodies or as things moved, action relates movement to 'acts' (verbs) which will be the design for an assumed end or result."[20] One subspecies of the movement-image, the action-image, is particularly prevalent in what has been called "classical Hollywood style," or realist American narrative cinema.[21] It allows for actions to be tied to situational causes as if in a behaviorist cycle: "An action . . . passes from one situation to another [or] responds to a situation in order to try to modify it or to set up a new situation."[22] The action-image ties movement to larger causal chains, as each action becomes a reaction to a previous situation and creates the possibility for future situations to arise. The continuity editing associated with the classical Hollywood style is eminently suited to asserting such causal claims, leading Deleuze to liken the action image to the American Dream.[23] The narratives that arise from such action-images provide support for notions of agency and mastery, as they allow subjects positioned within these narratives the ability to initiate and control actions and to understand their actions as having a tangible impact upon their surroundings.

(*opposite*) **10.** A photograph sequence by Eddie Adams of the execution of an unnamed Viet Cong suspect on the streets of Saigon during the Tet Offensive, labeled "Prisoner," "Execution," and "Death." Published in *New York Times*, 2 February 1968. Source: AP Photo/Eddie Adams.

We might elaborate "Saigon Execution" as an action-image by providing causality to General Loan's action, as seen in the quote that was distributed with this photograph: "They killed many Americans and many of our people." Many publications also published "Saigon Execution" alongside images of other events, seeming to restore movement to this frozen moment by animating it into a larger historical narrative. The *New York Times* juxtaposed "Saigon Execution" on its front page with an unrelated photograph of a South Vietnamese officer carrying the body of one of his children, apparently killed by Viet Cong "terrorists."[24] A similar narrative extrapolation occurs in *Time* magazine, which sandwiched Adams's photograph between two other images shot during Tet in other locations: to the left is a scene from Hue, with wounded marines lying on the sidewalk, and to the right is an image of Vietnamese civilians fleeing Danang, in which one man, presumably dead, is lying prone on the sidewalk with a pool of blood next to his head.[25] With the placement of Adams's photograph between images of American and South Vietnamese casualties, the Viet Cong prisoner executed by Loan is interpellated as guilty of committing these acts of violence hundreds of miles away— an instance of photographic montage collapsing spatial distance (Danang-Saigon-Hue) and creating a causal narrative where none existed. That the news stories in both *Time* and the *New York Times* accompanying these photographs remain silent on their connection only strengthens this montage effect, leaving the photographs to articulate what the text will not. In each case the narrative serves to contain the action depicted in "Saigon Execution" by justifying it, perhaps even making it mundane by juxtaposing it with other brutal acts of war.

Paradoxically when we restore movement to "Saigon Execution" by relating it back to its own series of images rather than to these external events, the perception of action actually diminishes instead of increases. For all the momentousness of this photograph as a symbol of the Tet Offensive or the Vietnam War as a whole, the action it depicts is quite subtle. For example, the *New York Times* also published a sequence of three photographs, all taken by Adams, on the inside pages of the same issue that featured "Saigon Execution" on the front page.[26] Labeled "Prisoner," "Execution," and "Death," the photographs concentrate what seems like the moment of death at the center of its temporal sequence. Taken together they attempt to trace the transition of a body from life into death as if in extreme slow motion. The slowing down of the image allows us, even forces us to contemplate the abrupt transition of the body from life to violent death. The images recall the fascination with movement that accompanied the birth of cinema from photography almost a century earlier, Eadweard Muybridge's movement studies and Leland Stanford's attempt to isolate the "moment when all four feet of a horse leave the ground."[27] Like the galloping horse, the dying body yields a tiny movement, imperceptible to normal vision; however, unlike the horse, the physical movement of death is entirely out of proportion to the secret of human existence it seems to reveal. What is most real in "Saigon Execution"—the death of the Viet Cong—is also that which is most elusive to vision, that evades the desire to isolate a moment of clarity and mastery. Without the master narrative of the war at large to lend significance to this moment it appears as an enigmatic signifier, addressing the viewer with a message not readily understood.[28]

The visual ubiquity of "Saigon Execution" might be understood not simply as a sign of the image's importance, but as a recognition of its enigma and an attempt to master it by imposing upon it the semblance of meaning. Linda Williams has named this visual obsession a "frenzy of the visible," apparent not only in early cinema but also in the modern genre of hard-core pornography. Pornography, which seems to be organized around a similarly obvious event, the sex act, actually struggles to make the essence of that act visible. Thus the cliché of the so-called "money shot," or ejaculation, is a hypervisible sign for masculine pleasure that actually masks the essential invisibility of another secret, that of "the woman's invisible and unquantifiable pleasure."[29] The moving-image footage of "Saigon Execution" that appeared on NBC's *Huntley-Brinkley Report* reveals a similar visual substitution that actually draws our attention away from the pivotal moment depicted in Adams's photograph. The footage covers about the same temporal span as Adams's three-photograph sequence, roughly fifty-two seconds, and its hundreds of frames hint at a plethora of visual information, although it lingers at different points of emphasis than the Adams photographs (fig. 11).[30] For the bulk of the sequence the Viet Cong suspect is unhurriedly escorted by General Loan's soldiers in what appears to be an ordinary arrest, with little to foreshadow the sudden death to come. The infamous gunshot itself is partially obscured by a soldier who walks in front of the camera just as Loan pulls the trigger, but after the gunshot the body crumbles to the ground, and we watch for several seconds as blood shoots several inches out of his head and pools on the ground. At the end of the footage the camera zooms in while another soldier places a cryptic label, "x27," on the chest of the Viet Cong.[31] As a pivot point the moment of the execution separates the film into two unequal halves, the first depicting the movements of an animated, living man walking to his death, and the second showing the stillness of the now dead body, motionless except for the blood spurting from it. But the pivot point itself is nearly

(*above and opposite*)

11. The NBC footage of "Saigon Execution," filmed by Vo Suu and Vo Huynh. Frame enlargements from "Tet (1968)," *Vietnam: A Television History.*

invisible, partly obscured and passing by too quickly to register fully, leaving only a sense of visceral shock in its aftermath. The kernel of the desired moment remains tantalizingly out of sight, with the focus of vision displaced onto symbols whose hypervisibility disavows the invisibility of these hidden moments: the ejaculation of blood standing in for the pain of death, mimicking the money shot in hard-core pornography. Far from supplementing the inadequacies of still photography, the technology of the moving image reveals the shared inability of photography and film to master the objects of their representation.

Just as enigmatic as the event of the execution is the identity of the anonymous victim, known only in photo captions as "Vietcong terrorist" or "VC spy."[32] Clad in civilian, Western-style clothing and nearly indistinguishable from the South Vietnamese civilians and soldiers, the Viet Cong confounds the tropes of war reportage and narratives, which demand a recognizable enemy as a symbol for collective hatred. Only a few weeks after "Saigon Execution" was published, on 20 February 1968, the correspondent Bernard Kalb began a CBS Report entitled "The Viet Cong" with the following voice-over, spoken over street scenes taken in Saigon:

> One of the most infuriating questions is the nature of the enemy himself, the most remarkable and most faceless foe in our history. Who is this man? This woman? This boy? What's in that basket? Behind those vegetables? Where does this man go when he leaves here? Enemies are usually instantly recognizable, and that is one of the reasons the war in Vietnam is so maddening, so exasperating for Americans. World War II had Hitler and Tojo, the swastika and the rising sun, and Americans knew them at a glance. But the enemy in Vietnam looks like the non-enemy. *Citizen of Saigon. Vietnam insurgent.* And who can tell the difference about an enemy that has emerged as a traumatic question mark?[33]

As Kalb speaks the descriptors "Citizen of Saigon. Vietnam insurgent," two photographs are placed side by side on the screen, both depicting nearly identical-looking elderly Vietnamese men in civilian clothing. While the military discourse surrounding the mysterious Viet Cong ostensibly derives from the material conditions of guerrilla warfare, the "traumatic question" for Americans, both at home and in country, was largely a racialized one. Civilians and insurgents, allies and enemies, even General Loan and his victim become obscured by a racializing gaze that cannot distinguish between them. Although its captions and framing narratives attempt to situate these characters into well-defined roles in the theater of war, the image of "Saigon Execution" ultimately cannot support this reduction. The small, casually dressed body of the Viet Cong suspect tells us nothing of the military threat he is supposed to embody, nor of the ideological differences that place him and Loan on opposite sides of the war. Unlike the public executions that stage a clear narrative about the workings of state power on its deviant subjects, this execution does little to clarify the "traumatic question mark" of the Vietnam War for American viewers.

As the action-image breaks down, along with the narrative relations that tie movement to causality and bodies to identities, so too does the mastery of the viewing subject over the spectacle presented before her. The situation of "Saigon Execution" can no longer be resolved through the reflex arcs favored by the action-image, leading to the "purely optical and sound situations" of the time-image; they "make us grasp *something intolerable and unbearable*. . . . It is a matter of something too powerful, or too unjust, but sometimes also too beautiful, and which henceforth outstrips our sensory-motor capacities."[34] However, this failure of action is not necessarily an ethical failure. In her discussion of death and documentary film Vivian Sobchack identified "Saigon Execution" as eliciting what she calls a "humane gaze," which cannot help but be "hypnotized by the horror it observes": "The frozen quality of the stare, the bodily paralysis and inertia it represents, suggests a recognition that there is *no* tolerable point of view from which to gaze at such a death yet that such horror must be witnessed and attested to."[35] For Sobchack the breakdown of "sensory-motor capacities" is itself the proper ethical response. It acknowledges the inadequacy of action to respond to "something intolerable and unbearable," for responding with action would be reinstating the fantasy of mastery that produced such a terror in the first place. The humane gaze also reveals the troubled relation of the human subject to death, which cannot be assimilated to any other experience. Phenomenologically death ties abstract time to human existence, defining the individual subject's temporality, durée, as finite, uneven, and specific. Bazin, who shares with Deleuze a Bergsonian influence, has remarked, "For every creature, death is the unique moment par excellence. . . . Death is nothing but one movement and another, but it is the last."[36] So while the death in "Saigon Execution" can be represented as various forms of movement—a bullet being fired, a body falling down—there are also aspects of that death that will always elude translation into mere movement-image. The paralysis of the pure optical and sound situation is not simply a lack of action but a refusal of action, a refusal to treat death as simply another action in a chain of events.

The resistance to accepting this state of nonaction is revealed by the debates over journalistic ethics that "Saigon Execution" aroused, wherein the photographer's inaction is questioned as morally dubious. Adams reports constantly being challenged with the question, "Why didn't you stop him from shooting?," to which he responds that he merely raised his camera to shoot without knowing what would transpire before him. In Haskell Wexler's *Medium Cool* (1969), a poster-size reproduction of "Saigon Execution" sets the scene for a confrontation between John Cassellis (Robert Forster), the cameraman protagonist, and his girlfriend Ruth (Marianna Hill; fig. 12). Although the photograph is never diegetically referenced, it looms on the wall at the beginning and end of this scene, thus allegorically framing their conversation about the Italian "shockumentary" *Mondo Cane* (1962):

> Ruth: Well, you remember that scene on an island, where they tested an atom bomb?
> John: Yeah.
> Ruth: Well, there were these big turtles, you know, tortoises, who at a certain time in their lives walk to the sea to lay their eggs. And they found with the radiation, they threw [off] the turtles' sense of direction. So instead of heading to the sea, they went inland and they died.
> John: Oh, I'm crying.
> Ruth: Dammit! Look it, somebody took those movies, right? I mean, do you think, did they, or didn't they, after they took those movies, did they reach down and turn those turtles around? Or did they put them on a jeep and drive them back?
> John: How the hell do I know what they did? Those were Italian cameramen.

The conversation eventually devolves into a naked pillow fight, which contributed to the film's x rating at the time of its initial release. It is interesting how the sexual obscenity of this scene overlaps with the ontological obscenity of the death haunting its background, as if one visual aporia were standing in for the other.[37] For John professionalism is one way of justifying inaction, aligning the photographer with a transcendental historical gaze that allows him to escape this situation of embodied but forced passivity. Philip Jones Griffiths, a Welsh photojournalist, has defended the ethical quandary which Adams and other cameramen have faced: "Your job is to record it all for history. You can't not feel involved, but you have to steel yourself and do your job, take your photographs."[38] This explanation attempts to convert viewing back into activity—an intervention, if not into the event itself, then into the larger historical processes into which this event is inserted—and thus disavows the uncomfortable passivity that accompanies the act of viewing. But both the

12. Violent and sexual obscenity meet: Adams's "Saigon Execution" decorates the wall in a scene of sexual foreplay. Frame enlargement from *Medium Cool*.

desire for intervention and the identification with historical authority evade the ethical demand to witness this traumatic event in its entirety. To "reach down and turn those turtles around," or reach toward Loan and turn his pistol away, is simply another way of turning away from the spectacle of death, flinching from the fact of the execution and all of its implications.

The paralysis of the viewer then becomes the condition of possibility for an ethical stance toward violence that one did not cause but is nonetheless implicated in. If we contemplate what might have happened if "Saigon Execution" had not been photographed and filmed, the importance of this ethical stance becomes clearer. ABC also had film cameras present at the execution, but their footage is incomplete compared to NBC's and Adams's. The anchorman Roger Peterson noted in his commentary after this footage aired, "As you noticed, he [our cameraman] got film before and after the execution but not at the actual moment of execution. Asked about that he said, 'I'm afraid of General Loan.' "[39] Turning away, the camera deprives its viewers of the opportunity to confront the violence of the execution, and ultimately to ponder the meaning of a war that can include such events. Deleuze's pure optical situation becomes a concrete illustration of the essential passivity of the American spectator posed in the previous chapter through the televisual primal scene. The phantasmatic relations of this primal scene differ from the narratives of the action-image because they do not claim causality or justification between social phenomena, but rather allow for new political imaginings and new possibilities for identification. As Deleuze explains, with the crisis of the action-image the viewer no longer needs to insert himself into the image in order to make sense of it: "What the viewer perceived therefore was a sensory-motor image in which he took a greater or lesser part by identification with the characters. . . . But it is now that the identification is actually inverted: the character has become a kind of viewer."[40] The inverse of this inversion is also true: all viewers, including photographers, are now also characters in the scenario, present before the fact of death if not at the scene of the execution.

It is important to note that these new possibilities for phantasmatic relations created by the crisis of the action-image are not inherently revolutionary or even progressive. As we will see with the images of the My Lai massacre and the "Napalm Girl," these imaginings can be used to shore up the same hegemonic ideologies supported by action-based narratives. While racial difference was somewhat submerged in "Saigon Execution" by the racial similarity of its two main figures, racial difference reemerges in the images of My Lai and the "Napalm Girl," as the American soldier becomes phantasmatically aligned with the American cameraman as an agent of harm. While the desire to stare at the death of the racial other may open one up to a closer imaged relation with that subject, it can also reveal an identification that allows one to come closer to one's own death and vulnerability. For antiwar veterans this translates into the death and trauma of American soldiers in Vietnam censored in the news media, while for the members of the nascent Asian American movement Vietnamese death figures their own vulnerability to racialized violence in the U.S.

The Victims of My Lai: "Massacre at My Lai" (1969)

If "Saigon Execution" might be thought of as a primal scene for the violence of the Vietnam War, taking the nation by surprise, the My Lai massacre is its nachträglich deflection, marking a belated response to this initial trauma. Although the My Lai massacre took place on 16 March 1968, at the tail end of the Tet Offensive, it was not revealed to the American public until over a year and a half later, when articles by Seymour Hersh and photographs by Ronald L. Haeberle, an army photographer, began appearing in the national print media, most notably in *Life* magazine, in a nine-page article accompanied by multiple, full-page color photographs.[41] The massacre occurred when a group of soldiers from the 1st Platoon of Charlie Company, 11th Infantry Brigade, Americal Division, U.S. Army, entered a hamlet of the village of Son My known to Americans as My Lai (4) and reportedly killed over three hundred of its residents, mostly elderly men, women, and children. But unlike the shock that accompanied "Saigon Execution," the My Lai massacre disturbed the public with its vivid portrait of civilian victims, and it also directly implicated American soldiers in the violence. Some letter writers to *Life* reacted by disavowing the article's veracity, while others cited the incident as symptomatic of the plague of violence infecting the United States domestically: "We have a thousand Mylais every day right here in America."[42] Such a response contrasted starkly with the reception of "Saigon Execution," which tended to exalt the moral visibility of violence while emphasizing its distance, both literal and symbolic, from American culture.

Although Haeberle's photographs seem to provide direct evidence of the victimization of the Vietnamese people as a result of American involvement in the war, they became instead symbols of a different sort of victimization, that of the American soldier. As exemplified by the figure of Lt. William Calley, the only soldier to be convicted of responsibility in the massacre, the American soldier emerged from discussions of My Lai as the primary victim of the Vietnam War, from both pro- and antiwar perspectives. Pro-war advocates believed Calley was the victim of a misguided trial that penalized soldiers for carrying out their patriotic duties, whereas antiwar advocates saw Calley as representative of a military culture organized around death and genocide. The period of Calley's trial, 1969 to 1971, saw not only this symbolic transformation of the role of the Vietnam veteran, but also the rise of a medical category, post-Vietnam syndrome (later to become posttraumatic stress disorder), to formalize the suffering of the American soldier. In the words of the historian Kendrick Oliver, "the war criminal became a martyr, the anti-hero a hero," and American soldiers like Calley eventually eclipsed the Vietnamese dead whose bodies were littered across Haeberle's photographs as the primary victims of My Lai.[43]

This reversal of roles from Vietnamese villagers to American soldiers is even more striking given that these photographs so directly linked Americans in the violence against the Vietnamese. Although the murder in "Saigon Execution" was also considered morally reprehensible, it nonetheless involved two active combatants in the war rather than civilian bystanders and could more easily be dismissed as a natural occurrence within the chaotic context of war. However, Haeberle's photographs depicted elderly men, women, and young children, figures far removed from the typical images of soldier combatants. Although many soldiers maintained that it was impossible to distinguish innocent civilians from Viet Cong collaborators, the photographs of My Lai seem to strengthen rather than confuse that distinction, showing a clear visual difference between American soldiers and their Vietnamese victims. Yet the moral outrage over the killing of innocents also obscured the active involvement of many women in combat roles on behalf of the Viet Cong or North Vietnamese Army, a fact celebrated by some in the New Left and the Asian American movement. As H. Bruce Franklin observed, after the success of the Tet Offensive "the dominant image of the Vietnamese [in the alternative antiwar press] would no longer be decapitated or napalm-mutilated bodies but triumphant fighters, not victims but heroes, as in the soon-to-be-famous picture of a woman guerilla wearing a rifle with fixed bayonet slung over her shoulder."[44] The female Vietnamese guerrilla challenged not only racial but also gender binaries associated with the war, and was thus embraced as a symbol of the Vietnamese struggle as anti-imperialist on multiple levels. Such images offered an alternative narrative of the war that was as much pro–North Vietnam as it was antiwar, portraying the resistance to American violence as noble and potentially justified.

However, in the mainstream press images of Vietnamese victimhood, as epitomized by the My Lai massacre, dominated representations of the violence of war. The eleven Haeberle photographs published in *Life* magazine established a clear dichotomy between American aggressors and Vietnamese victims, in part by mapping this difference onto not only race but also gender and age. The only two photographs that show American soldiers feature them in long shots, faces obscured, in classic scenes of military activity: jumping out of a helicopter in one and burning the food supplies of the village in another.[45] They frame the massacre, however disturbing, as a clear action-image, relating the event to visible movements performed by identifiable subjects. In contrast the eight photographs depicting Vietnamese offer what Oliver has tellingly called a "frozen tableau of terror and death."[46] Both time and action are halted here in disturbing ways, breaking the sensory-motor link suggested by the other action-images and offering abject examples of pure optical and sound situations. Four of these photographs depict Vietnamese subjects who are still alive; they are medium to close-up shots of mostly elderly persons, often framed by infants and children in their care, whose faces gaze directly at the camera. The viewer realizes only after reading the captions that these subjects are not posing for the camera, but are staring in helplessness and shock as they witness the death of their friends and family and await their own: "This man was old and trembling so that he could hardly walk. He looked like he wanted to cry. When I left him I heard two rifle shots."[47] The remaining four photographs are of Vietnamese corpses, always in multiples rather than as individual bodies. One of the most iconic of these images

13. Bodies on the road leading from the village of My Lai, from *Life*, 5 December 1969. Source: Ronald S. Haeberle/Time and Life Pictures/Getty Images.

depicts a group of over a dozen bodies lying in a tangled mass of overlapping limbs and torsos along a dirt road (fig. 13). The sheer number of these corpses, along with their arrangement in abstract rows and piles, make them resemble not so much human bodies as raw materials. The strong diagonal line of the road's edge, pointing toward a distant vanishing point, suggests the proliferation of these bodies outside of the frame of the photograph, further emphasizing the horror surrounding these multiplying corpses. Even in the absence of moving-image footage from My Lai, these eleven photographs appear like a storyboard of the massacre, illustrating the transition of the Vietnamese from living to dead through the intervention of American soldiers, whose faces appear like criminal mug shots in the small portraits accompanying the article.

Haeberle's photographs could not be used as evidence that a particular soldier had killed a particular villager. Yet in the absence of attribution of guilt onto a single soldier, these photographs implicate collective American responsibility, thus tainting voyeurism with guilt. The most damning descriptions of the massacre come not from Haeberle's photographs but from his narration. In his caption to a full-page color image of a weeping Vietnamese woman surrounded by other women and children, Haeberle reports, "Guys were about to shoot these people. . . . I yelled, 'Hold it,' and shot my picture.

As I walked away I heard MI6s open up. From the corner of my eye I saw bodies falling, but I didn't turn to look" (fig. 14). Seven pages later, buried in the text of the article, Haeberle explains that this photograph was taken after he interrupted an attempted rape of a teenage girl by several GIs; the image in fact depicts the girl "hiding behind her mother, trying to button the top of her pajamas."[48] This photograph is but an index of a moment of reprieve between two atrocities. In another graphic account Haeberle describes what occurred after he photographed a wounded young boy: "The GI fired three shots into the child. The first shot knocked him back, the second shot lifted him into the air. The third shot put him down and the body fluids came out. The GI simply got up and walked away. It was a stroboscopic effect."[49] Even from the vantage point of a direct witness, Haeberle uses the language of the camera apparatus rather than of natural perception to describe his visual experience; his perception is not fluid over time, but "stroboscopic," capturing the event in disconnected flashes. Although the textual details he supplies attempt to fill in the spaces between the photographs, they are unable to close the gap between spectacle and narrative and restore the sense of movement.

Like Adams, Haeberle cannot intervene in the massacre he obliquely captures on film; he is frozen by the ethical impossibility of acting in this situation. Unlike Adams, though, Haeberle shares with the soldiers doing the killing not only a racial and national identity, but also an institutional position, since he accompanied the platoon as an army photographer rather than a member of the civilian press. The scenario of the My Lai massacre does not allot the viewer a third position apart from the relations of violence, but implicates them quite directly, whether through Haeberle's own gaze or metonymically through the American-made weaponry, the MI6 rifle, to which such actions are attributed. As Michael Herr commented in *Dispatches*, his account of covering the Vietnam War, "You were as responsible for everything you saw as you were for everything you did. The problem was that you didn't always know what you were seeing until later, maybe years later, that a lot of it never made it in at all, it just stayed stored there in your eyes."[50] Looking is not merely a voyeuristic third position, as indicated in "Saigon Execution"; in the My Lai coverage looking is also identified with killing, despite, or perhaps even because of, the absence of continuous violent action before the camera.

With its implication of American responsibility, the My Lai massacre soon became a major rallying point for the antiwar movement. Haeberle's photograph of the corpses in the road became one of the iconic images of this atrocity. Not only was it reproduced frequently as a stand-alone image by newspapers and books referencing the massacre; it was also used as the basis

14. A crying woman is restrained, while a young woman buttons her pajamas, from *Life*, 5 December 1969. Source: Ronald S. Haeberle/Time and Life Pictures/Getty Images.

of a popular antiwar poster by the Art Workers' Coalition. Superimposed over the photograph were quotes from an interview by Mike Wallace of CBS with Paul Meadlo, one of the soldiers who took part in the massacre: "Q. And babies? A. And babies."[51] Hoping to help validate the charges against Calley and also turn public opinion against the war, the VVAW drew upon their own war experiences to fuel their performative protests against the backdrop of Calley's trial. In Operation RAW antiwar veterans acted out mock attacks on American towns and distributed leaflets that phantasmatically interpellated American citizens into the position of My Lai villagers: "A U.S. infantry company has just passed through here. If you had been Vietnamese, we might have burned your house, shot you and your dog, raped your wife and daughter, burned the town, and tortured its citizens."[52] Although these tactics seemed to focus on U.S. soldiers as the object of antiwar critique, they were actually intended to foster a sense of collective responsibility for these atrocities that would hopefully translate into collective action toward ending the war. For instance, the Art Workers' Coalition also manufactured thousands of masks featuring Calley's face to be worn at antiwar rallies, a gesture that suggested sympathy for Calley while signaling that all Americans were guilty for the crimes committed at My Lai through their support of a culture of militarism.[53] As veterans themselves, the members of VVAW were ideally poised to direct this critique at the military establishment, as their wartime experiences offered direct proof of the forms of indoctrination that turned ordinary American boys into "baby killers."

One of the symptoms of this culture of militarism was known by many veterans as the "gook syndrome." An index of the collision between violence and anti-Asian racism, it is encapsulated in the phrase "The only good gook is a dead gook" and Gen. William Westmoreland's offhand comment "The Oriental does not value life the way we do."[54] The term "gook" has a long history in the context of American racism, reaching back not only to the Philippine-American War of the early twentieth century, when the term was first used, but also the Indian Wars and the Haitian Revolution of the nineteenth century. Emphasizing the origins of the term as a racial epithet against blacks, Indians, and Asians alike, David Roediger remarks that this "broader pan-racist past of gook provides almost a short history of modern U.S. imperial aggression and particularly of the connections between racial oppression and war."[55] Thus the gook syndrome marks a continuity between present and past racisms. During the Vietnam War the epithet "gook" was applied not only to the enemy Viet Cong but also the allied South Vietnamese and South Korean soldiers who fought alongside the Americans.[56]

Although the gook syndrome was a form of dehumanization that stigmatized the Vietnamese enemy so as to enable American soldiers to kill them without guilt, the critique of the syndrome shifts sympathy from the "gooks" themselves to the soldiers afflicted by the syndrome. In *Home from the War* the psychiatrist Robert Jay Lifton traced the etymology of the term to its colloquial meaning of dirt or slime, thereby invoking a model of racial pollution by which Vietnamese deaths sully American lives: "The consequences are grotesque not only for Vietnamese victims but for American victimizers caught in the psychic slime of the gook syndrome."[57] Even African American, Latino, Native American, and Asian American soldiers were guilty of the gook syndrome, in effect aligning themselves on the side of whiteness against racial otherness. Lifton described this as part of "the melting-pot myth of leaving one's cultural-racial past behind and becoming totally an 'American,' which in this case meant joining in the collective American need, in that atrocity-producing situation, to victimize 'non-Americans.' "[58] But instead of blaming veterans for their complicity in killing Vietnamese, Lifton sought to turn the military culture of killing into a form of victimization itself, this time directed at American soldiers. The gook syndrome thus inverts into the "post-Vietnam syndrome," a provisional psychiatric disorder, later formalized as post-traumatic stress disorder (PTSD), that originated in part with interviews with My Lai veterans.[59] The racist hatred directed towards gooks turns inward, transforming into these veterans' guilt, self-loathing, and numbness.

A similar rhetorical tactic appeared in the VVAW's Winter Soldier Investigation, a three-day event which took place a month before Calley's guilty verdict was announced. Over a hundred veterans gathered in Detroit from 31 January to 2 February 1971 to recount the atrocities they either witnessed or committed themselves in Vietnam and to counter public skepticism that the My Lai massacre actually occurred.[60] While the majority of the Winter Soldier testimonies display a deep sympathy and regret for the mistreatment of Vietnamese, in some cases the sympathy shades into identification, as the atrocities committed on the Vietnamese become reflections of the "brainwashing" of the American soldiers. In the film documentary of the investigations, *Winter Soldier* (1972), one veteran, Carl Rippberger, presents a slide show of photographs from Vietnam, as if depicting his own personal My Lai. The first five slides show the mistreatment of Vietnamese POWs and casualties by various unidentified American GIs. He pauses on the final slide, presented in the documentary as a close-up that obscures the full content of the image until the camera pans downward, with the voice-over, "And the next slide is a slide of myself. I'm extremely shameful [sic] of it. I'm showing it in hopes that none of you people that have never been involved ever let this happen to you. Don't ever let your government do this to you. It's me, holding a dead body, smiling" (fig. 15). Rippberger reiterates what others in the investigation have described: that the gook syndrome not only dehumanizes the Vietnamese who are killed, but also "you," the Americans who are forced to do the killing. Yet the slide he shows points to a different kind of harm, that of the Vietnamese body being desecrated. If this photograph is meant to be visual evidence of the dehumanization of American soldiers, it accomplishes this by using the physical violence done to the Vietnamese body to symbolize the psychic damage suffered by Americans.

Another veteran, Mark Lenix, interviewed for the documentary outside the public testimonies, describes to the camera his descent into the gook syndrome through a similar identification: "They dehumanize you so much that the enemy is no longer a human being who has a wife and child, or has a family life. He just becomes the enemy. And therefore, when you're confronted with this, all you think of is it's just like another target, and they've trained you to shoot targets. . . . Then all of a sudden I realize, no, there is no justification, man. What I've done is wrong. I have to face it, I have to admit that what I've done is wrong. And now I have to try and tell other people before they make the same mistakes I've made." His words gain additional meaning against the foil of his surroundings: a living room draped with a large American flag, with his wife and young child playing in the background. The American "you" subtly elides into the enemy "him"; it is as if the American veteran himself "becomes the enemy" he has described, "with a wife and child." Although both the veterans of the VVAW and the psychiatrists allied with them intended to sympathetically unveil the anti-Asian racism at the heart of the war and show how such racism permeated American military culture, one result of these claims is a melancholic identification between Vietnamese and Americans that seems to erase Vietnamese suffering.[61] It is the dehumanization of the American soldier and not the dead enemy Vietnamese that takes center stage.

Ultimately even these flawed efforts to aid veterans were turned against them, as the existence of a psychological diagnosis enabled those in support of the war to brand such troubled veterans as isolated instances of moral failure rather than products of a systemic problem. In the end Calley was the only individual held responsible for the My Lai massacre; although two of his superior officers, Capt. Ernest Medina and Col. Oran K. Henderson, were also tried, they were eventually acquitted of all charges, thus frustrating attempts to hold the entire institution of the military responsible for the massacre. The

15. Vietnam veteran Carl Rippberger narrates a slide
show of personal photographs from Vietnam during
the Winter Soldier hearings, 31 January–2 February
1971. Frame enlargements from *Winter Soldier*.

Winter Soldier Investigation was largely ignored by the mainstream media, and members of the vvaw were dismissed as long-haired hippies masquerading as veterans.[62] The sociologist Jerry Lembcke has shown that the Nixon administration helped perpetuate the denigration of veterans as crazed "baby killers" in order to stigmatize and invalidate veteran dissent in the waning years of the war.[63] Both the revelations of atrocities like the My Lai massacre and the movement toward diagnosis of the post-Vietnam syndrome become fodder for a different scenario, one which pathologizes the antiwar veteran in order to create an idealized, heroic, pro-war veteran.

Ironically, for the administration that was trying to "Vietnamize" the Vietnam War by transferring more of the fighting to Vietnamese troops, the racialized figure of the Vietnamese fades into the background of this domestic dispute between political opponents, allowing the war to be brought home without its foreign, racialized referent. As Oliver astutely points out, the Vietnamese victims of the My Lai massacre quickly disappeared from public discourse, unable to testify at the trial of the massacre or even to be identified as distinct individuals who suffered a wrong: "They remained either a petrified presence within American culture, images on a page, or an alien one: strange Oriental figures, infrequently glimpsed, ghosts inhabiting a faraway land."[64] However, their invisibility bespeaks an altered form of presence; their ghosts are reanimated in the form of the American soldier, whose body bears the traces of their loss under a different racial guise. Eventually, as the post-Vietnam syndrome gave way to the general diagnosis of PTSD in the late 1970s, the racialization of that loss became even harder to trace, even as the loss spread beyond the veteran to the entirety of America society.[65] Thus the renewed calls in the 1980s for healing from the Vietnam War address not the wounded veterans themselves, but the nation as a whole. As the journalist Myra MacPherson declared, "America needs to cure itself of the post-Vietnam syndrome—so often attributed only to veterans."[66] Jan Scruggs, the veteran who conceived of the Vietnam Veterans Memorial, titled his book and subsequent television movie accordingly, *To Heal a Nation*.[67] Far from showing that the Vietnamese were forgotten, these displacements testify to a different form of remembrance, one of American identification with the same Vietnamese they pitied and loathed.

Becoming Like the Enemy: Asian American Antiwar Protest

From the first day to the last I was referred to as a "gook," "jap," "chink," etc., by the drill instructors. In classes, instructors called me "gook" and had me stand so the other recruits could see what the enemy looked like.

—Mike Nakayama, an Asian American Vietnam veteran,

"Nam and U.S.M.C.," *Gidra*, May 1971

As Asians living in America, we identify with the Asian people who for the last ten years have been killed, burned, and maimed by the American military machine in Indochina.

—Asian Political Alliance (Detroit), "Nixon's Look at Justice:

Backs Convicted Killer . . . Calley Jr.," *Gidra*, May 1971

If the gook syndrome helps us to understand the My Lai massacre as a tragic case of mistaken identity—of mistaking Vietnamese civilians for combatants —that same misidentification also proved to be central to the politicization and radicalization of Asian Americans in the Vietnam era. In fact the very concept of "Asian American" as a pan-ethnic collective identity arose against the backdrop of the Vietnam War, replacing the ethnic disidentifications and interethnic conflicts that appeared during the Second World War and the cold war.[68] But far from asserting the existence of a true identity apart from the false one produced by anti-Asian racism, the emergence of the Asian American movement was very much intertwined with the same phantasmatic processes that governed the emergence of the gook syndrome and other anti-Asian racisms. Against the backdrop of such images as "Saigon Execution" and the photos of the My Lai massacre, Asian Americans forged an antiracist, pan-ethnic identity that utilized the Vietnamese—and particularly the Viet Cong—as a phantasmatic bridge between the myriad forms of everyday racism experienced by Asians in America and the more spectacular forms of racism displayed in the military actions of the U.S. in Vietnam and broadcast in the mainstream visual media. These various transferences show the complexity of even the most obvious acts of racial identification—that of Asians with other Asians—and reveal that even "self" identification necessarily involves a structure of identifications with an "other."

The two sides of this Asian American identification might be conceptually broken into two separate processes, that of racial interpellation (being identified *as*) and what psychoanalysis would term identification proper (identifying *with*). However, these two processes are deeply intertwined, blurring the distinction between external and internal identification, between social compulsion and personal agency. While interpellation seems to originate outside of the subject being hailed—in Althusser's paradigmatic example, the policeman who yells, "Hey you!"—it ultimately depends on that same subject recognizing himself or herself in that form of address.[69] Likewise Laplanche reads identification in Freud as both conscious and unconscious, and in the case of the Oedipus complex identification may even precede and help constitute the subject as such.[70] If racial interpellation hails all Asians, regardless of nationality or ethnicity, into a single category, lumping together "gooks" with "japs" and "chinks," that interpellation also allows these subjects the possibility of recognizing their shared history of oppression and constituting themselves as a "race for itself," a consciously adopted racial identity that provides the conditions of possibility for contesting that racism.[71]

Visual media in particular provide instances of racial interpellation that can be transformed into political consciousness. The historian Sucheng Chan describes a kind of politicized "mirror stage" encountered by nascent Asian American subjects through the visual media in the Vietnam era: "With the help of the television evening news, an increasing number of Asian American college and high school students realized with a shock that the 'enemy' whom American soldiers were maiming and killing had faces like their own."[72] Likewise the Asian American folk music group Yellow Pearl sings of "watching war movies with the nextdoor neighbor, secretly rooting for the other side."[73] Thus what might seem at first to be a purely repressive form of racism turns out to be richly productive for the Asian American movement, radicalizing and providing a form of racial consciousness raising for a generation of Asian American activists. As the sociologist Yen Le Espiritu notes, "It is anti-Asian violence that has drawn the largest pan-Asian support. . . . Anti-Asian violence concerns the entire group—cross-cutting class, cultural, and generational divisions."[74] Certainly the Asian American movement that emerged in the 1970s was a multi-issue movement, encompassing resistance against U.S. militarism in Taiwan, Okinawa, and the Philippines, renewed interest in historical events such as Japanese American internment and the bombing of Hiroshima and Nagasaki, community-based activism against police surveillance, drug abuse, educational inequities, and the welfare of the elderly. At the same time the Vietnam War helped to crystallize these varying critiques of anti-Asian racism, becoming the primary lens through which many of these other issues were viewed.[75]

It is important to note, though, that this process of becoming Asian American was far from inevitable or natural. The Asian American identification with the Vietnamese did not necessarily mean that the Vietnamese were major partners in this pan-ethnic coalition. There were few Vietnamese in America before the end of the war—only 30,000 by 1975, or about 2 percent of the total Asian American population—and many of these Vietnamese, who came as students or diplomats, were neither antiwar nor engaged with the Asian American movement.[76] The historian Vu Pham points out, "Although Asian American panethnic identities formed around the Vietnam War, Vietnamese Americans themselves remained more interested in how the war affected their homeland than they did in America's racial landscape."[77] Furthermore the images that formed the site of this identification, including "Saigon Execution" and the My Lai massacre, were far from ideal models for political mobilization, considering that they portrayed situations of extreme immobilization that did not pave the way for clear reactions. But the Asian American response to these situations, especially My Lai, reveal the capacity of the Deleuzian time-image to create new political possibilities out of its ethical quandaries. Whereas the action-image associated with classical cinema assumes the existence, and thus representability, of "the people," the pure optical and sound situations of the time-image outline an empty space of potentiality and becoming from which a people might emerge. As Deleuze says, "If there were a modern political cinema, it would be on this basis: the people no longer exist, or not yet. . . . *The people are missing*."[78] The waning of action in the time-image allows these "missing" people to arise, as cinema is no longer bound to describe the politics of existing actions and agents, but can turn to the production of new political possibilities—in short, the politics of becoming.

The politics of becoming that Deleuze and Guattari describe in A Thousand Plateaus is necessarily a deterritorialization: "All becoming is a becoming-minoritarian."[79] "Minoritarian" differs from "minority" because it refers not to numerical quantity, but to an orientation toward power that resists its hegemony through the imposition of difference, nonequivalence, otherness. Thus "becoming-minoritarian" runs counter to what is often pejoratively called "identity politics" because it does not simply substitute one stable being (black, Asian, woman) for another (white man) but disrupts the very idea of stable and naturalized identities: "Even blacks, as the Black Panthers said, must become-black. Even women must become-woman. Even Jews must become-Jewish (it certainly takes more than a state). But if this is the case, then becoming-Jewish necessarily affects the non-Jew as much as the Jew. Becoming-woman necessarily affects men as much as women."[80] The political cinema associated with the action-image, with its fidelity to realist perception and behaviorist psychology, is too closed to represent these various processes of becoming. D. W. Rodowick asserts that "its goal is to represent the masses or 'the people.' They may be oppressed or in the process of liberation, alienated or awakened, but representation is nonetheless their right."[81] But the political cinema of the time-image—Deleuze's "modern political cinema"—departs from this injunction to represent what is, allowing it to explore what might be or is not. Such a political cinema must take on the task of "contributing to the invention of a people. . . . The missing people are a becoming, they invent themselves."[82] The political task of the images of Vietnam is not simply to address a ready-made constituency called "Asian America," but to usher in this community in its process of becoming. Thus we might reconfigure the temporal stasis of the Althusserian interpellated subject, who is "always-already" hailed as Asian American, to encompass the open-ended flow of a Deleuzian becoming, in this case becoming–Asian American. The task for this missing people is not simply how to respond to a specific atrocity, but how to open such events to historical connections and affective links beyond the chains of direct causality.

As the My Lai massacre proved, racial interpellation had particularly ominous consequences in the context of war, since subjects were being identified not only for the purposes of societal manipulation and control, but also for extermination. For the purposes of expediency American soldiers tended to collapse the question of identification into a clear answer: any Vietnamese, civilian or not, was to be treated as a potential enemy for the sake of protecting American lives. Varnado Simpson, one of the American soldiers present at the My Lai massacre, explained to Life magazine, "To us they were no civilians. They were VC sympathizers. You don't call them civilians. To us they were VC. They showed no ways or means that they wasn't. You don't have any alternatives. You got to do something. If they were VC and got away, then they could turn around and kill you."[83] The burden of resolving this lack of differentiation lay clearly on the Vietnamese themselves, rather than on the American soldier. Responding to Life's article on My Lai, one Vietnam veteran wrote, "The responsibility is on the Vietnamese people. They are alike, they dress alike and look alike. . . . They are trying to kill you."[84]

But the same interpellative gaze also fell on Asian American soldiers, many of whom were Japanese Americans whose parents had experienced a similar racial paranoia that resulted in the internment camps. Although their numbers were much smaller than those of African American or white soldiers, their inclusion validated the notion of a pluralistic and multiracial America putting forth a united front against its ideological enemy.[85] If this current group of Nisei and Sansei, like their ancestors from the heroic 442nd Infantry of the Second World War, viewed their military service as a pledge of loyalty to the American nation to counter such racist accusations, these same soldiers were being upheld as visual models of the Viet Cong for their non-Asian cohorts during their training, effectively becoming targets of the racial paranoia they thought they had left behind.[86] G. Akito Maehara related his experience as a young marine recruit during the Vietnam War: "The Drill Instructor stood me in front of the entire unit, and pointed, and said, 'This is what the enemy looks like! We kill people who look like him.' From that time until I left the service I was always being referred to as a friendly gook, Charlie Chan's cousin, Slant Eye, Yellow Belly and Zipper Head."[87] Not only did such interpellations expose Asian American soldiers as targets of racism, but they also fostered suspicions of potentially divided loyalties. As the white soldiers in an anecdote by M. A. Uyematsu exclaim, "Hey Gook, can't you kill one of your own?"[88] Such racial confusions assimilated Asian American soldiers into the long history of American racism, even as it manifested in new ways with the presence of "gooks" within the military itself.

This racial interpellation of Asian American soldiers was not limited to the relative safety of stateside boot camps, but continued into the combat zones of Vietnam, where they were suspected of harboring racial sympathies for the Viet Cong or simply mistaken for Viet Cong in disguise. In an article published in 1971 in the Asian American newsletter *Gidra*, Mike Nakayama described being denied medical care because other soldiers mistook him for a Viet Cong: "When I asked what was taking so long, the corpsman explained that he thought I was a 'gook.' They were treated last no matter how serious the wound."[89] Sam Choy, an ex-G.I. interviewed by the Asian American group I Wor Kuen in New York, reported that the racist abuse was worst when his fellow GIs returned from patrol and felt most vulnerable to attack: "They started asking me where I was born, where my parents were born, if I was a Communist. They even asked me what I thought about China. They thought I could turn traitor anytime."[90] The Asian American Vietnam veterans interviewed by Robert Nakamura in his documentary, *Looking Like the Enemy* (1995), reported similar instances of mistaken identity. Capt. Vincent Okamoto was almost thrown out of a helicopter when the pilot ordered the soldiers to "jettison the gooks" in order to gain more altitude, and was saved only by a black soldier who yelled out, "Leave him alone, he's American." Asian American soldiers were also vulnerable in the showers on base, where their lack of military uniforms increased the chances that they would be misidentified through their racial uniforms; Capt. David Miyoshi was attacked in the shower by a staff sergeant who assumed he was a Vietnamese who had snuck into American facilities. While many Asian American soldiers endured these indignities in silence, some did not, reflecting these projections of violence back to their source. After repeated harassment Choy eventually retaliated by throwing a knife at a mess sergeant who called him a "slant-eyed Chinaman, gook, chink"; by the time the military police caught Choy, he was so angry he "was thinking of joining the Viet Cong. At least they would trust me."[91]

However, the antiwar movement that emerged from the Asian American movement did not concentrate mainly on the mistreatment of Asian American soldiers, but instead focused its central critique on the anti-Asian racism inherent in the conduct of the war. As Paul Wong wrote in 1972 in an article for the Asian American periodical *Bridge*:

> The most widely accepted slogans in the white antiwar movement have been, "Give peace a chance," and "Bring the G.I.'s home." The Asian American movement, in contrast, emphasizes the *racist* nature of the war, using such slogans as "Stop killing *our* Asian brothers and sisters," and "We don't want *your* racist war." In the April, 1971, antiwar march in Washington D.C., the Asian contingent refused to join the main march because the coordinating committee would not adopt the contingent's antiracist statement for the march as a whole. In other instances, when Asian-Americans did join the white-dominated antiwar marches, such as the April, 1972, march in New York City, their appeals to use the podium to make their views known were met with hostility and rejection.[92]

Because of their exclusion from some of these national antiwar events, many Asian American activists organized their own rallies, addressed to their local communities rather than the national media and political leaders. Large antiwar events like the march in Washington, D.C. on 24 April 1971 (fig. 16) and events such as the Asian Americans for Peace rally in Los Angeles' Little Tokyo on 17 January 1970 featured slogans particular to the Asian American antiwar movement.[93] For example, the slogan "No Vietnamese Ever Called Me a Fat Jap" from the Little Tokyo march clearly invokes the black antiwar movement's mantra, "No Vietnamese Ever Called Me Nigger," but it also references Spiro Agnew's racist epithet to a Japanese American journalist on his campaign plane in 1968.[94] Other frequently used slogans also drew their meaning from specifically Asian American political issues, including anti-colonialist self-determination ("Asia for Asians"), the revival of the historical memories of anti-Asian racism in America and Asia ("Remember Manzanar," "No More My Lais"), and a rejection of model minority assimilation ("No

16. "No More My Lais!" Photograph of the Asian contingent attending an antiwar march on Washington, D.C., on 24 April 1971, following the VVAW's Dewey Canyon III protests. A reported 500,000 people demonstrated in this march, including contingents from women's liberationist and black and Chicano power groups. Copyright Corky Lee/Asian Media Collective.

Chiquitas Are We"). Some signs were written in untranslated Japanese and Chinese and thus were directed toward other Japanese or Chinese rather than to linguistic outsiders. As William Wei has argued, "the Vietnam War and the opposition to it unified Asian Americans psychologically and politically," becoming the focal point that united these various other Asian American critiques of American society and politics.[95]

But whereas the black antiwar movement chronicled in chapter 1 viewed the racism of the Vietnam War as an extension of the racism shown toward African Americans, the Asian American movement reversed the priority of these factors, as the spectacular violence of the war made manifest the more subtle racisms against Asians in America. Following the tactics of black power, early Asian American activists had tried to raise awareness of the marginalization of Asian Americans in American political and cultural life. But "yellow power," as articulated by Amy Uyematsu in an influential essay, struggled to articulate Asian American grievances against the backdrop of their seeming economic success as model minorities or "quiet Americans."[96] The Vietnam War gave visceral form to these psychological grievances, exteriorizing these symptoms into physical signs of violence. In particular the

My Lai massacre seemed to clearly illustrate the extremes of anti-Asian racism, producing an absolute binary between American aggressors and Asian victims. In advertisements for their rally in January 1970, Asian Americans for Peace included an Iowa housewife's comment about My Lai, "My Lai–Hiroshima—'it's no real loss,'" in order to call attention not only to the devaluation of Asian life by the U.S. military, but also to the widespread adoption of the gook syndrome by ordinary Americans.[97] In New York City in April 1971, during a demonstration against the incursion of U.S. bombings into Laos, a group of Asian American activists staged a reenactment of the My Lai massacre as a reminder of the human costs of the war (fig. 17). Interestingly Asian Americans played the part of both the victims and the aggressors, showing the fluidity of identification despite the polarization of roles. If Asians Americans sympathized with the victims of My Lai on racial grounds, they also embodied, however uneasily, their role as part of the American body politic, and it was this latter position which afforded them the agency to protest the war and American complicity with its violence.

Similarly in a speech following the Asian Americans for Peace march through Little Tokyo, Warren Furutani transitioned from talking about his Japanese American family to imagining them as victims of My Lai, using these familial relations to hail his listeners directly into the story of the massacre:

> But what, what if, you know, like my last name wasn't Furutani? What if my last name was like, ah, Wa or Lo or Pa or Minh or Nuyen or some other common Vietnamese name? And what if we didn't live in Gardena or Monterey Park or Crenshaw Square or Little Tokyo or Chinatown? What if we lived in a village like My Lai? Then what about my little brothers, my mother, and my grandmother? What future would they have? They would have none because they would be dead![98]

While similar to the rhetorical gesture made by the VVAW in Operation RAW, Furutani's speech does not simply bring the war home; it also defamiliarizes Little Tokyo and Chinatown, aligning them with My Lai as spaces where the violence of U.S. imperialism becomes manifest. This alignment of Asian America with Vietnam was particularly radical because it rejected the assimilationist approach of ethnic communities during the 1950s and 1960s, which strived to lessen racial discrimination by embracing the emerging "model minority" position.[99] Such sentiments showed the limits of assimilation in shielding Asian Americans from the hatred and suspicion being directed toward Asians. Unlike the citizens of the New Jersey and Pennsylvania towns visited by Operation RAW, the inhabitants of these Asian American ghettos

17. A reenactment of the My Lai massacre during an Asian American protest against the bombings in Laos. New York City, April 1971. Copyright Corky Lee/Asian Media Collective.

continue to be subject to the violence of racism even after they stop "imagining" themselves as Vietnamese. The striking repetition of familial metaphors in these slogans literalizes rather than disavows the racial bonds between the Vietnamese abroad and Asians in the U.S. Embracing interpellation as abject identification, these activists created an imaginative genealogy as well as an affective frame through which the atrocities of the Vietnam War, such as My Lai, would be experienced as the direct extension of anti-Asian racism in America. As a postcard from the Asian American antiwar movement put it, "Is this what they do to people who look like me?"[100]

To constitute a people around the shared experience of violence is a fragile and historically contingent process. As Wei notes, "When the antiwar movement ended in the United States . . . the major political focus for cooperative activity among Asian American activists disappeared as well."[101] At the same time this fragility is also a source of strength, in that such a conception of an Asian American people requires constant renewal, allowing it to respond to the exigencies of future political crises—the murder of Vincent Chin (discussed in the conclusion), economic violence, the war on terror—and even to expand and contract according to these circumstances. According to Patricia Pisters, the "class of violence" posited by Deleuzian political cinema differs from the given "violence of a (social) class," for it relates to "a shared feeling of refusal, intolerance, and impossibility" that cuts across seemingly neat racial, ethnic, and national boundaries.[102] Just as Furutani emphasized, the shared structure of feeling between Vietnamese and Asian Americans is not simply the result of the physical act of massacre itself, but stems from the temporal impossibility that various forms of racial violence creates: "What future would they have? They would have none because they would be dead!" But whereas the repressive power of the military state seems to foreclose the future, the process of becoming promises that alternative futures will flower from this historical obstruction. Most important, the formation of becoming–Asian American refuses the politics of healing and sympathy that falsely promises to resolve the problems of racial violence through the mirages of "proper" action. The Asian American protests against My Lai do not attempt to cover over the violence of the massacre or convert it into a sentimental narrative of overcoming. Rather they embrace abjection—not only the corpses of My Lai, but "My Lai–Hiroshima," an even larger historical scenario of mass extinction—that paradoxically allows Asian America to come into being.

A Child is Burning: "Napalm Girl" (1972)

By 1971 the specter of American guilt in Vietnam seemed to lessen as "Vietnamization," or the gradual replacement of American troops by South Vietnamese (ARVN) personnel, changed the character of the war for the U.S. from
ground-based counterguerrilla warfare to a supporting, high-tech role of
providing air cover to ARVN troops. Even though this move did not placate
antiwar protesters—in fact the expansion of the war into neighboring Cambodia in 1970 and Laos in 1972 sparked new waves of demonstrations, including the infamous one at Kent State—it did put an end to the type of face-to-face
war atrocities that the My Lai massacre and "Saigon Execution" symbolized.
Nonetheless one last iconic image of the Vietnam War emerged in this period,
one which did not so much shock American audiences as it did confirm their
feelings against the war. This image, variously referred to as "The Terror of
War," "Accidental Napalm," and the portrait of the "Napalm Girl," depicted a
nine-year-old girl, Phan Thi Kim Phuc, who had just been burned by napalm
from an airstrike by South Vietnamese Skyraiders on 8 June 1972, that hit her
family home.[103] Although images of Vietnamese burned by napalm were
common in antiwar literature since 1966, especially in protests against Dow
Chemicals, the manufacturer of this incendiary gel, the "Napalm Girl" has
both overshadowed and condensed these earlier images, becoming a belated
symbol of these earlier critiques of the war.[104] In one sense this image adds
little to our understanding of the Vietnam War, since the My Lai massacre
already drove home the point that babies had become victims of war. But in an
important departure from both My Lai and "Saigon Execution," the "Napalm
Girl" depicts a victim who survives her ordeals and thus points the way to a
narrative of healing that might restore the ethical paralysis brought on by
these earlier events. However, this promise of reconciliation ultimately reveals
a failure of responsibility, as the insertion of a narrative of action over this
image of pain obscures the larger crisis of action that the image precipitates.
In other words, healing prematurely and falsely sutures a historical wound
that ought to remain open to the larger implications of our culpability in the
violence of war.

The images by which the "Napalm Girl" came to be known were shot in
both still and moving formats by two different South Vietnamese cameramen,
both in the employ of American media outlets, as well as a British television
news cameraman: Huynh Cong "Nick" Ut, a photographer then employed by
AP, Dinh Phuc Le, who worked for NBC News, and Alan Downes, of Britain's
ITN.[105] Ut's photograph is perhaps the most recognizable, having won both

18. Huynh Cong "Nick" Ut's photograph of the "Napalm Girl," Phan Thi Kim Phuc, which appeared on the front page of the *Los Angeles Times*, 8 June 1972. Source: AP Photo/Nick Ut.

the Pulitzer and World Press Photo Prizes and appearing in countless publications (fig. 18). Like many newspapers, the *Los Angeles Times* initially paired Ut's photograph with another depicting the airstrike, and, in its captions tied the two together as a simple chain of events: "In photo above, napalm bombs dropped by South Vietnamese planes on North Vietnamese troops burst into flames at Trang Bang, South Vietnam. Below, South Vietnamese soldiers and children run down highway after one of planes accidentally dropped napalm on government infantry company and civilians trying to escape the cross-fire. Nude girl ripped off clothes after being burned on back."[106] Although the main event, the napalm bombing, is out of frame in the "Napalm Girl," this photograph remains an important, if deferred, index of the bombing, becoming like a reaction shot to the earlier establishing shot. The content of this image recalls the self-immolation of the South Vietnamese Buddhist monk Thich Quang Duc in June 1963 as a protest against the South Vietnamese regime of President Diem, another image of immobilized suffering burned into the American public imagination. The journalist Peter Arnett said of this earlier event, "I could have prevented that immolation by rushing at him and kicking the gasoline away. As a human being I wanted to, as a reporter I couldn't."[107] Duc's self-immolation garnered even more infamy when Madame Ngo Dinh Nhu, Diem's sister-in-law, belittled the protest as a "monk barbecue show"—a comment considered by some observers to be as obscene as the image itself because of its reduction of the human body to meat.[108] Both Duc's suicide and Madame Nhu's excoriation of it haunt the image of the "Napalm Girl," as General Westmoreland later dismissed Phuc's injuries as a "hibachi accident" that had nothing to do with the war.[109]

The composition of the "Napalm Girl" portrait, with Phuc's arms outstretched and her mouth open in a cry, recalls another infamous image, that of the Kent State shootings from the previous year, in which Mary Ann Vecchio screams over the body of a fellow student, Jeffrey Miller, who had been killed by National Guardsmen during a campus protest against the U.S. invasion of Cambodia. Significantly the implication of sound in both these images takes the form of an inchoate, embodied, and above all gendered scream, revealing what Kaja Silverman has called a "close identification of the female voice with spectacle and the body" as opposed to an invisible and anonymous male voice associated with voice-over and narrative authority.[110] Both female figures cry directly at the camera, as if addressing their pain and grief to an audience capable of redressing them. Robert Hariman's and John Louis Lucaites's close reading of both these images stresses their ability to stage a scene of public mourning and trauma, translating what seem like private sufferings for communal consumption.[111] But whereas the photo of the Kent State shooting symbolizes the collective cry of the antiwar movement, the "Napalm Girl" seems to speak the collective anguish of the Vietnamese people, again gendered as feminine against a male American norm.

Perhaps because of the gendering of the suffering in this image, the issue of obscenity haunts the "Napalm Girl" in a way that only tangentially affected the image of death in "Saigon Execution" or the indirect evidence of massacre in Haeberle's My Lai photographs. According to Horst Faas, a senior photographer for AP in Saigon at the time, other AP staffers worried that Ut's photograph would not be published in the U.S. because of the girl's nudity. Faas responded by asking a technician to shade Phuc's crotch to eliminate any shadows that might look like pubic hair, and the photograph was then wired to the U.S.[112] Although this act did not obscure Phuc's gender, it attempted to suppress any suggestions of sexuality in her prepubescent body, as if to disavow any connection between her injury and the explicitly sexualized violence suffered by women in the My Lai massacre. But a larger obscenity surrounded this photo as well as Adams's earlier "Saigon Execution," that of the violence depicted. Sexual and violent obscenity overlap to highlight the multiple transgressions of which the photograph is evidence. As Hariman and Lucaites point out:

> Girls should not be shown stripped bare in public; civilians should not be bombed. Likewise, U.S. soldiers (and many viewers mistakenly assume the soldiers are U.S. troops) are supposed to be handing out candy to the children in occupied lands, and the United States is supposed to be fighting just wars for noble causes. Just as the photograph violates one form of propriety to represent a greater form of misconduct, that breach of public decorum also disrupts larger frameworks for the moral justification of violence. . . . It is a picture that shouldn't be shown of an event that shouldn't have happened.[113]

In the case of the "Napalm Girl" obscenity becomes not a barrier to but rather an arousal of sight. As the elision between South Vietnamese and American soldiers suggests, many viewers experience Ut's photograph as a call to culpability, even if the facts of the bombing allow for an alibi of blamelessness. However, outrage over the image's sexual obscenity alone becomes a way of masking the discomfort aroused by its transgressive violence, and the issue of sexual obscenity comes to the fore as the outrage over the violence in the image fades into historical cliché. As recently as 1994 Ut's photograph was censored by the Texas Department of Criminal Justice, which prevented a Marxist newsletter, *Workers Vanguard*, from circulating in prisons because it reprinted the "Napalm Girl" and thus violated child pornography laws.[114]

As with "Saigon Execution," the moving-image footage of the "Napalm Girl" also troubles the interpretations of the still photograph, as the prolonged footage of Phuc's body disrupts the cause-and-effect narrative created by the juxtaposition of still photographs. Although Susan Sontag has famously claimed that Ut's photograph "probably did more to increase the public revulsion against the war than a hundred hours of televised barbarities," it is impossible to isolate the photograph from the context of moving images from which it emerged, including the moving image of the same event.[115] The footage taken by Le originally aired in the U.S. on NBC *Nightly News* on 8 June 1972 in a half-minute section at the end of a four-minute report on combat between the VC and ARVN troops in the area. The footage first depicts Phuc and her brother, Phan Thanh Tam, running in a diagonal line toward Le's camera, then cuts to a traveling shot following behind both children. If Phuc's silent cry is the overwhelming emotional center of Ut's photograph, in the moving-image footage she is strangely affectless—a chilling lack of reaction perhaps traceable to her third-degree burns, which do not cause pain because they kill the nerve cells in the skin. The cut in the NBC footage also excises the framing of full frontal nudity found in Ut's photograph, which was reportedly censored by NBC because it was "too racy" for television.[116] In place of her cry and anguish this footage concentrates on the bodily injury, as the shot from behind allows us to see the burned skin on her back and arm. Significantly the NBC footage also includes a sequence even more shocking. A ten-second sequence at the end of the broadcast shows Phuc's aunt, Nguyen Thi Xi, carrying the body of her nine-month-old son, Phan Can Cuong, who was burned so badly that pieces of his skin were falling off and dangling from his body. The narration that had accompanied the images of Phuc falls silent during these last seconds, letting this infant body speak its own pain. When set in motion the images of Phuc's and Cuong's burned bodies speak even more strongly than the still photographs of the impossibility of meaningful intervention that would undo this damage, showing even the cameramen transfixed by this spectacle.

Two of Phuc's cousins, including the infant Cuong, died from the injuries they sustained from the bombing, but Phuc herself miraculously survived, saved in part by the photographer Ut, who drove her in an AP van to a hospital soon after filming ended.[117] Phuc's survival sets in motion an alternative narrative of healing that attempts to replace the immobilized gaze found in both the moving and still images of her suffering. Thereafter the "Napalm Girl" became a running story in both television and print news, with Phuc's slow recovery followed by reporters for months, even years. Only a few weeks after her injury CBS Evening News broadcast a story about her transfer from Saigon Children's Hospital to the American-funded Center for Plastic and Reconstructive Surgery, also known as the Barsky Unit after its founder, Dr. Arthur Barsky, who had also established the Hiroshima Maidens project in the 1950s.[118] Like the Hiroshima Maidens, the "Napalm Girl" becomes the beneficiary of American generosity and technology, which is ironically called upon to heal the violence of national projects that derive from that same technological superiority. Thus despite the footage's disturbing portrayal of a Deleuzian pure optical and sound situation, a narrative of heroic action and survival supplants the horror of this act of witnessing, suturing Phuc's wounds as well as the viewer's investment in her outcome.

The transference between American audiences and the South Vietnamese pilots who were actually responsible for the bombing has its roots in the very start of the Vietnam War, insofar as Americans had attempted to shape both the government and the army of South Vietnam "in our image," as a CBS

News Special Report commented in 1970.[119] The similarities between ARVN soldiers and American GIs were not only ideological and tactical, but visual as well. Within a discourse that privileges visible identification, many South Vietnamese appear in American newscasts to be virtually indistinguishable from American soldiers from afar. Referring to the South Vietnamese Air Force in 1969, CBS News describes their nearly complete incorporation of Americanness, beginning with their uniforms and ending with the origin of their planes and bases: "*Unless you look closely, it's not easy to tell them from their American counterparts.* Except for their black air force combat coveralls, every item of their equipment—helmets, oxygen masks, parachutes, flak jackets—is American. The trucks that take them out to the flight lines are American. The concrete revetments that protect their new American planes are of American design and are built with American cement."[120] The visual association of technological modernity with America and the West extends beyond the military realm into the economic, as portrayals of civilian life in Saigon frequently emphasize the paradoxical hybridity of Vietnamese bodies consuming American commodities. Unlike the focus on male bodies in the description of South Vietnamese soldiers masquerading as Americans, such cultural economic hybridity is most frequently marked on female bodies: South Vietnamese women riding a "French-made motorbike, powered by American gasoline," wearing American miniskirts and beehive hairdos while dancing to rock-and-roll, or in crowded markets purchasing American products.[121] As a character in Stanley Kubrick's *Full Metal Jacket* (1987) remarks, "Inside every gook there is an American trying to get out." If American viewers of the "Napalm Girl" mistook South Vietnamese bombs for American, the confusion was natural, since not only were American bombers ubiquitous throughout the war, but even South Vietnamese bombers were essentially Americans in military technological drag.

In the antiwar documentary *Hearts and Minds* (1974), by Peter Davis, this identification becomes overt as an American veteran assumes responsibility for injuring Phuc as a way of narrating his remorse for participating in the Vietnam War as a whole. *Hearts and Minds* utilizes not Le's NBC footage but Downes's ITN footage, including some portions that were never broadcast on American television. *Hearts and Minds* places the "Napalm Girl" directly after a shot of General Westmoreland making his infamous comment, "The Oriental does not value life the way we do." The documentary splits the footage into several segments, each of which is interspersed with an interview with Randy Floyd, a pilot during the war. After beginning with the long shot of the bombs hitting Phuc's village, Floyd explains, "During the missions, after the missions, the result of what I was doing—the result of this, this game, this exercise of my technical expertise never really dawned on me. That reality of the screams or the people being blown away or their homeland being destroyed just was not a part of what I thought about." Immediately after these words we cut to a continuous sequence of this reality: Phuc and her brother, Tam, running down the road, first toward the camera, and then past and away from it—restoring the seconds cut from the NBC Nightly News broadcast— followed by another previously unseen sequence, of Phuc pausing before a group of American photographers, who give her a drink from their canteens and pour water on her wounds. Floyd returns on-screen to explain, "We as Americans have never experienced that. We've never experienced any kind of devastation" (fig. 19). The final segment from Downes's footage is of Phuc's aunt and baby cousin, beginning like the NBC segment but lingering on a traveling close-up of the skin falling off the baby's feet. Here Floyd's words overlap with Downes's images, as Floyd proclaims, "When I was there, I never saw a child who got burned by napalm. I didn't drop napalm, but I dropped other things just as bad." The intercutting between Floyd and the "Napalm Girl" footage creates the impression that he is reacting directly to Phuc's wounds, as if it were her image that sparked his reflections on his wartime activities. Floyd's admissions are both a disavowal and an affirmation; he knows very well that he did not do these things to her, but he acts as if he did so as to assume responsibility for this spectacularly publicized act in order to atone for other, unseen sins.

To complete the identificatory cycle Floyd inserts not only himself but also his own children into this scenario, allowing him to feel not only the horror of responsibility but the pain of the victims' suffering: "I look at my children now, and I don't know what would happen if, what I would think about if someone napalmed . . ." At this utterance the documentary and Floyd both fall silent for almost thirty-five seconds while the camera remains on him, an extraordinarily long interval that forces the viewer to contemplate the scenario Floyd has just offered. In this remarkable pause Deleuze's transition from the action-image to the time-image suddenly manifests: in the midst of Floyd's narrative, in which he constructs himself as a "subject of movement or the instrument of action," erupts "a little time in the pure state," both as the uncomfortable durée of Floyd's distress, and also as the Nachträglichkeit of the delayed anguish that failed to accompany his original acts.[122] But this moment is fragile, broken by the rare entrance of the off-screen interviewer's voice at the end of the pause, prompting Floyd to return to his narration, offer a moral to his story, and restore the primacy of action to the documentary:

19. Frame enlargements of the "Napalm Girl" ITN footage taken by Alan Downes and narrated by Randy Floyd. None of these shots was broadcast on the NBC *Nightly News*. Frame enlargements from *Hearts and Minds*.

"Do you think we've learned anything from all of this?" From there Floyd's claim of virtual responsibility and shared trauma—a powerful ethical moment, even if predicated on a set of problematic racial cross-identifications—degenerates into the commonplaces of the antiwar movement: the "criminality" of American "officials" and "policymakers," rather than the potential guilt of all Americans viewing Phuc's image.

This scene from Hearts and Minds has extraordinary resonance with the dream of the burning child, originally recounted in Freud's The Interpretation of Dreams but explicated by many later commentators, including Jacques Lacan and Cathy Caruth, as a parable about an "ethical relation to the real."[123] A child had recently passed away from an illness, and his father took a rest from the funeral vigil, during which he dreamed that the child was standing beside his bed, whispering to him reproachfully, "Father, can't you see I'm burning?" When the father awoke, he discovered that an overturned candle had set the child's clothing on fire. This disturbing dream condenses several themes present in Hearts and Minds: parental responsibility, unconscious guilt for deeds outside of one's control, and an uncanny overlap between the dream and the real. Although the father awakens in time to save his child's corpse from further mutilation, the dream reminds him that he was too late to save the child from the fever that consumed him the first time. Freud interprets this dream as a simple wish fulfillment; in the dream the father gets to be with the child who is no longer in his life, thus allowing the father to momentarily escape an unpleasant reality. However, Lacan views this dream as the Real reasserting itself through the unconscious, in the form of this traumatic command that calls the father out of the dream and back into the reality of his son's death: "Can't you see?"[124]

The "Napalm Girl" functions like a similar command to the Real, forcing Floyd to awaken to the results of actions he had turned away from. Yet in both cases the injunction is also phantasmatic: despite their guilty consciences, neither Floyd nor the father of the dream were actually responsible for the children being burned. Their remorse represents, not the desire to undo their own previous actions, but rather to undo a reality that was not of their own making, and thus to assert agency over their essential impotence through the affect of guilt. As Caruth offers in her own reading of this dream, the child "commands the father to awaken" in order to confront the reality outside the dream that he dreads, and thus attend to the burden of the real through the act of survival.[125] The ethical command is not to heal the child who is burning, but simply to bear witness, and thus attest to the reality of this trauma. The visual form of bearing witness is precisely the Deleuzian pure optical and sound situation, as sight, and not action, constitutes the grounds for ethical response in these impossible situations.

But as we saw in *Hearts and Minds*, it is difficult to refrain from stumbling back into action, attempting to make good through sensory-motor activity what the eye perceives as an intolerable historical reality. In 1996 another veteran, John Plummer, attempted to take responsibility for the napalm bombing that injured Phuc. However, unlike Randy Floyd, who had situated his remarks in the midst of an antiwar critique at a time when the war was still an open target of critique, Plummer's attempt at reconciliation was overdetermined by the narrative of healing and closure that has dominated the national memory of the Vietnam War since the early 1980s. Phuc, who had immigrated to Canada in 1992, was a very literal figure of this healing, as reporters and photographers continued to track her recovery, marriage, and even childbirth as an embodied index of the pastness of the Vietnam War. In contrast Plummer's life story told of the ever-present nature of the war for veterans, including PTSD-like symptoms such as nightmares, alcoholism, and the dissolution of his first marriage. The entire scene of their tearful reconciliation is captured in Shelley Saywell's documentary *Kim's Story: The Road from Vietnam* (1997), whose film crew happened to be following Phuc on the day of their encounter. Seeking personal absolution as much as historical closure, Plummer went to see Phuc at a Veterans Day ceremony at the Vietnam Veterans Memorial in 1996, where Phuc was addressing the crowd with words that framed her life story not as contingent on the specificities of the Vietnam War, but rather as a universal parable against war in general: "Dear friends, as you know, I am a little girl who was running to escape from the napalm fire. I do not want to talk about the war because I cannot change history. I only want you to remember the tragedy of war in order to do things to stop fighting and killing around the world. . . . Even if I could talk, face to face, with the pilot who dropped the bomb, I could tell him, we cannot change history" (fig. 20). Answering to her seeming interpellation of "the pilot who dropped the bomb," Plummer approached Phuc afterward with a note saying simply, "I am the one." Plummer recounted his role in Phuc's injury in *Kim's Story*:

> When we put in the airstrike, it was given to us, or the information that we received back was that the bombs were on target and everything was fine, and we felt very successful. . . . So when I went to bed that night, I was very satisfied that we had done our job. And then the next morning, when I woke up and went to the mess hall, and the *Stars and Stripes* newspaper was laying on the table, and it had Kim's picture, and underneath it, it said, "in

an airstrike at Trang Bang," and it hit me just like someone had hit me in the face with a baseball bat. That was that airstrike that I did yesterday afternoon. Every time I saw that picture, I guess it was a subconscious voice inside of me saying, *I did that to her, I'm responsible for that.*

Plummer's memory tells of a delayed reaction, as he learns of the consequences of his actions only through the media rather than through direct experience. But this distance does nothing to assuage his guilt for the airstrike, which he describes as an "open wound." Whereas Phuc and her scars situate her injury as "history," Plummer's narrative locates his trauma in the present.

Both Phuc's speech at the Wall and Plummer's explanation also personalize the Vietnam War in ways that make it difficult to resituate the war within a larger political context. In particular Plummer portrays the war as a personal rather than a national trauma, saving his "confession" for over twenty years for the individual he injured rather than addressing a national audience such as the vvaw's *Winter Soldier* or Davis's *Hearts and Minds.* As if to drive home the insular context of this reconciliation, the camera in *Kim's Story* pulls back from the one-shot of Plummer recounting his story to reveal a two-shot of Plummer and Phuc sitting together on a couch (fig. 21). Plummer turns to Phuc and says, "I needed you to look in my eyes, because I knew, when you saw that, when you saw the sorrow that I had, that you would know, you'd understand." The specter of Vietnam has faded into a scene of marital bliss, as former soldier and victim embrace and hold hands as if wooing. Plummer not only reclaims personal agency by asserting that he was the one who directly ordered the airstrike, but also disconnects the individual from the nation by isolating both himself and Phuc from the social relations that placed them on opposite sides of the war. His oversimplified action-image compensates for the troubling stasis embodied in the picture of the "Napalm Girl," demanding that her gaze recognize him as "the one," the real protagonist of this scenario.

Unfortunately for Plummer, his confession was exposed as a lie soon after *Kim's Story* was broadcast. The original reports on Phuc from 1972 never obscured the fact that South Vietnamese pilots dropped the bombs that injured her, but as *Hearts and Minds* showed, American audiences claimed Phuc as their child and projected themselves into the positions of attacker and healer, thus enabling narratives of guilt and absolution at the expense of a more complex story about collective responsibility for the dispersed actions of modern warfare. But the veterans who came forward to discredit Plummer

20. Kim Phuc speaks on Veteran's Day at the Vietnam Veterans Memorial in 1996. Frame enlargement from *Kim's Story: The Road from Vietnam*.

21. Victim and bomber reunited: Kim Phuc and John Plummer meet and reconcile after her speech at the Wall. Frame enlargement from *Kim's Story: The Road from Vietnam*.

were not interested in these ethical questions. Ronald Timberlake, the main antagonist to Plummer's would-be hero, wrote a number of Internet articles debunking Plummer's claims, and his rebuttal was eventually confirmed and publicized by the same media outlets that broadcast Plummer's confession.[126] With seeming amnesia for the My Lai massacre, Timberlake and other veterans seemed to take great offense at the very notion that Americans might have committed any such atrocities:

> The Girl In The Photo was accidentally burned by her own countrymen, who were fighting her future countrymen. The only American participants of any nature were the journalists who reported the event and made her famous, and the doctors who saved her life. If left to the care of her countrymen, it is unlikely that the little girl would have lived to market forgiveness to anyone, but Americans saved her, and Americans made her famous enough to forgive us for an accident in which no American participated.

The Vietnamese, strangely unnamed in this passage, are again portrayed as internecine combatants who not only target their own kind for violence, but are incapable of taking care of their people without the constant intervention of Americans. Timberlake also criticizes Plummer's distortion of the chain of command as an inflation of his importance during the war, causing Plummer to split semantic hairs in order to reclaim any sense of agency: "No, I didn't order the air strike in the military sense, I set into motion events that eventuated into an air strike."[127]

In both Plummer's confession and Timberlake's rebuttal ethical responsibility is reduced to a simple binary logic, linked to a factual debate about whether or not one man's actions directly caused the napalm bombing of Kim Phuc. The very nature of this debate reduces situations such as that of the "Napalm Girl" into a scenario that one either enters as a participant or disavows as a viewer. But the questions persistently raised by not only the "Napalm Girl" but also "Saigon Execution" and the photos of the My Lai massacre refuse these binaries, insisting not only that the viewer plays an inextricable part in these scenarios that cannot be reduced to mere action, but also that viewing itself is its own form of ethical response. On the simplest level these images raise the importance of witnessing trauma, of bringing what is normally unseen into the light of the public sphere for debate. More important, the Deleuzian critique of the action-image warns us of the inadequacy of action-based narratives to account for these traumatic events, and consequently the dangers of basing ethical judgments on these narratives alone. In Plummer's and Timberlake's drive to identify the "real" perpetrator of the bombing, and thus determine the true narrative of the event, they foreclose the possibility that the circle of responsibility might exceed these narrative chains, jumping out of the continuity of causality into more phantasmatic relations. Plummer's feelings of guilt, like that of the father in the dream of the burning child, point to something deeper than the mere fact of causation, whether or not he "ordered" the airstrike. They constitute the possibility of ethics, of care for the other, in the face of the impossibility of controlling everything that happens to the other.[128] Timberlake's refusal of responsibility becomes a strange mirror of Lieutenant Calley's defense in the My Lai massacre, as they both perpetuate a fantasy of control that disavows any relation, ethical or otherwise, to the dead and injured subjects in these photographs.

Chapter 3

RESTAGING THE WAR

Fantasizing Defeat in Hollywood's Vietnam

No one will go out of the house to see the Vietnam war on a movie screen. The American people don't want to confront the war yet. Every one of these movies will die.

—American movie executive, quoted in Earl C. Gottschalk Jr., "After Long Study, Movie Makers Find a New War to Fight," *Wall Street Journal*, 1 November 1977

Between 1964 and 1977 only a single Hollywood film, *The Green Berets* (1968), starring John Wayne, attempted to directly represent the Vietnam War. Considering the close collaboration between Hollywood and the government during the Second World War, which saw dozens of war films made during the war itself with the blessing and even help of the U.S. military and the Office of War Information, this paucity of Vietnam films may seem puzzling.[1] Perhaps it was the competition of the "living-room war," playing out for free on television screens over the course of the conflict, that dissuaded fictional films from competing with this constant flow of images. Or perhaps, according to the armchair psychology of various Hollywood executives, the war was too fresh a wound in the American psyche, putting a damper on the profit motive of the film industry. In any case Hollywood's diagnosis was a self-fulfilling prophecy, as studios and producers shied away from financing any venture that did more than obliquely reference the war, despite the circulation of numerous scripts and projects: Morrell's *First Blood* was optioned as early as 1972 by Columbia Pictures, and the original screenplay for what became *The Deer Hunter* was written in 1974.[2] Even as a "Viet Nam blitz" of films began to be slated for release in 1978, many doubted that these films would turn a profit. Echoing the traumatic violence of the war, these skeptics predicted that the films would "die," thus doubling the defeat of the war itself.

This is not to say that the Vietnam War was completely absent on American movie screens during this time. In fact Vietnam haunted many films made in this era, often through the presence of Vietnam veteran characters, even as the war was relegated to the background of these narratives. As Paul Schrader, the screenwriter of *Taxi Driver* (1976), itself a prime example of the Vietnam veteran genre and its avoidance of the war, said in 1975, "The war is still too close to most Americans for them to sufficiently detach themselves. . . . One must work in metaphors *for the moment* (i.e., Mexico is Vietnam)."[3] Among the metaphors employed to represent Vietnam were contemporary issues, such as street crime (*Dirty Harry* [1971]), rural poverty (*Deliverance* [1972]), racism (*Hi Mom!* [1970]), drug dealing (*French Connection* [1971]), and historical events such as the Indian Wars (*Little Big Man* [1970]), the Second World War (*Tora! Tora! Tora!* [1970]), and the Korean War (M*A*S*H [1970]). But just as the American 1968 belatedly emerged as a complex condensation of disparate events, the nachträglich appearance of the Vietnam War in Hollywood film revealed a very different Vietnam than the one viewed live through the flow of television. As Max Youngstein, an American consultant to the production company Golden Harvest, based in Hong Kong, explained:

> Did the American public want to hear about Vietnam—in any form? Forget about what position [they] took. . . . Did they want to see anything about it and be reminded of something that turned out to be probably the only losing war that American has ever been involved in? Plus all the sociological and human aspects of 50,000 young men killed in the prime of their lives, with the quarter of a million that nobody talks about being anything from quadriplegics to maimed to where they are totally dependent on somebody else for their life.[4]

The spirit of defeat in the body politic would be mirrored by the "maimed" bodies of American soldiers, both as filmic representations and as "sociological" referents. After the withdrawal of American troops in 1973 and the fall of Saigon to North Vietnamese forces in 1975, it would be impossible to represent the Vietnam War to American audiences except through the lens of defeat, and even the most heroic depictions of American soldiers would be marked by this melancholic tone.

A Tough Sell: Reviving the War in 1978

Golden Harvest eventually did produce the first film to be released in the U.S. which centered on combat during the Vietnam War, *The Boys in Company C* (February 1978). But such reservations revealed how the specter of Vietnam in these films was very much an embodied ghost, one which would compulsively restage the violence of the Vietnam War for audiences to reexperience. *The Boys in Company C* would quickly be followed by a string of other Vietnam War combat films: *Go Tell the Spartans* (September 1978), *The Deer Hunter* (December 1978), and *Apocalypse Now* (August 1979). Along with *Coming Home* (February 1978), a film that focused on the returned veteran, these films refuted the theory that trauma could not also generate profit. Although a few other films are often grouped with these five as part of a renewed Vietnam War genre—for example, *Rolling Thunder* (October 1977), *Heroes* (November 1977), *Good Guys Wear Black* (June 1978), and *Who'll Stop the Rain* (originally titled *Dog Soldiers*, August 1978)—these latter films continue to deal with the war as background or allegory, aligning them with earlier metaphorical displacements of the war. In contrast *The Boys in Company C*, *Go Tell the Spartans*, and *Apocalypse Now* focused their gaze squarely on the Vietnam War, and even though *The Deer Hunter* and *Coming Home* staged most or all of their narrative on the home front, they too concentrated on the war as a specific and visible historical object.

I focus on these five films in order to examine the politics of identification through historical reanimation. As part of this historical specificity, these films engaged with the iconic images that emerged from the reporting of the war—"Saigon Execution," the My Lai massacre, "Napalm Girl," and the fall of Saigon—at times even restaging such images directly, albeit with significant variations. The most notable of these variations was the substitution of killed and maimed American bodies for the wounded and dead Vietnamese found in the iconic images, thus literalizing the identifications found between antiwar veterans and the Vietnamese in the previous chapter. However, in these new filmic restagings the orientalization of the American soldier no longer carried an antiwar message, which was made obsolete by the conclusion of the war. Instead they reflect the dispersion of identification from the individual soldier to the American nation, which now mourns its loss of the war through the internalization of Vietnamese suffering.

This process of internalization was more than metaphorical, for the late 1970s also saw the influx of oriental bodies, both in the general increase of Asian immigration enabled by the reforms of the Immigration and Nationality Act of 1965 and in the multiple waves of Vietnamese refugees fleeing from the aftermath of war. Together with the wounded American veteran, these Asian immigrants constitute the embodied history of the Vietnam War, belatedly exerting their presence against the seeming pastness of the war. Even as the new Vietnam War genre attempted to master the trauma of the war by restaging it, these racialized bodies threatened to traumatize the nation anew in a new crisis of assimilation and incorporation. Most vividly, at the same time the Russian roulette scenes from *The Deer Hunter* reimagined "Saigon Execution" as a tragic game ensnaring American lives, the shooter in the original scenario, Gen. Nguyen Ngoc Loan, was fighting his deportation from the U.S. as a symbol of the orientalized violence the nation wished to expunge. In such debates over refugee policies the violence of the Vietnam War on the individual body is writ large as struggles over the contours of the body politic, both on the level of its contents (population) and on the control over its boundaries (immigration).

In order to hold together these various levels of analysis—material and representational, individual bodies and body politics, historical reality and fictional imagination—I return to the concept of fantasy alluded to in my introduction, fleshed out through Laplanche's work on a specific Freudian scenario, "A Child Is Being Beaten." While Freud's original case study focused on the mobilization of beating fantasies for sexual pleasure, the double meaning of "being beaten" as both physical violence and defeat comes through clearly in the fantasies of the Vietnam War being reenacted in this film genre. Laplanche's understanding of fantasy as not simply a narrative but also a structure and a syntax for desire helps us to analyze the complexity of substitutions and identifications in these varied restagings of historical material. In particular this model helps us understand the paradoxes of pleasure and pain found in such fantasies, which would seem to violate the ideological pleasure principle by which popular culture is assumed to serve the national imagination. If Hollywood's Vietnam cannot erase the loss of that war in the historical record, how does it make use of that loss?

A Nation Is Being Beaten, and I Am Looking On:
The Deer Hunter (1978)

Those horrifying Russian roulette games where a man's face must be watched in its madness as a pistol pointed at his temple threatens self-inflicted destruction are quite bluntly intended to mix subconsciously with the worst image we all have of Vietnam: that oft-published picture of Vietnamese police chief Nguyen Ngoc Loan blowing out the brains of a Vietcong cadre as television cameras grind away. Make no mistake: Cimino wants you to accompany his characters into that hellish place in war, and, perhaps, in our subconscious fantasies, where life is completely devalued, where savagery and total disregard for humanity rule.

—James Wilwerth, "The Deer Hunter: An Epic Film
of Myth and Reality," *Horizon*, March 1979

Look, the film is not realistic—it's surrealistic. . . . I used events from '68 (My Lai) and '75 (the fall of Saigon) as reference points rather than as fact. But if you attack the film on its facts, then you're fighting a phantom, because literal accuracy was never intended.

—Michael Cimino, quoted in Leticia Kent, "Ready for Vietnam?
A Talk with Michael Cimino," *New York Times*, 10 December 1978

Michael Cimino's *The Deer Hunter* is a peculiar condensation of the two main themes of the Vietnam War film subgenre, containing scenes of soldiers at war and of veterans returning to the home front. While its almost tender portrait of American working-class immigrant culture and the relationships between American soldiers has drawn praise from many critics, its depiction of the Vietnamese and the Vietnam War has been widely excoriated as "xeno-phobi[c]," "fatally oversimplified," and "herald[ing] a new wave of reaction-ary jingoism."[5] In many ways this divide retrospectively mirrored that between supporters and opponents of American involvement in the war. These two sides of *The Deer Hunter* are not contradictory but reveal the overriding logic of a single fantasy scenario: that of "Saigon Execution," "the worst image we all have of Vietnam." That portrait of a Vietnamese man shooting another at point-blank range is transformed in *The Deer Hunter* into the game of Russian roulette, played first by American and Vietnamese prisoners of war and later by Americans and Vietnamese for money (fig. 22). The film's construction of Vietnam as a particularly "hellish place" endemic with such brutal violence is necessary in order to produce America as a site of relative innocence and peace. But *The Deer Hunter* does not simply reveal Vietnam and America to be polar opposites. Rather it shows a deep and complex identification between the two national entities, involving both the *transference* of violence from Viet-namese to American bodies and the *condensation* of interpersonal violence into a self-reflexive act. Such permutations recall the structure of psychoanalytic fantasy, apt frameworks for scenes that Cimino himself deemed "surreal." If *The Deer Hunter* is an American fantasy of Vietnam, it cannot be a simple projection of historical desire to rewrite the war. Instead the transformations

22. "Saigon Execution" restaged as Russian roulette.
Frame enlargement from *The Deer Hunter*.

between "Saigon Execution" and other historical materials and its resulting restaging of the Vietnam War reveal a destabilizing and melancholic fantasy of America's own undoing. *The Deer Hunter* does not salvage American subjectivity in the face of defeat; it embraces defeat as the very condition of American subjectivity, after Vietnam.

The events of the Vietnam War at first seem to form a curiously detached backdrop in *The Deer Hunter* for the human drama that unfolds around the the three main characters, Michael (Robert De Niro), Nick (Christopher Walken), and Steven (John Savage). The film's tripartite structure sandwiches the war between two long acts set in Clairton, Pennsylvania, a rust-belt town filled with Russian immigrants and economically centered around a steel mill where Michael, Nick, and Steven work. "The war is really incidental to the development of the characters and their story," claimed Cimino. "It's part of their lives and just that, nothing more."[6] However, the earliest hint of the war, occurring in the elaborate Russian Orthodox wedding of the first act, already sets up the representational politics of the second act in Vietnam. "What's it like over there?" Michael eagerly asks of a Green Beret sitting at the bar next to the reception hall, and the veteran replies, "Fuck it," foreshadowing in this linguistic obscenity the aporia of representing the war. Accordingly the second act, which takes place in Vietnam, does not depict combat per se but focuses mainly on the characters' experiences in a VC prisoner-of-war camp, where they are forced to play Russian roulette with one another. After a dramatic escape they emerge in Saigon to experience military hospitals, Vietnamese brothels, and a unique gambling hall where the main attraction is Russian roulette again, this time played for profit rather than torture.

This part of the film provoked much consternation from both popular and academic critics, as it seemed to perversely invert the history of the war as seen through earlier news coverage. Although Russian roulette was never documented as a form of torture used by VC soldiers or the North Vietnamese Army (NVA), it was noted in eyewitness accounts of the My Lai massacre as a method American soldiers used to psychologically torment the villagers before shooting them: "We captured four suspects. . . . They were being beaten kind of hard and the kid named the older man as an NVA platoon leader. [Capt. Ernest] Medina drew his .38, took out five rounds and played Russian roulette with him. Then he grabbed him by the hair and threw him up against a tree. He fired two shots with a rifle, closer and closer to the guy's head, then aimed straight at him."[7] The My Lai massacre indeed haunts The Deer Hunter and other Vietnam War films as a phantom, although not in the form of direct quotation, as with "Saigon Execution": the first atrocity that occurs when The Deer Hunter shifts to Vietnam is not Russian roulette, but a Vietnamese soldier throwing a grenade into a bomb shelter where women and children are hiding. The historian Bruce Cumings referred to the Vietnam scenes in The Deer Hunter as revisionist "print negatives" which invert the power relations of the war: "it was the Vietcong terrorists who burned villages," not the U.S. Marines.[8] The New Yorker film critic Pauline Kael remarked, "The impression a viewer gets is that if we did some bad things over there we did them ruthlessly but impersonally; the Vietcong were cruel and sadistic. The film seems to be saying that the Americans had no choice, but the v.c. enjoyed it."[9] For such critics the historical inaccuracies of The Deer Hunter lead them to dismiss the film as irredeemably racist, thus foreclosing any further discussion of the relation between the film and its historical sources.

We can make sense of The Deer Hunter's inversion of "Saigon Execution" by considering its permutations of a deeper structure of fantasy, as alluded to in "A Child Is Being Beaten." In that case study Freud documented that many patients with hysterical or obsessive neurosis reported the fantasy of watching an unknown child being beaten as a source of masturbatory pleasure. Upon further analysis, Freud reveals that the fantasy is simply one stage of a larger fantasy structure that moves through several prior, repressed phases:

(1) My father is beating the child whom I hate.
(2) I am being beaten by my father.
(3) A child is being beaten (I am looking on).[10]

Although the manifest pleasure may occur in the final phase, in which the fantasizing subject imagines herself separate from the scene of violence, this pleasure is predicated upon repressed moments of imagined violence, in which the subject experiences the sadistic pleasure of violence being inflicted upon her rival, as well as the masochistic pleasure-pain of having that violence turned upon herself. The material basis of the fantasy is the child's frightening experience of the contestation for love and power between parents and siblings, and later between proxies for those familial roles, teachers and students. But when that history is converted into the materials for fantasized pleasure, there is a reflexive movement, which Freud describes as a "turning round upon the subject," by which the subject internalizes external events into a form of psychic reality.[11]

Freud's beating fantasy is a paradigmatic instance of Laplanche's and Pontalis's definition of fantasy as a dramatic scenario with shifting roles and a narrative line: the fantasy is "not an object that the subject imagines and aims at, so to speak, but rather a sequence in which the subject has his own part to play and in which permutations of roles and attributions are possible."[12] In such a model the self shifts from the privileged agent of fantasy to an object split off and alienated from the desires articulated therein. In one of the most basic forms of fantasy—the fantasy of heteroaggression, or violence against an other—the child does not achieve mastery over the other, but paradoxically emphasizes his or her own lack of power. As Laplanche remarks, "The very movement of fantasmatization [is] . . . to reflect the action, internalize it, make it enter oneself as fantasy. To fantasize aggression is to turn it round upon oneself, to aggress oneself."[13] Thus, far from being the mere prop of a will to power, fantasy becomes a tool for exposing the fallacy of mastery in the fantasizing subject and a way of interrogating the essential relationship between mastery and the history of suffering that it disavows. To fantasize is not simply to construct a narrative that fulfills the desires of the fantasizing subject; it is to expose the essential passivity of that subject to a history of violence that becomes the condition for his or her desires.

The structure of Freud's beating fantasy also forces us not to privilege any one manifestation of the fantasy as the "real" scenario, but rather to think of the logic that links together each of the phases of the fantasy. In each phase the position of the fantasizing subject shifts constantly, from being active to passive to voyeur, such that the focus of the scenario lies as much in the action taking place (beating) as in any individual role (the beater, the beaten). The beating fantasy emphasizes the importance of multiple and simultaneous sites of entry into the fantasy, rather than on a "one-to-one correlation between the subject and the protagonist in the fantasy."[14] Film theorists such as Carol Clover, Kaja Silverman, and D. N. Rodowick have used the beating fantasy to consider the possibilities of cross-gender identification.[15] The Deer Hunter invites a similar consideration of cross-racial identification, as the

Russian roulette scenes' rotating cast of players and complex relationship to "Saigon Execution" destabilizes the racial positions within this fantasy of violence. If we consider "Saigon Execution" as analogous to the third, manifest phase of the beating fantasy, depicting a distant violence for the consumption of American audiences, the inversion of The Deer Hunter's Vietnam scenes becomes more like a permutation of a deeper desire, in which Americans shift from watching the scene to being a participant in it. The critiques of Cimino's Russian roulette scenes as an inversion of "Saigon Execution" assume that American viewers will naturally identify with the American characters and thus absorb the racism implied in that positioning. However, that positioning is itself an index of an identification with the suffering Vietnamese body submerged in the photograph's permutation of the fantasy. Thus, like the fantasy of heteroaggression, the repetition of "Saigon Execution" in the form of Russian roulette enacts not the mastery of the American viewer over this historical trauma, but rather the subjection of the American nation to the reenactment of its original scene of defeat.

The first Russian roulette scene in The Deer Hunter demonstrates this relationship between voyeurism and subjection. As the film critic Janet Maslin wittily commented, "At this juncture, 'The Deer Hunter' . . . has introduced an element of genuinely unbearable violence, and still has two hours to go. Will you, the captive audience, spend the rest of that time being scared?"[16] Here the fantasy is less of domination than of the passive spectatorship that also characterizes the primal scene, another paradigmatic example of Laplanchian fantasy. The first victims forced to play Russian roulette are not even the American soldiers but two unnamed Vietnamese men. The audience's captivity parallels that of the American soldiers trapped in a watery cell beneath the action. Between the reactions of the diegetic prisoners of war and the extradiegetic audience, it is difficult to tell which is worse: being forced to listen to horrors one cannot see, or being forced to stare at these horrors directly. Even the camera's gaze is destabilized as a point of identification, and hence as a position of mastery. Michael, Nick, and Steven witness the events only in fragments, as revealed through point-of-view shots through cracks in the floor. Further disorienting the spatial logic of the scene, Cimino refrains from shot/reverse shot structures, forcing the spectator's gaze to bounce randomly about the hut and below to the prisoners. When the first death during the game takes place, the body of the Vietnamese man falls and he dies across three separate shots, interspersed with reaction shots from Michael and Steven, who cannot see the game but can only hear its gory end, as well as from another Vietnamese prisoner player (fig. 23). As the blood

spurs from the head of the man lying on the floor, recalling the "after" images of "Saigon Execution," the camera swivels ninety degrees, offering images that do not match either the eye lines of the reaction shots or the points of view of other identifiable characters. When Steven, Michael, and Nick later emerge from their watery cage to play the game, the camera frames them with the same composition that marked "Saigon Execution" and the first Russian roulette death: player facing the camera, gun directly to the left of the temple. This chain of substitutions, from "Saigon Execution" to Vietnamese prisoner to American soldier, makes explicit what the critique of inversion obscured: that the American soldier is not diametrically opposed to the Vietnamese (as represented by the VC in charge of the game), but is also taking the place of the Vietnamese (as prisoner of war).

The desire to fix the interpretation of The Deer Hunter on the basis of its historical veracity (or lack thereof) can also be understood as a desire to stabilize these shifting points of identification and to elevate a certain version of the fantasy of Vietnam as real. The trope of Russian roulette was actually created by the screenwriters Quinn Redeker and Lou Garfinkle in 1971, long before Cimino signed on to this project and even before Vietnam was chosen as the setting for this trope.[17] However, Cimino later embraced the idea as if it were his own, drawing upon anecdotal knowledge to ground the trope:

> I've been asked about the authenticity of the sequences depicting a Vietnamese version of Russian roulette and I can only say that I have no way of knowing how prevalent it was. There have been numerous reports in various Southeast Asian newspapers of exactly this sort of thing going on, and in the case of Vietnam, just about anything you can imagine taking place *did* take place in some form or other. As a matter of fact, the man who plays the role of Julien in the picture told me that he lost a friend playing a game exactly like that. Incidentally, that man who played Julien wasn't an actor at all, but a former French fighter pilot who fought at Dien Bien Phu and stayed behind to open a bar in Saigon.[18]

In other interviews Cimino played up his autobiography as a way of validating his film: "I was attached to a Green Beret medical unit. My characters are portraits of people whom I knew."[19] Among those who accepted Cimino's

---

(*opposite*) **23.** Three shots depicting the first Vietnamese prisoner to die during the Russian roulette game at the prisoner-of-war camp, intercut with two reaction shots from captured Americans Michael (Robert DeNiro) and Steven (John Savage) and an unnamed Vietnamese prisoner. Frame enlargements from The Deer Hunter.

credentials was David Denby, who deflected criticism from The Deer Hunter by stating, "Putting the 'correct' attitudes into a movie isn't so hard, especially now; what really counts is authenticity of experience, which this movie has by the ton."[20] Cimino's life story was later debunked by Tom Buckley in Harper's, and Cimino's lack of honesty regarding his personal history was brought to bear on his filmic treatment of national history. Ironically this same aura of authenticity abused by Cimino was also used by critics of the film to shore up their own version of historical truth.[21] Gloria Emerson, who called The Deer Hunter "the most racist film I have ever seen," claimed in her review for the Nation, "The most brilliant dissections of The Deer Hunter have come not from professional critics but from men who reported the war in Vietnam."[22] John Pilger, who renamed the film "The Gook-Hunter," began his editorial on the film by staging his own autobiographical credentials: "I have spent much of my adult life in Vietnam and the United States as a journalist and documentary-film maker. I have been with American soldiers when they were killed or maimed."[23] The Deer Hunter was being compared not only with other fictional films but with the entire genre of Vietnam news coverage, and accordingly the ultimate arbiters of truth were the journalists who produced that coverage in the first place.

This equation of news coverage with the "real" is particularly problematic on the issue of violence, which in American films after 1968 has been characterized by a certain hyperrealism to represent the effects of violence on the body. Using closely framed squib work (small explosives placed on the body to mimic gunshots), fake blood, and quick montage sequences, this style highlights the body's loss of control over its contents and its movements as a way of marking the rupture of violent death. Aljean Harmetz pointed out the contradiction between the hyperrealism of graphic details and the counterhistorical claims of the narrative itself: "The rising backlash against the movie may come partly from the increasing knowledge that the seemingly realistic sequences of violence are not based on any reality."[24] The graphic effects of violence, plus the camera's relentless, slow-motion stare seem to equate visibility with truth. Yet the style of The Deer Hunter's violent scenes owes as much to directors such as Sam Peckinpah and Arthur Penn as it does to "Saigon Execution" or other Vietnam War news coverage. Defending his use of hyperrealist, stylized violence in films like The Wild Bunch (1969) and Straw Dogs (1971), Peckinpah inverted the usual binaries and asserted that it is fictional film rather than news coverage that elicits the proper ethical response to violence: "We watch our wars and see men die, really die, every day on television, but it doesn't seem real. We don't believe those are real people dying on that screen. We've been anesthetized by the media. What I do is show people what it's really like—not by showing it as it is so much as by heightening it, stylizing it."[25] Although such stylization may conflict with the desire for unmediated visual representation in documentary news footage, these techniques were able to convey the affect of violence upon viewers, thus making violence "real" in an embodied sense. As one filmgoer retorted to critics of The Deer Hunter, "How is this film a distortion of history if it evokes, better than any other, feelings comparable to those of the total chaos and mind-breaking destruction that occurred in Southeast Asia?"[26] Realism becomes a matter of affect rather than factual accuracy, and the role of film is to evoke the proper structures of feeling associated with the Vietnam War rather than reproduce the war as a historical artifact.

The explicit violence of the Russian roulette scenes is not simply a form of racism, if what is meant by this accusation is the othering of a racialized group through distancing and distortion. The violence also functions as a form of address designed to draw American audiences into an affective relationship with its fantasy of violence, making that violence intimate and domestic. The extreme, even obscene nature of this hyperrealist visual style works in the service of this affective role, drawing viewers into a viewing relation that seems to be itself an act of violence. Vincent Canby of the New York Times compared the Russian roulette scenes' "simulated blood-and-guts" to a form of "theatrical blackmail" designed mainly "to elicit strong emotional responses," while Barbara Grizzuti Harrison in Ms. characterized the rhythm of violence in The Deer Hunter as "obscene," a form of "calculated foreplay" designed to manipulate the viewer's reactions.[27] The graphicness of this violence was so important to The Deer Hunter's reception that Universal Pictures initially marketed the film by implying that it received an x rating for violence.[28] The intimacy of such violence transforms the generalized and voyeuristic spectacle of "a child is being beaten, and I am looking on" into the individuated, masochistic form "I am being beaten," inserting the American spectator into the chain of equivalences already established between American and Vietnamese soldiers. In effect The Deer Hunter nationalizes the fantasy of "Saigon Execution," turning an image of Vietnamese-on-Vietnamese violence into the scene of the nation's trauma.

As Nick's suicide in the final Russian roulette game proves, this internalization of Vietnamese violence into the American body has tragic consequences. This final act of violence, which appears against the backdrop of the fall of Saigon—complete with real news footage of the frenzied evacuations— signifies America's withdrawal from the war through an implosion. Whereas the earlier scenes show American soldiers forced into the game as an act of torture, now Nick has willingly stepped into the game, played as a form of gambling entertainment in the heart of Saigon, as if eerily drawn to a re-capitulation of the death he cheated while in captivity. Nick even dons the white shirt and red headband of the other Vietnamese players, a visual assim-ilation to the Saigon milieu of the game. The Vietnam War does not kill Nick, for he dies by his own hands. However, the violence performed by his body is of an oriental origin, learned from the VC prisoner-of-war camp and from the Vietnamese gamblers in Saigon. As further evidence of Nick's complete bodily incorporation of orientalized violence, there are needle marks on his arm implying heroin use, another sign of Asiatic corruption. In effect Nick has identified with the whole of the beating fantasy; estranged from his own identity as an American soldier, he simultaneously becomes Vietnamese shooter, victim, *and* viewer.

In describing the inward movement from witnessed scene to imagined scenario, Laplanche argues that this "reflexive (*selbst* or *auto-*) moment [is] constitutive" of fantasy, a form of " 'autoeroticism' in which the object has been replaced by a fantasy, by an object *reflected* within the subject."[29] The reflexive syntax of Nick's suicide, "I shoot myself," reveals how fantasy itself has become an object violently penetrating the subject. The aggressive aspects of fantasy, wherein one inflicts violence upon another, also reflect an inherent self-aggression. Laplanche describes these permutations, "*introjecting the suf-fering object, fantasizing the suffering object, making the object suffer inside oneself, making oneself suffer,*" as related vicissitudes of fantasy that slide imperceptibly into one another.[30] If *The Deer Hunter* imagines suffering Vietnamese bodies, it also shows that suffering incorporated into the American subject, eventually surfacing as self-inflicted suffering when the self and the incorporated other become indistinguishable. The final Russian roulette scenes posit a self-dissolving fantasy in which visual fascination ends at a radical point of nonbeing. In encountering violence both *as radical* other and *through the racial* other, the American subject comes face to face with himself, through an internalization of the visual "style" of violence, and simultaneously implodes and explodes. When Nick takes the object, the oriental bullet, inside himself, he completes his assimilation to the abject fantasy provided by the executed VC in "Saigon Execution."

The final suicide complicates the critique of *The Deer Hunter* as a mirror narcissistically reflecting upon American identity and values and ignoring Vietnamese subjectivity. If it is a crude form of racist dehumanization that allows killings like My Lai to take place—*I can kill the other because the other is merely an object to me*—then that objecthood is brought uncomfortably close to one's own subjecthood through participation in violence; *If the other can kill me, I am thus potentially an object myself.* In such a structure that destabilizes human subjectivity so radically, what would it mean to "humanize" the victims of the Vietnam War? Even if we were to rectify the representational politics of *The Deer Hunter* by restoring Americans to the role of aggressor and Vietnamese to that of victim, as it "really" was in the war, this strategy cannot escape the permutational logic of the beating fantasy.

The Body Incontinent: *The Boys in Company C* (1978) and *Coming Home* (1978)

The other side of the spectacular infliction of violence is the effect of that violence on the body of the American soldier. The films *The Boys in Company C* and *Coming Home*, both released in February 1978, shift our visual focus from the violated Vietnamese body of "Saigon Execution" and the My Lai massacre to the "maimed" American bodies that John Kerry eulogized as the "filthy obscene memory" of the Vietnam War. The low-budget combat film *The Boys in Company C* substitutes drug addiction for the spectacular pyrotechnics of hyperrealist violence and their injurious effects on the body. *Coming Home*, a high-budget film featuring A-list actors, is centered entirely on the disabled veteran's body, to the exclusion of even a single scene of combat in Vietnam. Together these films outline the vicissitudes of what I term "the body incontinent,"a messy, leaky, and permeable physical body that also serves as a metaphor for the loss of control that the Vietnam War imposed on the American soldier on multiple levels. Certainly we see instances of the body incontinent throughout the Vietnam War genre as well: Steven in *The Deer Hunter*, who returns to the U.S. paralyzed; Colonel Kurtz, whose indolent, corpulent body is sacrificed at the end of *Apocalypse Now*; and the vomiting and shitting American GIs in *Go Tell the Spartans*. Hyperrealist violence in these films, with its visual attention to bodily ejecta, is itself an important vehicle for the representation of incontinence, as it transforms the human body from a volitional subject to a fleshly object subject to the control of external, physical forces.[31] But *The Boys in Company C* and *Coming Home* trace the effects of incontinence beyond the scene of injury, and thus link the physical violence of Vietnam to other societal upheavals of the late 1970s, in particular second-wave feminism and its reconfiguration of national desire and the continuing racialization of "law and order" through the specter of illegal drugs. In gesturing to these other contexts these specific incontinent bodies link the violence done to the individual soldier to the epistemic and sociological violence occurring on the level of the body politic.

Although incontinence is popularly associated with a medical pathological meaning—the inability to contain and control one's urine and feces—my use of the term invokes its larger etymological history, and in particular its deployment in ethical theories. In these theories incontinence is linked to the Greek term *akrasia*, found in Aristotle's *Nicomachean Ethics*, which is also translated variously as "impotence," "intemperance," "powerlessness," and "moral weakness." *Akrasia* refers to a complicated dialectic between the body and the rational or conscious mind to control one's appetites or desires. For example, an incontinent man might drink alcohol or pursue sexual activity to excess, yet he does so not by choice but because he cannot help himself. As Aristotle explains, he is "mastered by his pleasure" rather than asserting his reason to control these pleasures.[32] Foucault reads the problem of akrasia as not simply an issue of restraint, in which the mind suppresses the body—abstaining from alcohol or sex completely—but rather as a technique of active struggle between the mind and the body that envisions the embodied subject engaged in a project of "self-mastery" in order "to remain free from interior bondage to the passions."[33] In these martial metaphors the struggle with incontinence thus mimics the process of phantasmatization of "A Child Is Being Beaten," as aggression toward the self is mapped onto a battle over an external other.

This language of mastery and slavery ties the dialectic between incontinence and continence to the concept of self-sovereignty, one of the bedrocks of the concept of citizenship in democratic societies. For John Locke the sovereign individual is the polar opposite of the slave; he has complete dominion over his body, just as the sovereign state has dominion over its territories, and this self-mastery is the precondition of his participation in the state.[34] From this follows a body of U.S. case law that protects the boundaries of the body as if they were the borders of a state, not only from physical violence and assault but also from coercion by the state and other authorities. On the issue of medical coercion and consent Elaine Scarry comments, "The body is here conceived of not simply as something to be brought in under the protection of civil rights, but as itself the primary ground of all subsequent rights."[35] In other words, continence provides the condition of possibility for the sovereign citizen, while incontinence becomes a model for absolute subjection and lack of freedom. This link between the moral and the political further pathologizes the masochistic subject of the beating fantasy as one who paradoxically chooses his unfreedom, allowing his body to be violated in the pursuit of his painful pleasures.

Racial and gender difference have inflected the way sovereignty and continence have been distributed among American body-subjects. In fact the incontinent or unsovereign man resembles Freud's "feminine masochist," a man who desires to be treated as a woman, insofar as his body becomes violated, penetrated, and forced into submission, states which Freud considered natural to women but pathological for men.[36] Ironically it was in *Pratt v. Davis*, a case in 1905 in Illinois illustrating the gendered violation of self-sovereignty—a physician removed a woman's uterus without her consent in order to treat her for hysteria—that led to an influential decision which declared, "under a free government at least, the free citizen's first and greatest right, which underlies all others—the right to the inviolability of his person."[37] This assertion of the body's "inviolability" belies the violence done to the female body by virtue of its presumed incontinence and lack of self-mastery. Feminist scholars such as Elizabeth Grosz, Julia Kristeva, and Susan Bordo have traced this gendering of incontinence to the exclusion of female subjects from the political or social order.[38]

But incontinence and sovereignty are also highly racialized, as Locke's reference to slavery suggests. Contemporary racialized bodies in the U.S. remain vulnerable to violation, as evidenced by the Tuskegee syphilis experiment, body cavity searches of prisoners and immigrants, the involuntary provision of DNA and other bodily evidence, and the forced sterilization and contraception of minority women.[39] The iconic images of the Vietnam War are evidence of the Asian body's incontinence, in the form of not only violent death ("Saigon Execution") but also rape (My Lai) and disfiguration ("Napalm Girl"). The adversary in the dialectical struggle of the subject for continence is not simply the body's own internal appetites or propensities, but also a plethora of sociopolitical forces that impinge upon that body's sovereign boundaries from without. These struggles ultimately map onto the succession of scenes in the beating fantasy, as the subject is alternately the subject of and subjected to acts of violence that constantly remake the boundaries of that subject. The body incontinent, like the beaten body, is not the privileged endpoint of the beating fantasy, but one manifestation of a larger phantasmatic sequence that rehearses the various forms of subjection and mastery that the body encounters in its social existence. The manifestations of incontinence in *The Boys in Company C* and *Coming Home* reveal the particular roles that black male and white female bodies play in relation to the phantasmatic Vietnamese body.

While most Vietnam War films focus on incontinence caused by violence or bodily injury, *The Boys in Company C* substitutes drugs as the source of incontinence. In this film drug abuse and drug dealing represent the parallel yet intertwined discourses of individual and state sovereignty, employing the black American soldier as the proxy by which the oriental contagion corrupts the white American body politic. As the historian Paul Gootenberg has shown, public outrage over illegal drugs in the U.S. has often equated drugs with racialized minorities—Chinese and opium, Mexicans and marijuana, blacks and crack cocaine—thus tying the issue of personal incontinence to the traffic of immigrants and goods across national borders: "Mind-altering drugs transgress symbolic boundaries, such as race, along with real borders. . . . Certain states of consciousness themselves became criminalized, declared outside of the nation and its white body politic."[40] During the Vietnam War panic over drug abuse among GIs led to Nixon's declaration of a "War on Drugs" in 1971 and the founding of the Drug Enforcement Agency in 1973, enabling what Jeremy Kuzmarov has called a "narco-insurgency" that authorized the U.S. to expand its military operations into both Laos and Thailand, thus sanctioning the violation of other nation's borders through their pharmacological infiltration of the American soldier.[41]

In *Boys* the link between the orientalized Golden Triangle and the U.S. is embodied by the sole black protagonist, Tyrone Washington (Stan Shaw) from Chicago, whose street-smart, black power persona invokes the violence of the urban rioter as well as the racialized target of the discourse of "law and order," both from the 1960s, and thus connects the urban jungle to the jungles of Vietnam.[42] In the opening montage, as we are introduced to each main character by his brief farewell before departing for basic training, Tyrone is seen off not by family members or loved ones, but by his drug boss, Spoon (Cisco Oliver): "Some shit eating, turd packing, honky motherfucker is drafting my main man away, to send you off to kill chinks. Who's going to take care of business for me on the streets?" In the first half of the film, which depicts the recruits comically befuddled by the challenges of basic training, Tyrone is again set apart from his fellow recruits, as the street has provided him with experiences equivalent to fighting in Vietnam. His drill instructor, Sergeant Loyce (Lee Ermey, who later reprises this role in *Full Metal Jacket* [1987]), confesses to him, "I've got eight fucking weeks to teach these goddamn fucking people what it took you twenty years to learn on the streets." Even the film's publicity materials reinforce these links between black America and Vietnam; one article blurs the line between the film and the actor Stan Shaw's biography: "Karate classes kept him off the streets of Chicago's South Side, where cousins, and friends like Tyrone Washington, ran with the gangs."[43]

Even Tyrone's plan to traffic heroin from Southeast Asia back to the U.S. inside body bags is a plot device stolen from newspaper headlines, specifically news of a drug trafficking ring headed by an African American Vietnam veteran, William Henry Jackson, which surfaced around the same time Nixon initiated his War on Drugs.[44] In Boys Tyrone comes up with this plan after one of his platoon mates, Billy Ray Pike (Andrew Stevens), mistakes a body bag for a sleeping bag and gets stuck inside one, to the amusement of the entire platoon. Alvin Foster (James Canning), the budding journalist in the platoon and the narrator of the film, observes afterward, "The way they stick somebody inside one of those bags, seal it up and send it off? It's like a neat little convenient package, nobody even thinks about what's inside," to which Tyrone replies with a laugh, "Yeah, nobody ever looks inside." In this comic sequence, what begins as a critique of the censorship of the human costs of war becomes the impetus for the economic exploitation of that war. Set in 1967, before the Tet Offensive, Boys can simultaneously conjure a nostalgia for the innocence of the early years of the Vietnam War and ridicule that nostalgia through its cynical, morbid humor. To further solidify the Asian–African axis of war profiteering, Boys dramatizes Tyrone's initial attempts to broker a deal with his suppliers, who turn out to be two corrupt South Vietnamese officers, Col. Nolong Dong and Colonel Trang (played by Joe Mari Avellana and Vic Diaz, both veteran Filipino actors). "Doesn't it bother you to harm your own troops? Doesn't it bother you to put money in the pockets of your enemies?" Dong asks Tyrone during their initial meeting. "No? Good. Doesn't bother me either." African Americans and South Vietnamese are aligned as similarly failed national subjects, putting their self-interest before their identification with the nation and its call for self-sacrifice.

But Boys allows Tyrone to redeem himself and reenter the imagined community through his relationship with Billy Ray, the naïve teenager from Galveston, Texas, who inspires Tyrone's smuggling plot. Bridging the divisions between black and white, North and South, and urban and rural America, this friendship helps to redefine the main opposition of the film as national rather than racial, as Vietnamese against Americans rather than nonwhites against whites. Billy functions as a foil to Tyrone; his innocence contrasts with and yet complements Tyrone's street-smarts. Ironically, although Tyrone is the drug dealer, it is Billy who loses his self-control by becoming addicted to drugs, at first to the Demerol prescribed to him during boot camp, and later to illegal heroin supplied by another U.S. soldier in Vietnam. While Tyrone is negotiating with Colonel Dong, Billy nearly overdoses off-screen, and Tyrone returns from his meeting to find Billy collapsed on the ground. In a continuous shot that lasts for nearly a minute Tyrone eventually succeeds in reviving Billy by slapping him around, disrupting the narrative with this double spectacle of incontinence: Billy's drooling, flopping body and Tyrone's angry, emotional hysterics (fig. 24). Tyrone's overreaction is inexplicable to the other GIs, but the audience is meant to understand his anger as guilt for the drug negotiations bracketed by Billy's overdose. This dramatic irony is reinforced by a subsequent sequence in which Tyrone solemnly witnesses a procession of coffins draped with U.S. flags. No longer are the invisible bodies simply anonymous, abject matter; their sovereignty as national subjects is restored and reclaimed in this patriotic act of burial.

Subsequently Tyrone also learns the difference between "good" and "bad" Vietnamese subjects, modeling his own choice between becoming a "good" or "bad" American, when his troop is ordered to attack a village filled with women and children. Colonel Trang, the brother-in-law of Colonel Dong and the second South Vietnamese partner in the smuggling ring, arrives to interrogate a young Vietnamese boy whom the American GIs had saved earlier. As the boy is taken off-screen to the sounds of screams and a gunshot, Tyrone bitterly remarks to his inept commanding officer, who handed the boy to Trang, "You wouldn't have done that if that was a white boy back there, yeah, but to you, he's nothing but a gook, he's just a yellow nigger." In contrast to the black radical critique of the war, Tyrone's realization of his alignment with the "yellow nigger" leads him back into rather than away from the American imagined community, albeit one unified by its common abjection by the conditions of war. When Trang contacts Tyrone to finalize their deal, Trang's body is framed against a pair of body bags, American casualties from the previous battle. With his Fu Manchu–like fingernails and sinister disregard for human life, Trang is marked as other even to the mangled "Remains Non-Viewable" hidden within these bags (fig. 25). Tyrone's refusal of Trang's deal ultimately takes the form of a disidentification: "Yeah, man, my name is Washington. Half the niggers in the Marine Corps' name is Washington. You got the wrong man." Simultaneously invoking both the anonymity of racism and the nation's father, Tyrone escapes his pact with the enemy and returns to the national fold. Paradoxically his refusal of incontinence leads back to another form of incontinence, as he disavows his complicity in the Vietnamese boy's torture and Billy's overdose by choosing instead to be aligned with the other "boys" in their shared subjection to the dangers and absurdities of the war. In the final scene of the film, in the aftermath of a deadly ambush of a soccer game set during the Tet Offensive,

24. Tyrone Williams (Stan Shaw) tries to revive Billy Ray Pike (Andrew Stevens) from his heroin overdose. Frame enlargement from *The Boys in Company C.*

25. Colonel Trang (Vic Diaz) inspects the body bags marked "Remains Non-Viewable" that will carry heroin from Vietnam to the United States. Frame enlargement from *The Boys in Company C.*

Tyrone leads the surviving soldiers in a march off the field, recapitulating the marching chants from basic training at the film's start.

Following soon after the release of *Boys*, *Coming Home* focuses on the antiwar movement and the home-front experiences of injured Vietnam veterans, but its attempt to resignify the injury of the normative, sovereign white male body is heavily inflected through its own ambivalence toward the feminist movement. Although the rise of second-wave feminisms in the 1970s is complex and multifaceted, the feminism against which *Coming Home* reacts focuses mainly on the political and sexual empowerment of middle-class white women and the concomitant reconfiguration of masculinity in relation to this empowerment. The impact of this version of feminism on Hollywood is apparent in the Oscar-winning films that bracketed the success of *The Deer Hunter* and *Coming Home*; the previous year's best picture was *Annie Hall* (1977), featuring Diane Keaton as an iconoclastic woman with a predilection for menswear, and the following year's was *Kramer vs. Kramer* (1979), a melodramatic portrayal of divorce and single fatherhood that won over *Apocalypse Now*. *Coming Home* foregrounds gender through its central love story between the disabled veteran Luke Martin (Jon Voight) and the newly radicalized officer's wife Sally Hyde (Jane Fonda). In many ways Voight's performance embodies the reconfigured, "feminized" masculinity also found in the figure of President Jimmy Carter and his attempts to heal the national wounds of the Vietnam War.[45] At the same time the film reveals the phantasmatic force of racial otherness in defining the contours of white masculinity and femininity, and in particular the threat to American self-sovereignty posed by orientalized violence even within the relative safety of the home front. Thus even though "the closest 'Coming Home' gets to the front is an R&R in Hong Kong," the film nevertheless animates the absent presence of the war through its focus on these wounded veterans and their reclamation of a political and social existence.[46]

Ostensibly *Coming Home* is about the rehabilitation of the Vietnam veteran: his physical rehabilitation and restoration to sovereign individuality despite his disability, and his symbolic rehabilitation from psychotic criminal to heroic citizen. The main veteran protagonist, Luke Martin, reclaims his participation in the nation by becoming an antiwar activist, protesting the conditions at the VA hospital and speaking out against the war at local high schools. The film tries to redeem the antiwar movement by portraying it as sentimental politics aimed at reclaiming masculine sovereignty and empowerment, but at the expense of a more pointed critique of the war and its specific political and historical context. As the historian Jerry Lembcke points out, the screenwriter

Waldo Salt conducted his research for *Coming Home* by interviewing members of the Vietnam Veterans Against the War in Venice, California, including Ron Kovic (the subject of *Born on the Fourth of July* [1989]) and Bobby Mueller (a prominent interviewee in *Hearts and Minds* [1974]).[47] However, whereas the VVAW in the Winter Soldier hearings defined the wounding of veterans as a violence done to them by the U.S. military, *Coming Home* associates that wounding with the violence that veterans themselves did to the Vietnamese, ultimately implying the veteran's responsibility for his own injuries.

Coming Home opens with a panorama of injured American bodies, as a number of unnamed black and white veterans in wheelchairs and gurneys congregate around a pool table and debate the meaning of their wartime service. This rap session, filmed in a disjointed verité-like style, appears to be situated in the present of 1978, depicting a typical scene in VA hospitals around the country, but in fact represents an already distant past, a quaint moment from 1968, before the country has turned against the war. This temporal ambiguity disrupts the attempt to stage an honest reckoning with the costs of the war, because it disavows the hindsight gained between 1968 and 1978 and instead substitutes an ahistorical desire to justify the act of serving in Vietnam. One black veteran complains about hawkish veterans, "I can't see anybody . . . coming back to say that they would go again. I just can't deal with that," to which a white veteran replies, "Some of us need to justify to ourselves what the fuck we did there. So if we come back to say what we did was a waste, what happened to us is a waste, we can't live with it. . . . [We think,] 'I have to justify being paralyzed. I have to justify killing people. So I say it was OK.' But how many guys can take the reality, and say, 'What I did was wrong. And all this other shit was wrong,' and still be able to live with themselves because they're crippled for the rest of their fucking life?" In order to come to terms with their disabilities these veterans must reclaim the act of going to war as individually heroic, even if the act of war as performed by the nation-state was wrong. Otherwise, if going to war was a "waste," then by implication the veterans' own bodies are also potentially "waste," cast off from the body politic as what another film critic called the "detritus of war."[48] This separation of personal from national ethics not only depoliticizes military service, but also obscures the fact that, for many veterans, service was not a choice but a legal obligation. *Coming Home* holds at bay the historical memory of the violent protests over the draft by concentrating on a group of soldiers who mostly exercised the choice to enlist, and for whom the trauma of the war was about disillusioned patriotism rather than the coercion of the state against its own citizens.

Yet *Coming Home* cannot completely erase the violence associated with the war and with antiwar protests, and here the mirroring of these sites of violence in the metaphor "bringing the war home" is restaged along the lines of gender. The white female body becomes the site for the condensation of these intertwined fantasies of race and gender, both paralleling and contradicting the rehabilitation of the male veteran. Even as the veteran's own antiwar awakening is remasculinized, the "femininity" of the antiwar movement remains abject and excluded from this rehabilitation. In his review of *Coming Home*, the film critic Richard Turner compares Jane Fonda, the diegetic love-interest, with Ron Kovic, the extradiegetic disabled veteran:

> People wanted to look at Kovic about as much as they wanted to parachute into Da Nang. Guilt is too frail a word for the reaction he conjured up— what average American could look him in the eye and call him wrong? That he was eloquent didn't really matter. All he had to do was sit there, legs paralyzed, and the point was made.
>
> But Fonda—she was Kovic's photographic negative. As fiercely as they wanted to avert their eyes from Kovic, they wanted to confront Hanoi Jane—stare her down, look at her body, cut her tongue out, have her officially declared *persona non grata*. What was guilt and pain with Kovic was blind lusty rage with Fonda, sometimes from the left as well as the right.[49]

Here it becomes impossible to separate the film from its extradiegetic historical referent, and in particular Fonda's history as the antiwar activist who betrayed the nation, visiting Hanoi in 1972 and giving "aid and comfort" to the enemy.[50] The violence done to Kovic's body during the war becomes projected onto Fonda's body, whose symbolic dismemberment is erotically tinged. Yet although the responses to Kovic's and Fonda's bodies seem diametrically opposed as "photographic negatives," they both bear traces of the violence linked to the Vietnam War, demonstrating its emasculating effect on the American body politic.

We can see a similar juxtaposition in *Coming Home*, in the scene where protagonists Luke Martin and Sally Hyde first meet. Luke is multiply, excessively incontinent: drunkenly cruising around the halls of the hospital on a gurney powered by two canes, he crashes into Sally and his catheter bag squirts urine all over her, sparking a violent tantrum that causes the staff to physically restrain and then drug him into submission (fig. 26). His lack of self-sovereignty is further underscored when a male orderly must spoon-feed him while he is strapped to his bed; the only protest Luke can attempt in this position is to let the food dribble out of his mouth. Thus his initial resistance

26. After crashing into her on his gurney, Luke Martin (Jon Voight) spills urine from his catheter bag onto Sally Hyde (Jane Fonda). Frame enlargement from *Coming Home*.

against infantilization is to become even more infantalized, allowing food and urine to leak from his bodily orifices. Unlike the bloody Russian roulette scenes in *The Deer Hunter*, here the ejaculation of body fluids functions like a circuit of desire linking Luke to Sally, perhaps even anticipating their later sexual encounter. But as Luke gains both political and physical independence and mobility, these leaky bodily processes are pushed off-screen, presenting a self-contained body-subject, and leaving Sally's body to be the sole index of incontinence.

Following a vaguely feminist narrative of development, Sally too undergoes a transformation in this film, beginning as a repressed, uptight officer's wife and ending as the free-spirited and sexually uninhibited rebel we know extra-diegetically from films like *Barbarella* (1968). At first Sally's metamorphosis is tied closely to Luke's. Her volunteer work at the hospital leads her into Luke's life, but also starts her on the path toward independence from her husband. She in turn pulls Luke from his depression by providing him with an object to desire and thus a reason to become independent as well. As Luke gains mobility and independence—both essential features of self-sovereignty—Sally does as well. However, their metamorphoses part ways after the pivotal sex scene that consummates their relationship. Because Luke is paralyzed below the waist, he cannot have penetrative intercourse, so he instead performs cunnilingus on her, thus giving her her first true orgasm and also reclaiming his sexual potency. Feminist film critics such as Linda Williams have praised this film's refusal of "the dominant phallic discourse of sex" by portraying these nonnormative sex acts.[51] Ironically Luke's return to self-sovereignty is premised upon and in fact leads to Sally's loss of control in orgasm. The freedoms they gain from their relationship are very asymmetrical. While Sally gains freedom from her husband, Luke is freed from infantalization, impotence, and intemperance. Sally is politicized by wanting to write about the plight of mistreated veterans, but Luke becomes the poster boy for that cause, turning his disabled body into a form of protest by chaining it to a marine recruiting post and parading it before high school students eager to enlist. If Coming Home is at all invested in Sally's sovereignty, it is not to effect her entrance into a public sphere of political activity, as Luke does, but rather to enable her to make the choice between Luke, as the representative of "true" masculinity, and her husband, Bob Hyde (Bruce Dern), who still believes in the "false" heroics promoted by the military.

It is through Sally's character that the racialization of incontinence enters the narrative of Coming Home. One of Sally's first acts as a hospital volunteer is to feed a black veteran who is even more disabled than Luke; not only can he not lift his arms enough to feed himself, but he cannot even articulate his needs to Sally until she "transistorizes" him, or plugs an electronic amplifier into an opening on his trachea. This figure is reminiscent of the wounded black soldier Nick encounters in a Saigon hospital in The Deer Hunter, whose arms have been amputated above the elbows and who is almost completely wrapped in bandages. In both cases the black body is employed to display forms of bodily injury and violence that are too grotesque to display on the white body, and yet still preserve some sense of the Americanness of that wounded body and thus the audience's interest in potentially rehabilitating that body. At the same time the black body provides a phantasmatic bridge to oriental otherness. Also at the VA hospital is a black veteran with a ventriloquist's puppet that looks like a black body in Vietnamese drag (fig. 27). The puppet is a strange Doppelgänger of its puppeteer, mimicking his mustache, skin color, and paralysis from the waist down, but its performance of Vietnameseness also enables it to speak the illicit desires denied to its puppeteer. When this uncanny double cracks sexual jokes at Sally on her first day at work, it calls her "mamasan" and even tries to solicit "boom-boom" from her, such that it has to be verbally restrained by its puppeteer to "be cool." The puppet orientalizes Sally by framing her through the patois of Vietnamese prostitution, rendering both Sally and itself sexually incontinent figures.

The most obscene violence is reserved for the "real" Vietnamese body, which does not appear at all in Coming Home except as a linguistic referent in a war story Bob tells Sally in Hong Kong. Bob tries to express his estrangement from the behavior of his fellow GIs in Vietnam, behavior that departs from his

27. A black veteran with his Viet Cong puppet at the Veterans Administration hospital where Sally Hyde works. Frame enlargement from *Coming Home*.

expectations of a heroic and just war. One of his men asks for permission to mutilate enemy corpses: "Excuse me, sir, I'm sorry to bother you, but do you think it would be okay if we put the heads on the poles? You know, that really scares the shit out of the VC." But when Sally attempts to comfort Bob, he rebuffs her sympathy: "Is that the way you massage the basket cases at the hospital?" Bob's inability to come to terms with the violence of the war manifests as an attempt to separate his still unmarked body from the wounded bodies at the VA hospital, but this disavowal of violence ultimately explodes as an act of self-injury. He is discharged from the army after he accidentally fires his weapon into his foot on the way to the showers, but this ignoble accident makes him ashamed of the hero's welcome he receives upon his return to the U.S.

The overdetermination of feminine sexuality and orientalized violence comes to the fore when Bob confronts Sally about her affair with Luke. Although Bob calls Luke a "Jody," a common military epithet for antiwar hippies, he angrily denounces Sally as a "slope cunt," effectively aligning her sexual betrayal with the Vietnamese enemy. Luke eventually calms Bob down by explaining, "I'm not your enemy, maybe the enemy is the fucking war," but this alibi does little to negate either the racial epithet hurled at Sally or her infidelity. As Bob and Luke eventually find common ground in their shared experiences of being physically and emotionally wounded by Vietnam, Sally is shuttled aside in the narrative, as the only member of this triangle with no experience of Vietnam, but who is nonetheless aligned with it. Fonda's extra-diegetic role as Hanoi Jane only further compounds this alignment. The film pathologizes her as not only sexually but potentially racially other, and this undermines its antiwar politics. Even as it tries to restore a political and social normalcy to the disabled American veteran, *Coming Home* ultimately refuses the identification with otherness that its incontinent bodies suggest.

Going Native, or, The Return of the White Man's Burden: *Apocalypse Now* (1979)

Coppola makes his film like the Americans made war—in this sense, it is the best possible testimonial—with the same immoderation, the same excess of means, the same monstrous candor . . . and the same success.

—Jean Baudrillard, *Simulacra and Simulation*

Although it was the first of the Vietnam War films to go into production (in 1975), Francis Ford Coppola's *Apocalypse Now* was the last of this group to appear in theaters, going into general release in August 1979. In many ways the long-running story of its production was read by many film industry commentators as a recapitulation of the Vietnam War, and this analogy was also embraced by Coppola, who announced at the Cannes Film Festival in 1979, "My film is not about Vietnam, it *is* Vietnam."[52] Unlike Cimino, who drew upon his personal biography and the experiences of his actors to authenticate *The Deer Hunter*, Coppola transforms the film's production into a restaging of the Vietnam War. As he explained at Cannes, "The film was made the way the war was fought. There were too many of us, too much money, too much equipment." Publicity for *Apocalypse Now* often focused on the materials consumed by the film, a list that reads like an inventory of weapons: "1,200 gallons of gasoline burned in ninety seconds . . . over 500 smoke bombs, 100 phosphorous sticks, another 1,200 gallons of gas, 1,750 sticks of dynamite, 500 feet of detonating cord, plus 2,000 rockets, flares and tracers."[53] The massive expenditure, estimated at over $31.5 million, led the critic Sol Yurick to call the film "the Coppola complex," a military, cinematic, and industrial system that succeeds, like the war itself, in "redistributing wealth and power" and capitalizing on "expensive technological means" and the "psychic commodities" of trauma and loss associated with the Vietnam syndrome.[54] As a stunning example of vampire capitalism, *Apocalypse Now* not only recapitulates the labor involved in producing spectacular acts of mass violence, but it also submerges Coppola's cast and crew into the neocolonial power relations of Southeast Asia that organized the Vietnam War as well. Thus it is not only the well-known characters of Colonel Kurtz (Marlon Brando) and Captain Willard (Martin Sheen) in *Apocalypse Now* who go native and internalize the violence of Vietnam, but the film itself also restages a descent into primitiveness that marks its own peculiar version of the beating fantasy of Vietnam.

While many contemporaneous reviewers condemned *Apocalypse Now* along the same lines as they dismissed *The Deer Hunter*, insofar as both films' surrealistic tone and deviations from historical accuracy misrepresented the true horrors of the war, more sympathetic commentators have interpreted *Apocalypse Now* as a critique of American imperialism, by way of its allusions to Joseph Conrad's *Heart of Darkness*.[55] Interestingly what this link between the Vietnam War and European colonialisms from the nineteenth century obscures is a more direct comparison between *Apocalypse Now* and American colonialism, in particular the early twentieth-century colonization of the Philippines, where *Apocalypse Now* was filmed. It is worth remembering that Rudyard Kipling, another British author cited in *Apocalypse Now*, was referring to the U.S. invasion of the Philippines in 1899 after the conclusion of the Spanish-American War when he wrote his poem "The White Man's Burden." The film's citation of T. S. Eliot's "The Hollow Men" is also symptomatic of this repressed relation between American and European colonialisms; not only does Eliot's poem allude to Conrad in its epigraph, "Mistah Kurtz—he dead," but Eliot's early writings on primitivism were influenced by a visit to the World's Fair in St. Louis in 1904.[56] This fair featured the infamous Philippine Reservation, a human zoo that displayed nearly 1,200 Filipinos living in authentically "tribal," semibarbaric conditions and served to validate the paradigm of "benevolent assimilation" wherein the newly colonized Filipino subjects were unworthy of self-rule and yet were worthy recipients of American tutelage.[57] These links point to the historical depths of American empire in Southeast Asia, far predating the American intervention in the Vietnam War which *Apocalypse Now* ostensibly critiques.

In fact one might argue that the on-location filming of *Apocalypse Now* from 1976 to 1977 in the Philippines is itself proof of the continuing force of American imperialism in the independent Philippine state, both in the film's complicit relationship with President Ferdinand Marcos and in its choice of locations and local actors, themselves living ghosts of the Philippines' multiple colonial pasts. Coppola initially considered working directly with the U.S. Department of Defense for access to the military equipment he required to recreate the Vietnam War, but those negotiations ended when he made a deal directly with Marcos in October 1975.[58] During the film's production the Philippines was in the midst of a nine-year period of martial law (1972–81), which Marcos had initially declared to silence his opposition and overcome term limits on his presidency. Despite such political turmoil, Marcos gave Coppola's crew access to "40 Philippine armed forces 1968-era Huey helicopters, fighter jets, military trucks, an arsenal of M-16s, and other assorted material," charging only for expenses and insurance. He reserved the right to take back these resources at a moment's notice for use in his ongoing battles with Muslim insurgents in Mindanao Province and communist guerrillas in the New People's Army.[59] Marcos came to possess such military technology in the first place because of his neocolonialist relationship with the U.S., which supported his regime as an important cold war ally despite his authoritarian tendencies. Beginning in the colonial era of the the early twentieth century the Philippines was host to several large U.S. bases, which according to Benedict Anderson "had nothing to do with the defense of the Philippines as such, and everything to do with maintaining American imperial power along the Pacific Rim," including supplying and servicing the armed forces during the Vietnam War.[60] Along with another cold war neocolonial ally, South Korea, the Philippines also contributed token troops to the war in Vietnam, helping the U.S. justify the war as a multinational effort.[61] In short, Coppola's choice of the Philippines as a substitute for Vietnam is unintentionally befitting, as his patronage of Marcos's regime continued previous eras of colonial and neocolonial involvement and mimicked U.S. support for various South Vietnamese governments during the course of the war.

Coppola put his Filipino military resources to extensive use in his infamous scene of a village being napalmed, which begins with fifteen Huey helicopters flying in a row over the horizon toward the camera to the sounds of "Ride of the Valkyries." Lest we assume the music is part of the soundtrack, Lieutenant Colonel Kilgore (Robert Duvall), the commander of this air cavalry unit, explains that they blast Wagner from huge speakers on the helicopters because "it scares the hell out of the slopes." Thus not only technological but musicological modernity is employed to attack the Viet Cong, who reside in a bucolic, orientalist past, as a jump cut switches us from the noise of the helicopters and music to the silence of a peaceful Vietnamese town square in the calm before the attack. Vinh Dinh Drap, the Vietnamese village in this scene, was built from scratch by Coppola's crew in the remote coastal town of Baler, in Quezon Province, only to be destroyed almost in its entirety by the copious explosives Coppola had ordered (fig. 28). The production displaced local residents, swelled the population, and drove up the price of local goods in a display of what the political scientist Gerald Sussman derided as "Yankee showmanship."[62] For additional filmic veracity in the scene Coppola even employed Vietnamese refugees sojourning in the Philippines—the first wave of refugees from the fall of Saigon—even though their indexicality as real Vietnamese barely registers in the long shots of them fleeing from the helicopters' assault.[63] At the end of this scene Coppola filmed five F-5 jets flying overhead while his production crew ignited 1,200 gallons of gasoline along a tree line at the edge of the village. This spectacular destruction and expenditure seemed solely designed so that Kilgore could utter one of his infamous lines: "I love the smell of napalm in the morning. . . . It smells like victory."[64] In this one line Coppola resignifies the napalm that was the object of so many antiwar protests into an empty sign for the absurdity of the war, as a mere spectacle of violence without casualties or traumas. Incinerating flora and human fauna alike, napalm leaves nothing behind in the wake of its attack except for its scent, not even "one stinking dink body," as Kilgore reminisces about a previous battle, as if erasing the "Napalm Girl" from historical memory. And all this so that Kilgore can clear the riverbank and have his soldiers surf the waves, a plot device that infuriated some reviewers as a "California cliché that had nothing to do with the reality of South Vietnam."[65] In the film the military rationale for attacking this village appears as nonsensical as Coppola's motivation for diverting millions of dollars of resources into this scene.

Even more extravagant construction projects were undertaken in Pagsanjan, a popular tourist site in Laguna Province on the Laguna de Bay, where Coppola's crew built a faux-Cambodian temple for Kurtz's compound and a bridge for the Do Lung sequence, fashioned upon the bones of a structure destroyed by the Japanese during the Second World War.[66] The sets for these scenes were based on images of Angkor Wat from *National Geographic* that Coppola's production designer, Dean Tavoularis, had seen (fig. 29).[67] But the most uncanny relic of American imperialism in *Apocalypse Now* was its use of over two hundred extras from the Ifugao tribe to play the part of Montagnards, a French term for indigenous Vietnamese highlander tribes who were recruited into the war by the U.S. Special Forces. The Montagnards were reputed to be more savage than the South Vietnamese, and thus were prized as anticommunist fighters in the mountains near Cambodia; many Montagnards were persecuted by the Vietnamese after the war for their intimate collaboration with the U.S. As an American Green Beret describes them in a British documentary, *The Siege of Kontum* (1972), "The Montagnard is a very primitive type of person, they don't really understand modern technology. Special Forces trained them in modern weapons and gave them the weapons that they use. They paid them—the first time the Montagnards had ever seen money. They didn't even know what money could do. They gave them

28. The Vietnamese village of Vinh Dinh Drap, built and destroyed in Baler, Quezon Province, Philippines, and staffed with Vietnamese refugees as extras. The Huey helicopters in this scene were borrowed from Ferdinand Marcos's military. Frame enlargement from *Apocalypse Now*.

29. Kurtz's Cambodian temple compound, constructed in Pagsanjan, Philippines, and based on images of Angkor Wat. Frame enlargement from *Apocalypse Now*.

clothing, which the Montagnards had never had before. They were like fathers to them."[68] This combination of paternalism and primitivist fascination
also governs Kurtz's interactions with "his people," Montagnards "who worship him like a god and follow every order, however ridiculous."

The extras playing the Montagnard people were not recruited from Pagsanjan, but were brought in from the village of Batad in Ifugao Subprovince, over
two hundred miles to the north in the Cordillera mountain region. A casting
director, Eva Gardos, first encountered the Ifugao, a subgroup of highlander
peoples, while on a visit to the Nayong Pilipino, a theme park located in
Manila that reproduces tribal villages in a style similar to the Philippine
Reservation at the World's Fair. According to an Ifugao interpreter, Jerry
Luglug, Gardos "preferred pure Ifugao, and not 'hybrid Ifugao' born of
intermarriages and who didn't have 'the look' that the film required. She
didn't want Ilocano or Tagalog-looking Ifugao."[69] Thus *Apocalypse Now* recapitulates the logic of the early twentieth-century American colonial administrators in the Philippines, who also fetishized the "wildness" of these noble
savages over the hybridity of Christianized mestizo elites who were less
malleable to the cause of benevolent assimilation.[70] The Ifugao of *Apocalypse
Now* function much like the half-naked, dog-eating "Igorots" paraded at the
Philippine Reservation, which a contemporary Filipino American filmmaker,
Marlon Fuentes, skewered as America's "long awaited dream of Filipinos in
the flesh" in his film *Bontoc Eulogy* (1995).[71] Like American Indians in the late
nineteenth century, they designate what Philip Deloria has called an "authentic reality in the face of urban disorder and alienating mass society," in
contrast to assimilated natives who denote modernity's corruption of the
noble savage.[72] The politics of indigeneity in the modern Philippines were
deployed by Marcos in a similar fashion, as he was accused of helping to
orchestrate the discovery of a "new" and untouched Stone Age tribe, the
Tasaday, in the early 1970s in order to promulgate a source of Filipino unique-
ness untouched by Spanish or American influence. The continuing association of a history of headhunting and animal sacrifice with these modern
Igorot groups, including the Ifugao, mirrors the savagery of the Montagnards
which the U.S. Special Forces esteemed.[73] In effect Coppola has not only resurrected an old colonialist logic romanticizing indigenous peoples but also
connected it to neocolonial hegemonies in both Vietnam and the Philippines.

Colonel Kurtz, modeled on his namesake in *Heart of Darkness*, is the American in *Apocalypse Now* who has most explicitly gone native, as he has abandoned the U.S. military chain of command to conduct his own private Vietnam War with his Montagnard army in the mountains bordering Cambodia.

The American commanders who order Willard to assassinate Kurtz explain, "Out there with these natives, it must be a temptation to be God. . . . Walt Kurtz has reached his [breaking point], and very obviously, he has gone insane." The crime that Kurtz is officially accused of is ordering the assassination of four Vietnamese double agents, but his larger transgression is fighting the war "his way," essentially absorbing the amorality of the oriental enemy. When Willard finally reaches Kurtz's compound, Kurtz justifies his methods to Willard by way of a long anecdote about how the Viet Cong would cut off the arms of children that the Americans had inoculated against polio. Rather than shocking him, this example led to Kurtz's epiphany that the enemy was stronger than he was; they had the strength to realize the full extent of violence necessary to win the war. Kurtz rhapsodizes, "If I had ten divisions of those men, then our troubles here would be over very quickly. You have to have men who are moral, and at the same time, who are able to utilize their primordial instincts to kill without feeling, without passion, without judgment. Without judgment. Because it's judgment that defeats us." If the Americans must become the Vietnamese in order to be able to kill them, this suggests an intimacy between violator and victim often disavowed in critiques of violence. In a sense Kurtz's going native parallels *The Deer Hunter*'s allusions to James Fenimore Cooper's *The Deerslayer* (1841), whose hero, Natty Bumppo, enacts the mythos Richard Slotkin has called "regeneration through violence" through his identification with Native American hunting rituals.[74] But in *Apocalypse Now* the native Montagnard substitute for the Viet Cong, providing not only a link to the "primordial" violence shared by all Vietnamese but also signifying an ahistorical relationship to the land that bypasses the historical claims made by the Viet Cong and National Liberation Front on behalf of an anticolonial war.

While Kurtz may symbolize for Coppola the extreme absurdity of the Vietnam War that led to so many deaths on both sides, Coppola's reverent portrayal of Kurtz in these final scenes reveals the ambivalence of his critique. Shot in close-up with chiaroscuro lighting, Kurtz's face dissolves during his many monologues into a montage of gigantic carved idols and native bodies, lending a mythic rather than satirical quality to these identifications. These stylistic elaborations confused reviewers, who complained, "But all this exhilaration and lyricism of war . . . what is an allegedly antiwar filmmaker doing mucking around in this tainted ecstasy?"[75] Kurtz's death at Willard's hands is filmed with the same adoration. Coppola reportedly struggled for a way to end his film, and the Ifugao extras inadvertently provided him with a solution when they requested a carabao (water buffalo) for use in a ritual sacrifice.

30. A carabao (water buffalo) killed in an Ifugao ceremony stands in for the fallen body of Colonel Kurtz (Marlon Brando), who is never clearly shown in the film. Frame enlargement from *Apocalypse Now*.

Coppola ended up restaging and intercutting shots from the sacrifice, including documentary images of a real carabao being killed with machetes, with images of Willard attacking Kurtz with a machete, allowing the indexical images of the dying carabao to literally stand in for Kurtz, whose body remains in shadows during the entire sequence of his death (fig. 30).[76] In choosing this method of killing Kurtz, Willard not only takes on Kurtz's role as assassin but goes native as well, mimicking Kurtz's earlier appearance in camouflage makeup by emerging with his face smeared with mud as if in brownface. The anthropologists Deirdre McKay and Padmapani Perez liken Coppola's sponsorship of the Ifugao sacrifice to *cañao*, or ritual feasts, organized by American colonial administrators for highlander tribes as a way of channeling their primordial violent tendencies away from headhunting and tribal warfare and toward more "civilized" pursuits such as sports. But these American elites still valued the spectacle of primitiveness that these *cañao* offered, and often persuaded or coerced tribal leaders to perform exotic rites such as dances and animal sacrifice as a substitute for the censored headhunting rituals that fascinated American imaginations.[77] Because the carabao was a symbol of colonial power and beneficence, McKay and Perez suggest that the sacrifice was a way of "symbolically assassinating the imperial donor." Even as Coppola practices his American largesse on his Ifugao extras, extracting the surplus value of their ritual for his own creative use, he stages Kurtz's death as an invitation to the natives to kill their American benefactors by effigy, and Coppola's symbolic self-destruction mirrors the production of

Apocalypse Now and, by extension, the war as a whole. The end credits of the film scroll over footage of the explosive destruction of the set for Kurtz's compound after filming concluded, an ending that parallels the film narrative's implosion even as it satisfies the studio's demand for a use value to be extracted from the absurd expenditures of Coppola's production.

The Gook Comes Home: *Go Tell the Spartans* (1978)

The inverse of the fantasy of the American soldier going native might be called the nightmare of the gook coming home—the same Vietnamese who menaced American soldiers in Vietnam now follows that veteran back to the U.S. Here we see how American orientalism varies from its European counterparts, as the danger posed by the orient goes beyond the external threat embodied by a foreign "yellow peril" to include the internal threat posed by the specter of the Asian immigrant. In particular the Vietnamese immigrants' presence in the United States uncannily evokes the violent images disseminated in the years prior to their arrival in television, photojournalism, and film. If these news images anticipated the actual waves of immigration, delivering spectral Vietnamese bodies to American living rooms, Vietnamese immigrants and refugees were belated repetitions of this earlier trauma, reactivating debates and controversies that preceded them. A renewed debate about torture emerged in 1978, sparked by the effort to deport Nguyen Ngoc Loan, the infamous South Vietnamese general of "Saigon Execution," and by the release of Vietnam War films that restage those scenes of torture in the public sphere. While Loan is most visibly linked to *The Deer Hunter* and its restaging of his summary execution of a VC suspect, it is a minor film from that period, *Go Tell the Spartans*, that most vividly portrays the connection between Vietnamese torture and the American body politic.

Much has been written about the extraordinary character of Asian immigration after 1965, focusing on how the amendments to the Immigration and Nationality Act replaced the national origins quotas with a system favoring family members of U.S. citizens and skilled, middle-class workers—a system that helped create the phenomenon of the "model minority."[78] Lisa Lowe argues that these immigrants, who are predominantly from Vietnam, Cambodia, Laos, Taiwan, and South Korea, differ from the older waves of Chinese and Japanese migrants. Instead, they "come from societies already disrupted by colonialism and distorted by the upheavals of neocolonial capitalism and war. The material legacy of the repressed history of U.S. imperialism in Asia is borne out in the 'return' of Asian immigrants to the imperial center. . . . These immigrants retain precisely the memories of imperialism that the U.S. nation seeks to forget."[79] Vietnamese immigration both typifies and serves as an exception to these generalizations. Unlike the other major Asian American ethnic groups, practically all Vietnamese Americans arrived after 1965. In 1964 only 603 Vietnamese were living in the U.S., mostly students and diplomats; twenty-five years later there were nearly 615,000.[80] Of this population, 80 percent were born in Vietnam and had immigrated or left as refugees, and over 95 percent of these had arrived after the fall of Saigon in 1975, at first enabled by the Indochina Migration and Refugee Assistance Act of 1975 and later by the Refugee Act of 1980.[81] But the Vietnamese immigrant of the 1970s had little in common with the so-called "boat people" and other refugees who arrived after 1979 and whose images dominated media coverage of the post-war immigration.[82] The first wave of immigrants had many advantages over the later ones; they were largely educated, English-speaking, and urbanized, making them similar to the rest of the Asian immigrants after 1965.[83] Many also had contacts with Americans through their involvement with the South Vietnamese military or government, which allowed them the privilege of immigrating to the U.S. when so many others were left behind.

The production of *Spartans* derived its authenticity in part from this first wave of Vietnamese refugees, who played all the background Vietnamese roles in the film. Lacking the financial resources to film on location in Thailand and the Philippines, as *The Deer Hunter, Apocalypse Now,* and *The Boys in Company C* had done, the producers of *Spartans* constructed a Vietnamese village just north of the San Fernando Valley in southern California, filming its combat scenes at night so that the "deficiencies" of the location would be less visible.[84] However, the location did enable the production to hire sixty Vietnamese from the refugee population in the Los Angeles area.[85] The experience proved uncanny for many of these refugees, who played both South Vietnamese and Viet Cong roles, even though all of them were South Vietnamese who had fled to escape retribution by the communist government after the war. Some were ARVN veterans with combat experience who were able to advise the production on how to stage battle scenes realistically. Nghia Vo Trong, a former helicopter pilot who worked on the *Spartans* set, told the *Chicago Tribune,* "I think a lot of [refugees] like the filming because this area reminds them of Viet Nam. They didn't like the war; a lot of them lost their friends or husbands. But I think they like to look again, once again, at the war."[86] The process of re-creating the war for the film industry becomes an ambivalent source of pleasure for these refugees, as they are allowed to inhabit, albeit phantasmatically and temporarily, a country and a history to which they cannot return. "To look once again at the war" takes on a different meaning for these refugees than for the American public, for whom their bodies are simply indexical traces of acts of violence America seeks to forget.

Also among this first wave of immigrants was Nguyen Ngoc Loan, who arrived in the U.S. in 1975 and moved to the suburbs of Washington, D.C.[87] In 1976, after borrowing $8,000 from his "American army friends," Loan and his family opened a restaurant called Les Trois Continents, serving all-American fare in addition to Vietnamese and Chinese dishes. The subtitle from an article on Loan published in Esquire in 1979 encapsulates the absurd contrast between his previous infamy and current immigrant "success story": "Nguyen Ngoc Loan pulled that trigger in 1968 and became a symbol of the Sixties. Now he sells pizza. A symbol of the Seventies."[88] Details of his family-owned restaurant further built up his image as an ethnic business owner: his mother and wife spoke no English, but helped out in the kitchen; the children also worked there after school and spent their free time in the restaurant studying (fig. 31). Here is the model minority as what David Palumbo-Liu has called the homo economicus, a self-sufficient economic entity readily absorbed into the mainstream of American capitalism.[89]

Loan's ascension to model minority status and economic success seemed to mock the brutal act of violence he committed in 1968 as a proxy for the American military, as well as insult those American veterans who returned to a repressed economy. This contrast revealed the shadowy economic underside of the supposedly positive model minority myth. As Robert G. Lee explains, "The model minority has two faces. The myth presents Asian Americans as silent and disciplined: this is their secret to success. At the same time, this silence and discipline is used in constructing the Asian American as a new yellow peril. . . . The Asian American is both identified with the enemy that defeated the United States in Vietnam and figured as the agent of the current collapse of the American empire."[90] Whereas the threat posed by the oriental other in Vietnam was physical, this current "peril" is economic in nature—and Loan embodied both threats. The American economy that Vietnam veterans returned to in the 1970s was in recession, in contrast to the boom years that followed the Second World War. The effect of this recession was dramatized in 1978 in the CBS News Special "Charlie Company at Home," a follow-up to a program aired in 1970, "The World of Charlie Company."[91] Reviewing what became of the original soldiers featured eight years earlier, the program was a glimpse into the state of the American workforce and into the lives of Vietnam veterans. Some found jobs in the industrial sector, while others moved into middle-class, white-collar jobs. Most telling was the story of

Inset: The 1968 picture showing Loan, then chief of national police, executing a Viet Cong. Right: Loan today outside his restaurant.

The Villain of Vietnam

Nguyen Ngoc Loan pulled that trigger in 1968 and became a symbol of the Sixties. Now he sells pizza. A symbol of the Seventies

by Tom Buckley

Loan limped over to the booth where I was sitting, waiting for him. He stopped a few feet away, staring at me. "I remember you," he said at last, spacing the words out. He smiled his gargoyle's smile, and we shook hands.

Perhaps he did remember me, but it had been a long time. I first met Nguyen Ngoc Loan early in 1967. He was then chief of the national police, Prime Minister Nguyen Cao Ky's closest confidant, and one of the most powerful men in South Vietnam. I saw him again in 1971. By that time, the United States had pushed Ky from power and Loan had fallen too. He sat in an empty office in the Defense Ministry without an assignment.

That was the time Loan and I spent a morning talking and drinking the Hennessey he always had close at hand. I wrote an article about what had become of the most notorious figure of the war, the man whose filmed and photographed execution—or murder, depending on how you looked at it—of a bound and helpless captive during the early days of the Tet offensive in February 1968 had come to symbolize, in this country, at any rate, the bestiality and futility of the war.

Now we were sitting together once again in the restaurant he

Tom Buckley has written often for Esquire. A reporter for The New York Times, he covered Vietnam for that paper.

has been operating for the past three and a half years, Les Trois Continents, in a shopping mall in Burke, Virginia, about twenty miles from Washington and 10,000 miles from Saigon. Loan looked frail. His unbuttoned brown cardigan hung from his shoulders. His trousers bagged. There was a grayish cast to his yellow-ivory skin.

That dead Viet Cong suspect had arisen to haunt him. Two members of the House of Representatives, Harold S. Sawyer of Michigan and Elizabeth Holtzman of Brooklyn, had denounced Loan as morally unfit to be a citizen or even to continue residing in the United States. At their command, the Immigration and Naturalization Service had begun an investigation of his purported crime that could have ended in his deportation.

The press jumped on the story. Once again the papers ran the famous moment-of-death photograph. Loan in profile, wearing his flak jacket, with his arm holding the revolver fully extended, the prisoner, wearing shorts, sandals, and a sport shirt, facing the camera, his features distorted, his hair seemingly standing on end.

Television crews blocked the mall and besieged the restaurant. Reporters questioned his customers. Yes, they said, they knew who Loan was, what he was supposed to have done, but it was all a long time ago, he was on our side. After all, it had been a lousy war and a mistake all the way around, and anyhow, they liked him and his family, and they served good, cheap food. Loan

Photograph by Jim Moore/Gamma/Liaison; inset, Wide World

31. Nguyen Ngoc Loan in 1979, in front of his restaurant, and in 1968, in "Saigon Execution." From *Esquire*, 5 June 1979, 61.

George Rivera, who had been awarded thirteen medals but could not find a job when he returned to New York City, and instead moved back to Puerto Rico. The voice-over recycled the clichéd language of the war coverage, but this time applied it to economic abjection: "It is a life of a casualty, a wasted life." When compared with the entrepreneurial success of Loan, Rivera's story appeared even more tragic: Americans could not win the war in Vietnam, yet the Vietnamese could come to America and succeed at the American dream, beating Americans at their own game.

This irony was perhaps more than some could handle, for in November 1978, three years after Loan immigrated to the U.S., the Immigration and Nationalization Service, at the behest of two members of Congress, began proceedings to deport him on the grounds of "moral turpitude," based on the summary execution captured in the "Saigon Execution" photograph.[92] As coverage of the proceedings spread through television and print news, Adams's photograph was resurrected and recirculated only three months after *Spartans* was released and a month before *The Deer Hunter* premiered in New York. Although the *New York Times* editorialized that Loan's actions were clearly "morally indefensible," a surprising convergence of liberal and conservative commentators jumped to his defense.[93] Both William Buckley Jr. of the *National Review* and Murray Kempton of the *Progressive* pointed out the hypocrisy of blaming Loan while the real villains went unpunished—although for Buckley these villains were the Vietnamese communists, while Kempton pointed the finger at the secretaries of state and of defense.[94] A similar pattern of ideologically contradictory responses appeared in the letters to the editor responding to the *New York Times;* two letters displaced Loan's "moral turpitude" onto an interesting pair of villains from the right and the left: Lieutenant Calley and Jane Fonda.[95] In all of these responses Loan was present only through his photographic proxy. Loan eventually was allowed to remain in the U.S., not because his past actions were proven to be morally justified, but because President Carter pardoned him to avoid a larger public relations scandal.[96]

The grounds for Loan's deportation, moral turpitude, were designed to protect the American body politic from moral contagion. When the principle was first introduced into American immigration law in the early 1900s, it was justified by the need "to devise some system by which undesirable immigrants shall be kept out entirely."[97] The concept lacks a statutory definition in the legal code and refers "generally to conduct that shocks the public conscience as being inherently base, vile, or depraved, contrary to the rules of morality and the duties owed between man and man."[98] The idea of a public conscience summons an image of a unified nation, into which all individual subjects and their moralities must be assimilated. Because moral turpitude is not limited to any particular crime, it becomes a subjectively wielded instrument of public morality. The message sent by the proceedings is, in a sense, a repudiation of Loan's apparent assimilation: it rejects his successful economic assimilation on the grounds of his inadequate moral assimilation.

Spartans uncannily anticipates many of the arguments made against Loan. This small-budget film, partially eclipsed by the higher profile releases of *Coming Home* and *The Deer Hunter* that same year, centers on Vietnamese torture as a cause for American incontinence, on the level of both the individual soldier and the U.S. military as a whole. Based on a novel published in 1967, *Incident at Muc Wa*, by the journalist Daniel Ford and set in the early years of the war, before Tet, *Spartans* nonetheless adopts a tragic tone toward such incontinence, as seen in the elegiac (and orientalist) reference in its title to the Battle of Thermopylae in 480 BCE, where three hundred Spartan soldiers died while trying to hold a pass against a massive invading Persian army. As the paradigm of American orientalism suggests, the threat to the U.S. military lies both within and without. The struggles of the American commanders in the film are as much against the South Vietnamese allies whom they control as they are against the unseen Viet Cong hordes who overrun the village and kill all but a single soldier at the film's end. Maj. Asa Barker (Burt Lancaster) grapples with the violent tendencies of their local ARVN soldiers, and in particular a South Vietnamese translator nicknamed Cowboy (Evan Kim) with a penchant for torturing and dismembering VC. The film suggests that our Vietnamese allies are "savages" who pervert the logic of war by returning to a premodern paradigm of spectacular violence and public torture, and thus delegitimizing the war in the eyes of a weak-stomached American public.

In the opening scene Cowboy and two other ARVN soldiers are torturing a VC suspect by dunking his head repeatedly into a bucket of water, only to be stopped by Major Barker, the commanding officer of the base (fig. 32). Cowboy explains his actions: "He say he not Cong, we make him say he Cong." But the verbal confession is superfluous, since it is clear that the South Vietnamese are interested only in the truth of the tortured body itself, its violation tautologically confirming its status as "Cong." Even after pulling the suspect out of the water, Cowboy continues to slap and kick him and threatens to slit his throat, prompting Barker to call Cowboy a "goddamned gook" and order him to return the prisoner to his cage. Barker, nicknamed "World War Two" by his communications officer and played by Lancaster, who is famous for his starring role in *From Here to Eternity* (1953), seems to

32. In the foreground South Vietnamese soldiers led by Cowboy
(Evan Kim) use water torture on a Viet Cong suspect as Major
Barker (Burt Lancaster), standing in the background, tries to
intervene. Frame enlargement from *Go Tell the Spartans*.

stand for the obsolescence of the moral perspective of previous wars, whereas
the ironically named Cowboy indicates the Vietnamization of the John Wayne
maverick celebrated in earlier war films such as *Back to Bataan* (1945) and *Sands
of Iwo Jima* (1949). Cowboy's water torture also recalls several prominent
scandals about the treatment of enemy combatants during the Vietnam War,
including a photograph of waterboarding featured on the front page of the
Washington Post in 1968 and the exposé of "tiger cages" at the South Vietnamese Con Son Prison in *Life* magazine in 1970.[99] While both reports reveal
the complicity of the U.S. military in these acts of torture—the *Washington Post*
photograph depicts an American soldier helping to hold down the suspect
being waterboarded—they suggest, in a departure from My Lai, that the
source of the violence is ultimately the Vietnamese, who savagely disregard
the rules of warfare on both sides of the insurgency, and thus draw Americans
into their morass of violence. As one reviewer of *Spartans* points out, echoing
Westmoreland, "Indeed, the film at times seems to support the racist notion
that life is cheaper in the Orient."[100] If anything, *Spartans* inverts the structure
of violence in these photographic referents, showing American soldiers attempting to contain rather than encourage the spread of oriental violence,
even at the cost of their own lives.

The two possible ways for American soldiers to respond to such violence
are modeled by the weak-stomached Lt. Raymond Hamilton (Joe Unger) and
the stoic Corporal Courcey (Craig Wasson). The fate of Hamilton, the eager

volunteer whom Barker assigns to the village of Muc Wa, mirrors the disintegration of American military control of the Vietnamese countryside. While
driving to the village they come upon a crude roadblock with a bomb on a
tripwire, and the ARVN soldiers capture a VC hiding in the jungle next to the
roadblock. Hamilton calls for Cowboy to interrogate their captive, and when
no information is forthcoming, turns to walk away, assuming that the suspect
will be restrained and taken to the village with them. However, Cowboy
interprets his command differently, choosing to decapitate the prisoner with
his machete after the interrogation is over. Instead of a hyperrealist staging of
the bloody beheading, we watch the violence from the prisoner's point of
view, the camera rolling with the fallen head as the only sign of the actual
decapitation. In a reaction shot both Hamilton and Courcey look on with
disgust, although only Hamilton physically responds, running into the trees
to vomit off-screen. Cowboy is confused by their reactions, since it was
American soldiers who gave him his orders to "sat Cong" (kill communists).
For the remainder of the film until his death, Hamilton remains physically ill,
ducking out of drills and staff meetings to run to the outhouse. Both his
diarrhea and his vomiting, while comic signifiers of his inability to adapt to
Vietnam, are also symptoms of his loss of control over even this small platoon. Yet Hamilton's incontinence is simply a corporealization of the impotence of his commanding officer, Barker, who has remained at the rank of
major despite having served in two wars prior to Vietnam because of his
weakness for "booze and pudenda." Neither Hamilton nor Barker is able to
control his own body much less those of the South Vietnamese soldiers under
their command.

The sole survivor of the attack on Muc Wa, and a stark contrast to Hamilton's loss of bodily control, is Corporal Courcey, a quiet draftee under Hamilton's command who quickly befriends the South Vietnamese villagers, in a
role nearly identical to the Vietnamese sympathizer Bisbee in *The Boys in
Company C*. But Courcey does not so much overcome the weakness of Hamilton and Barker as he seems to escape their fates by accident. Shot during the
final, doomed battle for Muc Wa, Courcey tells Barker that he feels blood
running down his leg. Barker muses, "Maybe you just crapped your britches,"
and Courcey replies dead-pan, "I have very strong sphincter muscles, sir."
Barker's death is as unremarkable as his career; wounded in the same attack
that injured Courcey, Barker simply slumps down while trying to hold up his
rifle, murmuring, "Oh, shit," before quietly passing away. The obsession with
feces in *Spartans* recalls Anglo-American anthropologists' attempts to explain
Japanese militarism in the Second World War as a result of anal-sadistic toilet

training rituals, except here the failure of the U.S. to win seems linked to the opposite: American soldiers' insufficient anal discipline, an inability to "hold their shit together."[101] Ultimately, though, it is not Courcey's sphincter control that saves his life, but an old Vietnamese man he rescued during an earlier patrol. This old man drags Courcey into the bushes, where he inexplicably survives the attack that kills every remaining defender of Muc Wa, American and South Vietnamese alike, and leaves all American soldiers' corpses stripped bare.

If the process of assimilation is modeled upon the nation as a body, the recurring theme of incontinence in Spartans and other Vietnam War films parallels the anxieties over Loan's deportation ordeal. In both cases the violent transgression of a boundary destabilizes the identity of the body within, forcing an equally violent expulsion of the foreign, poisonous element. In her analysis of American literature Anne Cheng describes the assimilation of racialized subjects in terms of a bodily schema of incorporation and expulsion modeled upon eating: "Freud's notion of this uncomfortable swallowing and its implications for how loss is processed and then secured as exclusion lend provocative insights into the nature of the racial other seen as 'the foreigner within' America. In a sense, the racial other is in fact quite 'assimilated' into—or, more accurately, most uneasily digested by—American nationality."[102] Loan and other first-wave Vietnamese refugees represent immigrants who could not be fully digested by an American nationality that desired to forget its participation in a failed imperialist endeavor; they are recalcitrant elements that cause the nation to gag. These metaphors of eating are even more suggestive when viewed against Loan's restaurant, premised upon the fusion of cultures and cuisines to be fed to American consumers. If Loan's act in 1968 provoked a national gagging response of disgust, that response resurfaced in 1978 as a complete rejection of that violence. The lack of control of feces endemic throughout Spartans is but a variation of this basic symptom, of the inability to assimilate and digest the violence of the Vietnam War, but this time to the detriment of the American body politic through which these threatening elements pass.

Although Loan's deportation was eventually halted and he was allowed to remain in the U.S., the stigma of his moral turpitude never wore off. When he died in 1998 "Saigon Execution" was trotted out again to summarize his life. Eddie Adams later regretted having taken the photograph because of its effects on Loan's life, visually freezing him into the role of the perpetual Asian enemy.[103] The problem of being the "foreigner within" never faded away for this particular Asian American immigrant, forever seen in terms of the oblique threat he and his country of origin posed for the American body politic. His obituary showed that, even as late as 1991, Loan was plagued with ramifications from an act neither he nor America could put behind them: "As a message scrawled on a restroom wall [in his restaurant] put it, 'We know who you are.' "[104] How could a nation which could not define itself in relation to the Vietnam War recognize its reputed enemy so easily? Precisely because it saw itself reflected in and absorbed into this scenario of the oriental obscene.

Chapter 4

KUNG FU FIGHTING

Pacifying and Mastering the Martial Body

I'm here a week now, waiting for a mission, getting softer. Every minute I stay in this room I get weaker. Every minute Charlie squats in the bush, he gets stronger.

—Captain Willard, *Apocalypse Now* (1979)

At the beginning of *Apocalypse Now*, as Capt. Benjamin Willard (Martin Sheen) awaits his new orders in a Saigon hotel room, he passes the time drinking, smoking, hallucinating, and practicing what appear to be martial arts forms (fig. 33). This momentary glimpse of kung fu, in the midst of a major film about the Vietnam War at the close of the 1970s, gestures toward a hidden link between the Asian martial arts and America's Vietnam syndrome. Willard's "soft" body, weakened by ennui, idleness, and alcohol, stands in contrast to the imagined but unseen Viet Cong body, hard and strong from its martial labors. Thus Willard's attempt at drunken kung fu, which ends violently when he punches at his own image in a mirror, is an attempt to recapture that hard body through a different mode of orientalized violence. Kung fu becomes another form of going native, different from the descent into primitive, tribal violence as intimated by the flash-forwards in this scene to the end of the film, where Willard dons Montagnard "brownface," emerging from the river slick with mud, to assassinate Kurtz. Whereas brownface allows Willard to access a primordial violence that takes him outside his white American body and permits him to sacrifice Kurtz, the violence of martial arts in this opening scene is directed inward, toward the self. After smashing the mirror he grasps his bloody hand and rubs it all over his face, as if trying to awaken from his drunken daze and his nightmarish memories of the Vietnam War. If kung fu can create a hard body for the traumatized American soldier, it

33. Captain Willard (Martin Sheen) practices kung fu in his Saigon hotel room as he awaits orders at the beginning of the film. Frame enlargement from *Apocalypse Now*.

does so by redirecting that soldier's violence back onto himself through the oriental obscene, through the phantasmatic scenarios now provided by Asian martial arts.

Chop-Socky as Vietnam Syndrome

Asian martial arts entered the mainstream of American popular culture many years before *Apocalypse Now* appeared, just as the violence of the Vietnam War began to fade from popular consciousness with the signing of the Paris Peace Accords and the withdrawal of American troops in 1973. The "kung fu craze," also referred to in film industry journals as "eastern Westerns," "Chinese actioners," and "chop-sockies," features what appears to be a new brand of film violence: actors engaged in direct hand-to-hand combat, their violence originating and ending in the unadorned body itself.[1] Such fights differed from the traditions of American stage and film violence; they employed a baroque repertoire of weapons, poetically named their moves "Flying Tiger" and "Iron Fist," choreographed their movements to an almost dance-like rhythm, and, most shocking to some, emphasized prolonged bodily contact and showed its effects on the body in gory, fantastic detail. American audiences flocked to urban, second-run theaters to see these cheaply made and wretchedly dubbed productions. Their enthusiasm for kung fu film's kinetic energy spilled over into other areas of popular culture, where kung fu became a hobby, a sport, a diet, a disco dance, a means of self-defense and feminist empowerment, an initiation at Christian youth camps, and even a motivator for urban students' reading scores.[2] Between 1972 and 1978 it was perhaps no exaggeration to claim, after Carl Douglas's hit song of 1974, that "everybody was kung fu fighting."

But what exactly does this historical conjunction between the end of the Vietnam War and the beginning of the kung fu craze mean? David Desser described this conjunction as "coincidental," but he goes on to qualify, "Surely it is not coincidental that interest in the Asian martial arts increased with continued, ongoing and intense exposure to Asia, what I termed the 'encounter with Asia.'"[3] Tracing the sporadic appearance of Asian martial arts in American popular cinema over and against U.S. political and military involvements in East Asia, Desser understands this cultural movement as also an epistemological project, to "know" Asia and Asians through their martial arts. What differentiates the martial arts that appear in the film craze of the 1970s from the snippets that appear in earlier films, such as *Bad Day at Black Rock* (1955), *The Manchurian Candidate* (1962), and the James Bond film *You Only Live Twice* (1967), is that the fighting styles in the 1970s are increasingly linked to China rather than Japan. The difference is between kung fu and karate, for those in the know, although the differences are more diffuse than this nomenclature might indicate. And the dissemination of martial arts through American popular culture would be increasingly linked to an epistemological project, as knowledge of kung fu, karate, *hapkido*, and the various national styles translated indirectly to knowledge about China, Japan, and Korea as their respective nations of origin.

Knowledge about Asia was in short supply, as the American media painfully learned not only when covering the Vietnam War, but also when covering Nixon's groundbreaking visit with Mao in communist China in 1972. Television broadcasts of documentaries such as *China, An Open Door?* and Michelangelo Antonioni's *Chung Kuo*, the television series *Kung Fu*, a cartoon based on Charlie Chan, and even an American tour by a Chinese *wushu* troupe were all part of what the television critic Benjamin Stein called "the current fascination with things Chinese," with each text and performance contributing to the overall puzzle of communist China.[4] The films of the kung fu craze, no matter how low-brow or violent, fed this thirst for knowledge. In 1974 the reporter Alex Ben Block speculated, "If Mao hadn't brought China together, if Nixon hadn't gone there, if acupuncture's time hadn't come, if mysticism weren't on revival, if martial arts weren't an answer to crime in the streets, if kung fu didn't fill such a obvious void for a physical culture with socio-religious overtones, Bruce Lee might never have gotten beyond the Mandarin film circuit in South Asia."[5] Yet the interest in communist China was overshadowed by the continuing war against communist Vietnam. Desser called the kung fu craze "just one cinematic signifier of a post-Vietnam stress disorder on the cultural level."[6] Building on that observation, I argue that the character-ization of martial arts as a response to the Vietnam War not only entails a further slippage between one group of Asian bodies and another, but also continues the cross-racial identifications I have traced in previous chapters, of assuming the "trauma" of the racial other as part of one's own subject formation. Vietnam's trauma had become America's own, and its symptom was the proliferation of another form of orientalized violence within Ameri-can borders. But Desser's comments also suggest another interpretation of martial arts in the 1970s: not only as a symptom, but as a potential remedy to the trauma of Vietnam.

In this chapter I define the martial arts genre somewhat narrowly, discuss-ing only those films which went into general release in the U.S. as part of the kung fu craze, mainly between 1972 and 1978, and which were advertised explicitly as kung fu, karate, or martial arts films. This definition and chronol-ogy necessarily deviates from a study of the martial arts film in its original contexts of production and distribution in Asia.[7] Martial arts films were often released in the U.S. much later than they were produced, which jumbles the chronology between film production and consumption. I also exclude the Japanese samurai genre and the Hong Kong swordplay films that preceded the kung fu craze, in order to concentrate on the human body as the weapon of choice. I reserve Bruce Lee as a special case study for chapter 5 because of his unique position as both an American and a Hong Kong film star—a transnational liminality that affects the interpretation and identification with his star persona.

As the earlier example from *Apocalypse Now* suggests, Asian martial arts offer a racial fantasy that is intimately linked to and yet very different in form from the fantasies of defeat and suffering that preoccupied the Vietnam War films of the late 1970s. Those films were themselves a belated response to the violent traumas portrayed during the war itself. But the kung fu film craze offers a different response to that trauma, one that approximates what Freud describes in *Beyond the Pleasure Principle* as an impulse toward mastery through repeated and willed exposure to unpleasurable stimuli. These impulses do not so much overcome the originary traumas that plague the subject as they transform the scenario of that trauma into a bearable form, shifting through the roles available within that scenario to find a more stable subject position. Thus the nation is not so much being beaten in martial arts as it is learning to beat itself and others in new ways, and the *body mastered* takes the place of the body incontinent found in Vietnam War films. Through Asian martial arts the American national subject comes to understand the violence that plagued it throughout the Vietnam War and also adopts a project to internalize and redirect that violence into a form of self-mastery. But, as with the more direct Vietnam War representations, the martial arts continue to preserve the troubling phantasmatic elements of the oriental obscene within the national imaginary. Just as the American soldier of the Vietnam War film modeled his trauma on the figures of Vietnamese suffering that pervaded news coverage of the war, the American martial artist overcomes his bodily trauma by drawing on the repertoire of the Asian martial arts. The martial artist introjects these orientalized styles of violence, just as the American nation continues to incorporate Asians and Asian Americans into its body politic. These phantasmatic Asian elements offer different fantasies of mastery for different American subjects, including Asian Americans, who use the cross-racial identifications of the oriental obscene to stage their own political claims on these body politics. Nonetheless the multiple selves constructed through martial arts continue to be interwoven with strands of otherness, racial and otherwise, that ultimately undermine these projects of mastery. Like subjection, mastery also remains dependent upon such phantasmatic otherness. If the martial arts are to be understood as an overcoming of the Vietnam syndrome, it is a solution even more intimately bound to the oriental other than the fraught scenarios of subjection and incontinence of the previous chapters.

The Militarism of the Martial Arts: Billy Jack (1971)

If you have eyes to see and a paper to read you may observe that the mysteries of the Orient in the varied forms of Kung Fu, Tai Chi, Savat, and related martial arts have taken the town the way Hong Kong tailors, Asian fly, and the Vietnam war once did. They beat us over there (or at least we didn't beat them), and . . . we demand to know why. Our POWs are home and now America needs to know.

—David Freeman, "Karate Flicks: What It All Means," Village Voice, 17 May 1973

In a short satirical piece accompanying a review of Five Fingers of Death (1973), the first of the Asian kung fu films to receive national distribution, David Freeman jokingly linked the emerging kung fu genre not only to the Vietnam War, but to Asian immigration and other perverse pestilences wrought upon America. While Freeman's tone is largely ironic, critiquing as much as perpetuating the racism and orientalism surrounding the uptake of the kung fu genre, his polemical statement highlights how America's confusion and frustration over the war was displaced onto an orientalist mystique surrounding the North Vietnamese and Viet Cong. Bill Brown commented upon Freeman's body politics, "[Kung fu's] guerrilla tactics replicate what was taken to be the strategy by which U.S. forces were defeated—which might be best understood not as knowledge about why 'we' lost, but as knowledge about how 'they' won."[8] With American troops' superior weaponry and training, how could the Vietnamese communists, described by the American news media as primitives fighting in "black pajamas" and using crude weapons such as sharpened bamboo sticks dipped in feces, possibly overtake us? As Freeman goes on to say, the answer must lie in a "secret weapon" whose source was inaccessible and lay within the body of the racial other. "And now we know," Freeman explains, mimicking the voice of the American public and recalling hysterias in the early twentieth century about cheap coolie labor. "Them gooks punched our boys full of cut-rate gook smack and then kung fooed them. Now I understand."[9] As Freeman's repetition of "know" and "understand" suggests, this epistemological project was geared at not only understanding this other who "kung fooed" American soldiers in Vietnam, but also obtaining this knowledge as a route to self-mastery, thus ensuring that such a defeat would never occur again.

Ironically the appearance of martial arts in American popular culture did not come about because of Asian militarism in Vietnam, as Freeman suggests, but rather because of U.S. militarism in the Pacific between the Second World War and the Korean War. Bud Buonocore, a columnist in *Black Belt* magazine, commented, "No group of Americans has done more to promote the Oriental martial arts in the United States than Armed Forces personnel."[10] The different histories of Chinese, Japanese, and Korean martial arts map directly onto the particular military and political interactions between those nations and the U.S. Long before there was a kung fu film craze, there was a slow dispersal of martial arts as a sport, led by Asians such as Kano Jigoro, the founder of modern judo, who was engaged in a cultural nationalist project of modernizing Japanese traditions at the turn of the twentieth century.[11] This dissemination was greatly aided by American soldiers, who picked up karate and judo while stationed in East Asia after the Second World War and then taught the sport to their peers in the military and in law enforcement, including such notable figures as the film star Chuck Norris (U.S. Air Force, Korea) and Robert Trias, founder of the U.S. Karate Association (U.S. Navy, Solomon Islands).[12] While Chinese American communities also practiced martial arts, because of perceived racial hostilities they rarely opened their academies to non-Chinese. But as the sociologist Ying-Jen Chang notes, these communities began to open up in the 1970s, in response to the rise of the kung fu film craze and Nixon's visit to China.[13] Thereafter the martial arts would refer to this conglomeration of East Asian traditions in an "imaginative geography" reminiscent of orientalism's conflation of cultures.

Many martial arts biographies emphasize the passage of knowledge from master to acolyte, thus situating American students as the phantasmatic offspring of their oriental instructor fathers. The Americans who were able to enter these martial arts cultures were also portrayed as native informants with access to mysterious oriental knowledge, even as they were challenged by newly radicalized Asian Americans who resisted such stereotypes of their communities. The controversy over a *Black Belt* magazine article in 1974 on Bob Campbell, a martial arts instructor in Boston, is symptomatic of the rise of such tensions. Campbell, who had a background in karate and had begun to study kung fu with Master Henry Chan in Boston's Chinatown, was described as an exceptional figure who was able to pierce through the veil of mystery and xenophobia that supposedly characterized Chinese American enclaves: "He holds the distinction of being one of the few whites who belong in Chinatown. . . . For literally hundreds of people in Chinatown, and especially for the Chinese-American kids stranded on the shaky bridge that attempts to connect two radically different cultures, he is a last link between the traditional ways of the Chinese elders and the contemporary lifestyle of urbane Bostonians."[14] As the consummate insider Campbell not only speaks Chinese and eats real Chinese food (not off the "tourists' menu"), but is closer to authentic Chinese culture than those Chinese American youths whose hybridity draws them away from the traditions of their elders. As seen in a photograph of Campbell clad in a silken kung fu uniform with elaborate trim and bearing archaic swords, his main claim to authenticity lay in his embodied knowledge of martial arts, but this claim was predicated on a view of kung fu as a repository for an unchanging Chinese culture untouched by modernity.

Ten students from the Asian American Cultural Society at the University of Massachusetts, Boston, wrote to *Black Belt* to criticize such representations of Campbell "as a 'white-god figure' who has decided to save the fate of Chinese youth."[15] These students were in turn rebutted in a subsequent issue by Ronald D. Yee, president of the Chinatown Neighborhood Supportive Committee; Davis Woo, a resident of Chinatown; William J. Bray, executive director of the local Chinese YMCA; and Campbell's own students.[16] This controversy reveals struggles not only between white insiders and Chinese Americans, but also within the Chinese American community itself. The students' self-identification as Asian Americans signals an awareness of the media stereotyping that the Asian American movement began to condemn in the early 1970s.[17] The rebukes by Yee and Woo reveal some of the power struggles between Chinese Americans for the authority to speak for their community in the public sphere, especially between university students and community members. These contradictory responses by Chinese Americans indicate the difficulty of recapturing the meaning of martial arts as a form of Asian American culture from its persistent orientalization in American popular culture.

It was through this orientalism that martial arts was linked back to the Vietnam War. As the term "eastern Western" suggests, the diegetic settings of the kung fu film, like the "in country" of Vietnam, were read as replications of the American Wild West, inverting the eastness of Asia into an extension of America's western frontier.[18] Despite the absence of proof that the Vietnamese used martial arts in the war, this association attempts to give form to the otherwise inexplicable and invisible triumph of Vietnamese guerrillas against a technologically advanced American military. Some members of the antiwar left had romanticized the Viet Cong as the antithesis not only to American hegemony but also to Western modernity in general. For example, Marianne DeKoven describes Frances FitzGerald's Pulitzer Prize–winning *Fire in the Lake: The Vietnamese and the Americans in Vietnam* (1972) as an attempt to "[construct] Vietnamese culture as a postmodern alternative to a failed Western colonialist modernity."[19] But as DeKoven's use of "postmodern" in the place of "antimodern" suggests, this did not mean that the Vietnamese guerrilla's body was devoid of technology as such. While the American soldier in Vietnam was inserted into the technologized, collective machinery of the American military, the imaginary Viet Cong who had mastered the martial arts represented a body penetrated with technology from within. In a similar vein Jachinson Chan speculated about the appeal of martial artists like Bruce Lee: "At a time of anti-war sentiments, it may have been refreshing to witness an Asian hero who uses his own body to resist the technological advancement of the West."[20]

In this sense we might say that the "arts" of martial arts are a form of technology, harkening back to the ancient Greek root of technology as *techne*, which Heidegger has linked to the idea of *poiesis*, the act of creation often associated with the fine arts.[21] The object which the martial arts seeks to create is the martial body, remade through a process of self-discipline and mastery that Foucault has referred to as a "technology of the self."[22] The martial arts body counters the American soldier's body not by refusing the violence of war, but by turning that violence inward, in an almost sadomasochistic reflexivity, in order to create a stronger, more invincible body. However, that body is no longer simply a naturalized body standing outside of culture, ideology, and technology, but is fully penetrated with technology from within. The opposition of nature against technology persists, however, perhaps because of the way this binary maps onto the racial oppositions between Western and non-Western nations. Within this binary racialized American subjects occupy both spaces: they are presumed to be closer to nature and the natural body, and yet they are completely imbricated in the technologically saturated culture of the U.S. As a result these hybridized subject positions offer access to dual fantasies of the body, as both the beneficiary of and the challenge to the technologies offered by American modernity.

The film Billy Jack (1971, rereleased in 1973) offers an interesting vision of this Vietnamized martial body as inflected through the complexities of a multiracial American body politic. The main character, Billy Jack (Tom Laughlin), is a part–Native American former Green Beret who originally appeared as a character in Born Losers (1967), one of a number of motorcycle gang films in 1967–71 that featured the Vietnam veteran as a violent, psychotic outlaw.[23] Billy deviates from this pattern; in both Born Losers and Billy Jack he uses his military training to resist violence through violence, fighting back against the motorcycle gang in the former film and assaulting a corrupt Arizona sheriff in order to protect a multiracial, progressive "Freedom School" in the latter. Jean Roberts (Delores Taylor), the head of the Freedom School and also Billy's love interest, describes him as a "war hero who hated the war," and although the film is quite violent and even called "obscene" by some viewers, its plot attempts to situate Billy in the antiwar movement and the general youth counterculture.[24] This countercultural aspect may explain the film's use of martial arts long before the kung fu craze officially took off. The hapkido instructor Bong Soo Han, whom Laughlin hired to choreograph the fight scenes, had in fact taught hand-to-hand combat to American troops in Vietnam as a member of the South Korean military before he emigrated to the U.S., providing a possible rationale for Billy's knowledge of martial arts.[25] However, the absence of such a backstory in the film implies that Billy learned these skills by fighting the Viet Cong.

This internalization of the enemy's violence parallels the "gone native" tropes of later films like The Deer Hunter and Apocalypse Now, but with an important exception: the American soldier who experiences martial arts is not killed by that exposure but becomes stronger, and the encounter with the enemy proves to be merely a lesson in a longer journey toward self-mastery. Celebrated retroactively by Black Belt magazine, the Green Berets become "American 'guerilla forces,'" the U.S. military's equivalent to the Viet Cong.[26] Thus the film fulfills paradoxical desires, both celebrating the veteran and his martial violence and aligning him with anti-establishment themes. The film critic Rex Reed even lauded the film for drawing together such disparate issues as "the Calley case, the fight for Indian affairs, returning Viet Nam veterans, the militant right vs. the pacifist left, the generation gap, the public attitude towards hippies."[27]

In a further concatenation of political meanings, Billy Jack also condenses multiple cross-racial identifications, not only with Asians (through martial arts) and Native Americans (through blood ties), but also with the Mexican Americans who populate the backdrop of the film and with African Americans through persistent references to black power and civil rights tropes. The first time Billy unleashes his "Green Beret karate tricks" is to defend the Freedom School's Native American students, who are barred from entering the town's ice cream parlor because of prohibitions similar to Jim Crow laws. Some white patrons harass the children by pouring flour on them, in effect "whitening" them, but the students follow the rules of nonviolent protest and do not retaliate. However, Billy is not bound by their pacifist ethics and is able to take revenge on behalf of the students by confronting their attackers outside the parlor, dispatching them with a swift series of kicks filmed in slow motion (fig. 34). The press book for the film highlights this scene by noting that "Mr. Han painstakingly trained Mr. Laughlin so that the truth of the explosive and fascinating karate episode is clear and unmistakable."[28]

Later in the film, after the corrupt rancher's son, Bernard Posner (David Roya), rapes Jean, Billy again exacts revenge through martial arts, killing Bernard with a single karate chop across the neck. But Jean, representing the Freedom School and its pacifist impulse, rebukes him for murdering her attacker, telling him, "You just can't keep making your own laws." Billy responds by pointing out that "turn[ing] the other cheek" failed to save the lives of Jean's heroes, Martin Luther King Jr. and Bobby and Jack Kennedy. But Jean's sentiments prevail in the end, and she convinces Billy to surrender to the police rather than suicidally fight them off. As Billy is handcuffed and led off, the students of Jean's school raise their fists toward him in a black power salute. The sequel, The Trial of Billy Jack (1974), connects Billy even more explicitly to the antiwar movement, flashing back to My Lai during his trial and even restaging a massacre of the Freedom School students reminiscent of the killings at Kent State.

Although Laughlin's multiple performances of the character Billy Jack

34. Billy Jack (Tom Laughlin) unleashes his "Green Beret karate tricks" to defend the Freedom School's Indian students from white racists. Frame enlargement from *Billy Jack*.

show an attempt to convert the troubling, anarchic violence of the Vietnam War into a more focused form of political critique, this connection between Vietnam veterans and the martial arts was not always a progressive alliance. Years later, as the kung fu craze evolved from Laughlin's primitive hapkido choreography to more elaborate fight scenes, the alliance between Vietnam and the martial arts became more threatening than enabling. David Bain, who attended a screening of Sonny Chiba's *The Killing Machine* (1975) in New York City, described one audience member's response to the film: "Seated directly in front of us were two men who had recently returned from overseas duty in the United States Army. We knew this because they were both very drunk, and talking loudly, but we didn't object because we were in a Times Square movie palace, watching a kung fu double feature. Near the climax of the film, one of these men decided to climb up on the apron of the stage and do battle with Sonny Chiba's projected image."[29] In Bain's scenario the crazed Vietnam veteran, filled with hidden aggression and lacking rational constraint, confronts the Asian martial artist of the kung fu craze as if he were a manifestation of the Viet Cong, and the film, an invitation to restage the Vietnam War. Seemingly unable to grasp the difference between representation and reality, this paradigmatic martial arts fan turns the theater into a potential warzone; when dissenting audience members shout insults "in at least three languages," the fan threatens them with a gun hidden in his pocket. Bain, who attended the screening only because he had helped with its English dubbing, beats a hasty retreat, running away from both the violent film and its violent fans. Even after the war has ended, the popularity of Asian martial arts threatens to put the wartime eruptions of "bringing the war home" into an infinite loop.

Although the cultural repetition compulsion of the Asian martial arts film is addressed to the trauma of Vietnam, we must view the martial arts' attempt at mastering the body as a fantasy equivalent to the fantasy of traumatic suffering brought on by representations of the war itself. Far from simply working through this trauma, martial arts imply a knowledge about the oriental body that is itself potentially traumatizing. Nonetheless they add to the iconography of the oriental obscene a new way of representing embodied trauma, both visually and narratively. When the kung fu craze and its army of flailing Asian bodies reached American theaters, they offered a complex array of new pleasures and pains for the viewing audience. The Asian bodies were simultaneously beating and being beaten; consequently, identifying with those bodies offered both active and passive pleasures. As a result of the emphasis on embodiment in the martial arts, these pleasures were less about voyeurism and scopophilia than those we find in "Saigon Execution" and The Deer Hunter, where the camera provided a mediating distance between viewers and the violent spectacle. By fetishizing the seemingly unadorned body, martial arts films phenomenologically activated viewers' fantasies of their own bodies, their arms and legs becoming weapons of combat. As the choreography and staging of the martial arts became more complex and extravagant, the pleasures of identifying with its fantastic bodies increased as well.

Pleasure, Pain, and the Ars Violentiae: Deep Thrust— Hand of Death (1972) and The Street Fighter (1974)

Nearly two years after Billy Jack the first Hong Kong "chop-socky" films were released in the U.S. by national distributors. The first of these, the Five Fingers of Death (produced by the Shaw brothers and released in Asia in 1972), was on the top of the U.S. box office charts throughout April and May 1973, and it was soon followed by the Golden Harvest production Deep Thrust—The Hand of Death (also first released in 1972).[30] Unlike Five Fingers of Death and many other chop-socky films, Deep Thrust featured as one of its martial arts leads the hapkido expert Angela Mao, who also appeared as Bruce Lee's sister in Enter the Dragon (1973). But the choice of the title Deep Thrust over the title used in Hong Kong, Lady Whirlwind, seems to displace Mao as the headliner of the film and focus instead on her costar, Chang Yi, who wields the deadly "hand of death" of the American title. The title also seems designed to profit from the notoriety of *Deep Throat* (1972), Gerard Damiano's feature-length hard-core pornographic film that hit the top of *Variety's* box office charts a year before the release of *Deep Thrust*. This wordplay also points to a deeper connection between the martial arts genre and pornography. As a reporter for *Variety* observed in the midst of these releases, "Recent rash of Kung-Fu-karate imports indicates, of course, that sheer violence remains as potent at the [box office] as is sheer sex. The fact that the former generally draw R's from the Motion Picture Association of America while the latter uniformly pull X's is clearly a sign of the moral times."[31] Both explicit sex and violence were deemed "obscene" by the Catholic Film Bulletin, pornography for perhaps obvious reasons, but martial arts films were also condemned for the amoral universe of their settings, their copious use of blood and gore, and their choreography of bodily violence that was "too realistic, too savage to be either cleverly amusing or comfortably entertaining."[32] Yet as *Variety's* review of *Deep Thrust* pointed out, pornography consistently received x ratings from the Motion Picture Association of America (MPAA) and was frequently subject to obscenity charges in the courts, whereas kung fu films received more lenient R ratings and were sometimes even praised by critics for their "balletic" acrobatics.[33] By what cultural logic would martial arts and pornography simultaneously be linked and yet separated for their visual and cinematic treatment of the body and its affects?

The explanation for this paradoxical link may lie in the respective truths they seem to tell about the body, as well as in the racialization and gendering of that body and its contours in the cinematic visual imaginary. What I mean by "truth" is what Foucault traced in his three volumes of *History of Sexuality* as the knowledge which the body yields through various modes of self-examination. Foucault's argument as it relates to sexuality and desire has been persuasively glossed by many other scholars, but here I turn to his schema of the *ars erotica* and the *scientia sexualis* as a way of understanding what violence and its accompanying affect, pain, might reveal about the body and the construction of embodied subjectivity. Drawing on Foucault, Linda Williams argues that hard-core pornography such as *Deep Throat* offers the "money shot," or male ejaculation, as the truth of the hidden and unseen pleasure of their female actors.[34] Likewise a dialectic of hiddenness and revelation operates in *Deep Thrust*, revealing what its advertisements emphasized as the power of its own naked (as in "unaided") body. By drawing an analogy between sexuality and violence I am not arguing that they are derived from one another, an argument often heard in the condemnation of sexuality and violence in film. Instead I propose that sexuality and violence are parallel systems with the aim of producing embodied subjectivities. The violence employed in martial arts forms the basis of something like an *ars violentiae* that transforms, reshapes, and remakes the body into an object of mastery. However, the system of difference that drives desire in the ars violentiae is not gender but race. The oriental exoticness of martial arts differentiates their violence from the more familiar forms of fisticuffs and brawls found in other violent American film genres. When martial arts in the kung fu film are detached from their historical origins and reattached to the Vietnam War, as in *Billy Jack*, they are able to take on even more phantasmatic and elaborate forms, drawing more exoticness from the Asian bodies performing the movements on American movie screens.

The link between violent pain and sexual pleasure can also be found in Freud's model of trauma. One of the central enigmas he addresses in *Beyond the Pleasure Principle* is the question of the repetition compulsion: Why would a subject obsessively repeat an unpleasant experience, either in dreams or reminiscences?[35] This seems to violate the economic principles Freud developed in his earlier *Three Essays on the Theory of Sexuality*, in which an increase of excitation is experienced as unpleasurable, while the evacuation of excitation is experienced as pleasurable. This economic model is at odds not only with the war neuroses, where patients continually flash back to memories of endangerment or injury, but also with the eroticized practices of sadism and masochism and the commonplace notion of sexual pleasure as excitation. This becomes the problem of the pleasure principle which Freud moves beyond in this essay.

One of the solutions that Freud offers is a doubling and splitting of key terms such as "pleasure" and "pain" through the introduction of the death drive as distinct from the life-preservation instincts. As Laplanche explicates these concepts, the death drive is aligned with the primary processes and the unconscious, and thus the type of pleasure associated with it is a pure evacuation of cathexis toward an inorganic (dead) state, a "zero principle" of this economic system. In contrast the life-preservation instinct is bound up with the secondary processes of consciousness and requires that the libido be held in a reserve of energy (i.e., the ego), which is maintained at a constant level and can be drawn upon to do the work of life; Laplanche calls this the "constancy principle."[36] Accordingly pleasure becomes two very different entities in each of these systems. In the life instincts, pleasure serves sexuality as Eros or "the preserver of all things" and is aligned with reproduction and the constancy principle, while in the death drive there is a pure "pleasure of discharge" of energy which Laplanche calls "a kind of antilife as sexuality, frenetic enjoyment [jouissance]."[37] Pain undergoes a similar splitting in these systems and becomes distinct from unpleasure. The intensity of pain is mixed up with the evacuative jouissance of the death drive, but it can also be a site of binding, a "wound" (either psychic or literal) which draws freely flowing libido toward it and "masters" it. This accounts for the paradox in which people who were actually injured during the war did not develop traumatic neuroses, whereas people who were not injured did develop them. Wounding, seemingly a physical violence done to the subject, becomes paradoxically a form of mastery that guards against the more dramatic psychic violence resulting from unmasterable traumas.

Deep Thrust provides an interesting model for how martial arts can provide for such forms of mastery as a response to trauma. The film is essentially a double revenge tale typical of its genre. Miss Tien (Angela Mao) comes into town to seek revenge on Ling Shi Hou (Chang Yi), a man who jilted her sister and caused her to commit suicide. But Ling himself is on a revenge quest to kill the Japanese gambling boss, Tung Ku (Pai Ying), whom Ling used to work for and who wounded Ling and left him for dead three years ago. We enter these cycles of reciprocal violence in medias res, but it is clear that each violent act comes into existence only in response to an earlier act. Tien agrees to let Ling live long enough to exact his revenge, and much of the humor of the film revolves around her intervening to save his life, even when she wants to kill him herself. Violence is the sole medium and occasion for social relations in this film; when Tien is not fighting with Ling herself, she is fighting off his enemies or refraining from violence in order to allow him to fight. This lawless world, which provides the milieu for many martial arts films, is similar to the western, and in particular the "spaghetti westerns" which were popular in the 1960s before the rise of the martial arts film. Relocated to the orient, this world becomes situated outside of historical, Western time, and is posited as a primordial period, when one entered into social relations with little more than one's body.

The mysticism of oriental violence becomes even more pronounced when we see Ling learn the "deep thrust" of the title from an old Korean herbalist he encounters in the woods. This common plot device, of the master who maintains and transmits the secret technique necessary to defeat the enemy, also resonates with the mode of transmission in Foucault's ars erotica, in which "the relationship to the master who holds the secrets is of paramount importance; only he, working alone, can transmit this art in an esoteric manner."[38] Indeed this master carries a single pamphlet with hand-drawn diagrams of the human body, which contains this esoteric art. And what is the secret he

35. Ling Shi Hou (Chang Yi) practices tai chi chuan techniques on a boulder. Frame enlargement from *Deep Thrust—Hand of Death*.

reveals to Ling? It's tai chi, one of the softer and more meditative "internal" styles of kung fu, used in many Asian communities as a form of morning calisthenics. But in *Deep Thrust* tai chi becomes something else altogether, a method for becoming a killing machine. "Its power is limitless, beyond description," proclaims the Korean master, yet he goes on to describe it in a series of vague aphorisms: "It confuses your opponent. It weakens him and so puts him off guard. You must shadow the enemy's every move. So that wherever he moves fast, be ready to beat him. Never relax for one moment. Keep your body taut. Wait for him to move, and watch out for an opening. Throw from the shoulder, kick from the hip, then you'll get more power. Poise yourself ready, just like an arrow on a bow. Do not bend the body and keep your balance." These mystical terms reveal little of the actual techniques of tai chi, compounding the mystery associated with the art and deepening the inscrutability of the master. In the training sequences that follow we see Ling progress by first thrusting his hands straight into an urn full of ashes, then one full of small rocks, and then large rocks—the montage of urns implying the swift passage of time. Finally Ling proves his mastery by impaling a falling boulder onto his outstretched fingers (fig. 35). Like Freud's *fort/da* game, martial arts training becomes a repetition compulsion that one willingly engages in, with the goal of mastering its pains and transforming it to a form of pleasure. But the technique is not fully revealed in the film until Ling is suddenly attacked while meditating. Using his new hand/weapon, Ling thrusts his fingers deep into his opponents' abdomens, creating bright red wounds that gush copious amounts of blood. Here the ars violentiae reveals the double truth of the body: that it is mortal flesh, mere meat waiting to be violated, but that it can also become the weapon of that violation, strengthened through ordeals into an instrument of mastery.

The achievement of mastery was most spectacularly shown through the effects of the body's mastery on other bodies. One achieved mastery by subjecting one's body to pain and withstanding the assault; other bodies represented the failure of mastery by their vulnerability to violation. In the gory violence of The Street Fighter (1974), a rare Japanese entry in the hand-to-hand combat martial arts genre, the emphasis is on the pain that Terry Tsurugi (Sonny Chiba) inflicts upon his opponents, rather than on the pain he endures to achieve his mastery. Lacking a training sequence, The Street Fighter is about pure external force; in addition to the usual karate fights, Tsurugi rips out the (clothed) genitals of a would-be rapist and bashes the head of another opponent, illustrated by a cut-away to an x-ray image of a skull being crushed before returning to a shot of the opponent's mouth gushing blood (fig. 36). Such an effort to bring the cinematic apparatus inside the body represents the flip side of the visual treatment of the body incontinent, where the body's contents are brought outside of the body to meet the camera. (Both styles of violence are present in this film.) Tsurugi's self-contained complex of body, machine, and weapon acts upon other bodies as if they existed in a purely mechanistic system governed only by external forces rather than internal will: blood pours from his victims as if he had turned on a faucet, and bodies fly from his path as if launched by a catapult. Interestingly The Street Fighter was the first film to receive an x rating for nonsexual violence under the MPAA system.[39] What seems obscene about this film is not the specific acts of violence it represents, which are commonplace throughout the martial arts genre. Instead the film emphasizes the pain experienced by Tsurugi's victims through their bodily ejecta, not only the "gushing gallons of synthetic gore" derided by one critic, but also vomit interspersed with broken teeth, and even innards ripped from an opponent's throat.[40] Tsurugi's body mastered attains special prominence when contrasted with the incontinent bodies that surround it; it becomes the calm center around which a storm of acrobatic violence rages.

In effect the ars violentiae of martial arts showed the body mastered and the body incontinent to be dialectically linked. While the development of mastery over one's own body reveals that body to be merely an object to be refined, the attainment of mastery shows the superiority of one's control over that body-object in relation to other body-objects. In Deep Thrust Ling is at first weak, out of control; when beaten by the villain and his cohort in the opening sequence he flops around like a rag doll. But after his encounter with the tai

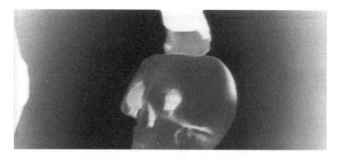

36. After Terry Tsurugi (Sonny Chiba) punches his opponent on the top of the head we see an x-ray of the effect on the inside of the body, then the usual reaction shot, a gush of blood, to indicate the inside of the body coming out to meet the camera. Frame enlargements from *The Street Fighter*.

chi master he attains mastery by subjecting his body to the very violence he could not endure before, and then overcoming it. Thrusting his hand first into rocks and then bodies, he discovers the equivalence between them, and also between his hand and other objects. But these lessons are less transformations of so-called Western metaphysics separating body and mind than they are insertions of alterity into it, maintaining the otherness of the orient which provides these teachings. Recalling the orientalism of other countercultural trends of the 1950s and 1960s, such as yoga and Zen Buddhism, these truths of the martial arts are received as fetishized foreign curiosities. The reception of martial arts in the U.S. was never far from these orientalist metaphysical fantasies, even when they relied upon seemingly factual accounts of what Asian religions or cultures entailed. Ultimately such fantasies do not so much deconstruct the mind/body dichotomy as set up the orient as the "body" to the Western mind. Ironically the bodily mastery offered by martial arts is as much a yellow peril as the violence of the Vietnam War it is meant to counter.

Although fantastic, the strange and impossible techniques seen in the martial arts film occupy a continuum with the actual techniques of martial arts promoted in nonfictional cultural texts. Some of these books simply report the fanciful techniques shown in films and described in Asian folklore without questioning their truth value. In *Kung Fu: History, Philosophy, and Technique*, cowritten by David Chow, the martial arts choreographer for the *Kung Fu* television show, photographs of actual Chin Na maneuvers demonstrated by Chow are followed by a section on traditional kung fu techniques, illustrated with line drawings resembling Chinese paintings. These techniques seem fantastic: how to pulverize rocks into sand and kill without touching using the Red Sand Palm, how to draw one's testicles up into one's body, how to climb up a wall like a gecko. The only caveat Chow writes to accompany these techniques is this: "Some of the following Kung methods are certainly possible to accomplish, but others must be viewed as fantasies designed to astound. Although it must be said that the impossible goes only as far as man's determination."[41] Although some of the techniques Chow describes, such as breaking boards or bricks with one's hand or head, are commonplace in martial arts practice, they too were viewed as mysterious and fantastic by the general public. Yet even unattainable and imaginary techniques such as the Red Sand Palm held symbolic value, representing the potential of "man's determination" to transform his body. These fantasies made manifest the latent power of the human body over itself and its environment, objects as mundane and vulnerable as baskets, walls, sand, and even one's own testicles.

Many live martial arts exhibitions also combined the realistic and the fantastic within a forum recalling the carnivalesque. One exhibition in 1974, called "Oriental World of Self Defense," organized by a martial arts instructor, Aaron Banks, and held in New York City, exhibited martial artists sparring and breaking bricks alongside "Ralf Bialla, the German who promises to catch a bullet in his teeth; Joseph Greenstein, the 93-year-old vegetarian billed as the Mighty Atom, who bangs spikes through four inches of plywood with his bare hands, and Jack Walsh, who supposedly has lifted 732 pounds with one finger."[42] In this carnivalesque atmosphere the emphasis was on the spectacle of the body pushed to its limits, whether or not that body's skills were scientifically verifiable. As explained by one black belt whose performance consisted of lying on a bed of nails while cement blocks were broken across his stomach, the more visible the display of bodily mastery, the greater the invisible "reserves of 'inner power' " were assumed to be.[43] The audience brought to this exhibition the same suspension of disbelief they took into the theaters which showed martial arts films. Such spectacles, like the line drawings in Chow's volume, were offered as the end result of arduous training which transformed the body-subject's mode of being. Even if taken as unreal, such bodies symbolized the hidden potentiality available to all bodies, if one was willing to incorporate these Asian techniques of mastery.

Despite the availability of real martial artists in sporting events and exhibitions, the cinematic apparatus remains particularly suited to the work of unveiling the hidden potentiality of the body. Whereas still photographs in martial arts books privilege the frozen gesture, cinema reveals the body in motion, a crucial aspect of bodily mastery. Even when represented in a print medium, images of the martial arts used various visual techniques to emphasize the moving mastery of ars violentiae. Most common was the juxtaposition of multiple images in a sequence, outlining a movement from beginning to end. But the use of stroboscopic photography also aids in the discovery of the secret of the body's movements in the print medium. Featured in magazines as disparate as Esquire and Scientific American, such photography used a repeating flash and multiple exposures to capture several images on a single piece of film, creating an almost ghostly image of a body's copies morphing into one another.[44] These stroboscopic images represent an extension of slow-motion cinematic techniques, simultaneously extracting the secret of the body's movements while testifying to the reality of such movements. Ironically the scientific rhetoric of these articles did little to dispel the mystery associated with such movements; if anything, by verifying such feats as possible they moved the martial arts from being impossible fictions to being deceptively simple realities. Collectively these myriad representations of the ars violentiae fostered a belief that such potential found in The Street Fighter or Deep Thrust was available within every human body. However, particular racialized subjects had an easier time of extracting such potential from their bodies because they were "closer" to their bodies to begin with. Once such potential was unmasked by the cinematic apparatus, these martial bodies became available as sites of identification and objects of mimicry, allowing them to leave their diegetic worlds of ancient rivalries in exotic settings and enter the more familiar spaces of American culture.

Martial Arts in the Living Room: Kung Fu (1972)

At the same time the Vietnam War was made more intimate for American audiences through its representation on television news, martial arts played on the small screen in the form of the show Kung Fu, starring David Carradine in the role of Kwai Chang Caine, a biracial Shaolin monk wandering in exile through the Wild West. Although Kung Fu debuted as an ABC made-for-TV movie on 22 February 1972, over a year before the kung fu craze appeared in mainstream American theaters, its creators were very much influenced by the early martial arts films that had been circulating in Hong Kong and in Chinese American ethnic enclaves in the late 1960s.[45] Thus *Kung Fu* was very much a part of the larger phenomenon popularizing Asian martial arts and bringing the ars violentiae into mainstream American culture, even if its appearance before films like *Deep Thrust* and *Five Fingers of Death* seems to reverse the causal relation between them. One of the only television shows in this genre, its run from 1972 to 1975 mirrored the rise of the martial arts film on the big screen. *Kung Fu* was an "eastern western," transposing the stylistic elements of orientalized violence into the milieu of the nineteenth-century American West and borrowing the traditional western themes of "the call of the frontier," rugged individualism, and "mastery over the natural order."[46] Its cast drew upon an older generation of Asian American actors such as Philip Ahn, Keye Luke, Benson Fong, and Richard Loo, whom *Variety* called "the cream of Hollywood's Oriental actor colony," thus recalling earlier formations of Hollywood orientalism found in Charlie Chan films and films of the Second World War.[47] Even Caine's name, taken from his American father, shows the influence of biblical iconography and thus alludes to Christian missionaries and their role in early Chinese American communities.[48] While Hong Kong kung fu films may have been oriental lenses through which American audiences refracted their fantasies about the Vietnam War, *Kung Fu* the television series was very much an American text, a condensation of the country's troubled history with Asians in America rather than Asians abroad.

Although, as a broadcast television show, *Kung Fu* never reached the heights of explicit violence for which kung fu films were criticized, it also attracted more scrutiny from media critics because it could reach an audience of all ages rather than appearing in theaters under the age-restricted MPAA ratings system. A month before the pilot movie aired, the U.S. surgeon general released a report titled "Television and Growing Up: The Impact of Televised Violence," sparking a debate in Congress led by Senator John Pastore, chairman of the Senate Communications Subcommittee, over what came to be known as "TViolence."[49] Concerned with the ways violence spreads beyond the bounds of rational society, this discourse on violence became a *scientia aggressionis* in counterpoint to the ars violentiae, enabling a scientific gaze to fall upon the body in violence and reinscribing it as an object of knowledge categorized under criminology, sociology, and medicine. However, the discourse of the scientia aggressionis, as discussed in the following section, would land more heavily on the bodies of racial minorities, while the ars violentia was associated more with white counterculture. *Kung Fu* aligned itself with art over science by surrounding its violence with a heavy veneer of mysticism, in particular through the character of Caine and his flashbacks to his Shaolin temple training in China. As one reviewer ironically described the show, "This pacifist, vegetarian priest beats the holy moses out of three frontier bullies."[50] Furthermore because Carradine was not trained in the martial arts, the fights staged on the television show were much less physical than those featured in the martial arts film genre: bodies rarely connected, and when they did their boundaries were never visibly violated. As if to compensate for the lack of authenticity in his martial artistry, Carradine privileged a gestural vocabulary that conveyed the pacifist mysticism of the ars violentiae, which held violence in check, in the position of a pure potentiality rarely actualized. After his success in Kung Fu Carradine became an "anti-Establishment, antimaterialist, antimilitarist . . . anti-hero" who played the guitar, slept on the floor on tatami mats, smoked marijuana, and cohabitated outside of marriage with Barbara Hershey and their son.[51] This celebrity backstory added as much to the orientalist, mystical aura surrounding the show as any knowledge about Asian religions or martial arts on Carradine's part.[52]

Kung Fu's mysticism drew upon what one critic derided as "night-school notions about Buddha, Confucius, and Lao-tse," translated into aphoristic, pseudo-poetic language very similar to the dialogue used in the Charlie Chan films of the 1930s.[53] One reviewer, Stephen Sansweet, complained that Caine "spouts more aphorisms than a bushel of fortune cookies," but he also praised the television show for its high-quality production values and writing in comparison with other martial arts films.[54] Frank Chin, an author and fifth-generation Chinese American, excoriated the dialogue on Kung Fu, accusing its orientalism of negatively influencing everyday perceptions of Asian Americans: "Being Chinese means doing strange things in the workaday world of white people. . . . The Chinese of 'Kung Fu' obviously are not the kind of people who'll give anyone directions to the bathroom in anybody's workaday world without a few plodding words so profound they hurt the head. People love it. The more brilliantly meaningless the lines, the more wooden, stilted and archaic the English, the more Chinese they think it is."[55]

Chin's arguments against Kung Fu are an extension of the critique of "racist love" he raised in his introduction to the anthology Aiiieeee!, where he rails against "effeminate" stereotypes of Asian American men as well as against Asian American acceptance of those stereotypes.[56] In the case of Kung Fu, as with older caricatures such as Charlie Chan and Fu Manchu, Chin sees Asian Americans again portrayed as "passive, docile, timid, mystical aliens." When Ed Spielman, one of the creators of the show, responded to Chin's criticisms, he made recourse to an orientalist system of knowledge production that attempted to invalidate Chin's critique by portraying Chin as the inauthentic Chinaman. Spielman defended the dialogue on the show from charges of racism by touting the authority of his source materials—"the books of Confucius, Lao-tzu, Chairman Mao"—and also by boasting about his own scholarly credentials: "I invested 10 years of my life in the research that allowed me to bring 'Kung Fu' into existence."[57] Such a defense not only tries to legitimize the content of the show, but also authorizes the white scholar or cultural agent to bring this portrayal into America on behalf of Chinese culture, a position made even more significant by Kung Fu's position at the beginning of the martial arts genre's entrance into American popular culture.

Like its enigmatic main character, Kung Fu contains contradictory elements of a mystifying orientalism and a nascent Asian American sensibility that a figure like Chin might appreciate in other settings. While Caine's pacifist nature may seem docile, especially in comparison with the brutal protagonists of Deep Thrust and The Street Fighter, he is no mere coolie, as Chin's complaint implies. Throughout the series the show vacillates between two historical and geographic worlds: the China of Caine's childhood, represented by Shaolin temples, saffron-robed monks, and stilted aphorisms, and the America that Caine travels to as an adult after being forced to flee China. In the pilot movie, "The Way of the Tiger, the Sign of the Dragon," Caine comes to the aid of Chinese laborers working on the transcontinental railroad, an important episode in Chinese American history that was little known to most Americans. Although over ten thousand Chinese laborers worked on this railroad, their contribution was essentially erased in the iconic photograph of the Golden Spike ceremony in 1869 linking the Central Pacific and Union Pacific branches of the route, which depicted only Irish American laborers. As David Eng points out, restoring that Asian American history and presence became the literary project of writers like Chin and Maxine Hong Kingston, who write from the perspective of those effaced laborers in Donald Duk (1991) and China Men (1980), respectively.[58] Although this history is peripheral to Kung Fu's narrative concerns, the film resurrects this episode as a way of differentiating Caine as an exceptional Asian American. In the first scene of the pilot movie set in the U.S., Caine enters the saloon of a railroad town, only to encounter a racist white who objects to his presence. The white man barks at an older Chinese man, Han Fei (Benson Fong), "You know I don't like any slant-eyes in a white man's saloon," and then attacks Caine, progressing from fists to chairs to knives. But Caine is not like Han Fei, who defers to whites and fails to defend himself against such insults. He calmly and silently deflects each of the white man's attacks, using no more than his bare hands and a mug of water that never spills. This early scene appears to set Caine up as a defender of his race, one who might belatedly respond to the historical injustices that helped to emasculate early Asian American subjects.

The logic behind Caine's techniques is explained in a later flashback to his Shaolin training, as one of his teachers, Master Kan (Philip Ahn), lectures Caine on the proper uses of his skills: "Perceive the way of nature and no force of man can harm you. Do not meet a wave head on: avoid it. You do not have to stop force: it is easier to redirect it. Learn more ways to preserve rather than destroy. Avoid rather than check. Check rather than hurt. Hurt rather than maim. Maim rather than kill. For all life is precious nor can any be replaced." Although such training ostensibly makes men into killing machines, this violent potentiality is held in check by the religious and philosophical orientation of the temple. Such pacifist philosophies contain the violent content of Kung Fu, emphasizing *ars* over *violentiae*, and ultimately blunt the potential subversion of its Asian violence. In a later flashback another of Caine's teachers, Master Po (Keye Luke), is killed by the emperor's nephew, who is in turn killed by Caine. The visual staging of this scene of violence reveals the ars violentiae at work even more clearly than the spoken aphorisms. Po, who is blind, stands still while the guards of the emperor's nephew attack him, deflecting a fist with a flick of his hand, tripping another by sticking out his foot. Caine enters the fight only after Po is shot by the nephew. Caine kills the nephew by throwing a spear at him (fig. 37), but again this action appears simply as a reaction to the nephew's original gunshot, and is shown through a shot-reverse sequence that emphasizes this reciprocity. Caine is impassive until pushed over the edge by another's act of violence. The killing forces him to flee from the imperial authorities to the U.S. Yet Caine makes for a strange action hero, for the killing is simply a reaction to the forces that surrounded him, both ideologically and physically.

One might even call Caine's use of martial arts nonviolent, reminiscent of the tactics of the mainstream civil rights movement. The opening scene in the saloon allows the white racist to expose his prejudice to the audience's disapproval, just as numerous sit-ins and marches revealed the violence of southern racism for northern audiences. But by winning over the audience with such seemingly liberal racial politics, Kung Fu constructs an alibi for its mystification of Chinese culture, romanticizing Caine's nonviolence as oriental wisdom that sets him apart from the rabble-rousing laborers in the camp. Just as nonviolent protest came under attack by both black radicals and white racists, Caine's refusal to engage more directly in the structure of oppression

37. Enraged by the murder of his teacher, Master Po (Keye Luke), Kwai Chang Caine (David Carradine) reacts by throwing a spear at the Chinese emperor's nephew, an act which sets into motion his exile. Frame enlargement from "The Way of the Tiger, the Sign of the Dragon," *Kung Fu.*

that plagues the Chinese laborers makes him vulnerable to violence from both the Chinese and the Americans. One Chinese laborer, Fong (Robert Ito), angrily denounces Caine's passivity in the face of outright exploitation by the white foremen and tries to egg the other workers on to revolt. As Caine counsels the laborers to wait, Fong snaps back, "For what? Starvation? The tunnel?" It was precisely these conditions that Caine refused to protest that brought on his capture, for another Chinese laborer, Hsiang (James Hong), betrayed Caine to the boss Dillon (Barry Sullivan) in exchange for a chicken drumstick. Even Raif (Albert Salmi), Dillon's foreman, notices that Caine holds himself apart from the other Chinamen: "I get the feeling that you think you're better than the rest of them. Maybe you can lay ties around the clock. Maybe you don't feel the cold the way they do. But I'm gonna show you you can bleed the way they do." Although Caine is sympathetic to the other Chinese laborers, his exceptional bodily mastery means that he has difficulty experiencing their suffering and weaknesses. Fong is shot by Dillon's men only moments after he calls for revolt, and Han Fei is captured along with Caine and shot in the back while trying to escape. It is Han Fei's death that sparks Caine's flashback to Master Po's death, drawing a parallel between both men's position as mentors to Caine and Caine's impotence to prevent either death despite his superior fighting skills.

Frank Chin's criticism that *Kung Fu* portrays "yellows as too cultured, too philosophical, or too spiritless to pick up their shovels when a white man threatens them" is technically disproved by the ending of "The Way of the

Tiger," yet the spirit of his observation remains on point. Caine and other Chinese meet the violence of white racism with violence, but not in any sustained fashion that might alter the social relations within the show's diegetic world. Caine escapes again to wreak havoc in the camp and ultimately arms the remaining Chinese laborers to rise against Dillon, who is abandoned by his white workers and held hostage in his own camp. This collective action hints at various labor strikes initiated by Chinese laborers in the late nineteenth century, including a major railroad strike in 1867 against the Central Pacific, belying their reputation as docile workers.[59] But the revolt in Kung Fu's pilot film fails to bring about tangible change. Although the workers revel in the temporarily reversed power dynamics, they win no concessions from the railroad for their safety, wages, or well-being, as the strikers in 1867 did. Also Caine does not remain with this early Chinese American community for the remainder of the series, choosing instead to wander alone in the mold of the individualistic western hero. Although he has led this rebellion *for* the workers, he ultimately does not join *with* them in their larger struggles. In an ideological restaging of the principles of redirection of energy found in martial arts, Kung Fu posits the martial artist as a nonviolent fulcrum of the violent forces raging around him. If violent action happens to pass through his body, it is simply because he refracts and redirects violence that originates elsewhere. At the center of a sociopolitical reaction arc, the philosophical martial artist participates in a culture of violence but uses his mastery over his own body to remain at a distance from this violence. As Chin suspected, Kwai Chang Caine makes a poor model for contemporary Asian American politics, offering only a temporary detour from the origin myth of coolie passivity. In this domesticated, pacified version of kung fu the martial artist essentially stands apart from politics, and his orientalist origins in a mythic, ahistorical tradition remove him from the ordinary concerns of historically concrete people.

Feminist and Third World Anger

A woman is kicked in the face: score one for ERA. . . .

Karate can turn into pretentious anti-Western egg-role-playing. . . . Half the contestants and more than half the audience are black or Hispanic: karate is Third World anger-release. Anyone can guess the unspoken implication: that those little, wiry yellow folk are superior. That we lost in Vietnam because Russia supplied Ho Chi Minh with shin kicks and palm chops and 60 mm Zen kuans [sic].

—D. Keith Mano, "Kung Phooey," *National Review*, 2 May 1980

The martial arts were not limited to the visual mass media, but had a lively existence as wider cultural practices such as sports and dance. How do the martial arts change when they leave the screen and become part of social practice? For one, the body in question changes from an individual body concerned with its relationship with itself, to a social body or a body politic, a society conceptualized as a body and concerned with regulating the relationships between its constituent parts. Despite being set up as "half-breeds," characters like Billy Jack and Kwai Chang Caine were essentially white men played by white actors, representing a domestication of martial arts' more anarchic qualities. However, when practiced by women and nonwhites, the martial arts symbolizes a potential challenge to the monopoly of violence held by white men as proxies for state power. Although organized under the sign of self-defense, martial arts in these contexts and communities do not simply shore up the normative self but may also present a new weapon—sardonically called "anti-Western egg-role-playing" and "Third World anger-release" by the conservative magazine *National Review*—against existing social arrangements and meanings.[60] As celebrated by second-wave feminists and black power and yellow power activists, martial arts take on a utopian tone as a possible techne for social liberation.

For many radical activists martial arts were the popular manifestation of Third World political alliances being formed in the antiwar and larger anti-imperialist movements. Vijay Prashad finds the roots of a multicultural Afro-Asian alliance in the martial arts, emphasizing the constructed nature of these identifications so as to challenge the naturalizing collapse of culture onto race.[61] Black radical activists' fascination with a phantasmatic orient maps readily onto the images of Third World triumph found in Asian martial arts films. These films appear like the photographic negatives of the images of the Vietnam War, both real and fictional, which depict the Asian body as always already violated. Fred Ho, an Asian American activist from the 1970s who was briefly a member of the Nation of Islam, speculates that "black and brown youth" were drawn to the images of "nonwhite dominance" found in Asian martial arts films, identifying with these "yellow" heroes and their unlikely triumph against corrupt Manchu officials, evil Japanese colonialists, and the occasional British, Russian, or American villain.[62] No doubt such cross-racial identifications provided a source of pleasure, but a more overt symbol of black empowerment was the transference of these bodily masteries into black characters themselves. Numerous critics have noted the popularity of Asian martial arts films among urban black audiences; in the blaxploitation genre of the 1970s martial arts became part of the popular iconography of black

38. Jeff Gerber (Godfrey Cambridge), in the center of the third row, embraces his newfound blackness by practicing karate. Frame enlargement from *Watermelon Man*.

power.[63] Even an early film such as *Watermelon Man* (1970) found a ready signifier for race consciousness and militancy in the black martial arts. Directed by Melvin Van Peebles, who would later produce what some consider the first blaxploitation film, *Sweet Sweetback's Baadasssss Song* (1971), *Watermelon Man* is a comedy about a white man, Jeff Gerber (played by the African American actor Godfrey Cambridge in whiteface), who wakes up one morning to find that he has inexplicably become black. While Gerber resists his racial transformation at first, he finally gives in to pressure by his white neighbors, coworkers, and even family members and leaves his white life behind. To mark his embrace of blackness, the film's final scene shows Gerber in a bare-bones inner-city dojo that advertises karate as "a fine oriental art," where he and other African American men learn to brandish a broom as a weapon (fig. 38). For a film so conscious of racial performativity, it is interesting that Gerber's learning karate does not suggest a form of yellowface mimicry. Although the audience is supposed to find humor in the incongruity of Gerber's attempting to act white even after his body has become black, his adoption of martial arts is part of his return to racial authenticity.

The black embrace of Asian martial arts in the 1970s must be situated within the longer history of the civil rights movement, when African Americans contesting racist police forces and extralegal white supremacist violence turned to armed self-defense for the protection of their communities and activists. In the 1950s and 1960s groups such as the Deacons for Defense in Jonesboro, Louisiana, and the local NAACP chapter led by Robert F. Williams in Monroe, North Carolina, used organized groups of legally armed black citizens to defend themselves from violent attack by the Ku Klux Klan, whose actions were condoned by and whose members often included local white law enforcement officials. These black self-defense groups, which predated the better known Black Panthers, were often composed of working-class black men whose experience with firearms derived from military service in the Second World War and Korea—the same source of much African American knowledge about Asian martial arts. As Williams explained in his manifesto *Negroes with Guns* (1962), blacks did not "*introduce* violence into a racist social system—the violence [was] already there"; he declared nonviolence "suicidal" when blacks were being threatened with direct violence out of the spotlight of the national press and organized protests.[64] Although mainstream civil rights groups abhorred these methods—Williams was expelled by the national NAACP leadership after telling the press that he would "meet violence with violence"—the use of armed self-defense was an important, if unacknowledged, element of the civil rights movement.[65] In his history of the Deacons for Defense, Lance Hill argues for the importance of such efforts in exposing the inadequacy of the law in protecting black citizens, and also in providing a rhetorical foil for mainstream civil rights organizations to appear more moderate in their claims.[66] Hence Asian martial arts was neither the first nor the primary means of African American self-defense, but it quickly entered the repertoire of defense techniques, not only because it was accessible to those of limited means, but also because its training provided organizational and disciplinary structures useful to cultural nationalist groups such as Ron Karenga's "US" Organization in Los Angeles and Amiri Baraka's Black Community Defense and Development group in New Jersey.[67]

Self-defense was also the primary rhetoric used to describe martial arts within second-wave feminism. The martial arts were viewed as a method for protecting women from sexual violence and also as a form of bodily discipline that would help women overcome their ingrown bodily habits of submission. Martha McCaughey notes that many nonfeminist self-defense tracts from the 1970s, which were often written by men in law enforcement, discouraged women from fighting back against their attackers, thus reinforcing "gendered body-codes" regarding the weaker sex and women's need for the protection of others.[68] In contrast a conference organized by the New York Radical Feminists in 1971 included karate demonstrations and discussions about arming women with ordinary objects such as scissors, corkscrews, and hammers, with the following rationale: "Since you are living in a jungle and no one may help you, be self-reliant. . . . Everyone has a tiger inside of her."[69]

Situated within a larger discussion about rape and street crime, feminist martial arts also served to train women to have a different relationship with their own bodies. The "tiger inside" every woman was not necessarily an exceptional martial artist capable of breaking rocks with her bare hands. Instead she was a woman who simply inhabited her normal body more fully. Three female students of martial arts outlined the reasons they wanted to learn self-defense, at first framing their response as freedom from fears about rape and assault, but concluding with more ordinary pleasures: "Karate has made us feel much healthier and stronger. . . . [It] gets us out of the house. . . . [It] has mentally increased our confidence in ourselves as human beings."[70] In *Against Our Will: Men, Women and Rape* (1975) Susan Brownmiller described her experiences in jujitsu and karate classes in a similar vein: "I learned I had natural weapons that I didn't know I possessed, like elbows and knees. I learned how to kick backward as well as forward. I learned how to fight dirty, and I learned that I loved it."[71] An article in *Ms.* summarizes these transformations: "A fist becomes a political act: an assertion that you are a physically competent woman. . . . I now see my body as a potential weapon. . . . I'm not a victim anymore."[72] In all of these accounts the production of bodily mastery through martial arts counters the sexual objectification of the female body. Although the language of weaponry may seem to imply an instrumental relationship to the body, the assertion of self-empowerment arose from women's self-possession of these weapons: "our bodies, ourselves."

However, as the references to street crime suggests, the utopian work of the martial arts was contained by its absorption into existing patterns of social relations. The feminists who advocated martial arts training and promoted awareness of sexual violence were largely white and middle class and often reproduced stereotypes of racialized violence in their descriptions of their imagined attackers. The illustrations accompanying a *Sports Illustrated* article on self-defense courses cast this racialized dichotomy in stark terms, contrasting the naïve, beautiful white woman emerging from her "Instant Karate Kung-Fu Tai-Chi Killer" course and confronting a gang of menacing, urban male denizens, including a black man with a large Afro.[73] Interestingly the raised fist, a political symbol associated with Black Power and signifying a collective resistance to the state, becomes transformed into a reconsolidation of the power of the individual self when raised by the woman in the cartoon. In light of this symbolic appropriation, it is especially disturbing that Brownmiller's text, a classic polemic of the feminist movement of the 1970s, recasts the African American man as an archetypal rapist against which the (white) feminist must guard herself. She describes Emmett Till's whistling at a white woman as an instance of "a deliberate insult just short of physical assault," and even aligns Till with one of the men who murdered him, J. W. Milam, as both sharing an "understanding" of women's sexual objectification.[74] Angela Davis takes Brownmiller to task for her distortion of these and other examples, noting that Brownmiller denies the possibility of fraudulent rape charges against black men as another form of social control equivalent to men's use of the threat of rape to control women's behavior.[75]

Blaxploitation films after Sweetback, which were largely studio productions that sought to profit from the segmenting of urban black audiences, also perpetuated sexist and racist social relations that contradicted the utopian meanings posited by many of its practitioners. The main characters in films like Cleopatra Jones (1973) and Black Belt Jones (1974), both distributed by Warner Brothers, are hip and stylish variations of white law enforcement stock figures, whom one reviewer derided as an "attempt to wed elements of James Bond with Super Fly."[76] The action sequence accompanying the credits of Black Belt Jones depicts its protagonist, played by Jim Kelly (who also appeared in Enter the Dragon [1973]), dispatching a multiracial gang of Asians and Latinos for no reason except to display his martial arts prowess to the film audience. The cops-and-robbers plot features FBI-like undercover agents squaring off with the Italian mafia, and Jones's karate dojo in Watts is merely caught in the cross-fire. Similarly the main character in Cleopatra Jones, played by the former model Tamara Dobson, is a secret agent whose main associates are other white, male secret agents and whose main task is to take down a white female drug lord named Mommy (Shelley Winters). The awkward black power salute that Cleopatra's white boss gives her after the successful completion of her mission only underscores the distance between these black martial artists and the sociopolitical conditions from which black self-defense arose. In these films black martial arts are less about the defense of one's civil rights and more about the conversion of the black body into a weapon to be wielded by white power. Both Joneses become fetish objects whose potential subversion is held in check by putting their violence in the service of the maintenance of law and order.

Thus the liberatory potential of martial arts is attenuated by the development of discourses that contain such violence by making it an object of study in sociology, criminology, and psychology. In response to the ars violentiae these social scientific disciplines absorb martial arts into something like a scientia aggressionis, a counterpart to the Foucauldian scientia sexualis, that uses knowledge-power to categorize and delineate the proper and improper uses of violence within the social body.[77] Many of these investigations into violence in the mass media situated martial arts as a matter of public health and moral hygiene, recalling earlier efforts by the Catholic League of Decency to institute the Hollywood Production Code in the 1930s and Fredric Wertham's jeremiad against comic books in the 1950s.[78] By conflating identification with direct imitation, critics saw media such as film and television as pedagogical vehicles for such a science of aggression, such that the Washington Association of Mental Hygiene convened a meeting on TV violence in 1972, "Television— The Home Course in Violence," and framed the issue as a "public health problem."[79]

In particular, the TV violence debates demonized black and Latino youth as naturally prone to violence and especially susceptible to the mimicry of televised violence. The surgeon general's report on TV violence in 1972 concluded that there was a "preliminary and tentative indication of a causal relation between viewing violence on television and aggressive behavior," but it also qualified that this causal relation applied only to "some children who are predisposed to be aggressive" and "only in some environmental contexts."[80] Such terms, correlated with other contemporaneous news items on youth violence, were clearly euphemisms for children from African American and Latino families of low socioeconomic status.[81] Films were likewise targeted as "manuals of crime," giving new forms to expressions of antisocial violence by racialized audiences who were "poor, black and stuck."[82] This same racialized audience was blamed for a "melee" in which the audience for an unnamed kung fu film started a fight in the theater which "spilled over into the street."[83] It was feared that the racialized Asian bodies in the martial arts film might give a visual form to the racial tensions present in America in the 1970s, allowing the violence within the film to spill into the social reality outside the film. In response to the spread of martial arts, Georgia and New York began to require all black belts to register with the state as "deadly weapons," while other cities such as Baltimore and Detroit banned martial arts paraphernalia such as nunchaku, the stick weapons popularized by Bruce Lee.[84] These juridical responses treated the racialized body-weapon as an object of regulation.

This scientia aggressionis reveals an "incitement to discourse," both textually and extratextually. In a self-reproducing cycle representations of violence on television, in the news, and in film respond to and reproduce the increasing violence found in the world, which in turn claims to be incited by replications of violence in representational media, as well as in those news media covering this issue. A two-page ad placed in Variety by several television stations justifies the increasing violence in news coverage by recourse to statistics which quantitatively prove the rise of violence in the world.[85] Yet as some social scientists argue, the increased representation of violence leads to the impression that the world is "even more dangerous than it really is," creating a culture of victimization that encourages an increase in social violence.[86] Violent texts are leaky vessels; their representations of bodies being violated find their way into bodily practices of violation. The texts themselves even violate the bodies of their viewers. In the wake of the surgeon general's report, a member of the Federal Communications Commission even accused television networks of "molest[ing] the minds of the nation's children," conflating the violence portrayed in the shows with the violence done by the shows.[87]

Yet the same spread of martial arts into predominantly white and middle-class portions of American society aroused few anxieties, and was even hailed as helping to contain the contagion and growing disorder within racialized ethnic communities. Articles in business magazines such as *Fortune* and *Dun's* describe white-collar employees turning to martial arts as mental self-discipline, at the same time using the physical self-discipline of martial arts to shape their bodies into a normative masculinity.[88] The white body is perfected to a level of mastery in which actions can take place without thought, and the resulting body-subject does not transcend Western binaries of mind and body, but rather elevates the body to the level of the mind as a seat of subjectivity. These body-subjects are not so much transcending the self as they are perfecting it. This is the apotheosis of Western individuality, and it is mobilized to protect the rights and properties of that body. Instead of using martial arts to transform the body as object, the body *as subject* incorporates all manner of private property within its boundaries and protects them as if they were part of the body itself—a perverse inversion of the logic of the ars violentiae. Like the popular illustrations accompanying female self-defense courses, martial arts classes are portrayed as part of a city dweller's arsenal against violent economic crime and featured alongside articles on locks and alarms, security guards, and the strengthening of "tough on crime" laws.[89] The same weapon that racialized youth are accused of wielding is legitimized and turned against them by the white middle class.

Because of these pathologizing discourses we must be wary of celebrations of martial arts as an essentially Third World cultural form that is inherently resistant to dominant formations of state and economic power. This warning extends to the naturalization of the identification of African American and Latino audiences with Asian martial artists, as if all people of color automatically recognize themselves in one another and share a single political stance toward racism and imperialism. Amy Abugo Ongiri has critiqued this alignment of racialized audiences with spectatorial blood-lust as reductive, arguing that these simplistic theories of identification overemphasize the degree to which African American audiences saw their experiences reflected in the plots of Asian martial arts films. Instead, Ongiri argues, "the stylized action of the martial arts genre readily spoke to an African American audience's history of violence and violation in which acts of spectacularized violence would become the central visual metaphor for African American cross-identification."[90] Rather than a direct identification between the oppression of African Americans in America and of Chinese in colonial China, Ongiri posits the visual stylization of violence as the site of identification. The spectacles of violence in martial arts, separated from their narrative content, mirrored the treatment of the African American body in American entertainment and news media. Yet the techne of mastery also offered a response to this visual abjection of the African American body, showing the "transcendent beauty of the mastery of the body and its assertive possibilities."[91] Ultimately these oscillating dynamics show Asian martial arts as an ambivalent site of identification, for at the bottom of the "transcendent beauty of the mastery of the body" is a traumatic core of bodily suffering that can be traced back more immediately to the brutal training of the Asian martial artist, and finally to the Vietnam War as the origin for these secret truths of the body.

As they spread out into such a diverse set of cultural practices, the martial arts remain a nexus of anxieties over race and gender, but what seems to disappear once the martial arts leave the screen is the specificity of the Asian body. What remains is the violence which such Asian bodies taught to Americans, a gestural vocabulary that retains an Asian cultural residue through periphery symbols: the use of Asian terminology, such as *sensei* or *sifu* for teacher, even when applied to non-Asians; costumes of white karate *gi* robes and kung fu outfits with Mandarin collars; a mystical lore combining Buddhism and other Asian religions with the American counterculture. When martial arts are transferred from the screen into cultural practice the meaning of orientalness becomes severed from the Asian body. The body mastered of martial arts answers the body incontinent of the Vietnam War by displacing that Asian body which these two tropes have in common—displacing by essentially taking its place, the American becoming the oriental object by proxy. In Vietnam War films the American body is orientalized by assuming the position of suffering previously occupied by the Vietnamese body. In the kung fu craze the American body is orientalized by learning the "secret" technologies of the Asian body and using those technologies to transform itself into an object that can no longer be violated. Unlike American movie stars, Asian martial arts stars such as Angela Mao, Lo Lieh, and Sonny Chiba do not serve as direct points of identification, but are conduits for this style of violence that flows through them and into the audience as kinetic energy. The one exception to this exclusion is the figure of Bruce Lee, whose persona offers further insight into just how this orientalized violence makes its way into American bodies without those bodies becoming overtly racialized as Asian.

Chapter 5

BEING BRUCE LEE

Death and the Limits of the

Movement-Image of Martial Arts

Hong Kong—Bruce Lee, star of violent action films that have become known as "Eastern westerns," died here Thursday night, police said Friday.

The 32-year-old hero of films such as "Five Fingers of Death," which featured dazzling displays of Oriental martial arts, died shortly after admission to a Hong Kong hospital.

—"Bruce Lee, Hong Kong Film Star, Dies at 32," *Los Angeles Times*, 21 July 1973

Bruce Lee has come to symbolize the martial arts film genre for American spectators, looming above all other martial arts stars in terms of name recognition and visibility. But at the time of Lee's death, on 20 July 1973, the genre and Lee himself were largely unknown outside their target audience base of martial arts enthusiasts and fans of exploitation action film. The obituary for Bruce Lee distributed by the Reuters wire service was symptomatic of this level of ignorance. Referring to the genre as "Eastern westerns" rather than "kung fu films," the obituary writer apparently viewed these films as an offshoot of an established Hollywood genre rather than a distinct group of films with its own conventions and audience. It also tellingly misattributed another popular martial arts film, the Shaw Brothers' production *Five Fingers of Death* (1973) starring Lo Lieh, to Bruce Lee, who never appeared in the film. This slippage between genres and stars highlights the foreignness of the Asian martial arts film at the time of its initial American reception—with one kung fu star indistinguishable from another—but it also signals one of the first of many attempts to assimilate this foreign element into the mainstream of American popular culture.

Exit the Dragon

At the center of this assimilation is Bruce Lee. Nicknamed Li Xiao Long ("Little Dragon"), Lee was the only martial arts star of the 1970s to have a career in both Hollywood and Hong Kong. His best-known film, *Enter the Dragon* (1973), was a Hong Kong–American coproduction and involved a multiracial, multinational cast quite unlike casts in the majority of martial arts films. His other films, which also departed from the typical narratives of Ming-Ch'ing political intrigue in Chinese martial arts films, reflected the conditions of the Chinese diaspora in the twentieth century, presenting "stories of Chinese who live in places dominated and controlled by non-Chinese."[1] Lee himself was a diasporic subject; the son of a Cantonese opera performer who was touring the U.S. on the eve of the Japanese invasion of Hong Kong, Lee was born in San Francisco's Chinatown but raised in Hong Kong, and he returned to the U.S. as an adult and eventually maintained residences in both countries. All these factors enabled Lee to be claimed by both Hong Kong and American film cultures as one of their own icons. As a transitional figure between the Asian martial arts film (made by Asian actors for Asian audiences) and the later American martial arts film (made by white American actors for American consumption), Lee marks the movement of the oriental obscene in martial arts from a foreign, exteriorized style of violence to a violence made familiar through its incorporation into American bodies. The object of assimilation is not simply the static image of Lee, frozen in time on a movie poster, but rather a style of movement: the combination of choreography and cinematography that produced the dynamic images of bodily movements identifiable as Bruce Lee. Thus Lee seems to provide an exemplary instance of the Deleuzian movement-image, since his star persona appears to be completely enmeshed with the mapping of his body moving through space onto the temporal medium of the cinema.

But whereas the movement-image posits a stable body from whom these motions and actions emanate, the figure of Bruce Lee also troubles this organic wholeness, largely because his star persona is a posthumous one, a cult of personality arising after his premature death during the height of his popularity and physical powers. Not only is there a motif of death running throughout the films Lee worked on before his passing, but his death itself becomes the driving force for an explosion of film narratives and texts that attempt to understand and exploit this fact. Just as it haunts the martial arts genre as a whole, the Vietnam War shadows the movement-images of Bruce Lee as well, appearing on the edges of films like *Enter the Dragon* through Vietnam veteran characters such as Williams (Jim Kelly) and Roper (John Saxon), and emerging in the colonial settings and battles of his other films: *Fists of Fury* (1971), filmed in Thailand and depicting the exploitation of Chinese contract workers; *The Chinese Connection* (1972), based on a true story of a Chinese martial arts school in Shanghai during Japanese colonial rule; and *Return of the Dragon* (1972), set in a Chinese immigrant community in Italy.[2] If the martial arts film genre is obsessed with the mastery of death and injury through violent action, Lee's death is a reminder of the intimate link between violence and death, between these polarized yet dialectically linked signifiers of activity and passivity. Despite being one of the iconic figures of the kung fu genre, Lee disrupts its narratives of mastery and signals the limits of the ability of martial arts to respond to the mass death and suffering of the Vietnam War.

In chapter 2 I examined the disruption of the movement-image through a "crisis of the action-image" brought about by forms of stillness: the fixing of death and injury in the still photograph, the failure of narrative to give meaning to these deaths, and the paralysis of the viewer's ability to respond to those events in a way that might restore his or her historical agency. These elements of stillness can also be found in the literal disruptions of Lee as movement-image. If the moving image signals life through the animation of the body, then death emerges as still images extracted from this sequence: Lee as photograph, Lee as poster, Lee as corpse. In this chapter I am interested in a different form of departure from the movement-image, one which Deleuze celebrates as " 'a little time in the pure state' . . . ris[ing] up to the surface of the screen."[3] This direct presentation of time in the cinema, which Deleuze calls the time-image, no longer subordinates time to movement but allows time to emerge through the ruptures of memory, thought, history, and—as I propose—death. The cinema of the time-image does not simply represent death on screen or show a psychological reaction to death; rather it registers something of the ontological effects of death on notions of time, causality, narrative, and identity. Death introduces discontinuity or "false continuity" into the movement-image of Bruce Lee through the processes of extraction, replication, and reordering, as film texts visually register the fact of his death even while their narratives attempt to smooth over his absence. An army of Bruce Lee clones arise from this disorder: Bruce Le, Bruce Li, Dragon Lee, and even the old Bruce Lee, reanimated in bits and pieces from the preserved remains of his previous films. These acts disrupt the identity of Lee as film star as well as the organic wholeness of his movements, viewed as actions emanating from a living body-subject. As a result Bruce Lee is a movement-image wholly permeated with death, and as such is an unstable site of imitation and identification. When the oriental obscene embodied in Lee's movement-image is called upon to shore up an impermeable, idealized American masculinity, it reveals the contradictory ways that race and culture are written on, and then defaced from, Lee's body.

Thus "being Bruce Lee" is not the imitation of a stable ego ideal of masculinity and agency; it is a contradictory and multiple set of identifications with both movement and stillness, activity and passivity, life and death. These contradictions are carried through to the racialization of Lee's body as well, such that he comes to embody both the transcendence of racial categories and the epitome of racialized masculinity. I investigate these contradictions in the Bruce Lee star persona as they play out in Lee's "posthumous" work, a set of films created in the absence of Lee, yet invoking his presence through a number of strategies such as the use of body doubles (credited and un-credited), the recycling of older footage of Lee, and the circulation of the legend of Lee through fan culture. Unlike previous American films which featured what the sociologist Eugene Wong called the "Asian death theme" of scores of dead oriental bodies, where death is seen as a dead-end in the production of narrative around the Asian male body, the deadness of Bruce Lee's body generates a seemingly endless stream of narrative production in the martial arts genre.[4] Lee's persona is posthumous in the archaic sense of the word: not only surviving Lee's death, but literally "late-born," birthed from a womb that is essentially a tomb.

The textual hinge of this chapter is the enigmatic film *Game of Death* (1978), the only posthumous Bruce Lee text produced by a major Hollywood studio. Essentially a Bruceploitation film capitalizing on a work left unfinished at Lee's death, it combines footage from previously released Lee films, un-released footage filmed by Lee before his death, and new footage featuring a Lee body double. This film is an exemplary text of discontinuity; it not only violates the codes of continuity editing established by mainstream Holly-wood films, but it also undermines the continuity of identity implied in Lee's movement-image through its direct and indirect invocations of his death, exploiting the rumors surrounding his death and even utilizing his funeral as narrative fodder. Its various methods of reproducing Lee—as extradiegetic referent, as diegetic character, as indexical presence and absence—directly mirror the multiple facets of Lee's persona that are fetishized by worshipful fans. Far from diminishing the film's popularity, these discontinuities and ruptures are incredibly generative, sparking multiple attempts to piece together Lee's authorial intent and retrieve his auratic presence. As the ghost of Bruce Lee surfaces, I read these false continuities not as the errors of inadequate film technique, but as the interaction between ahistorical, mythic presentations of Lee on film and the particular historical circumstances of his stardom and life.

As one of the first Asian film heroes embraced by American cinema, Lee exemplifies the transference of the oriental obscene from the oriental body to American bodies, both Asian American and otherwise. His movement-image appears to offer yet another example of the body mastered and the ars violentiae, waiting to be taken up by American spectators weary of failures of the body incontinent exhibited in the Vietnam War. However, the tragedy of Lee's death links the mastery of his style of movement with the ultimate limits of the human body and ties the ars violentiae to death. Between the activity of violence and the passivity of death, Lee's movement-image points to the inextricability of violence and death, but also the incommensurability between the two—the inability of violence to make sense of death, and ultimately the failure of the body mastered to take the place of the body incontinent.

Bruce Lee as Movement-Image: *Enter the Dragon* (1973)

You know how after you watch a kung fu movie, you feel like you're a mad motherfucker? You go outside and kick trash cans and maybe you fight your friends, because you feel like nothing can stop you, like you're Bruce Lee? Well, tonight you're all going *to watch Bruce Lee*. And tomorrow you're all going to pass that test, because you're going *to be Bruce Lee*.

—Sergeant Vasques, drill instructor

Given the numerous and ardent fan cultures of impersonation surrounding figures such as Marilyn Monroe, James Dean, and Elvis Presley, the cult surrounding Bruce Lee would seem to be no different. But becoming Bruce Lee seems to entail a form of mimesis different from simply copying Lee's awkward bowl haircut, chiseled musculature, or comic accent. Writing in *Jump Cut* on martial arts action films, Aaron Anderson relates an anecdote from when he was in basic training in the military. The night before a big physical training test, Anderson's drill instructor screened *Enter the Dragon* and instructed his students to "be Bruce Lee."[5] While Anderson uses his anecdote to critique the overemphasis on static bodily physique in action genre criticism, what Yvonne Tasker has termed "musculinity,"[6] his example also reveals the difficulty of isolating what Bruce Lee is. When one identifies with, imitates, impersonates Bruce Lee, what exactly is this object of mimesis?

The enigmatic nature of the command to "be Bruce Lee" importantly reveals just how being Bruce Lee differs from impersonating stars such as Elvis or Marilyn. As Eric Lott explains in his ethnographic study of Elvis impersonators, all celebrity impersonation relies upon an Oedipal contradiction between desire and identification, in which "appreciation, deference, spectatorship, and emulation compete with inhabitation, aggression, usurpation, and vampirism."[7] To mimic a star is to elevate that star into an impossible ideal of adoration at the same time that one attempts to absorb or partake in some of that celebrity and social status by proxy. Thus to "be Elvis" is to become someone other than oneself, often by adopting the ostentatious clothing and hairstyle that signified Elvis's status as a celebrity. However, the point of "being Bruce Lee," as Anderson argues, is not simply to shape one's body into Lee's image or to copy Lee's mode of dress, hairstyle, or facial expressions—none of which Anderson and his fellow recruits even thought to imitate. (Imagine the absurdity of these recruits showing up for their physical training dressed in Bruce Lee yellowface!) Rather it is to bodily inhabit the "physical virtuosity" which Lee's film image presents, but within the physical and visual parameters of one's own body-image.[8]

Even more complicated for potential Bruce Lees, his physical virtuosity cannot be reduced to a simple catalogue of specific movements and gestures, although there are many such gestures that became associated with him, such as the "one-inch punch" he demonstrated at the Long Beach International Karate Tournament in 1964, the animalistic yells that punctuated *Enter the Dragon*, and the flying high kick that adorned American advertisements for *Fists of Fury*. The difficulty of impersonating Lee became apparent in a set of open auditions for a Bruce Lee look-alike held in Los Angeles in April 1975 by the director Robert Clouse for a potential biopic, *Bruce Lee: His Life and Legend*. Although five hundred people of all races, genders, ages, and shapes turned out for the auditions, flanked by larger-than-life film stills of Lee posted on the walls of the studio, very few were able to perform their movements quickly enough or with adequate control in the thirty seconds given to them.[9] Responding to the inadequacy of Lee impersonators, a South Korean film company proposed in the first decade of the twenty-first century to "resurrect" Lee through computer animation for a live-action film tentatively titled "Dragon Warrior."[10] But as evidenced by one fan's complaints about a video game, *Quest of the Dragon* (2002), also based on a computer-animated Bruce Lee, even modern CGI technology may be inadequate to capture his elusive aura: "Any Bruce Lee fan worth his salt knows that the Dragon has a certain style to his movements. There is that noticeable swagger that is the essence of Bruce Lee. This game has none of that. The only way you know that the character is supposed to be Bruce Lee is by the clothing and a face that bears a resemblance to him."[11] This quality of movement, which this fan terms a "style," describes a relationship between the body and its movements, an ability to inhabit the body through such movements. Hence the object of mimesis is not a static image, Bruce Lee frozen in midmovement on a movie poster, but rather a dynamic series of motions, strung together by a particular visual syntax that makes such moving pictures recognizable *as* Bruce Lee. As a result Bruce Lee is not so much a character, a psychological depth, or a mere visual icon, as he is a potential for movement and agency.

This is not to naturalize the movements of Bruce Lee, for they are first and foremost filmic representations of movement. As much as fans idolize him as the quintessential street fighter, his moves were not unified actions carried out in real life, but highly stylized movements reassembled into a whole in film through careful montage. One of Lee's major contributions to the martial arts action genre was an understanding of how fight scenes should be choreographed, framed, and edited. Hong Kong martial arts films of the 1960s were characterized by what Sek Kei called "credible exaggeration," using special effects such as trampolines and wires to portray hyperbolized versions of ordinary actions such as kicking and jumping, but staying within the bounds of cause and effect in the physical world.[12] In contrast Hsiung-Ping Chiao describes Lee as attempting to de-emphasize such "Oriental fantasies" and visual illusions in favor of "western realism," evidenced by long shots showing the completion of movements without excessive editing to hide the use of special effects.[13] In the opening fight scene of *Enter the Dragon*, Lee and a fellow Shaolin student (played by Sammo Hung) spar before their teacher and fellow monks. While the monks in the background are dressed in exotic costumes, Lee and Hung wear only tight black briefs, cloth shoes, and boxing gloves, their exposed bodies not only showcasing Lee's tight musculature (in contrast to Hung's chubbiness) but also testifying to the lack of wire harnesses and padding that might make the sparring seem artificial and aligning the fight with Western-style sports. The fight concludes in a fifteen-second long shot that also highlights the direct bodily contact between Lee and Hung, as Lee deflects Hung's kicks and flips him to the ground three times before forcing him to submit with a judo-style armbar.[14]

Yet Lee's realism is not the same as the Bazinian total reality created through the enlargement of the frame and the absence of editing. Lee's long shots and long takes were meant to focus on the reality of the body as it accomplishes these movements without the aid of trampolines, wires, or other special effects, but it did not diminish the artificiality of the movements as products of intense planning and detailed choreography. Choreography is by no means opposed to editing and montage, for the timing of martial arts movements, even within a single shot, creates a music-like rhythm that the film critic Stuart Kaminsky likened to dance in the 1970s.[15] In the martial arts film, choreography assists montage in organizing temporal relations. The rhythm of linked shots often accentuates the rhythm of movements within shots. A review of Fists of Fury (1971) referred to Lee's fight scenes as "balletic fisticuffs," recalling earlier descriptions of Peckinpah's The Wild Bunch as a "blood ballet," but in Lee's case it is his body, not the fluids ejecting from his body, that star in this ballet.[16] Even as a display of violence, Lee's martial arts movements emphasize his volitional mastery over his body rather than evidencing a lack of control usually associated with the display of aggression or anger. Lee commented on the difference between violence and action in his films:

> I don't call the fighting in my films violence. I call it action. Any action film borders somewhere between reality and fantasy. If I were to be completely realistic, you would call me a bloody violent man. I would simply destroy my opponent by tearing him apart or ripping his guts out. I wouldn't do it artistically. . . .
>
> In a way I perhaps anesthetize violence by the way I move my body so that the audience calls it, not violence, but body control.[17]

The artifice of Lee's "artistic" violence not only makes the body and its movements more visible, but emphasizes the body's "control" over its own motions. Lee aligns the dichotomy between art and reality with a similar binary between orderly and chaotic bodily movement, implying that real violence leads to a naturalistic chaos while action lies in the orderly realm of art and culture.

Hence Lee's description of action and body control fits right into Deleuze's conception of the movement-image as the dominant element of narrative cinema. Through techniques such as continuity editing and point of view, narrative cinema reinforces the sense that movement derives from stable actors executing identifiable actions within a framework of linear, causal time. In fact by fetishizing the complexity of movement, Lee's martial arts films intensify the fantasy of agency that the movement-image propagates. As implied by Lee's use of the term "body control," actions not only begin but also end in that same body, a body that is both subject and object of the act, without any other mechanical or technological elements intervening. This narcissistic circuit is reflected in the prevalence of shots of Lee performing actions alone, his opponent either absent or off-screen. In *Enter the Dragon* he plays a character simply named Lee, collapsing the difference between the diegetic persona and the star. The film ends with Lee fighting in a hall of mirrors, which reflect his movements from multiple angles and magnify our gaze on his body as a seat of action. This multiplication of Lee as movement-image does not even allow for a second body, that of the villain Han (played by Shih Kien, a famous Hong Kong swordplay star of the 1960s), to register as the primary destination for Lee's strikes and blows. Rather these actions are directed toward the camera alone, for the audience's viewing pleasure. The object of our focus is an image that becomes iconic of Lee: his naked, muscular torso. This image exposes Lee to the kind of eroticized gaze usually associated with the female body in Hollywood cinema. The film critic Tony Rayns has referred to Lee's mirror scenes as "onanistic," revealing both Lee's libidinal investment in his own body as well as our libidinal investment in his movement-image.[18] Desire and identification blend together: we not only want to "be Bruce"; we also want to "have Bruce," to possess that body. Even if most fan discourses, like Anderson's basic training anecdote, suppress the threat of queer sexuality in this scenario by conflating desire and identification, such desires are made explicit in responses such as Lynne Chan's trans-gendered Lee impersonator, "JJ Chinois" or Nguyen Tan Hoang's fantasy of Bruce Lee encountering the gay porn star "Brandon Lee."[19]

But Lee's naked torso in *Enter the Dragon* is a difficult object of identification and desire, since it is also a sadomasochistic image of suffering transformed after the fact into mastery. Han, who is stalking Lee in this scene, wields a prosthetic hand that has been fashioned into a set of razor-sharp claws—a violation of the ethic of unaided bodily mastery in Lee's martial arts films, which ultimately condemns Han to failure. As Han and Lee fly past each other in a slow-motion confrontation, Han's mechanical claw slashes Lee across his abdomen. In an infamous gesture Lee touches his hand to his wound and lifts it to his mouth to taste his own blood (fig. 39). In effect Lee fortifies himself for his subsequent attack by consuming himself, literally converting the abject fruits of his bodily suffering into the source of his bodily mastery. Even more directly than the scenes of arms and fists being forged into weapons in films like *Deep Thrust—Hand of Death*, this movement-image of Bruce Lee posits a cycle of wounding and self-fortification that feeds upon the body in a

39. Wounded on his abdomen by a blow from Han's (Shih Kien) metal claw, Lee (Bruce Lee) tastes his own blood before retaliating and eventually killing Han. Frame enlargement from *Enter the Dragon*.

potentially infinite loop. Unlike the images of wounding from the Vietnam War, this cycle offers a regenerative fantasy in which the body confronts violence but never succumbs to it—the ultimate image of mastery.

The discourse of volition and self-control associated with Lee's body appears to be aligned with the temporal relations that his movement-image presents and manages. Yet the relation between filmic time and historical time is disrupted by Lee's death, which also challenges the discourse of bodily control and the fantasy of infinite regeneration. What I term "historical time" refers not only to time outside the film, but also to what phenomenologists focus on as the finite temporality tied up in the duration of the human body in life.[20] In death the body changes from a seat of volitional movement articulating its own relationship to time, to brute inanimate matter that exists outside of historical time. Although Lee's action films narrativize the results of intentional action upon the world around him, his death acts as an absolute limit to the powers of action. Lee died only a month before the theatrical release of *Enter the Dragon*, in the midst of the publicity campaign for the film, and it was difficult for Warner Brothers to sustain a narrative of invincibility and self-control when his death contradicted the fantasy of mastery perpetuated by his films. Like the paralysis engendered by "Saigon Execution" and photographs of the My Lai massacre, Lee's death also provoked a crisis in the action-image, disrupting the ability of the martial arts film genre to repair the damage done by the Vietnam War. *Enter the Dragon* and *Return of the Dragon*, the two films released in the U.S. after Lee's death, appear as spectral images, movement-images no longer tied to a body-subject that can guarantee their wholeness.

Even the subsequent stories of Lee's life were fundamentally structured

punches, and leg exercises and kicking. He also did sit-ups and leg raises, but the main benefit derived from the simple act of continually practicing. He was constantly kicking and punching—everything, in fact, depended upon repetition as with a pianist or other musician who spends hours and hours every day practicing the same notes. Gradually, he came to develop several pieces of equipment that he hoped would help him. I often saw him sit down and draw ideas for special equipment on a piece of paper; he would then get somebody to build the apparatus. He constantly sought more *realistic* equipment, for heavy bags and dummies, after all, cannot fight back. So he tried to develop equipment that would increase reaction speed—equipment that would not come back at him in a set pattern but from different angles, forcing him to change, move, be aware, active. But even the best equipment cannot simulate real combat conditions—which is why he did as much unrehearsed sparring as possible.

Bruce was never orthodox—he was always the innovator; the skeptic; the iconoclast. Right from the beginning, for example, he set his face against the kind of rankings that exist in karate. A few years later, when he had become a nationwide celebrity, he was asked by an interviewer if there were any rankings in gung fu. He

77

40. A flipbook of images of Bruce Lee taken from *Enter the Dragon*, from Linda Lee's *Bruce Lee: The Man Only I Knew.*

around his death. The biography *Bruce Lee: The Man Only I Knew*, published soon after his death by his widow, Linda, is as much a writing of his death as of his life, beginning and ending with the story of how Lee died. The relation between death and Lee's movement-image is uncannily invoked by the flipbook contained at the center of this biography. It offers a sequence of grainy, still images from *Enter the Dragon* accompanied by the instructions, "Turn the book sideways. Hold the binding in your left hand. Flip the pages with your right thumb, and watch BRUCE LEE FIGHT AGAIN!" (fig. 40).[21] This sequence of images recalls the "cinematographic illusion" which Deleuze critiqued as deriving the semblance of movement from essentially "immobile segments": "the regulated transition from one form to another, that is, an order of *poses* or privileged instants, as in a dance."[22] Such "privileged instants" were frequently deployed in martial arts instruction manuals such as Lee's own *Chinese Gung Fu*, in the form of still photographs, sometimes marked by hand-drawn arrows, that distilled the complexity of movement into poses that could be more easily imitated.[23] However, in this flipbook the still images are not derived from deliberately held poses but are film stills extracted from a dynamic sequence in which Lee defends himself from and strikes down twelve attackers in a row. Although the flipbook purports to resurrect Lee by reanimating his movement-image at a moment of triumph, it actually illustrates the fundamental dissolution of that movement-image back into immobility and passivity. The reanimation of the immobilized body of Bruce Lee is poignant precisely because he cannot "fight again."

As Jacques Lacan described the act of mourning, "Only insofar as the object of . . . desire has become an impossible object can it become once more the object of his desire."[24] Being Bruce Lee, having Bruce Lee—this love object is also a lost object, a desire made impossible by death, but nonetheless built into the mimetic imperative surrounding his movement-image. Lee's star persona serves to focus the potential for self-mastery and self-making represented in the martial arts genre as a whole, but his particular relationship to violence and death reminds us of how the body exceeds the conscious project of self-making. As many fans point out, Lee's early death recast him as a martyr or saint, magnifying the spiritual and religious associations of the martial arts themselves. Being dead, his persona seems to reside outside of historical time and the time of the individual, and instead enters the temporality of the mythic or epic: Bruce Lee, The Legend (1977), as one documentary frames it. Lee's death leaves what the film critic Kwai-Cheung Lo poetically calls "the hole punched out by Bruce Lee's body."[25] For Lacan death and loss create just such a hole, a gap in the Real which sets into motion the process of mourning to repair the corresponding gap in the Symbolic. If Lee's body leaves behind a hole, a literal absence in the material world, then we attempt to fill that hole with new signifiers—films, images, narratives, even actors—in hopes of making the signifying chain whole again.

Quantitatively speaking, Lee's posthumous film career was even more prolific than the work he created during his lifetime. The vast majority of the films made to mourn Lee had little connection to him, and often to humorous effect: thinly veiled body doubles to substitute for Lee, sensationalist "documentaries" or biographies, and blatant citations of Lee's previous images and film narratives. The low-budget production values and exploitive character of these films, fictional and factual alike, led some fans to coin the term "Bruceploitation," recalling both the sexploitation and blaxploitation genres.[26] Bemoaning the critical neglect of this large and colorful genre, Brian Hu asserts, "If we are to understand Bruce Lee's star persona, we must consider 'Bruce Lee' not only as an individual who starred in a discrete number of films, but as a star discourse that lived on, though the actor did not."[27] Paradoxically nearly all of these films deviated from the various qualities of Lee's movement-image outlined in the previous section, many devolving into a yellowface minstrelsy seeming to take advantage of non-Asian fans' inability to distinguish among little yellow fighting machines. Lee becomes the Oedipal father for the Hong

Kong martial arts genre, waiting to be displaced by Sammo Hung in *Enter the Fat Dragon* (1978) or Jackie Chan in *New Fist of Fury* (1976). In *Bruce Lee Fights Back from the Grave* (1976) his death gives birth to the film, as the opening scene begins with lightning striking Lee's grave and the actor Bruce K. L. Lea jumping out of it. Although Lea's character bears no resemblance to Lee, he is literally burdened with death, carrying the ashes of a former teacher in a large box hanging from his neck for nearly half of the film. The stage names of those who attempted to fill the hole left by Lee cleverly demonstrate their slippage from the original signifier: Bruce Li, Bruce Le, Bruce Lea, Bruce Leong, Bruce Rhee.[28] In the aptly named *The Clones of Bruce Lee* (1977) an entire pantheon of Bruce Lee imitators—Bruce Le, Dragon Lee, Bruce Lai, and Bruce Thai—is ostensibly cloned from Lee's DNA in order to combat international crime syndicates. At one point the clones even fight one another, literalizing the battle over Lee's proper name.

arts found themselves listening to him intently.' Luckily Ed Parker filmed Bruce's demonstration—this was to prove a fortunate break.

In the audience that evening was a Hollywood hair stylist named Jay Sebring—later among the victims of the Manson gang when they invaded film director Roman Polanski's home and murdered his wife, Sharon Tate, and other guests. Sebring, who later became a good friend of Bruce's and was instrumental in introducing him to Steve McQueen, one of the first of Bruce's 'celebrity' students (Roman Polanski became another) was highly impressed with Bruce's vitality and presence and, when, a few months later, he was cutting the hair of a TV producer called William Dozier, he mentioned Bruce's name. Dozier had said he was looking for someone to play the role of Charlie Chan's number one son in a new TV series he was planning. Jay mentioned that he had seen Bruce in action and believed Dozier should seriously consider him. He thought he had definite charisma, had a great sense of humor and ought to come across to audiences very well. Dozier took Jay's tip and at once got in touch with Ed Parker, who took his film of Bruce's demonstration over to the 20th Century-Fox studios. Dozier liked what he saw and immediately put in a call to our home in Oakland.

79

The plentitude of Lee-like bodies and films might even lull one into forgetting that Bruce Lee had died in the first place, leaving one unable to work through the trauma of his passing. But as Laplanche reminds us, mourning cannot so easily compensate for the death of a loved one. As the scenario of haunting suggests, we are confronted by the enigma of the (dead) other, confounding the efforts to close the gap left by his absence. The ghost that floats up in his place is an absent presence, tormenting those left behind with questions of unfinished desires: "What does the dead person want? What does he want of me? What did he want to say to me?"[29] Mourning shades into melancholia, as the enigma of the ghost allows us to preserve the lost object by transforming this riddle into a ritual of fulfilling his last wishes. For what could Bruce Lee want more than to "fight again"? As we incorporate the lost object of Bruce Lee into ourselves—an uncanny version of "being Bruce Lee"—our desire *for* the dead becomes the desires *of* the dead, taken as our own desires. It is love for Bruce Lee that fuels the drive to complete the movement-images that have been stilled by his premature death. No other celebrity cult of impersonation has inspired such a morbid drive, obsessed not only with remembering the dead celebrity in his pastness but also resurrecting that celebrity in an eternal present. However, the opacity of the dead resists such easy closure, throwing us back to what Laplanche has called the "otherness of the other."[30] The lost body of Bruce Lee hangs heavily on the attempt to reanimate his movement-image, casting its inertia upon the fantasies of power and control we may wish to dream in his place.

Playing with Death: *Game of Death* (1978)

John Barry has written some good music that might work if Jan Spears' script or Robert Clouse's direction could compensate for the fact that *Bruce Lee was simply not alive to complete the picture*. Unfortunately Lee died back in 1973 in the midst of making the film and *no amount of doctoring could hide it*. Obviously, there were a number of people who thought they could.

—"Review: Game of Death," Variety, 13 June 1979 (my emphasis)

Interviewer: Won't it be obvious that it's someone else playing Bruce Lee?
Ronney Kurtainbaum: Film reality, my man, it's made in the editing room, you
know? Hey, Eisenstein, you know, he taught us that with associative editing, and
that was fifty years ago! We're only limited by our own imaginations.

—Finishing the Game: The Search for a New Bruce Lee (2007)

Tantalizingly Lee left behind an unfinished project that would reignite the energies of fans and filmmakers alike, a project uncannily titled *Game of Death*. Lee conceived of the project after he finished *Return of the Dragon* in 1972 and had begun filming a few fight scenes when he was interrupted with the opportunity to make *Enter the Dragon*. In fact the project was so well known that rumors circulated that Lee's death was simply a publicity stunt to promote *Game of Death*.[31] Because of these circumstances, as well as the provocative title of the project, *Game of Death* became a phantasmatic object for those mourning Lee's death, offering both a potential narrative with which to make sense of his passing and an actual commodity that would continue to generate surplus value from Lee's aura. While many Bruceploitation films and clones would attempt to do the same, *Game of Death* had a different status within the genre, seeming to carry the direct imprimatur of Lee's authorial hand as well as eagerly awaited, previously unseen indexical movement-images of Lee himself. Yet the existence of Lee's footage would also complicate the completion of this film, as any Lee double willing to take on the role would be literally haunted by Lee's presence in the film, bearing the burden of unfavorable comparisons with the late martial arts master as well as the difficulty of merging one's own movement-image with that of another's. Even the most high-profile and financially successful of these attempts, *Game of Death* (1978, released in the U.S. in 1979), would be plagued by the problem of Lee's absence, which, as one reviewer sardonically pointed out, "no amount of doctoring could hide." Justin Lin would parody this blithe disregard for continuity and realism in his mockumentary *Finishing the Game: The Search for a New Bruce Lee* (2007). A fictional young director, Ronney Kurtainbaum, naïvely explains away these continuity errors as Eisensteinian "associative editing," blaming the conventional filmgoer for a lack of "imagination." In fact the tagline for the advertising campaign for *Game of Death* invited us to watch as "Bruce Lee challenges the underworld to a 'Game of Death'" in the present tense, as if Lee had never died.[32]

what thoroughness and business acumen Bruce had set about the job of making his *kwoon* a success. A student of psychology, he had an instinctive awareness of the kind of thing that would attract customers. He made selling points of the exclusivity of his *kwoon*—that it was limited to honored members only; that it was the only one of its kind in the world; that all lessons were personalized and so on. He listed the motives for taking lessons in kung fu—for good health, for securing the admiration of others, for amusement, self-improvement and, above all, peace of mind. He was able to provide prospective customers with statistics of crimes such as mugging and rape and other assaults and asked, 'What would *you* do if and when you are attacked? What *can* you do when your loved ones are with you during an unprovoked attack?'

There was never any question but that as American violence increased and more and more men and women thought about equipping themselves with some method of self-defense, that Bruce and James could have made a great deal of money. But to Bruce, this would have meant prostituting his art. He was determined to proceed along the lines he had originally envisaged; that is, to teach every class himself, so far as possible, realizing that it was necessary that each pupil understand that the

81

At the same time *Game of Death* offered a unique opportunity for the Bruceploitation genre to register Lee's death, not simply as a fact to be represented, but as an enigma that would reveal cinema's relationship with temporality, both historical and personal. *Game of Death* provides a vision of Deleuze's time-image: a "direct" image of time that troubles the organic unities of agency, narrative, and causality that governed the "indirect" presentation of time in the movement-image.[33] As Deleuze explains, the time-image arises when "time ceases to be derived from the movement, it appears in itself and itself gives rise to *false movements*. Hence the importance of *false continuity* in modern cinema: the images are no longer linked by rational cuts and continuity, but are relinked by means of false continuity and irrational cuts."[34] In false continuity the use of montage does not simply assert the wholeness of movement across time, but allows for linkages that emphasize nonchronological or causal relations, such as those of memory, thought, desire. Thus as if anticipating Justin Lin's parody, Deleuze borrows from Eisenstein the phrase "impossible continuity shots," drawing upon Eisenstein's own theory of montage as a technique that allows for the juxtaposition of radically different elements in the service of creating the new.[35] While Deleuze generally associates the time-image with avant-garde or auteurist cinema that deliberately experiments with the conventions of classical Hollywood film—for example, the work of Godard, Renais, Ozu, Kubrick, Welles, and Rossellini—the time-images of *Game of Death* emerge from the body of a seemingly conventional Hollywood action film, almost as if against the will of its creators. The use of multiple body doubles, convoluted nested stories, and extensive cross-cutting between different film texts in *Game of Death* foregrounds a false continuity that subverts the narrative's attempt to make Lee, and his unfinished film, whole again.

Lee had originally conceived *Game of Death* to demonstrate the essence of his "Jeet Kun Do" (way of the intercepting fist) method, showing off the flexibility and hybridity of his fighting style against masters mired in the rules and traditions of their own martial arts schools. The narrative outline he left behind describes his character fighting his way through a multilevel pagoda, each level guarded by a different martial artist using a different style. In the scenes he filmed before his death, the guards are played by Dan Insanto, a Filipino *escrima* fighter; Chi Hon Joi, a Korean hapkido expert; and Kareem Abdul-Jabbar, a seven-foot-two basketball player and former student of Lee's, portraying a "giant who fights unpredictably."[36] In these scenes Lee wears a striking, bright yellow jumpsuit rather than his usual silken kung fu uniform in order to emphasize his transcendence of traditional martial arts styles and claim a modern, American-influenced individualism. Although he left behind a hundred-page working script and four hours of rushes and other footage, the production in 1978 discarded all but eleven minutes of his film, replacing the rest with a generic action plot reminiscent of a second-rate James Bond film. Like Dr. Frankenstein, the director Robert Clouse and the coproducer Raymond Chow (both of whom were involved in *Enter the Dragon*) dismember the bodies of several films—not only Lee's *Game*, but also significant portions of *Return of the Dragon* and *The Chinese Connection*, all films well known to fans—in order to assemble this *Game*. To reanimate Lee, Clouse uses three body doubles: a Korean martial artist named Kim Tai Chong, who is credited for the fight scenes, but also two uncredited actors, a Hong Kong martial arts actor, Yuen Biao, to double Kim for acrobatic scenes, and a Hong Kong businessman named Chen Yao-Po for a few dialogue scenes.[37] Hence the monster produced by these procedures is both a film body, an aggregate text masquerading as an organic whole, and Lee's body, a split identity held together by the name "Billy Lo" in the new narrative.

In the plot of Clouse's *Game* Billy Lo, like Bruce Lee, is a martial artist and actor working on a film that turns out to be *Return of the Dragon*, featuring a famous fight scene between Lee and Chuck Norris, which is being "filmed" in the opening scene. However, unlike Lee, Lo is being harassed by a mafia-like crime syndicate led by Dr. Land (Dean Jagger). This "underworld," as the ads characterize the syndicate, outlines a theme of death and resurrection, presenting the diegetic space of *Game of Death* as a Hades for Bruce Lee and his body doubles to traverse and overcome, even while avoiding explicit reference to Lee's extradiegetic death. When Lo refuses to pay protection money the underworld sets out to harass his white American girlfriend, Ann Morris (Colleen Camp)—a character modeled on Lee's wife, Linda Emery—and even tries to kill Lo on the set of another of his movies, modeled on and using clips from the final scene of *The Chinese Connection*. After Lo

thereby ceases to expand or to grow. He is a mechanical robot, a product of thousands of years of propaganda and conditioning. One must be uninfluenced and die to one's conditioning in order to be aware of the totally fresh, totally new. Because reality changes every moment, even as I say it.'

Many of these realizations sprang from his reading and subsequent understanding of the forces of nature; others were the product of his own experiences. Once he realized the physical limitations of the Wing Chum style, he rapidly began to branch out, to explore, to test new movements, to re-think the traditional styles. He did not do this by jumping about from style to style or instructor to instructor, but rather by searching inwardly for the best within himself, rejecting the unsuitable and retaining the appropriate. He may have found this easier than most people because he had always felt a personal obligation to himself to be the best at whatever he did—not the biggest or most successful—but rather to express himself to the highest degree of which he was capable. His goal was never to be wealthy or famous but to produce quality work. And, in the end, he managed to arrange his life so that it became like his—Jeet Kune Do—simple, direct, effective. In fighting he achieved this by never being bound by rules or limitations—indeed, he made the slogan of his

83

is injured, he and his journalist friend, Jim Marshall (Gig Young), decide to fake his death (here the film uses scenes from Lee's actual funeral) so that Lo can continue to investigate the crime syndicate and take his revenge. This plot twist exploits the mysterious circumstances that surrounded Lee's death, which even today are the subject of debate; although his autopsy report listed the cause of death as a fatal drug allergy, many fans put forward theories far less mundane, and more "oriental." (Among the theories that Alex Ben Block's sensationalistic biography enumerates: that Lee was murdered by jealous movie business people; that Lee was poisoned by Japanese ninjas; that Lee was given a "Chinese karate death touch" on his nerve points; that Lee received the "Malaysian vibrating palm" technique, which caused a delayed death; even that Lee was still alive, using his death as a publicity stunt to promote his films.)[38] To bridge this narrative with Lee's footage, Clouse sends a motorcycle gang in yellow jumpsuits after Lo. Lo kills his assailants and eventually dons one of their yellow jumpsuits as a disguise. He finally seeks out Dr. Land at the top of his multistory Chinese restaurant and criminal headquarters, dispatching three sets of guards on each floor of the restaurant—the scenes featuring Insanto, Chi, and Abdul-Jabbar that were taken from Lee's orphaned footage.

By using footage from Lee's films and basing the plot on his biographical details, Clouse draws upon an extradiegetic, collective memory of Lee's movement-image to infuse the character of Billy Lo with new life, making the fine print at the end of the opening credits particularly ironic: "The characters and incidents portrayed and the names used herein are fictitious, and any similarity to the name, character or history of any persons is entirely coincidental and unintentional." But Billy Lo is not simply Bruce Lee, reanimated. The "realness" of Billy Lo as a character oscillates between the visual fetish of Bruce Lee and the lack of equivalence with its replacement, (usually) Kim Tai Chong, and is often framed through the metafilmic device of a film being created within the film we are watching. An example of this oscillation and framing appears in the manipulation of shot/reverse shot sequences between Billy Lo and other characters. The first shot to appear after the opening credits is an old fight sequence between Lee and Norris taken from *Return of the Dragon*, the last film Lee was seen in by American audiences. The six years between Lee's death and *Game* are collapsed in this opening, with *Game* seeming to pick up the thread of Lee's life where he left off at death. This is immediately followed by a (new) shot of a film crew and camera, reframing this old footage as a movement-image being created anew by this diegetic apparatus. But the fissures in the continuity of this old movement-image appear as soon as Kim takes over for Lee. A lighting fixture drops to the floor, almost striking Kim, and he looks up, his back to the camera. The very next shot, presumably a reaction shot, shows not Kim's but Lee's face looking up (with the backdrop of *Return*'s outdoor location, the Roman Colosseum, surrounded by blue skies), followed by a point-of-view shot of the (indoor) ceiling from which the fixture dropped. Although this sequence seems to follow the grammar of continuity editing, the false continuity between the old, reused footage and the new footage is readily apparent, a humorous disjuncture that makes this film a cult favorite. As one reviewer put it, "The name of the real game in this movie is which Bruce Lee is really Bruce Lee?"[39]

However, the premise of this question is suspect, presuming the existence of a real Bruce Lee to uncover. The relationship between Lee and Kim is not simply reducible to that of original and copy. Kim can step into the Lee persona only through the intermediary of Billy Lo. Taken as a visual and narrative creation, Lo is literally a split subject, split by the doubling of this role by two actors: Lo/Lee and Lo/Kim (and even more in other scenes). Lo/Lee gives a face to this subject, appearing mainly in facial close-ups and frontal medium-shots, but he almost never speaks. Lo/Kim provides a voice for this subject, interacting with other characters in shot/reverse shot sequences, yet he is rarely seen, often filmed from behind or hidden beneath oversized sunglasses or disguises such as a fake beard. The living body of Kim remains faceless, while the visage of Lee hovers over his image like a death mask. But rather than viewing the lack of continuity between Lo/Lee and Lo/Kim as a careless error or simply the product of bad filmmaking, it is possible to see the splitting of Billy Lo as revealing the splitting of time itself, giving rise to what Deleuze celebrates as a "labyrinth of time": a temporality both Borgesian and Leibnizian, "passing through *incompossible presents*, returning to *not-necessarily true pasts*."[40] Like the multiple worlds of Leibniz's philosophy, cinema does not simply record what has happened, but gives rise as well to what has not, cannot, or will not happen. False continuity participates in the process of becoming and the creation of the new, which Deleuze cele-

realized that I had been preventing myself from achieving my best by being all tensed up and tightened up. The first thing I learned was to free myself from mental tension.'

Many of his students —among them were well-known martial artists and national karate champions in their own right—were convinced that Bruce had a sixth sense. Louis Delgado once described Bruce as 'quite baffling—almost as though he had ESP'. I know that I myself was continually impressed by Bruce's perceptions; I often used to try to catch him off-guard by making a quick movement when he seemed to be immersed in a book or even watching TV, but I always failed. Yet Bruce himself pooh-poohed such nonsense. He told his students, 'Don't disregard your five natural senses in the search for a so-called sixth. Just develop your five natural senses.' He emphasized that all he had done personally was to raise his own senses to their highest pitch.

Danny Inosanto makes the point that Bruce 'really set new standards. He was like a Roger Bannister—like an Einstein, Edison or Leonardo, if you like, so far as the martial arts were concerned.'

Another friend insists, 'Bruce was never pompous, either. Oh, sure, he had human weaknesses—like he wanted admiration and he wanted respect. But he got

85

brates as the "powers of the false."[41] The coexistence of impossible temporalities in *Game*—Bruce Lee is dead, Bruce Lee is alive—also produces the multiplicity of subjects parading beneath the name of Billy Lo. Thus in the place of the unified subjects whose agency grounds the movement-image, the false continuity of the time-image produces "an irreducible multiplicity, 'I is another' [*Je est un autre*] has replaced Ego = Ego."[42]

This is not to say that *Game* has embraced the false continuity of the time-image intentionally. After all the film is meant to be a commodity, a genre film that strives to fade into its genre rather than break out of it as an exception. What strikes me as most interesting about *Game*, though, is the way it is forced to confront the *multiplicity* of Billy Lo and the *incompossibility* of its narrative, simply through the fact of Bruce Lee's death. Like "Saigon Execution," *Game* registers death on both a formal and a representational level: the formal through the time-images generated out of its false continuity, and the representational through its narratives of attempted murder, faked deaths, and revenge killings. However, unlike "Saigon Execution," *Game* does not simply show the breakdown of the movement-image into stillness and paralysis, but creates new images of time that show the generativity of death. Movement does not freeze in *Game* because the actions it represents are ethically intolerable, as with "Saigon Execution." Rather it becomes "false," "aberrant" movement, and this reflects the absurdity of continuing the fantasies of mastery and control that Bruce Lee represented as a living movement-image.[43] The powers of the false in *Game* do not mourn Bruce Lee, nor do they resurrect him; they in fact create a Lee that is simultaneously real *and* fake, alive *and* dead. This differentiates *Game* from films such as *Dragon: The Bruce Lee Story* (1993), in which Lee appears as a coherent subject, but at the cost of being relegated to the past as a dead object. In *Game* the Bruce Lee of the past coexists with a Bruce Lee that never existed, all taking place under the exigencies of a present in which Bruce Lee is dead, illustrating Deleuze's attempt with the time-image to "[bring] together the before and the after in a becoming, instead of separating them."[44]

The movement-image does not only break down into the time-image through violations of continuity editing. *Game* is rife with dead objects—a corpse in a funeral, a life-size cardboard figure masquerading as Lee, a photograph of Lee defaced by Kim with a black marker, and a ceramic head placed in a false grave—that mimic the stillness of the freeze-frames of "Saigon Execution," but they do so within moving shots in which time continues to flow. These objects are meant to stand in for Lee/Lo, but in ways that supplement and exceed the labor put in by Kim Tai Chong and the other body doubles. The scene in which the cardboard cutout appears utilizes this dead object in the midst of moving images from both Lee and Kim, all of which participate in the illusion that Bruce Lee is interacting with another character. After the opening "accident" that threatens Lo's life, Steiner (Hugh O'Brien) from the crime syndicate appears in Lo's dressing room to threaten him. At first we see Lo/Kim walking into his dressing room with his back to us. In the very next shot Lo/Lee is addressing Steiner from the front, with the camera doing a 180-degree turn. Likewise the medium shot which establishes Steiner and Lo/Kim in the same room shows Lo/Kim with his back toward Steiner, yet the conversation features shot/reverse shot sequences between Steiner and Lo/Lee as if they were facing one another. Rather than reinforcing Billy Lo as a center from which these actions emanate, these cuts decenter him, chopping up the space of the dressing room and literally oscillating from one implicit camera position to another. The culminating shot is an infamous one, in which Steiner points his blade at a life-size cardboard cutout of Lo/Lee (fig. 41 on p. 234). Presumably the lack of technology to combine a moving Lee with other characters led to this nonsensical substitution. However, it is interesting that the desire to place Lee in the same physical space as another actor overrides the violation of realism in this shot, creating an inadvertently comic Brechtian effect. Although the cardboard figure resembles Lee more closely than Kim, it completely lacks any potential for movement, and as such signifies the lack of Bruce Lee in this film even more strongly than the presence of Kim, the "fake" Lee.

Even in its recycling of previous footage of Lee *Game* confronts the formal dilemma of the breakdown of the movement-image as these old images are placed into new temporal contexts. *Game* aligns Lo's character with Lee's own film career, presenting Lee's finished films as Lo's works in progress. The film-within-a-film motif is again used when the syndicate tries to assassinate Billy Lo. The scene which Billy is ostensibly filming is the final scene from *The Chinese Connection*, the strongest statement of cultural nationalism among Lee's four films.[45] *The Chinese Connection* famously ends with a freeze frame of Lee, in midleap toward the camera, at the

Based on one of the most successful American radio serials of the 1930s, *The Green Hornet* was intended to show the exploits of Britt Reid, a crusading newspaper editor-publisher who donned green clothes at night and turned crimefighter. As Kato, his manservant and assistant, Bruce was to catapult to stardom overnight in America. Later Bruce cracked to a newspaper interviewer: 'The only reason I ever got that job was because I was the only Chinaman in all California who could pronounce Britt Reid.'

SIX

The Green Hornet was destined to become one of the more forgettable shows on American TV—which may be saying a lot. Yet even before the show premiered, it became clear that if any person or anything about it had a chance of capturing the public imagination, it was Bruce and the art of gung fu.

Bruce made several personal appearances around the

87

moment before colonial police shoot him down for murdering the Japanese karate master who killed his teacher. *Game* takes this image and literally unfreezes it. During the shooting of this scene a member of the crime syndicate hides among the extras playing the police and fires a "real" bullet at Lo/Lee, and we see the extradiegetic aftermath of the diegetic freeze frame, as Lo/Kim falls onto a mattress after the famous leap (fig. 42 on p. 235). The way *Game* makes use of *The Chinese Connection* gives the lie to the aura of invincibility that surrounded Lee, not only emphasizing the centrality of violent death in Lee's films, but also using the frame story to illustrate the real threat of violence that accompanies movie stunt work and gives staged violence its corporeal weight. This metanarrative from *Game* masquerades as more real than the film clip from *The Chinese Connection* it surrounds, by surrounding the suspended animation of the clip's freeze frame with a temporal sequence that engulfs it and frames it. By showing the violent aftermath of the staged death scene *Game* also breaks with the heroic tradition in Lee's previous films and presents Billy Lo as vulnerable, thus alluding to Lee's own vulnerability to death. Lo/Lee begins this sequence with a volitional leap into the air, yet the body that completes the downward trajectory of the leap is one vacated of volition.

In a further condensation of film death and real death, *Game* stages Billy Lo's fake funeral by exploiting documentary footage of Lee's actual funeral, depicting tearful mourners restrained by police and lining up to view Lee in his casket, and even offering a brief glance of Lee's corpse under a pane of glass.[46] The false continuity in this scene is not a violation of continuity editing, but a layering of virtual and actual pasts that Deleuze would call "crystalline," wherein "the real and the imaginary, the actual and the virtual chase after each other, exchange their roles and become indiscernible."[47] At the same time that the film's plot insinuates that Lee's real-life death was faked, it also capitalizes upon the audience's knowledge of Lee's death and tries to present the actual funeral as if it were fictionalized. As a result of this multilayered reflection on the death of Lo/Lee, it becomes difficult to separate real events from film narratives, compounding the effect of incompossible presents. Furthermore such false continuity jumbles the sequence of time, as when the press kit for *Game* claims that its narrative, six years after the fact, "prophetically parallels the mysterious rumors which swirled around Lee's actual death"[48] What was visual evidence of an outpouring of grief by Hong Kong audiences for Lee's death becomes recast as the elaborate staging of false grief. By presenting the fictional text of *The Chinese Connection* as a creation of its own plot, *Game of Death* aligns its narrative with the real, projecting its own fiction onto the real footage of Lee's funeral and leading unsuspecting audience members to take this scene as a dramatic re-creation. Fakery makes the diegetic stunt death more real, while casting an air of artifice onto the documentary trace of real death. Even the realness of this corpse disappears in a later scene, when the crime syndicate exhumes Billy Lo's grave and finds only an empty ceramic head, which Steiner smashes in frustration. Like the audience, the crime syndicate is confronted with an increasing plethora of Billy Los/Bruce Lees that elude their ability to pin him down and kill him off.

In death the still body of Bruce Lee converges with the still images that stand in for him in *Game of Death*. The funeral of Lo/Lee is crosscut with scenes of Lo/Kim undergoing plastic surgery, a procedure whose name underscores the plasticity of Bruce Lee's body within these narrative and formal manipulations. After the surgery Lo/Kim evaluates the success of the procedure by comparing his image in the mirror with a publicity headshot of Bruce Lee, on which he draws a beard with a black marker (fig. 43 on p. 236). Like the earlier still image of Lee in cardboard, this photograph bears a greater likeness to Lee than Kim himself, yet both images extract Lee from his movement-image and write his corporeal absence back into the film. The comparison between Kim and the photograph is especially ironic because, despite the narrative collapse of Kim and Lee into their shared role, the visual equivalence between the two is an impossibility that invites disidentification with either image. Staring at the photograph, Lo/Kim must deface "his" own image in order to see himself in it. The photograph is a frame which abstracts and separates Bruce Lee from the larger narrative frame that surrounds Billy Lo. In contrast the cardboard and ceramic figures attempt to re-insert Lee back into this narrative frame, and their failure to do so appears to kill Lee off again even while denying his death as a basis for mourning. The same cane carried by Steiner, which threatened the cardboard Lee earlier, shatters the entombed ceramic Lee near the end of the film, revealing the utter passivity of dead matter within the arc of violent action. The comic absurdity of these substitutions seems to imply that Bruce Lee, so closely identified with his movement-image, could not possibly reside in these still replicas which crumbled so easily; Bruce Lee is not here, he is elsewhere in the film, elsewhere in the world.

tended to stage long drawn-out battles to achieve the maximum effect of gore and violence. Bruce, instead, insisted that on any level—not only on the effective but artistic — a u d i e n c e s would be far more impressed with the sudden, deadly strike, the overwhelming, annihilating effect of gung fu. Provided the essence of his own expression was retained, he was prepared to allow a certain poetic or theatrical license— which was why viewers saw him perform flying jumps he would never indulge in in real life.

As another interviewer wrote: 'The object of gung fu is to send a foe to the nearest hospital in the shortest possible time, what Lee calls "a maximum of anguish with a minimum of movement". This is accomplished with knees, elbows, fingers in the eyes, feet in the teeth.' The same interviewer managed, I think, to catch part of the essence of Bruce's multi-sided character and personality when he added: 'When he isn't playing the cold-eyed Kato, Lee is the complete ham, alternately the pixie and the tough kid down the block. He puns unmercifully, performs dazzling feats of speed and coordination, wades bravely into the riptides of a language he is trying to master. Sample Lee wit: "Seven hundred million Chinese cannot be Wong", "I don't drink or smoke. But I do chew gum, because Fu Man Chu." '

89

Poised around the absent center that is Bruce Lee's corpse, *Game of Death* fabricates entangled and multiple layers of real and fake, fictional and nonfictional, and living and dead Bruce Lee that shift our attention away from action and narrative. The game of *Game* is not the sequence of fight scenes that culminate at the end of the film, but rather the play of identities and temporalities that dangle so many possible and impossible Bruce Lees before our eyes. Whereas the movement-image centers actions on stable body-subjects, the time-image that emerges in *Game* denies this possibility, as space and time lose their continuity, movement itself decomposes, and "bodies no longer have centres except that of their death."[49] Deleuze's claim is not an elegy for the loss of the body-subject, but a celebration of the possibilities freed by this loss. If *Game of Death* was intended as an expression of mourning for Lee, it reveals a grief tinged with joy and mischief, irreverently propping up Lee's corpse and toying with the very mythology constituting his aura.

Two, Three, Many Bruce Lees

Many Bruce Lees proliferate throughout the Vietnam era and beyond, in various shades of racialization and political affiliation. For his fans in the Asian American movement, Lee's films dramatized the oppression of the Chinese diaspora and working class. As one Asian American fan wrote shortly after Lee's death:

> Ah, Mr. Lee, Mr. Lee,
> how the people cheer you. We cheer be—cause you are one of us, a yellow
>   man
> trashing any and everyone
> white/black/yellow who didn't
> say you was boss man of all martial
> art, being the world's greatest.[50]

But while Lee allowed these Asian Americans to recognize their "yellow-ness" by claiming him as one of their own, such an identification was not the only one available. *Enter the Dragon* and *The Chinese Connection* played alongside blaxploitation films like *The Black Godfather* (1974) and *T. N. T. Jackson* (1974) in urban theaters catering to African American audiences, and they even inspired blax-Bruceploitation hybrids such as *The Black Dragon* (1974) and *The Black Connection* (1974).[51] One can see why the writer Darius James might claim, "My nomination for the greatest blaxploitation hero of all time starred in *The Chinese Connection*."[52] Lee could be a fellow "blaxploitation hero" in the vein of Shaft or Sweetback, giving bodily form to the existing grievances of a global racialized underclass.

More recently the first public monument to be dedicated to Lee was not erected in Los Angeles, Seattle, or Hong Kong, but in Mostar, Croatia, the site of intense violence in 1992–95, during the wars in the former Yugoslavia. A political art collective called Urban Movement erected a bronze statue of Bruce Lee in Mostar, Croatia, in 2003. Veselin Gatalo, one of its members, explained that "out of all the ethnic heroes and those who have a material interest in acting as victims, we have chosen Bruce Lee. Now they can rack their brains trying to decide whether he is Bosniak (Bosnian Muslim), Croat, or Serb."[53] For the leaders of Urban Movement, Lee was a symbol of peace who transcended the ethnic and religious divisions that still persist in the region, although, ironically, they chose to enshrine an image of Lee from *Enter the Dragon* in midbattle, holding nunchucks under one arm and raising his other hand to strike. Nino Raspudic, the cofounder of Urban Movement, explained to the international media, "We chose Bruce Lee for a reason. We want to honor him personally but also as a true symbol of the fight against injustice."[54]

perhaps useless to deny that many other martial arts instructors must have felt highly annoyed with Bruce, although the very best of them, such as Jhoon Rhee, however much they disagreed with Bruce, respected him for his honest views and integrity and became his life-long friends. His use of nunchakus, however, led to other kinds of criticism. These are two rods, connected by a piece of leather or chain and are generally used to flair at an opponent in extreme cases one could even strangle an opponent with them). Their use, of course, is banned in many parts of the world and in some states of the U.S. even their possession is a felony. Bruce, however, was solely concerned with their dramatic and theatrical appeal. His library contained many books about weapons, both ancient and modern, Oriental and Western, and he saw the nunchakus as nothing more than a diverting prop—and no more likely to encourage youngsters to violence than the use of a rifle by John Wayne in a western.

Bruce, like other colorful, larger-than-life personalities, full of zest and almost demonic energy, unquestionably enjoyed the fame and adulation that came from his appearance in *The Green Hornet*. He basked in the sunshine of personal appearances, various openings and he even rode on processional floats dressed in the black

91

In all of these invocations of Lee there is the superimposition of the contradictory fantasies of mastery and suffering that characterize the oriental obscene throughout the Vietnam era, producing a phantasmatic Lee who embodies both the instigation and the resolution of violence. But most important, this phantasmatic Lee is simultaneously the apogee of Chineseness or Asian Americanness and also the denial of racial specificity in favor of cross-racial affiliations. As with Deleuze's false continuity, these contradictory fantasies coexist without being resolved into a logically coherent narrative. The "yellow man," the "blaxploitation hero," the Croatian "symbol of the fight against injustice"—these racialized personas of Bruce Lee occupy his body-subject like the myriad clones who animate the Bruceploitation genre. In the act of re-viewing Bruce Lee these fans re-member his dead body and form it into new configurations in the service of their own particular racialized identities and politics. This resulting multiracial Bruce Lee becomes an index that links the fantastic narratives of Bruceploitation films back to the political and historical contexts that produced them.

If we follow Deleuze's logic of the powers of the false, then we must consider these various racial deployments of Bruce Lee not as appropriations of an existing racial identity, but as identifications that produce "race" as an effect—a process of continual creation, of "becoming" rather than "being" Bruce Lee. Such identifications are not simply clones of a stable subject, but take on the ruptures, paradoxes, and discontinuities of Lee as time-image. Just as *Game of Death* showed that there was no real Bruce Lee behind each of the fakes parading through the film, the existence of this multiracial Bruce Lee casts doubt on the notion of a stable racial identity. For what is Bruce Lee? Even the seemingly obvious answer—Chinese—is fraught with controversy, invoking contested notions of race, ethnicity, and nationality. Lee's biography provides no easy answer, since he was born in the U.S. to a Eurasian mother

41. After speaking to Billy Lo (Kim Tai Chong), Steiner (Hugh O'Brien) threatens a cardboard cutout of Billy Lo (Bruce Lee). Frame enlargements from *Game of Death*.

and Chinese father, emigrated to Hong Kong, and became an international film star. Stephen Teo and Kwai-Cheung Lo read Lee as embodying an "abstract" Chinese nationalism, an "imaginary and void China" devoid of historical or political specificity that responds to the desires of a wide-flung Chinese diaspora.[55] This is the Lee of *Fists of Fury* and *Return of the Dragon*, defending Chinese laborers in Southeast Asia and Italy against local exploitation. But Lee is also strongly identified with Hong Kong, where he spent most of his childhood, launched his film career, and died. Characterized by Poshek Fu and David Desser as "caught between East and West, between China and Britain, a crown colony with a hybrid culture . . . Hong Kong presents a theoretical conundrum," one that complicates the phantasmatic unity of China as a place of origin and highlights the diversity of diasporic Chinese cultures.[56]

Lee's popularity with non-Chinese Asian audiences—in South Korea, Japan, the Philippines, and India—invokes a different fantasy of pan-Asian identity, an offshoot of the Third World internationalism that animated many anticolonial movements and potentially included all peoples of color in Asia, Africa, and Latin America. His alliance with Jim Kelly and John Saxon in *Enter the Dragon* seems to represent the possibility of such a multiracial coalition. Yet

42. Unfreezing Bruce Lee's suicidal final freeze frame from
The Chinese Connection to show Billy Lo (Kim Tai Chong) falling
onto a mattress. Frame enlargements from *Game of Death*.

this pan-Asian or Third World Lee comes into conflict with the Chinese nationalist Lee of *The Chinese Connection*, highlighting the history of Asian colonizers (in this case, Japan) and their rhetorical abuse of pan-Asian unity in the service of imperialism. When such internationalism is situated within U.S. racial politics it takes on the character of Asian American pan-ethnicity— yet another version of pan-Asian unity, this time drawing on a shared history of immigration and personal discrimination rather than of colonialism and uneven development. This Asian American Lee is the immigrant worker found in a Seattle Chinese restaurant in Paisley Rekdal's *The Night My Mother Met Bruce Lee: Observations on Not Fitting In* (2000), or the young man interpellated by stereotypes while watching Mickey Rooney's yellowface character, Mr. Yunioshi, in *Breakfast at Tiffany's* (1961), a biographical incident dramatized most famously in the biopic *Dragon: The Bruce Lee Story* (1993). Thus when Vijay Prashad claims that "Bruce, in the context of the Red Guards and of the North Vietnamese army, appeared on the screen to young Asian Americans as 'the brother who showed [America that] Asian people can kick some ass,'" his statement collapses into a single identification that is in fact a series of very distinct identity claims with very different political implications.[57]

43. After plastic surgery to change his identity, Billy Lo (Kim Tai Chong) defaces a photograph of "himself" (Bruce Lee). Frame enlargement from *Game of Death.*

It is the Asian American Lee who is vigorously debated in two documentaries on Asian American masculinity: Jeff Adachi's *The Slanted Screen: Asian Men in Film and Television* (2006) and Janice Tanaka's *No Hop Sing, No Bruce Lee: What Do You Do When None of Your Heroes Look Like You?* (1998). On the one hand, Lee was celebrated by some Asian Americans as a signifier of the lost masculinity denied to them by mainstream American society. As Phillip Rhee, a martial artist, actor, and director, relates in *The Slanted Screen,* "Of course, growing up, as a young man, the influential actors were Clint Eastwood, Charles Bronson. For me, it was always the action heroes that left a great impact on my life. But at the same time, I realized something that was missing. I realized that all the hero figures that I was looking up to were Caucasians. And I did not really have a strong model until this gentleman came on board called Bruce Lee. And I said, wow, he's like me! Or I'm like him!" The heroic genealogy of Eastwood, Bronson, and Lee replaces the abject genealogy provided by the impotent, servile characters of Charlie Chan, Hop Sing (*Bonanza*), and Mr. Yunioshi (*Breakfast at Tiffany's*), allowing Rhee and others to reclaim an "Asian male pride" that allows them to "walk down the streets with our heads up." Rhee not only places Lee in the role of racialized ego ideal, but also learns to constitute himself as a masculine subject through such an identification. Similarly, in his autobiographical essay, "In Search of Bruce Lee's Grave," Shanlon Wu writes of a "hunger for images of powerful Asian men" that would "surprise and frighten" him by its intensity.[58] Wu, who claimed he watched *Enter the Dragon* twenty-two times during his adolescence, situates Lee in a different heroic genealogy, this time including the Japanese American soldiers of the 442nd Combat Team and

Minoru Genda, the Japanese general who ordered the attack on Pearl Harbor. However, Wu's easy slippage from film hero to war hero to war villain turns his celebration of masculine agency into worship of a racialized will to power, although for Wu this embrace of a yellow peril is preferable to the emasculation he felt when watching other stereotyped images of Asian men in American popular culture: "I know that they [these heroes]—like me—may have been flawed by foolhardiness and even cruelty. Still, their lives were real. They were not houseboys on 'Bonanza.'"

As the comparisons drawn by both Rhee and Wu show, the Asian American valorization of Lee suggests a retrenchment of what Jachinson Chan has called hegemonic American masculinity, tainted with the presumptions of whiteness, heteronormativity, and misogyny.[59] Chris Berry has characterized this as a "double-bind" between "a compulsion to respond to the challenge of modern American masculinity on the one hand, and a homophobic and racially marked self-hatred that is a precondition for that ability to respond on the other."[60] In their particular embrace of Lee, Asian American men such as Rhee and Wu have adopted a version of masculinity that both suppresses the foreignness of Lee and reinforces the exclusion of femininity and queerness from Lee's mythology. This heroic genealogy adopts an amnesia toward Lee's own career, which was characterized by roles no different from the Hop Sing or Charlie Chan type that they disavow. For example, No Hop Sing, No Bruce Lee situates Lee as Hop Sing's descendent, another face of an Asian American stereotype that sparks disidentification from the Asian American men it interviews. Tanaka's documentary reminds us of Lee's servile past by choosing an image of Lee that predates Fists of Fury, when he played the sidekick and side-kicking Kato on the television show The Green Hornet (1966). This, says Tanaka, is the origin of martial arts stereotypes such as the crazy servant Cato (Herbert Lom) in Peter Sellers's The Pink Panther Strikes Again (1976), the mysterious Chinatown magician Lo Pan (James Hong) in Big Trouble in Little China (1986), and the inscrutable Mr. Miyagi (Pat Morita) in The Karate Kid (1984). These films show Lee to be part of a different family line, descended more from Charlie Chan than the heroic 442nd.

The dangers of the hypermasculinity Lee represents are similar to those of the emasculation he purportedly refutes. Bobby Lee, a comedian and actor best known for his work on the sketch comedy television show MADTV (2001–9), complains in The Slanted Screen that Bruce Lee became an impossible ego ideal for him: "Bruce Lee definitely made it harder for Asian men, in terms of the bar of what people saw you as. People would come up to me, 'Hey man, do you know karate?' But no! But it's because of Bruce that people think I know

44. Jun (Johnny Yune) implores his posters of Bruce Lee to make him stronger. Frame enlargement from *They Call Me Bruce?*

karate." Bobby Lee's comedy often draws on physical humor exploiting the unruliness of his short, portly, and out-of-control body, and his comments in *The Slanted Screen* betray an anxiety that Bruce Lee's idealized masculinity will pose a new disciplinary regime on his own nonnormative body. The film *They Call Me Bruce?* (1982) dramatizes this dilemma through a Korean domestic named Jun (Johnny Yune), who allows himself to be mistaken for Bruce Lee as a form of self-defense. Although Jun knows no martial arts, he performs an elaborate pantomime when confronting black muggers and white bullies alike, taunting them with verbal threats that substitute for the bodily violence he cannot perform: "With this hand, I can poke out your eyes. With this, I can break your neck. Take a good look at my face, I'm an Oriental." Although this performance succeeds in warding off violence, Jun's masquerade shatters when he cannot use his body to enforce the heterosexual prerogatives accorded to the typical action hero. "Bruce," Jun says to the wall of Bruce Lee posters which cover his bedroom, "if I was half as good as you, I could have fought those guys in the bar, and I would be with that girl" (fig. 44).[61] Being mistaken for Bruce Lee can also create the very conditions of anti-Asian violence that Jun sought to escape. In *No Hop Sing, No Bruce Lee* Stephen Stickler, a mixed-race Korean American photographer, recalls how he was attacked as a child by some white American students and was able to defend himself because he knew tae kwon do. But his knowledge of martial arts did little to neutralize the trauma of racist bullying: "Even though I escaped and beat them or won the fight or whatever, it was so traumatic to me." More insidiously, in 1997 Kuanchung Kao, an engineer living in northern California, was shot to death by a white policeman who assumed Kao was a dangerous martial artist.[62] Lee's image may remasculinize Asian American males to such an extreme that the resulting ideal itself threatens them with a renewed racism.

Thus an Asian American Bruce Lee is fundamentally an ambivalent and unstable identification, marked by a double consciousness vacillating between an internalized racial ideal and an externalized racist gaze. The biracial Chinese American performance artist Kip Fulbeck calls attention to this double consciousness in his parodic remake and tribute film *Game of Death* (1991). By placing his own subtitles over the opening credits and first scene of Clouse's *Game of Death* Fulbeck tries to articulate the thoughts that lie latent in these images.

> Bruce Lee is a Chinese legend—a chinaman who made it in America.
> America loved him.
> And the Chinese loved him.
> Or maybe they loved America loving him.
> question:
> why do we want to keep Bruce Lee alive?
> is the question really about keeping this one love alive

This legend of Bruce Lee is not about Shaolin mythologies or other exotic Chinese folklore; instead his is a typical American story of immigrant success. But the legend itself carries the taint of racism, as Fulbeck's use of the racist epithet "chinaman" suggests. By separating this "love" into two separate statements, Fulbeck implies that what America loved him for, his mastery of movement, is separate from what the Chinese loved him for: his racialized body, standing in for their own. Furthermore as a racialized hero Lee may be more an object of mimetic desire than simply a figure of identification. If the Chinese "loved America loving" Lee, this desire is triangulated between a Chinese viewing subject, an American viewing subject, and Lee. By recognizing himself in Lee, a male Chinese subject imagined how he himself might also be "loved" by America. This heteroracial triangle centered on Lee rests upon a disavowal of racial difference as well as of homoerotic desire.

Lee upholds this triangle because he can serve both as a metonym for the Chinese as a racialized group and also as an honorary white, a figure of masculine power who transcends his racialized status and is assimilated into existing structures of power. This fantasy of assimilation by proxy is echoed in "A Fistful of Yen," a film-within-a-film parody of *Enter the Dragon* from *Kentucky Fried Movie* (1977), featuring Evan Kim (who later appears in *Go Tell the*

45. Loo (Evan Kim) awakens in Kansas from his dream of "being Bruce Lee" at the end of the mini-movie "A Fistful of Yen." Frame enlargement from *Kentucky Fried Movie*.

Spartans) as Loo and Bong Soo Han (the martial arts choreographer of *Billy Jack*) as the villain Dr. Klahn. Unlike the gestures toward black–Asian alliances in *Enter the Dragon*, "A Fistful of Yen" clearly aligns orientalness with whiteness and away from blackness, where Detroit signifies a violence more frightening than the rogue martial arts tournament taking place in Hong Kong. The entire mini-film is itself framed as a dream sequence mimicking *The Wizard of Oz* (1939), as Loo clicks his ruby slippers after defeating Klahn and wakes up "back home, back to Kansas," in a final scene framed exactly like the ending of *Oz*. Loo's martial arts adventure turns out to be nothing more than a bad dream, and he awakes as Dorothy—an absurd act of racial and gender cross-dressing—surrounded by Klahn and other Asian characters from his nightmare, also masquerading as white members of Hometown U.S.A. (fig. 45). Like Fulbeck's film, "A Fistful of Yen" suggests that the dream of *Enter the Dragon* finds its fulfillment not in the embrace of Lee's foreignness and racial difference, but in the erasure of these elements in a full assimilation to mainstream American culture, even if this means a return to the emasculation that Lee tried to refuse.

As a result the Asian American Lee may not be far from the Lee constructed by white fans such as the Urban Movement group in Croatia, who focus on his supposed transcendence of race and ethnicity. Aaron Banks, a martial arts instructor, claimed that Lee was killed for allowing the "secret" of kung fu to spread beyond the Chinese community. "There's a lot of jealousy, naturally, and also a lot of Orientals still resent anyone who popularizes or teaches Westerners the martial arts."[63] Lee's biographer, Bruce Thomas, also emphasizes Lee's willingness to teach non-Chinese students and his refusal of national martial arts styles in favor of a synthesized, individual style, as signs of Lee's color-blindness.[64] Both these claims locate racism in Chinese rather than in American culture and depict Lee as overcoming his own culture's xenophobia and thus becoming "American" in the process. In his autobiography Davis Miller describes how Bruce Lee replaced the white heroes of his youth:

> Among other "biological" movements in which Lee had a role: the post–World War II Western ideal of the superior Christian, Anglo-Saxon, mannerly tough guy (à la Duke Wayne and Rocky Marciano). Humbled by the Koreans, crippled by Ali, and resolutely de-limbed by the Viet Cong, this bad old white boy was killed dead, and replaced in the public consciousness, by little bitty Bruce Lee.
>
> As millions of tiny twits like me—whether we were yellow, black, white, or brown—first saw Lee on big, enveloping movie screens, we no longer felt so little, so powerless. Lee even managed to help a few of us swim out of our bowls of sad soup and find something resembling real dry-land lives.[65]

Although Miller's memoir concentrates mostly on the specificity of his white, working-class background, here he invokes a cross-racial imaginary audience which converges around Lee through a shared experience of powerlessness. However, the racial unmarkedness of these feelings of impotence are exposed as white when they are placed into their history of defeats: by Koreans, by Viet Cong, by Muhammad Ali. This is the specific powerlessness felt by white hegemony at the loss of its previous dominance rather than the suffering of racialized groups terrorized by long histories of repression. Miller's move from mourning the death of the "bad old white boy" to being reborn through an identification with Bruce Lee is not simply about racial transcendence, but represents a reconfiguration of orientalness as a form of honorary whiteness, cleansed of its more troubling connotations.[66] Here one form of the oriental obscene, suffering and traumatized, is suppressed in favor of another, triumphant and powerful, when in fact the two forms are intimately linked in one racial phantasmatic.

The cross-racial teachings of Bruce Lee as oriental master are translated quite differently by two coming-of-age narrative films from the early 1980s: No Retreat, No Surrender (1986) and The Last Dragon (1985), featuring a white and a black protagonist, respectively. Together they belie the easy narrative of racial transcendence and postmodern identities that the cross-racial Lee seems to promise. No Retreat is an obvious reworking of The Karate Kid (1984) and the

46. The ghost of Bruce Lee (Kim Tai Chong) trains Jason Stillwell (Kurt McKinney) in the shadow of posters of Lee from *Game of Death*. Frame enlargement from *No Retreat, No Surrender*.

Rocky series (in particular *Rocky IV* [1985]), centered around a teenage Bruce Lee fan, Jason Stillwell (Kurt McKinney). Unlike Daniel LaRusso in *Karate Kid*, who is being raised by his single mother, Jason is part of a nuclear family. But Jason's father, a karate instructor, turns out to be a powerless figure who backs away from a confrontation with a violent mafia and admonishes Jason that "karate is not to be used aggressively." The entire family relocates from Los Angeles to Seattle, conveniently allowing young Jason access to a new father figure, Bruce Lee, whose grave Jason frequents in quasi-religious pilgrimages. While Jason suffers the usual adolescent torments—bullies from the local karate dojo, humiliation in front of his girlfriend—his dad remains hobbled from the attack by the mob and is forced to give up teaching karate to tend bar, suffering what seems to be an economic and psychic demotion. When Jason and his father argue one night about Jason's fighting, the confrontation becomes a clash over competing laws of the father, as Jason calls his father a "coward" and the father responds by ripping up the boy's Bruce Lee poster. That night, as Jason relocates his Bruce Lee paraphernalia to an abandoned house, "Sensei Lee" (played by a Lee double, Kim Tai Chong from *Game of Death*) appears to him for the first time, bringing reciprocity to their previously one-way conversations and channeling Jason's unfocused aggression into effective attacks (fig. 46). Lee's spirit enables Jason eventually to defeat the Russian fighter (Jean Claude Van Damme) who crippled his father and to regain the affections of his girlfriend, the admiration of the bullies, and the respect of the karate dojo that ostracized him. Thus the spirit of Lee is resurrected to restore the privileges of whiteness that Jason temporarily lost with the emasculation of his father.

However, the production history and subplots of No Retreat complicate the erasure of racial specificity that the film's narrative tries to perform. The film was directed by Corey Yuen and produced by Ng See-Yuen, two Hong Kong martial arts film luminaries and members of the Seven Little Fortunes, a Hong Kong performance troupe trained in Chinese opera acrobatics whose other illustrious members included Jackie Chan and Sammo Hung. As a result it is difficult to dismiss No Retreat as simply an appropriation and whitening of Bruce Lee's legacy, when in fact the film serves as an early bridge for Chinese directors and actors to enter Hollywood, anticipating later transnational productions with Chan, Yuen, Hung, Jet Li, Michelle Yeow, Chow Yun-Fat, and Ang Lee. Meaghan Morris has argued that we should reverse the usual national hierarchies that center on the American film industry and frame transnational works as derivative: "Instead of seeing No Retreat, No Surrender as a Hong Kong ripoff passing as American, we can just as well say that it remade The Karate Kid for people who like Hong Kong films."[67] We might extend Morris's claim to the characters in the film as well: rather than viewing the film as simply Americanizing Bruce Lee as an honorary white paterfamilias, it might also orientalize Jason through his imagined relationship with Lee, whom he addresses as "Lee da ge" (big brother Lee). Lee's first lesson to Jason is not a martial arts move, but the etymology of the Chinese character wu (meaning "martial"): "The character wu is made up of guo, which means violence or force, plus this character ji, meaning stop. We call it martial arts. We practice how to stop violence. What you learn from me is for defense only and should never be abused." As Jason internalizes Lee's teachings he does not necessarily become overtly orientalized—he never alters his appearance along the lines of a yellowface minstrel—but he does adopt Lee's bodily gestures, yelling with Lee's high-pitched kiais and beckoning his fallen opponents with Lee's characteristic outstretched hand. And No Retreat retains something of Lee's cross-racial coalitions, pairing Jason with an African American best friend, R. J., whom Jason defends from harassment when he incurs the wrath of the karate bullies. While Lee empowers Jason to regain his father's and his own dignity, it is R. J. and a pair of African American dancers who restore his heterosexual relations with his love interest, maneuvering Jason and the girl together on the dance floor. The universe of No Retreat is replete with instances of multiracial affinities that are missing in The Karate Kid's version of wounded white masculinity, even though it ultimately follows Davis Miller in privileging Lee as a fantasy of personal mastery.

Like No Retreat, The Last Dragon (1985), produced by Motown's founder, Berry Gordy, provides a vision of Lee that lies somewhere between an essentially Asian Bruce Lee and a nonracial (i.e., white) Bruce Lee. However, the stakes are different in envisioning an African American Bruce Lee, since racial difference is not being erased but is instead reimagined, as the orientalness of Lee is inflected through blackness. Bill Brown has speculated that Lee's popularity among African American audiences was due to his "generic ethnicity" as a man of color rather than his "ethnic specificity" as Chinese, thus inviting the audience to "translate the ethnonationalist conflicts staged within the kung fu film into the conflict of class."[68] However, what Brown ignores is that the ethnonationalistic impulse in Lee's films is already a translation of the class conflicts experienced by diasporic Asian workers, which map onto racial difference as well as onto nationalism. Thus the analogies made between the Chinese in Lee's films and African Americans are not as remote as the historically and geographically distant settings of the films might suggest, and they are mediated by the histories of racialization in the U.S. that have marked both blacks and Asians as racial rather than ethnic formations. What emerges in The Last Dragon is not so much a postmodern, postracial utopia of floating identities, but rather a phantasmatic relationship between orientalness and blackness that reveals a surprisingly specific shared history of repression and co-optation.

The Last Dragon is set in Harlem, a location symbolically associated with African Americans but actually encompassing a wide range of cross-racial interactions in modern New York City, including the presence of working-class Asian Americans in this segregated urban landscape. The film translates black-on-black urban violence into the language of nationalistic conflict, referencing the hostilities between Chinese colonists and Japanese colonizers from The Chinese Connection. Bruce Leroy (Taimak), nicknamed "the chocolate covered yellow peril" by his own brother, walks around Harlem dressed in a Chinese peasant outfit and straw hat and searches for the "secret" of Bruce Lee's power—or, as Leroy calls it, his "glow." Leroy takes on this search because he lacks a master, having outgrown his old kung fu teacher but still unsure of his mastery over himself. Leroy comes into conflict with an African American gang leader named Sho'nuff, also known as the "Shogun of Harlem" (Julius Carry), recalling an earlier historical alliance between Asians and African Americans.[69] Whereas Leroy's family seems to be following the model minority path to socioeconomic success—his father, Leroy Green (Jim Moody), has opened a pizza parlor in Harlem—Sho'nuff is bent on a path of pure destruction, at one point trashing the elder Leroy's restaurant in order to spur the younger Leroy to fight. The interclass conflict between Leroy's family and Sho'nuff mirrors the generational and class differences produced in Asian America by the Immigration Act of 1965, as newer, professional-class Asians embraced the model minority label that older Asian Americans eyed warily. But even the intraracial structure of this conflict is insistently multiracial: Sho'nuff's gang resembles a coed rainbow coalition, Leroy's dad adopts an Italian American rather than African American theme for his restaurant, and Leroy's best kung fu student is a biracial Asian American kid named Johnny Yu (Glen Eaton). If The Last Dragon is a black film, it depicts a blackness that is deeply imbricated with whiteness as well as orientalness.

The consumption of Bruce Lee as movement-image provides a constant backdrop for the narrative of The Last Dragon, highlighting the role that commodity culture plays in facilitating the development of racial identity. Like the Black Panthers' relationship to the Vietnamese, Leroy's relationship to orientalness does not arise from interactions with Asians around him, but rather from an imaginary repertoire derived from visual culture. Leroy and the Shogun's first confrontation takes place in a movie theater screening Enter the Dragon, where Leroy is eating popcorn with chopsticks. Later the night-club owner Laura Charles (Vanity) woos Leroy by assembling a montage of Bruce Lee film clips into a music video and educating the asexual Leroy by showing him an image of his master kissing Nora Miao in Return of the Dragon. When Leroy finally achieves the "glow" by invoking Lee's auratic star image and accomplishing a visual mastery of movement, it is signified by parallel slow-motion sequences of Lee's and Leroy's hands moving through the air and leaving a trail of afterimages that hypnotize their viewers. It is clear from these specifically filmic invocations that Lee is not simply a deity to be worshipped in the abstract; his power over Leroy is specifically based on the cinematic medium. Unlike No Retreat, where Bruce Lee enters the film in the form of a ghost, in The Last Dragon Lee is not a character but a movement-image derived from film alone, and Leroy has no access to Lee except through film spectatorship. In some ways this levels the playing field for Leroy, as it suggests that Lee is equally available to fans of all races, and that no imagined relation with Lee is more authentic than any other.

The various forms of racial drag in The Last Dragon also acknowledge the inescapability of racial markings on the body, but at the same time imply that there is no naturalized identity, that even an African American playing an African American character in some ways adopts a form of drag or masquerade. As one reviewer commented, "In the world of 'The Last Dragon,' racial style isn't something you're born with—it's something you choose."[70] The

47. "Bruce" Leroy Green (Taimak) encounters the Chinese workers of the Sum Dum Goy fortune cookie company. Frame enlargement from *The Last Dragon*.

central gag of *The Last Dragon* is the incongruity between Leroy's black body and milieu and the Chinese attire and mannerisms he adopts in order to be like Bruce Lee. But all of the characters in the film engage in acts of drag or passing: Sho'nuff's samurai-esque armor, Leroy's dad in an Italian-themed chef's hat, the three Chinese brothers from the Sum Dum Goy factory (a reference to restaurant Cantonese and Yiddish) who act black and speak "jive" (fig. 47). Although racial drag is meant to illustrate the lack of a racial essence to mimic, the humor or incongruity of such masquerades often reinforces the essentialism of one's given race. However, the multivalent cross-dressings in *The Last Dragon* posit both end points of the masquerade as equally unstable identity positions.

In one scene, inspired by Bruce Lee's disguises from *The Chinese Connection*, Leroy attempts to pass for black in order to gain entrance into the Sum Dum Goy factory. Leroy puts away his chinoiserie, dons a plain shirt and pants, and practices getting the intonations of black English into phrases such as "Hey, my man, what it look like" and "I am the soul brother like no other." Meanwhile the three Chinese brothers, whose speech, mannerisms, and dress signify a stereotypical blackness that ironically seems more natural than Leroy's attempts at passing, interrogate Leroy's disguise in self-racializing terms. When they ask him, "You the same fool that came dressed as a coolie?," Leroy answers, "No, no, we all just look alike, my man, brother." The double attempts at passing invoked by this set of characters—Leroy for Chinese, the Chinese brothers for black—intersect in this scene to highlight the stereotypical absurdity of both "authentic" and "inauthentic" identities and yet underscore the backdrop of racism that both attempts at passing try to traverse. By calling Leroy a "coolie," the brothers refuse to neutralize the history of racial denigration that has accompanied Chinese immigrants and their supposed inability to assimilate into the American cultural landscape in the nineteenth century. Yet Leroy's response does not disavow this racist history, but in fact acknowledges the entirety of the racial discourse it implies: "We all look alike," he says, invoking the typical racist refrain directed at Asians in America. Leroy follows this with the black colloquialism, "my man, brother," which in this scene has two meanings: that we are both black *and* that we are both Chinese. "Black" and "Chinese" do not signify pure racial identities to be defended from encroachment, but subject positionings of abjection and subjugation that allow for cross-racial affiliations without erasing the historical realities from which these positions arise.

This is not to claim a privileged political meaning for cross-racial identifications with Bruce Lee, for such identifications can easily reify the racial positions they cross from and into, as seen in the autobiographical writings of Shanlon Wu and Davis Miller. But *The Last Dragon* offers a space within which mimicry is neither simple appropriation nor assimilation, but serves to highlight the painful histories which racially mark the subject even in the present time. For such identifications with otherness—and here I count the Asian American identification with Bruce Lee, as well as Leroy's black Bruce Lee and Miller's white Bruce Lee—are ultimately identifications with wounds, even if the manifest content of these movement-images is one of mastery. Like the Bruce Lee of *Game of Death*, the Bruce Lee of *The Last Dragon* gestures toward a gap that Lee himself cannot fill—in *Game of Death*, his own death, and in *The Last Dragon*, Leroy's lack of a master. *The Last Dragon* moves us into a historical moment *past* Vietnam, not in the sense of having necessarily worked through the national trauma which Vietnam represents for America, but by moving into a historical periodization in which the Asian presence in America is more than a synecdoche for the Vietnam War and opens into other relations and juxtapositions, particularly through the circulation of ethnic styles in a system of commodification and consumption. Leroy is not simply Jim Kelly from *Enter the Dragon* reincarnated; he is not the Vietnam vet returned from the Asian heart of darkness who views the Asian-black relation as reflected through a global ghettoization. Leroy represents the possibility of thinking about the links between racialized positions, black and Asian, without the explicit mediation of Vietnam—for thinking about the woundedness of racialization in America without the primordial wound of the Vietnam War.

RETURNING TO 'NAM

The Vietnam Veteran's Orientalized Body

I would really like to become a white Bruce Lee.

—Chuck Norris, quoted in Richard Zimmerman, "Chuck Norris:
A Glimpse of Greatness," Black Belt, December 1977

Just as John Wayne saved several generations of movie-goers, Chuck Norris always comes through.

Pat H. Broeske, "Chuck Norris—An All-American Hit,"
Los Angeles Times, 19 May 1986

In the late 1970s Chuck Norris was just another martial artist in Hollywood hoping to capitalize on the posthumous yet still potent stardom of Bruce Lee. Given a small role in Lee's Return of the Dragon (1972, released in the U.S. in 1974, after Lee's death), Norris came to notoriety as one of the few non-Asian adversaries to spar at length with Lee on screen, as the American karate expert Colt hired by the Italian mafia to harass a Chinese restaurant in Rome. Lee was aware of the heavy symbolic value that such a pairing would project; he reportedly told his mother after casting Norris, a former World Middle-weight karate champion, "I'm an Oriental person, therefore I have to defeat all the whites in the film."[1] The Norris-Lee fight scene itself offers many stark contrasts in racial phenotypes, portraying Lee's short, wiry, and smooth body next to Norris's comparatively hulking and hairy mass, highlighted in one shot by Lee grabbing and ripping off a tuft of Norris's chest hair (fig. 48). Nonetheless as Lee and the martial arts culture of the era offered a seeming antidote to the traumatized, victimized aura surrounding American mas-culinity, it made sense that Norris, like the fictional and real-life imitators

48. Tang Lung (Bruce Lee) pulls out a handful of Colt's (Chuck Norris) chest hair. Frame enlargement from *Return of the Dragon*.

described in the previous chapter, would strive to "become a white Bruce Lee." The reversal of the usual terms of racial mimicry—the comparison of Asian and Asian American stars with their white norms that Frank Chin derides as the "Chinese Fred Astaire" effect in his novel *Donald Duk* (1991)— seems to signal a progressive inversion of racial hierarchies, momentarily inserting an Asian body in the midst of a positive national fantasy.

However, this moment passes quickly. Just when the Norris-Lee fight from *Return* is resurrected in the opening scene in *Game of Death* (1978), Norris's career starts to take a different turn. *Good Guys Wear Black* (1978), the first of Norris's post-Lee films to attain commercial success, situates Norris within an American cinematic tradition characterized by guns, cars, and explosions and a white masculine genealogy populated by figures such as John Wayne, Clint Eastwood, and Charles Bronson. *Good Guys* also anticipates the Vietnam subgenre that would later be popularized by Sylvester Stallone's *Rambo* (1982– 89) and Norris's own *Missing in Action* (1984–88) series: the POW/MIA film, revolving around the shared premise that the U.S. government left American soldiers behind in Vietnam as they were negotiating the ignominious end of the war. Even as he courted Lee's martial arts fan base with his "white Bruce Lee" comment to *Black Belt* magazine, Norris began to distance himself from this orientalized ego ideal in the mainstream media, telling the *Los Angeles Times* that same year, "Bruce Lee movies were all karate with a little story stuck in. . . . I want to have a story with some karate scenes."[2] Narrative development, along the lines of the action-images that Deleuze associates with American cinema, becomes a marker of the quality of Norris's new films, over and against the primitive, nonnarrative spectacles of violence purportedly dominating Lee's work. By 1986, when Norris is promoting his tenth film after *Good Guys, Invasion U.S.A.* (1985), Bruce Lee is no longer the main point of reference for his career. Instead, as another *Los Angeles Times* profile reveals, Norris is now the reincarnation of John Wayne, whose name is evoked four times on the first page alone, and Norris's films in the mold of "modern-day Westerns."

The White Oriental

From Bruce Lee to John Wayne—this reverse genealogy of the Hollywood action hero seems to undo the orientalization of the Vietnam veteran, replacing both the body incontinent of the traumatized soldier and the body mastered of the Asian martial artist with an earlier warrior figure more often associated with the violent oppression of racial difference on the edges of the U.S. nation-state (cf. *The Sands of Iwo Jima* [1949] and *The Searchers* [1956]). However, the soldier-heroes played by Chuck Norris, and later by Sylvester Stallone, represent a differently orientalized body, one neither fully traumatized nor invincible, but rather the condensation of both fantasies simultaneously, resulting in an ostensibly white body whose origins are thoroughly oriental. This whiteness is shot through with otherness both in the form of its bodily comportment—fighting techniques borrowed straight from the mysterious ars violentiae of Asian martial arts—as well as its specular form, descended from the bloody naked torso of Bruce Lee, revealing its vulnerable embodiment as Wayne, Clint Eastwood, and Charles Bronson never did. If such films "remasculinized" a working-class, white American male subject seemingly abandoned by the racial and gender politics of the 1970s, as scholars such as Susan Jeffords and David Savran have argued, they did so by making Vietnam into the crucible for a new white masculinity.[3] But it is simplistic to subsume race within gender, as though the racism of the war could be mapped onto sexism, or what David Desser once summarized as "vc-as-woman."[4] If anything the trajectory of the oriental obscene has been to privilege the racial phantasmatic as the site from which masculinity is engendered, not the other way around. The beleaguered white male hero of the 1980s is born of two fathers: the Vietnamese guerrilla and the Asian martial artist, both giving form to the suffering that white masculinity faces. The resulting miscegenated figure resembles the modern-day blackface minstrelsy found in Norman Mailer's "White Negro" hipsters or Elvis Presley's gyrating crooner, having shed the obvious signs of burnt cork but maintaining the rest of the "cultural dowry" of phantasmatic blackness.[5] Norris's and

Stallone's Vietnam heroes are white orientals, performing a yellowface minstrelsy sans yellowface, in order to reinvigorate a whiteness that has lost both its hegemonic wholeness from the protests of the 1970s and its masculine vigor from the Vietnam War. But since the oriental source of this minstrelsy is phantasmatic to begin with, such a masquerade is ultimately less a theft of authentic Asian culture than a reflection of the original fantasy of the oriental obscene that produced such scenarios.

We can see the outlines of this white oriental in Norris's character from *Good Guys*. Now sporting straight, blond hair and appearing even more Aryan than his hirsute persona in *Return*, Norris plays John T. Booker, a former army commando officer who is now a Ph.D. student in political science in Riverside, California. But unlike the countercultural roots of David Morrell's characterization of Rambo in his novel *First Blood* (1971), and in contrast to the more serious Vietnam films released that same year, *Coming Home* and *The Deer Hunter*, *Good Guys* manages to simultaneously celebrate and critique the war. The ultimate villain of the film is a career diplomat, Conrad Morgan (James Franciscus), who as under secretary of state sent Booker and his secret squad of Black Tigers on a fake mission to rescue American POWs during the Paris Peace Talks of 1973, and who is later responsible for ordering the assassination of the remaining Black Tiger veterans to cover his tracks as he comes up for nomination as secretary of state. Booker redeems the failures of the Vietnam War by exacting revenge on the politicians that led him and his soldiers astray. Such a narrative structure allows Booker to attack this corruption of state power while maintaining the ultimate goodness of the American nation and its soldiers. However, the style of Booker's violence owes more to *Billy Jack* and *Enter the Dragon* than to the white vigilantism of *Dirty Harry* (1971) or *Death Wish* (1974). Even the name "Black Tigers" evokes the exotic styles of Chinese kung fu and references the Chinese title of the Golden Harvest production *Slaughter in San Francisco* (1974)—*Huang Mian Lao Hu*, or *Yellow Faced Tiger*—that Norris headlined soon after Bruce Lee's death. Just as the Negro's "life of constant humility and ever-threatening danger" taught Mailer's white hipsters how to love and fear again after the anesthetizing experience of the Second World War, Vietnam and the Asian martial arts provide Norris's character with the form and impetus for his newfound heroism.[6] However, the histories of Asian Americans and African Americans are not analogous, for the racial phantasmatic of the Vietnam War is itself refracted through triangulating whiteness between oriental and black otherness, as comparisons between the civil rights movement and the Vietnam War revealed. The blackness of Booker's Black Tigers is itself a condensation of these racial fantasies, recalling not only the Viet Cong and Hong Kong martial arts, but also the Black Panthers and black nationalism.

Yet *Good Guys* contains little martial arts until the climactic fight sequence between Booker and Mhin (a misspelling of the Vietnamese name Minh) Van Thieu (Soon-Tek Oh), the South Vietnamese major hired by Morgan to lead the Black Tigers into the ambush in Vietnam and brought to the U.S. by Morgan to finish off the surviving Black Tigers.[7] Mhin seems to be the filmic analogue of Gen. Nguyen Ngoc Loan, the South Vietnamese executioner turned immigrant restaurateur, whose deportation case surfaced around the time of *Good Guys'* release. Like Loan, Mhin carries the violence of the oriental obscene behind the guise of the model minority, relocating to San Francisco after the war and finding employment at a Chinese restaurant, all the while carrying out a series of brutal murders with the help of his diminutive but deadly wife. Thus when Booker confronts Mhin after he has blown up the plane carrying Booker's love interest, Margaret (Anne Archer), Booker is not only defeating the Vietnamese enemy who eluded him during the war, but also carrying out the expulsion of the violent foreign other that the U.S. government welcomed into its borders and then failed to eject. Herein lies one key difference between the white oriental and the white Negro: whereas the white Negro identifies with a blackness learned through a three-hundred-year history of social and cultural intimacies, the white oriental of the 1970s rests upon a disavowal of any relationship between the U.S. and its Asia. Booker does not seek intimacy with Mhin and his like; the explicit narrative of their encounter is to sever any possible relation or similarity between the two, to make a clean break between America and its defeat in Vietnam.

This fight between Mhin and Booker is the mirror image of the fight between Norris and Lee in *Return*: here the large white body defeats the small Asian body (fig. 49). Earlier fight scenes featured Booker assaulting his enemies with machine guns, grenades, pistols, and car chases; this scene allows Booker to unleash the full extent of his karate skills, as he engages in hand-to-hand combat and finally kills Mhin with a flying kick through a windshield. But during this fight it is Mhin rather than Booker who appears to be in racial masquerade, sporting a blond wig and gray three-piece suit that mimics the appearance of Booker as well as Mhin's American handler, Morgan. Mhin's disguise seems to symbolize the unsuccessful attempts of Vietnamese refugees to assimilate into the American body politic, superficially adopting the values of American capitalism and commodity culture but still maintaining their old ideological conflicts and allegiances from the war. Thus in this scene it is the Asian immigrant rather than the Vietnam veteran who appears to be

49. Booker (Chuck Norris) spars with a former South Vietnamese major, Mhin (Soon-Tek Oh), disguised here in a gray suit and blond wig. Frame enlargement from *Good Guys Wear Black*.

wrongfully appropriating the culture of his other. Nonetheless the fight is ultimately a contest between two versions of orientalized violence, one (Mhin) deemed a fake by virtue of his disguise and ultimate defeat, and the other (Booker) appearing natural and organic in a seamless embodiment of martial technique. But while this fight might appear on the surface to be an act of racial cleansing—removing yet another yellow peril from American society—it also performs a racial mixture through the stylization of violence. If in earlier versions of the fantasy of the oriental obscene the racialized roles of victim and aggressor appeared to be separated, here they are merged into one: instead of an implosive act of self-destruction, as seen in Nick's suicide in *The Deer Hunter* or the death of Kurtz in *Apocalypse Now*, there is a triumphant cannibalization of the oriental other under the banner of white American masculinity, reinvigorated by its cultural miscegenation with oriental violence. In the death of the ostensibly real Asian body another phantasmatic oriental body emerges, with white skin and blond hair but racially hybrid in every other way. Reversing the claim later made in *Full Metal Jacket* (1987) that "inside every gook there is an American trying to get out," *Good Guys Wear Black* seems to show that inside every American is a gook waiting to emerge.

By the time Sylvester Stallone adopts the pose of the white oriental in *Rambo: First Blood Part II* (1985), we can see more clearly the outlines of the martial arts body mastered erupting through the shell of Rambo's white ethnic body. (To follow this genealogy we must temporarily set aside the Rambo of the earlier film, *First Blood* (1982), which is more of an artifact of the traumatized veteran than his reinvigorated alter ego.) As epitomized by Bruce

Lee's naked torso in Enter the Dragon (1973), this martial body seemed to offer a compensatory fantasy against the passivity and vulnerability that characterized the incontinent body traumatized by the Vietnam War, consuming its own blood and wounds to harden itself against further violence. However, these Asian martial artists are living ghosts, their racial difference referencing the invisible Vietnamese guerrilla who serves as both source and object of the violence of Vietnam and whose corpse can barely be imagined within this visual economy of mastery. As ghosts, the dead Asian martial artists are reborn in Rambo's glistening "hard body," which Susan Jeffords reads as a synecdoche for the U.S. national body during the Reagan era and perhaps a proxy for Ronald Reagan himself ("Ronbo"), or in the muscular torsos of Jean-Claude Van Damme, Arnold Schwarzenegger, and other action stars.[8] This white body effaces the racial history behind its dialectic of suffering and mastery. Even as early as Rocky (1976) we can see how such training sequences might be reinserted into a narrative of the self-made American man who sheds his ethnic particularity for access to hegemonic whiteness, a path unavailable to Lee. In fact the film portrays Rocky as what Matthew Frye Jacobson has called a "poster boy for white victimization," triangulating Rocky between the blackness of his opponent, Apollo Creed (Carl Weathers), whose similarity to Muhammad Ali references Ali's militant antiwar stance ("No Vietnamese ever called me nigger"), and the orientalness of the specter of Vietnam which lies behind them both.[9] Although Rocky lost his fight to Creed, and the U.S. its war to Vietnam, both he and the nation access a moral superiority through defeat that allows them to cast their opponents as the villains in an unfair fight, thus cleansing Rocky and the U.S. from the stigma that might otherwise accompany their complicity with violence.

But a quick glance at how Stallone performs this bodily posture in Rambo: First Blood Part II belies the hard body's claim to racial and national purity. As Rambo, Stallone's body is even more of a spectacle than in Rocky, drawing it even closer to the nonnarrative spectacles of violence found in the Asian martial arts films that Norris attempted to repudiate. Rambo's tanned, glistening, and chiseled chest more closely resembles the smooth body of Bruce Lee than the pale, hairy chest sported by Norris in their iconic fight, as if emphasizing the Asian origins of this hard body. But this body is bared only in the act of torture, placing Rambo in an abject position that disrupts the fantasy of pure mastery. We catch a glimpse of Rambo's tortured torso in First Blood, as he is stripped by the local police to be hosed down and shaved. "Holy shit, look at this!" the young officer Mitch (David Caruso) exclaims at the sight of deep scars running across Rambo's back. "What the hell's he been

50. John Rambo (Sylvester Stallone) strips down after his arrest for vagrancy, revealing unexplained scars from his time in Vietnam. Frame enlargement from *First Blood*.

into?" (fig. 50). But the physical violence that Rambo suffered in Vietnam can scarcely be imagined in *First Blood*, focused as it is on the traumatized veteran back in the U.S., and Rambo's hard body takes a backseat in this earlier film to his psychological trauma.

In contrast, the physical violence of Vietnam becomes the central narrative trope of *Rambo: First Blood Part II*, as the bureaucrat Marshal Murdock (Charles Napier) sends Rambo back to Vietnam to look for evidence of American POWs. Not only is Rambo's mission a chance to redeem the loss of the original war—Rambo famously asks, "Do we get to win this time?"—but it also allows him to reexperience the violence of the war, when he is captured and tortured by a Soviet colonel, Podovsky (Steven Berkoff). Although white like Rambo, Podovsky becomes infused with the orientalism of his Vietnamese setting, adopting the randomness and cruelty seen in the Russian roulette scenes of *The Deer Hunter*. In a series of "experiments" Podovsky submits Rambo to leeches, electric shocks, and burning knives, but the only torture that Rambo cannot endure is when Podovsky threatens to brand another American POW before Rambo's captive gaze. Rambo's immobilization thus explains not only his trauma in *First Blood*, but also recalls the experience of the American national body during the war, subjected to living-room as well as big-screen spectacles of suffering and defeat. Even in 1985, as Hollywood attempts to win the Vietnam War, the repetition compulsion of the war's trauma leads us back to the restaging of suffering, holding the nation's audiences captive again even as the actual threat of oriental violence recedes into the past.

Missing in Action

Missing in action is an accounting limbo. It reflects a lack of knowledge concerning an individual rather than being truly descriptive of his condition.

—Capt. Douglas L. Clarke, *The Missing Man: Politics and the* MIA (1979),
quoted in Hawley, *The Remains of War*

"Missing in Action" was a personal movie. . . . I lost a brother in Vietnam, and also there are 2,500 men missing still. I know where my brother is—I saw the body. But what if he was still a MIA? It creates turmoil in the lives of the families. The movie is a kind of tribute to these people.

—Chuck Norris quoted in Dolores Barclay, "Star Watch: Aging Boy Next Door
Chops His Way to Stardom," Associated Press, 25 February 1985

The Vietnam War was not the first nor the last war in which U.S. soldiers' bodies were left behind on the battlefield. Nearly half of the bodies of soldiers killed during the Civil War (over 300,000) remained unidentified or unburied at the end of the war, due to the lack of identification markers such as dog tags as well as few procedures for systematically recording and burying the dead.[10] Even in more recent conflicts such as the Second World War and the Korean War, in which concerted efforts were made to repatriate the bodies of dead soldiers, approximately 78,000 and 8,100 soldiers' bodies, respectively, remain missing.[11] The conditions of modern warfare, with its myriad ways of killing and dispersing the human body, make it difficult to recover soldiers' remains, even while forensic science develops new techniques of identification. What emerged in the Vietnam War was not a new phenomenon of soldiers missing in action, but rather a new political response to the situation. Scholars such as H. Bruce Franklin and Jerry Lembcke have argued that the Nixon administration fostered rumors of the North Vietnamese holding American MIAs as prisoners of war as a way of both manipulating pro- and antiwar sentiment in the U.S. as well as prolonging peace negotiations with the North Vietnamese.[12] But these rumors persisted even after Nixon resigned in disgrace and the war concluded, as families of these soldiers demanded the "fullest possible accounting" of their whereabouts in light of the false hopes that the Nixon administration had raised.

In his book-length study of the search for MIAs from the Vietnam War, Thomas M. Hawley asserts that these absent bodies represent "the most material indication of the defeat that occurred in Southeast Asia," and that the efforts to recover these bodies (numbering approximately 2,500 in 1975) continue to eclipse the needs of the Vietnamese, dead and living, in the eyes of subsequent U.S. administrations.[13] Indeed U.S. aid to Vietnam for the recovery of American soldiers' remains far outpaces spending to ameliorate the continuing effects of the war on current-day Vietnamese citizens, such as medical devices, decontamination of Agent Orange pollution sites, and the relocation of wartime orphans.[14] One might conclude that the American MIA has taken the place of the traumatized Vietnam veteran in subsuming the role of the "true" victim of the Vietnam War from the Vietnamese themselves, continuing the circle of identifications initiated in "Saigon Execution" and the My Lai massacre and restaged in Hollywood's Vietnam.

However, the body of the MIA is an ambivalent symbol of healing, which fails to restore the wholeness of the American body politic wounded by the Vietnam War. The category of the MIA itself is unstable, referring to an ontological aporia somewhat akin to Schrödinger's cat—neither dead nor alive, but both. The U.S. military itself prefers to move soldiers out of the category of MIA into either that of POW, which implies a confirmation of the soldiers' survival, or the category "killed in action, body not recovered," which asserts epistemological certainty of the fate of such soldiers even in the absence of material remains.[15] Thus the fusion of the categories MIA and POW by veterans' families and their advocates evinces a deep-seated optimism that forecloses not only the possibility of mourning these soldiers' deaths, but also the very acknowledgment of the wound represented by the Vietnam War itself. While 591 living POWs were repatriated to the U.S. after the signing of the Paris Peace Accords in early 1973, only a single POW, Robert Garwood, has returned after the end of the Vietnam War, leaving doubt that any surviving MIAs remain in Vietnam.[16]

However, for POW/MIA advocates the Vietnam War still continues, in the form of Vietnamese treachery in actively detaining and hiding American POWs. The POW/MIA issue helped sustain the continuation of a U.S. trade and diplomatic embargo against Vietnam until 1994.[17] Moreover such optimism is founded upon a fundamental absence, the missing soldier, since the discovery of remains would dash all hopes of reclaiming these soldiers as members of their families and of the national community. After the Vietnam War the search for what Hawley calls the "unaccounted-for" body of the MIA soldier is no longer about creating an account, a narrative explanation for what happened to that soldier, but rather of recovering a phantasmatic body that magically makes whole what has been lost in its absence.[18]

As a result the very notion of a subgenre of POW/MIA films sits uncomfortably within the action genre it purportedly belongs to. The action film, as a prime example of the action-image Deleuze defined, depends on the ability of narratives to make causal links between agents and their actions, thus imputing agency to the transformation of situations and circumstances. The American action-image had already suffered several crises during the Vietnam era, including the destabilization of causality in understanding wartime actions such as the My Lai massacre or the burning of the "Napalm Girl," as well as the proliferation of false actions and dead actors in the cult of Bruce Lee. Although narrative cinema in the U.S. was hardly being displaced by a non-narrative avant-garde in this era, this crisis of the action-image fomented the replacement of meaningful action with meaningless activity: "For the cinema of the action-image had itself engendered a tradition from which it could now only, in the majority of cases, extricate itself negatively. The great genres of this cinema, the psycho-social film, the film noir, the Western, the American comedy, collapse and yet maintain their empty frame."[19] The excess of spectacular violence of the so-called action genre recalls the dream of the Wolf Man from Freud's case study "From the History of an Infantile Neurosis," wherein "the perfect stillness and immobility of the wolves" in the dreamscape are a cipher that hides the "most violent motion" of the primal scene.[20]

But in the case of the action film the symptom is reversed, and the furious action of explosions, gunfights, and car chases forms an "empty frame" that hides the lack at the center of the genre: the radical absence of the MIA. As the POW/MIA film attempts to account for the MIA's "unaccounted-for body," it cannot return a narrative of that body's fate—how he was captured, why he was detained, and how his release changes the world he returns to—but can offer only an image of that body that cannot speak for anything but its mere existence. In effect the POW/MIA film is not a restoration of the action-image, but another symptom of its breakdown; not only are the people missing, but so is the action that might have given these people meaning.[21] However, rather than embracing the disruption of prior narratives as an opportunity for new political possibilities, the POW/MIA film attempts to reinsert the image of the MIA body into older narratives of national renewal and unity, as if the presence of the body itself could regenerate the body politic around it.

Norris's *Missing in Action* films (1984, 1985, 1988) demonstrate the dynamics of this breakdown of action. The films are offered in the spirit of mourning, as Norris dedicates them to his younger brother, Wieland, who died in Vietnam in 1970, but he also offers them to the families of MIAs as solace for the "turmoil" they experience in the absence of their loved ones' bodies. As Norris sympathetically imagines himself in the place of these families, image and presence are elided as balms for their epistemological anguish: "I know where my brother is—I saw the body. But what if he was still a MIA?" Thus the goal of the film is simply to furnish this body and thus validate the suspicions of the POW/MIA movement. But paradoxically the appearance of this body does not put an end to the mourning process of these families, but rather throws them into a state of continuous melancholia, fueling the morbid optimism that more and more bodies might be found. Thus the plot of the first *Missing in Action* mirrors the accusations of the POW/MIA movement that the Vietnamese are continuing to hide the presence of living American POWs in Vietnam, and that the U.S. government is impotent to help find these soldiers.

Norris's character, Col. James Braddock, was himself a POW who managed to escape, and now he finds himself with an American delegation negotiating with his former captors and torturers. Because the negotiations are stalled by the deceit and obfuscations of the communist Vietnamese, Braddock must act outside of official governmental procedures, breaking into the home of General Trau (James Hong) to find the location of the American MIAs, and then teaming up with an arms trafficker (M. Emmet Walsh) to storm the POW camp and rescue the American soldiers himself. The end of the film provides the clearest wish fulfillment of the genre's manifest desires, producing the unaccounted-for body whose existence the Vietnamese and U.S. governments denied. Just as the head of the Vietnamese delegation announces, "In conclusion, then, we categorically deny that there are any living MIAs in the People's Republic of Vietnam," Braddock marches into the negotiations with an American POW in tow, and the film concludes on a freeze-frame of this image. A similar ending appears in Stallone's MIA film, *Rambo: First Blood Part II*, in which Rambo is sent to present-day Vietnam to obtain photographic evidence of American POWs and instead returns with the actual POWs he has rescued. In both films the POWs who are saved are mute bodies, emaciated and pitiful compared to the brawny, hypermasculine heroes who rescue them. Though no longer missing, these POWs are ghostly presences, mere objects to be acted upon. It is telling that in *Missing in Action* the film freezes on the return of the POWs, as if the continuation of their lives back in the U.S. and the resolution of this diplomatic stalemate are moot for the purposes of this fantasy.

Like the POW/MIA movement that spawned it, the MIA film subgenre also produces a retrograde politics that suspends the myriad developments of the 1960s and 1970s—in particular the activism of racialized communities, of women, and of gays and lesbians—in favor of a moral calculus nostalgically located in the pre-Vietnam period. This POW/MIA is literally missing from

51. A Vietnamese communist bayonets wounded Americans soldiers, as seen from the vantage point of Braddock (Chuck Norris) in a flashback nightmare from the Vietnam War. Frame enlargement from *Missing in Action*.

American history, frozen into a political subject position untouched by the conflicts and the potentialities of this period, as if trapped in those filmic flashbacks so frequently called upon to signify the trauma of the Vietnam War. The case of Lt. Everett Alvarez and his family illustrates the contradictions produced by the disjuncture between the historical temporalities of the POW/MIA and the U.S. he left behind. As one of the first American POWs to be captured in 1964, and one of the longest to be held by the North Vietnamese, Alvarez was celebrated by the Chicano antiwar movement as a symbol of the exploitation of brown soldiers, and his sister Delia became a prominent antiwar and Chicana activist. But Everett saw Delia's work as "giv[ing] comfort to our enemies," and throughout his captivity maintained a belief in the "core values" of the nation—"duty, loyalty, unity, honor"—untouched by the dissension of the era.[22] Just as Anna O., one of Freud's earliest case studies, exhibited her traumatic hysteria in part by behaving as if she were reliving her experiences from exactly one year past, the POW/MIA film, although largely set in the present tense of the 1980s, seems to occupy the historical space of the previous decades.[23]

Missing in Action reaches even further back in history to borrow from an earlier iconography of the "yellow peril" in American culture: the Second World War film. The film begins with an extended flashback dream sequence: Braddock is attacking a Viet Cong POW camp and comes upon a VC bayoneting wounded Americans (fig. 51), which enrages him and causes him to jump onto the VC with two grenades in his hands. Abruptly the dream "death" awakens the real Braddock, who is lying in a hotel room in Ho Chi Minh City, listening to an American television news anchor describe the current MIA crisis. The flashback is doubly retrograde, drawing on imagery from the Second World War while situating the film's present-tense negotiations over POW/MIAS as a compulsive repetition of Braddock's failure to save them in the past.[24] The genre's return to Vietnam may appear on the surface to be simply a fantastic assertion of mastery on a past defeat, but it must also be understood as a traumatic compulsion betraying passivity as much as activity. The attempt to redo Vietnam is an attempt to escape the death drive of the flashback and emerge fully into the present, but remains stuck in a limbo between past and present, like the freeze frame that ends the film and prevents it from joining the contemporary moment.

The discourse of trauma, both historical and personal, links the POW/MIA with the Vietnam veteran, whom some have labeled "our stateside MIAS."[25] Stallone's *First Blood* focuses entirely on the stateside experiences of the veteran John Rambo, but deviates from its source in Morrell's novel by making even more explicit its cross-identifications with racial otherness, both black and oriental, described in chapter 1. The film's executive producer, Andrew Vajna, explained how the film adaptation responded to the mood of the 1980s, which was more forgiving toward the Vietnam War and its veterans: "Instead of [Rambo] being a total lunatic running around the countryside killing everybody, we made him a victim of circumstances."[26] To that end the film reinvents Rambo as a racially miscegenated character, supposedly of Native American and German descent (and eerily reminiscent of Chuck Norris's actual Irish Cherokee descent).

To contrast with Rambo's aimless wanderings in the novel, the film also frames the narrative with Rambo's search for a newly invented character: the African American veteran Delmar Barry, who served with him in Vietnam. Rambo is trying to track down Delmar in the film's opening scene, but is told by Delmar's widow that he has already passed away, presumably from cancer derived by exposure to Agent Orange. If Delmar is a physical casualty of the war, Rambo is by implication a psychological casualty, one of the "forgotten warriors" that the POW/MIA movement attempted to recover. But this parallel with Delmar also emphasizes race as the grounds for Rambo's melancholia. His jailhouse tortures include another plot element added by the film: he is hosed down in his jail cell after he refuses to take a shower, thus recalling the posture of African American abjection in scenes of fire hoses turned on civil rights protestors in Birmingham, Alabama. Yet the jailhouse torture is also what leads Rambo into his single flashback of the Vietnam War, a brief glimpse of his bare chest being sliced by a uniformed North Vietnamese soldier. Victimization thus draws from a racial phantasmatic wider than the war itself, reinforcing Morrell's imagined memory that the Vietnam War and racial strife in the U.S. were one and the same conflict.

The end of the film *First Blood* contains its most significant departure from the novel: a melodramatic monologue written mostly by Stallone himself, which situates Rambo firmly within the pattern of white male victimization. Weeping and confessing his psychological anguish to his former commander, Colonel Trautman (Richard Crenna), Rambo reveals the sources of his current traumatized state. But Stallone's hysterical performance belies the rhetoric of remasculinization by practically embracing his abjection. After a speech that lasts three and a half minutes and ends in tears, Rambo wordlessly reaches out to Trautman and cries into his shoulder. This scene not only breaks the fast-paced action sequences that dominate the rest of the film, but also breaks Rambo's near silence during the entire film. Stallone explained how he created this soliloquy: "I thought, what would it be like if a person hadn't been able to talk for five years, and then someone said, 'OK, you've got one minute to sum up everything you've gone through?' "[27] The result reads like a mini-history of the Vietnam War era. Like Booker in *Good Guys*, Rambo is the last remaining survivor of his platoon, and his trauma is partly survivor's guilt; as he tells Trautman, "Back there, I had all these guys who were my friends. Back here, there's nothing." Another cause of his trauma is the antiwar movement: "all the maggots at the airport, protesting me, spitting, calling me a baby killer and all kinds of foul crap." Yet another source of abjection is his current economic disenfranchisement: "Back there, I could fly a gunship, I could drive a tank. I was in charge of million dollar equipment. Back here, I can't even hold a job parking cars."

But the violent kernel of this trauma goes back to orientalized violence, as Rambo's friend Billy is blown up outside a Saigon bar by a bomb hidden in a Vietnamese child's shoe-shine box, a scene Rambo recounts in a frenzy:

> Billy's body is all over the place. He's laying there and he's fucking screaming, there's pieces of him all over me, and I'm trying to pull him off, you know, and—my friend! He's all over me! He's got blood and everything, and I'm trying to hold him together, and put him together, it's like his insides keep coming out. And nobody would help! No one helped! He said, I wanna go home, I wanna go home, he keeps calling my name, I wanna go home, Johnny, I wanna drive my Chevy, and I said, what, I can't find your fucking legs! I can't find your legs. I can't get it out of my head. It's been seven years. Every day it hurts. I can't talk to anybody.

As Rambo relives this traumatic memory, he rips the bandolier off his chest as if to brush Billy's viscera off his body, and crouches into a fetal position. Yet this fantasy of the incontinent body is itself modeled on images of the Vietnamese as victimized corpses, dissolving the integrity of the living body into abject waste. The rap groups and activism that established the PTSD diagnosis imagined these Vietnamese bodies contaminating the psyches of surviving American solders—a "gook syndrome" that eroded first their morals and then their sanity, threatening to turn veterans into dead gooks themselves.

This breakdown of the hard body is captured in First Blood in a series of long takes, focusing on Stallone's muscular physique now crumpled and weeping (fig. 52), and broken up periodically by brief reaction shots from Trautman, who is rendered speechless by Rambo's therapeutic confession. This is a confusing ending to an action film purporting to follow the narrative arc of escape and capture, yet climaxing in an emotional catharsis that results in physical and narrative paralysis. Linda Williams has identified First Blood as a genre hybrid between women's melodrama and the male war film, using the melodramatic mode "as a means of 'solving' problems of moral legitimacy."[28] Yet the film's solution is far from a cure for the Vietnam veteran's trauma, and the racial melodrama disrupts the empty frame of the surrounding action narrative. If earlier in the film Rambo had seemed to go native by showing complete bodily mastery—camouflaging himself with leaves, living off the land, ambushing the police chasing him—in this monologue his racial identification with the Viet Cong turns him into an incontinent being, emotionally out of control and phantasmatically covered with another soldier's body parts. Although it is convenient for many cultural commentators to focus on Stallone's and Norris's hard bodies as a symptom of the retrenchment of white masculinity in the early 1980s—indeed Rambo's pectorals receive far more attention than his emotional breakdown—these bodies are the end product of an earlier fantasy structure, the oriental obscene, that forever links them to their racial others and to the scene of their own undoing.

The transition from the emotional breakdown at the end of First Blood to the mission to return to Vietnam and rescue POW/MIAs in Rambo: First Blood Part II is in essence an attempt to displace this fundamental crisis of passivity with the semblance of activity. The MIA of the first film, Rambo, is rescued from himself, allowing the film series to project his "missing" status onto the other bodies whom he then must protect. But action, both as a filmic genre and as a mode of being, fails to recover the agency that we imagine ourselves, as a nation, to have lost along with the Vietnam War. As the imagined origin of

52. John Rambo (Sylvester Stallone) weeps as he confesses his wartime traumas after having laid siege to the small town that tried to jail him. Frame enlargement from *First Blood*.

that loss, Vietnam is itself a momentary diversion from a larger historical genealogy of trauma to the nation. Reportedly "puzzled by the controversy" over the POW/MIA rescue plot of *Rambo: First Blood Part II*, the director George Cosmatos responded, "We weren't trying to do a 'Deer Hunter' or an 'Apocalypse Now.' We wanted to make a movie about a hero. A warrior—like an American Indian warrior, or a Viking, or a gladiator from Rome.' "[29] The mythic past, outside of the march of history, is the only place left to locate the contemporary action hero away from the decay of the American action-image and its supporting master narratives.

Likewise the other films featuring Stallone's Rambo and Norris's Braddock never quite manage to move into present-day America, instead putting their heroes into ever more distant settings, both temporally and spatially. Although *Rambo: First Blood Part II* seems to conclude triumphantly with the return of American POWs, the opening of *Rambo III* (1988) finds Rambo hiding in Thailand among Buddhist priests, abandoning both the U.S. and the POWs he rescued. *Missing in Action 2: The Beginning* (1985) is a prequel, returning to the source of Braddock's trauma in his incarceration in a North Vietnamese POW camp. Paradoxically it depicts Braddock as POW freeing himself and his fellow Americans from the camp, a narrative which would seem to obviate the necessity of rescuing POW/MIAs in the first film. *Braddock: Missing in Action III* (1988) has Braddock returning to Vietnam to rescue the Amerasian son he left behind during the fall of Saigon, apparently during an alternate past in which he was never captured as a POW, and also in an alternate universe where he can escape across the border from Vietnam into Thailand, skipping over Laos and Cambodia altogether. As Rambo and Braddock depart further from the Vietnam War and its legacy in the U.S., they lead the action genre into more and more fantastic and allegorical territory, perhaps best exemplified by Arnold Schwarzenegger's battle with the Viet Cong as alien bounty hunter in *Predator* (1987).

But even the acknowledgment of Vietnam as a national trauma is far from an ethical reckoning with that war, for it ultimately plays into a larger fantasy that the nation was pure, good, and whole before its recent fall from grace. The brief eruption of the Second World War into the Vietnam combat scenes of *Missing in Action* foreshadows the recuperation of the "greatest generation" and the "good war" out of the ashes of Vietnam. As if to prove the emptiness of the action-frame of the POW/MIA, *Variety* magazine reported in 1985 that pirated videocassettes of *Rambo: First Blood Part II* were circulating in the Middle East with subtitles that transformed the setting from Vietnam to the Philippines during the Second World War, and the Vietnamese into the Japanese.[30] On one hand, the global interchangeability of the yellow peril with the oriental obscene in the 1980s shows that these older racial fantasies were not displaced by the Vietnam era but always lay latent in the background. On the other hand, this historical déjà vu may not signal the collapse of racial fantasies into one another but rather the emergence of new political fantasies, new constellations of imagined relations, and perhaps new traumas, in the context of the 1980s: Vietnam 1975, Iran 1978, and Japan, not simply reincarnated from 1941 but a new threat in 1985 to the already fragile economic landscape of the U.S.

Good Asian Americans, Bad Orientals

We'come a Chinatown, Folk! Ha. Ha. Ha. . . . Hoppy New Year! Fred Eng, "Freddie" of Eng's Chinatown tour'n'travoo.

"We tell Chinatown where to go." Ha ha ha. I'm top guide here. Allaw week Chinee New Year. Sssssshhh Boom! Muchee muchie firey crackee! Ha. Ha. Ha. . . .

You wanta see the Chinaman albino the color of Spam, and the sights only Chinatown's topguide can show ya. I might show-em to ya tonight, folks.

You make me feel good. I like ya. Goong Hay Fot Choy. . . .

—Frank Chin, *The Year of the Dragon* (1974)

There are those who liken Chinatown to a skating pond. On the surface, we see a lovely picture-postcard landscape of snowflakes and skaters. But underneath, the cannibal fish: the gangs. The sharks: those who control the gangs. And the whales:

the big bosses. All move in deadly swarms. These bosses, some people are beginning to say, are tied into an international crime network with its headquarters in
Hong Kong.

—Michael Cimino, *Year of the Dragon* (1985)

I end this book in the 1980s in part because this period marks the end of the
politics of cross-racial identification that made the oriental obscene possible.
Against the backdrop of the Vietnam War the Vietnamese symbolized a combination of threat and promise for a variety of American political movements,
as the utopian possibilities of identifying with oriental otherness was linked
to the danger that actual orientals posed to the existing sociopolitical order in
the U.S. But slogans such as "No Vietnamese ever called me nigger" or "My
Lai–Hiroshima" would be increasingly unthinkable in the era of neoconservative multiculturalism, as Asian Americans were identified more with capitalist success than with military threat or abjection. The 1980s were also a very
different decade than the 1960s for Asian Americans in particular. Rather than
a "missing" people in formation, Asian Americans as such became a recognizable entity within the larger U.S. body politic, making inroads into mainstream electoral politics and gaining access to social services and academic
professionalization. As Yen Le Espiritu has documented, the pan-ethnic organizing of the 1960s resulted in the naming and recognition of "Asian Americans" or "Asian Pacific Islanders" as legible political categories, and thus as
entities available to be courted by coalition politics and government fund-
ing.[31] Furthermore many of those radicalized in the 1960s went on to become
cultural producers, establishing a body of self-consciously Asian American
novels, plays, and films that would fuel the development of Asian American
studies as an academic discipline. And the effects of the Immigration and
Nationality Act of 1965 began to register not only in the numerical increase of
the Asian America population through new immigrants, but also in the shift
of that population from low-wage laborers to the middle- and upper-class,
white-collar professionals that the act favored.

However, the result of this domestication of the oriental obscene is not a
full-scale incorporation of Asian Americans into the American body politic.
The timing of these developments also coincided with the rise of what has
been called a post–civil rights or neoconservative racial politics, casting multiculturalism as a discourse of individual rather than collective rights while
denigrating many of the prior political strategies of racial minorities as mere
"identity politics."[32] Whiteness itself was reconfigured to take advantage of
the moral legitimacy of multiculturalism while denying its politics of collec-

tive redress, as a resurgence of interest in ethnicity allowed white ethnics to disavow any complicity in the hegemony of white dominance. The deproletarianization of Asian America even led some to view Asians as "honorary whites," implying that racial difference was reducible to socioeconomic disadvantage and could be erased through upward mobility. These strategies attempted to separate Asian Americans from African Americans and Latinos, leaving the latter minority groups to bear the stigma of racial pathology while celebrating Asian Americans as "model minorities" that proved the viability of the political status quo. In the 1980s the "good" Asian American (Americanized, mainstream, middle-class) would increasingly be set apart from the "bad" oriental (foreign, disruptive, violent) that was idealized during the Vietnam era. This symbolic bifurcation would mirror a widening demographic gap within Asian America that separated prosperous Chinese, Filipino, and Asian Indian immigrants from the refugees of the various Indochinese wars—Vietnamese, Cambodians, Laotians—who proved to be less ideal models of immigrant success.

The recuperation of Chinatown as a symbolic space within rather than apart from the U.S. is part of the movement away from the oriental obscene and toward the inclusionary claims of multiculturalism. Two significant Asian American texts, Frank Chin's play The Year of the Dragon (1974) and Wayne Wang's film Chan Is Missing (1982), attempt to deconstruct Chinatown as a racist fantasy disconnected from the complex and heterogeneous lives of the Asian Americans within its geographic boundaries. Both texts center on workers in Chinatown's tourism industry—in The Year of the Dragon, tour guide Fred Eng, and in Chan Is Missing, taxicab drivers Jo and Steve—all laboring to produce this phantasmatic space for consumption by its mostly white American visitors, often through what Chin derides as "food pornography."[33] In their opening monologues both Fred and Jo bemoan the banality of these exchanges. Jo jokes that his passengers will invariably ask, "What's a good place to eat in Chinatown?" within three seconds of entering his cab, and Fred proclaims in his fake pidgin tour guide accent, "I'm gonna take ya where I eat, 'The Imperial Silver Jade Empress.' Good home cookin and souvenir chopsticks."[34]

Even as these contemporary tourists go beyond chop suey in search of more authentic cultural treats, the hunt for food pornography satisfies the desire for otherness without a threatening encounter with actual otherness, and Asian American cultural peddlers oblige by trading on their dual status as native informants and (partly) assimilated familiars to their fellow citizens. Such liminality reflects the placement of Chinatown as a segregated ethnic enclave nonetheless embedded within the hearts of major American cities, or what Trinh T. Minh-ha has characterized as the phenomenon of "the Third World within the First."[35] But the very role of the Chinatown tour guide is itself phantasmatic, playing up to a fantasy of authenticity and alterity defined from the point of view of mainstream America. As Chin explained to a newspaper critic, the tour guide is "a Chinaman playing a white man playing Chinese . . . a minstrel show."[36]

Both of these texts strive to go beyond this image to illuminate some kind of truth about Asian American lives and experiences, one that connects them to American rather than foreign histories. Chin explained that he based the character of Fred on Chinatown tour guides he knew in San Francisco: "I watched one in Portsmouth Square, when I was a kid. He looked down the front of his tourists' summer dresses and pointed out Chinatown people as if they were rocks and trees in Yosemite National Park."[37] Ironically this treatment of Asian Americans as scenery situates them firmly within a national imaginary—Chinatown as Yosemite, both landscapes of wild otherness—even as it relegates the residents into objects for consumption, including the tour guide himself. Thus the main narrative of *The Year of the Dragon* is not only to peer behind this "pack of lies" told by the tour guide, but also to examine the effects of such alienating self-reification on its purveyors.

One of Fred's foils is his sister Mattie, who has managed to escape Chinatown by marrying a white man and parlaying her reification into economic mobility; she and her husband, Ross, produce wildly popular cookbooks and newspaper columns under the pseudonym "Mama Fu Fu"—a domesticated version of Fu Manchu—and have moved to the heart of WASP America, Boston. While Fred mocks Mattie's productions as low-brow, he seems to long for a similar measure of economic freedom, to become a creative writer rather than simply a peddler of tales to tourists. Mattie even offers Fred a chance to join her in Boston: "Out there we'll be able to forget we're Chinamen, just forget all this and just be people and Fred will write again."[38] Yet despite his disgust, Fred cannot dismiss Chinatown altogether; the reality of the place is too intimately tied to its complex history and interactions with white America, and the erasure of the tourist fantasy threatens to dissolve the remainder of the city built around it, including his father, the self-proclaimed "mayor of Chinatown." Although Mattie accuses Fred of clinging to Chinatown like "some ugly new breed of rat who can't live without poison," Fred reclaims it at the play's end as "my Chinatown," haunted by the ghost of his father, who dies in the last scene, and by the historical specters of railroad workers, starving laborers, left-behind wives, and paper sons.[39]

Similarly Wang borrows from the generic structure of film noir and detective stories to create a whodunit—the disappearance of a cabbie, Chan Hung—whose investigation allows the film to visit the disparate denizens of San Francisco's Chinatown, both Chinese and non-Chinese. Unlike the POW/MIA film, *Chan Is Missing* never resolves its central enigma by actually locating Chan Hung. Instead it dwells on what Peter Feng has called, in Deleuzian terms, "the challenge of becoming Asian American," refusing the fixity of identity in favor of a shifting negotiation of multiple roles.[40] Because the plot of the film meanders through its unsolved mystery with little progress, the main focus of the spectator's attention becomes the images of Chinatown life: the kitchen of the Golden Dragon Restaurant; a midday dance at the Manilatown Senior Citizens Center; the single-room-occupancy Hotel St. Paul, where Chan Hung lived; the benches at Portsmouth Square, where many elderly Chinese gather. Although the film may refuse identities, it fixates on spatial locations that bear the heterogeneous traces of Asian American life.

Yet these locations do not add up to a stable subject position that might readily be incorporated into a symbolic mapping of the U.S. as inclusive of Chinatown. If Chan Hung is meant to stand in for all Asian Americans, Jo's final comments in the film trouble the coupling of the politics of identification with visual representation: "The problem with me is that I believe what I see and hear. If I did that with Chan Hung I'll know nothing because everything is so contradictory. Here's a picture of Chan Hung but I still can't see him."[41] Even if the film has labored to produce a visual record of the real Chinatown, these indices do not produce a usable knowledge for the purposes of political representation, at least by the realist logic that animates electoral politics. By the time *Chan Is Missing* was produced, these images were already past, indexing the significant icons and locations of 1970s Asian American activism that had disappeared by the 1980s. These images cannot produce the body of Chan Hung or of Asian America, as *Missing in Action* triumphantly produced American POWs on screen. But in contrast to *Missing in Action*, *Chan Is Missing* gestures toward a politics of becoming that is not trapped in the fantasy of presence. Its images of Chinatown point to absences that refuse mere historical nostalgia or repetition. Having seen the real Chinatown, we leave behind the narrative action-image to locate a space for the becoming of the time-image.

Tellingly the film's closing montage is set to the tune of "Grant Avenue" from the Broadway production of Rogers and Hammerstein's *Flower Drum Song* (1958), a utopian cold war musical which also attempted to situate Chinatown at the heart of the U.S. nation: "Grant Avenue, San Francisco,

53. The Transamerica Pyramid, completed in 1972, hovers over San Francisco's Chinatown, symbolizing the encroachment of corporate capital into this ethnic enclave. Frame enlargement from *Chan Is Missing*.

California, U.S.A." Yet the images of this montage explicitly deny the narrative described in the song's lyrics, and in particular collide with the optimistic vision of food pornography proposed by Mattie in *The Year of the Dragon*: as the song saucily proclaims, "The girl who serves you all your food is another tasty dish," *Chan Is Missing* focuses on an anonymous elderly Chinese woman, rocking back and forth on the balcony of a nondescript building. We also witness the hybridity of Chinatown, bordered by other ethnic enclaves such as Little Italy and lying in the shadow of the prime symbol of economic power and urban renewal in San Francisco, the Transamerica Pyramid (fig. 53). The recognizable intersection of Jackson Street and Grant Avenue alludes to the tumultuous protests over the demolition of the I-Hotel in the heart of Manilatown just a block away, a battle that began in 1968 and did not end until 1979 and galvanized pan-ethnic activism in the city.[42] Thus even if indistinct, the Chinatown of *Chan Is Missing* is intimately linked to multiple strands of American society and history even as it marks Asian America as an absent presence within that history. Further linking the film to Chin's earlier project, the song is performed by the actress Pat Suzuki, who starred as Fred Eng's mother in the premier of *The Year of the Dragon* at New York's American Place Theater in 1974. Suzuki's role in Chin's and Wang's texts seems to mark both a generational gap and a continuity between pre– and post–Vietnam era Asian American cultural productions. While Wang and Chin may deny the assimilationist politics of the cold war era associated with *Flower Drum Song*, they each strive in their own way to place a rediscovered Chinatown within the boundaries of the U.S. The uniquely Asian American formations they outline are born as much from collisions with the U.S.—racist stereotypes of Charlie Chans and FOBs (immigrants fresh off the boat), allusions to John Wayne and the Lone Ranger—as from a distant Asia.

These earlier Asian American texts illuminate a more recent and well-known version of *Year of the Dragon* (1985): the film directed by Michael Cimino and starring Mickey Rourke as the aptly named Detective Stanley White, who endeavors to clean up another iconic Chinatown located in New York City. This film was derided by some critics as a racist "Rambo Goes to Chinatown" which treated White's assignment to rein in Chinatown gangs as "Vietnam II."[43] In many ways Cimino's film seems to be a repetition of the obsessions of the POW/MIA film, combined with the dark racial violence of his earlier work, *The Deer Hunter*, and scholars such as Robert Lee and Gina Marchetti have provided incisive critiques of the film's regressive racial and sexual politics.[44] But the film is equally a product of the multiculturalism of the 1980s and uses the Chinatown so contested by Chin and Wang as a way of separating good Asian Americans from the bad orientals lingering from the Vietnam War. This is most visible in the film's preproduction, as Cimino and the producer Dino de Laurentiis brag in their press materials for the film:

> In telling this story, "Year of the Dragon" presents a vivid portrait of a society that is both a part of and apart from the American mainstream. Seldom examined by artists, academics or journalists, and never before the setting of an American motion picture, New York's Chinatown reflects the growing vitality of the Asian community in the United States today. . . . Director Michael Cimino prepared himself by reaching far beyond the starting point of Robert Daley's 1981 novel, *Year of the Dragon*. Cimino traveled to New York to meet the people of Chinatown face to face—its ordinary citizens, its prosperous merchants, its street gangs—and to visit places few outsiders have ever seen—its private nightclubs, its secret gambling dens, and its basement soybean factories.
>
> Cimino's research included a study of immigration laws, the methods of the New York Police Department, the records of drug enforcement agencies, and the fascinating but often tragic history of the Chinese people in North America.[45]

This research into topics well known to Asian American studies—immigration, labor, bachelor societies—seems at odds with the allegorical transformation

54. Detective Stanley White (Mickey Rourke) studies up on Chinese America before his meeting with a television journalist, Tracy Tzu (Ariane Koizumi). Frame enlargement from *Year of the Dragon*.

of Chinatown into the Vietnam War, which Cimino and his co-screenwriter, Oliver Stone, appended onto Daley's original novel. While the press release still maintains the familiar exoticism associated with the Chinatown of Sax Rohmer's early twentieth-century Fu Manchu novels, it also gestures toward a potentially progressive historiography, as if to situate the Chinese alongside other white ethnicities recently recuperated within American history. Cimino reportedly told the playwright David Henry Hwang that he hoped his film would "speak truthfully about the Chinatown community."[46] Might this film be more accurate in its ethnic history than its military history?

The specific deployment of this knowledge reveals that multiculturalism restores more political and social capital to White (and to whites) than to the Asian Americans it purports to sympathetically reveal. One of the first history lectures of the film takes place while White is courting a television correspondent, Tracy Tzu (Ariane Koizumi), over dinner. When Tzu arrives at White's table, the camera reveals a series of books—Milton Meltzer's *Chinese Americans* (1980), Rita Aero's *Things Chinese* (1980), and Loren Fessler's *Chinese in America: Stereotyped Past, Changing Present* (1983)—which prompts Tzu to tease, "Are you doing your homework?" (fig. 54). But when Tzu attempts to relate her family history in California to White, he interrupts her, "Yeah, I know the story," and then proceeds to open *Things Chinese* to the infamous photograph of the Golden Spike ceremony in Utah at the completion of the Union Pacific and Central Pacific Railroads in 1869. The omission of Chinese laborers from this photograph—a phenomenon the activist Helen Zia jokingly calls "MIH— Missing in History"—became a point of contention for many Asian American artists and historians, and this photograph featured prominently in the novels

China Men (1980) by Maxine Hong Kingston and *Donald Duk* (1991) by Frank Chin.[47] Yet in White's version of this history the omission is less a tragic exclusion than yet another symptom of Chinese inscrutability: "There's not one single, solitary Chinaman. They weren't even asked to show up. They died anonymous. Goddamn people, you keep everything a secret." Hence passivity is rewritten as sinister agency, and the secrecy of the Chinese in 1869 continues today, as White accuses the residents of Chinatown of hiding Chinese criminals from the white police, thus furthering their own exclusion from the body politic.

A similar tactic occurs when White taunts one of his fellow police officers, Herbert Kwong (Dennis Dun), as "a tough kid from Kwangtung whose ancestors used to hang in baskets in the Sierras poking dynamite in cliff faces." Kwong explodes in a diatribe meant to refuse White's knowledge and power over him:

> What do you know about [my ancestors]? We were traders, shipbuilders, explorers! We taught you agriculture. We gave you the orange, the grape, your irrigation system. We dug your gold and silver, Stanley. We taught you how to fish the Pacific. And still we were barred from American citizenship until 1943. We worked so hard to build your railroads, then when our opium didn't come on time, we were so desperate, we helped each other kill ourselves. But I'm not gonna kill myself for you, Captain Stanley. No more Chinaman Joe. Those days are over.

Yet for Kwong to refuse White's monopolization of historical knowledge is not the same as freeing himself from the other forms of power that White wields over him. The history that Kwong relates, especially in its celebration of working-class Chinese immigrants, replicates the heroic, masculinist history that Frank Chin himself attempted to recuperate, especially in his non-fiction essays.[48] However, Kwong cannot sustain the bravado of his historical interpellation. In the very next scene he returns to the undercover job that White had assigned to him, hauling slabs of raw pork in the restaurant owned by the gangster Joey Tai (John Lone), as if cast back into the servile history he had hoped to overcome. And despite his protests, Kwong does end up dying for White, shot in the back by one of Tai's minions after being betrayed by a dirty cop in Tai's employ, Alan Perez (Jack Kehler). The greatest threat to Asian America, it seems, are other minorities and other Asian Americans. The only good oriental in *Year of the Dragon* is the dead one, the one who can be symbolically included in the nation precisely because he can no longer make any other political or social claims.

Another aspect of this film's strategic deployment of multiculturalism is its focus on white ethnicity. This move echoes Cimino's earlier fascination with working-class Russian Americans in The Deer Hunter and the European immigrant settlers in Heaven's Gate (1980). Throughout the film Detective White insists on calling himself a "stupid Polack," a self-deprecation that seems to lessen the sting of his other racist slurs. But this insistence on ethnic specificity also separates White from any overarching category of white privilege that such ethnic groups had previously claimed in the course of their assimilation. Such white ethnic claims also situate "Chinese" and "Polish" as equivalent categories, and thus sever "Chinese" from race as well as from any claims to racial redress. When Joey Tai tries to defend crime as his cultural patrimony, saying, "The citizens of Chinatown regard what you call extortion and bribery as part of the cost of doing business, and have felt that way for thousands of years," White admonishes him, "You're not special, and you're not beyond the law any more than the Puerto Ricans or the Polacks." This rhetoric could have been plucked from any number of contemporaneous descriptions of Asian Americans as model minorities and thus exempt from any form of affirmative action as remuneration for their previous exclusion. Echoing Cimino's press release, Asian Americans are both *apart from* the U.S., with their "Confucian values" and superhuman study habits, and *a part of* the nation, joining the ranks of hegemonic whiteness to deny white ethnics as well as black and Latino minorities their fair share of the national bounty.[49] Although White's character borrows much from the stereotype of the traumatized Vietnam veteran, unlike Nick or Michael in The Deer Hunter White ultimately refuses the traumatic cross-racial identification that drives these earlier veterans. By imagining his own whiteness as wounded, White can imagine himself as equivalent, but ultimately unrelated, to the Chinese.

Strangely these insertions of historical knowledge and multiethnic diversity seem designed to counterbalance the overt racism for which Year of the Dragon was critically excoriated, by offering positive as well as negative representations of Chinese Americans. On the surface this aligns the film with Chan Is Missing and Chin's The Year of the Dragon, offering a seemingly broad portrait of the heterogeneity of Chinatown. This struggle against stereotypes, mostly viewed as negative, infused many multicultural critiques of the media, as seen in the rhetoric of the National Asian American Media Arts Conference at UCLA in 1985.[50] Cimino's Year of the Dragon plays on this common line of critique, having the gang leader Tai lecture Tracy Tzu about her negative media coverage: "But why do you media people insist on emphasizing this sinister Charlie Chan image? Why don't you talk about the chair in Chinese history our association has endowed at Yale University, or our twelve-million-dollar fund for our ten thousand members, our free meals for the aged and the unemployed, free burials, things like that? Positive things." However, this critique merely serves as camouflage for Tai's criminal activities, which have come under attack by Tzu's investigative journalism as well as White's official (and unofficial) policing. The multiculturalist gambit of Year of the Dragon undoes itself by offering such claims as part of the dissimulating otherness of the Chinese underworld. Despite these mini-lessons in Asian American history, Chinatown for Cimino remains tied to Chinese history and ultimately to China.

Ironically the failure of Cimino's multiculturalism became a boon for Asian American activism. Chinese Americans protested both during and after Year of the Dragon's production, picketing the on-location shooting in New York, refusing to cooperate with the casting of extras in Durham, North Carolina, and even filing a $100 million class-action libel suit after the film's release.[51] Los Angeles City Councilman Michael Woo, himself a beneficiary of the entrance of Asian Americans into mainstream electoral politics, eventually helped to negotiate with Cimino's studio, MGM/United Artists, to settle the lawsuit and insert an unprecedented disclaimer in the film: "This film does not intend to demean or ignore the many positive features of Asian-American and specifically Chinese-American communities. Any similarities between the depictions in the film and any association, organization, individual, or Chinatown that exists in real life is accidental."[52] But while these negotiations and protests provided proof of the growing political power of Asian Americans, they also denied the more utopian possibilities of phantasmatic identification found in the oriental obscene. By insisting on both realism and "positive" representations, this disclaimer forces fantasy to deny its equal participation in both reality and fiction, and thus limits politics from partaking in the potential power of phantasmatic formations.

Even the martial arts strand of the oriental obscene fantasy is eventually rehabilitated along these multiculturalist lines. In the teen drama The Karate Kid (1984), set in the multiculturalist paradise of southern California, good and bad orientals are not even represented by Asian characters, but by styles of violence: the bad violence of the Cobra Kai dojo, led by John Kreese (Martin Kove), and the good violence of Mr. Miyagi (Pat Morita), who ends up training the film's protagonist, Daniel LaRusso (Ralph Macchio). Again white ethnicity occupies a middle ground between hegemonic whiteness and racial otherness, as Daniel's Italianness and working-class background align him with Stallone's "Italian Stallion" underdog rather than with the privileged, blond WASP-ness of the Cobra Kai teacher and his students. Bad violence is also associated with the Vietnam War, if not with the Vietnamese: Kreese is a Special Forces Vietnam veteran and is played by the same actor who piloted the helicopter that abandoned Rambo in Vietnam in *Rambo: First Blood Part II*. When we first meet Kreese he is leading his Cobra Kai students through something like a military cadence call, screaming together that fear, pain, and defeat "[do] not exist in this dojo," while Daniel looks on in fear and admiration at Kreese's framed portrait, which proclaims him "U.S. Army 1970–1972 Karate Champion."

The good violence associated with Miyagi is part of a patriotic history. We learn that Miyagi was part of the 442nd Regimental Combat Unit of Nisei soldiers in the Second World War, even while the nation detained their families in internment camps. Pat Morita apparently viewed Miyagi as a positive and complex role compared to his first film appearance, as an anonymous Asian henchman in *Thoroughly Modern Millie* (1967); he stated in a press release, "We never get to play people like this" and even changed his stage name to the more ethnic-sounding Noriyuki "Pat" Morita after *The Karate Kid*.[53] David Henry Hwang called the role one of "the most sympathetic portrayal[s] of an Asian-American" among recent films.[54] Yet the revelation of this patriotic history within *The Karate Kid* is somewhat suspect, emphasizing passive acquiescence to racism over active participation in the nation. The scene where we learn of Miyagi's past follows Daniel's humiliation at the country club at the hands of his privileged rival, the Cobra Kai student Johnny Lawrence (William Zabka). As Daniel rushes away from the club to Miyagi's home, he finds Miyagi wearing an old army uniform and drinking in honor of his anniversary; he learns that Miyagi's wife passed away during childbirth in the internment camps because she was denied access to proper medical care. After Miyagi collapses in bed, the audience learns along with Daniel about the rest of this history through a series of documents he leaves on the coffee table, including old issues of the *Los Angeles Tribune* detailing the evacuation and internment of Japanese Americans (fig. 55).

Despite his painful past, Miyagi is a gentle and pacifist role model, giving credence to the original formulation of the model minority by the sociologist William Petersen in 1966, who celebrated Japanese Americans as rising above not only the grievances of "problem minorities" such as African Americans, but also the complacency of white Americans:

55. Daniel LaRusso (Ralph Macchio) gets a history lesson on the Japanese American internment after a drunken confession from his karate teacher, Mr. Miyagi (Pat Norita). Frame enlargement from *The Karate Kid*.

> Barely more than 20 years after the end of the wartime camps, this is a minority that has risen above even prejudiced criticism. By any criterion of good citizenship that we choose, the Japanese Americans are better than any other group in our society, including native-born whites. They have established this remarkable record, moreover, by their own almost totally unaided effort. Every attempt to hamper their progress resulted only in enhancing their determination to succeed. Even in a country whose patron saint is the Horatio Alger hero, there is no parallel to this success story.[55]

Anticipating the model minority discourse of the 1980s, Petersen even casts the Japanese American internment in a positive light, as an adversity which merely "enhanc[es] their determination." Miyagi's tribulations serve as an object lesson in the endurance of suffering more than a recuperation of Asian American history: if he can survive the Second World War, the internment camps, and the death of his family without complaint, then Daniel's shame in front of his rich classmates cannot be indulged.

The climactic fight between Daniel and Johnny at the All Valley Karate Championship is thus a battle between these two styles of being oriental. The revenge- and power-obsessed Kreese orders his students to fight dirty in order to win, almost as if he were making up for the Vietnam War in each adolescent duel. "No mercy," Kreese sneers at one student who balks at following his orders to disable Daniel so that he cannot fight, while another student shouts at Daniel, "Get him a body bag!" after Johnny attacks Daniel's injured knee with an illegal move. Unlike *No Retreat, No Surrender* (1986), where the legacy of Bruce Lee points to a fantasy of liberatory violence and rebellion inherited from the black power and radical feminist movements, the martial arts violence in The Karate Kid is aligned with a disgraceful war and its repudiated tactics. Daniel triumphs instead with the graceful crane technique that he committed himself to master after Miyagi's drunken confessions. Daniel's orientophilia harkens back to early twentieth-century Japonisme and its obsessions with a feminized and aestheticized exoticism, which was itself revived as the "geisha-ization" of defeated Japan in the cold war era.[56] This domestication of the violence of the oriental obscene counters the masculine yellow peril of both the Japanese in the Second World War and the Viet Cong in Vietnam and becomes the price that Asian Americans pay to be part of the body politic of the multiculturalist 1980s. It is in this domesticated form that Miyagi can be cast as the father figure in Daniel's multicultural family, assimilating Daniel and his single mother from their New Jersey ethnic particularity into the multiculturalism of southern California. Associated with aesthetics rather than racial discrimination, Japaneseness in The Karate Kid becomes an ethnicity no different from Daniel's Italianness.

However, the ultimate reconciliation in the film takes place between whites (Johnny) and white ethnics (Daniel), rather than the two versions of oriental violence. With the privileges of whiteness Daniel does not need to suffer quietly as the model minorities do, and instead uses Miyagi's karate to win the respect of his upper-class schoolmates, ascending to his rightful place in the social hierarchy. The masculinity that Daniel inherits, and that accounts for his popularity as a teen idol, rejects the wounded and miscegenated masculinity of Rambo and Braddock in favor of a new masculinity predicated on a purified white ethnicity. If Daniel's lack of trauma is a sign that the nation has healed from the wounds of Vietnam, then it also indicates that the U.S. has forgotten the lessons of Vietnam in its encounters with foreign and racial others. Daniel does not have to assume the mantle of the white oriental because he has bypassed its traumatic history. According to the logic of multiculturalism, learning karate is no different from eating Chinese food, for both are ways of partaking in racial difference without threatening racial hierarchies or acknowledging racist histories. These practices of consumption might even reinforce white privilege by underscoring its ability to move between hobbies, spaces, and objects while remaining fundamentally unchanged. Thus learning karate does not bring Daniel closer to Asian America; like Detective White's experience with violence in The Year of the Dragon, or the white tourist's patronage of Chinatown, it makes him feel more white.

The Karate Kid thus reveals the rise of multiculturalism as a discourse that ultimately benefits whites by tempering the claims of racial minorities, yet it still retains traces of the oriental obscene. The tenuousness of this separation between good Asian American and bad oriental is shown in how easily the model minority falls back into the gook syndrome in the 1980s. As Robert G. Lee argues, "The Vietnam War story, told as the tragedy of America's lost innocence, works as a master narrative of national collapse while defining the post-Fordist crisis as a product of invasion and betrayal."[57] The Rising Sun symbol, which Daniel wore so innocently as a headband in The Karate Kid, becomes a harbinger of invasion for American laborers caught up in the narrative of a trade war with Japan in the 1980s. One reader complained to the Los Angeles Times, "[Prime Minister] Nakasone and his bureaucratic leaders mean to win the war Japan lost in 1945. . . . Continue to buy Japanese cars and Japan will have won that war," and a political cartoon published in 1985 titled "Hirohito's Revenge" portrayed planes dropping cars instead of bombs onto the U.S.[58] This new anti-Asian sentiment, couched in the rhetoric of the Second World War, likely fueled the murder of Vincent Chin, a second-generation Chinese American, by two unemployed auto workers in Detroit who may have mistaken him for Japanese.[59] Indeed Asian Americans continued to be subject to violence and exclusion through their association with foreign nations, and the indiscriminate lumping together of all Asian ethnicities echoed the pan-ethnic organization of the Asian American movement in an ominous fashion. Asian American groups protested not only the killings but the light sentence Chin's killers, Ronald Ebens and Michael Nitz, received: a $3,000 fine and probation. But the protesters remained within the boundaries of the idealized nation-state as framed by the language of civil rights, rather than the revolutionary rhetoric of the Vietnam era. The post–oriental obscene era ultimately shies away from violence as a critique of the nation-state, casting its lot instead with the inclusionary politics of multiculturalism as the guarantor of rights and freedoms.

Ultimately I do not intend to romanticize the politics of the oriental obscene, for it was a violent racial phantasmatic that offered its own horrors of exclusion and expulsion. However, I have tried to show how complex and potentially powerful these cross-racial fantasies and identifications proved to be. These identifications were not merely masquerades waiting to be displaced by a more culturally accurate model, for the rhetoric of appropriation implies that certain things are "proper" to one race and not another, and that identification is a form of psychic or historical dispossession. But as psychoanalysis teaches us, otherness cannot be purged but is constitutive of the self, and the constant appearance of cross-racial identifications is evidence that, psychically, all of our racial identities are premised upon racial otherness. If Rambo and Braddock, Daniel LaRusso and Detective White are in any sense white orientals, they are othered from within, by their exposure to a phantasmatic violence that precedes them. They represent the end of a historical arc through the various fantasies of the oriental obscene from nearly twenty years earlier. But LaRusso and White show how easily these earlier fantasies and identifications can be repressed by the emergence of a new racial phantasmatic, a new historical periodization. We can trace the movement of identification by recovering the complex histories behind these texts and narrative tropes. Only in this way can the racial unconscious of the nation become manifest, and only thus can we understand the importance of otherness in the construction of our national selves.

Notes

Introduction

1. Stephen C. Fehr, "Veterans Applaud Surge of Support for Gulf War Soldiers," *Washington Post*, 4 March 1991; Peter Applebome, "Sense of Pride Outweighs Fears of War," *New York Times*, 24 February 1991; "Gulf War Finally Heals Wounds Left from Vietnam, Bush Says," *San Diego Union-Tribune*, 1 March 1991; Helen Thomas, "Bush Praises U.S. Troops," United Press International, 2 March 1991. For an overview of the uses of the Vietnam syndrome in U.S. foreign relations and military actions in the 1980s and 1990s, see Issacs, *Vietnam Shadows*, 65–102.

2. Geyelin, "The Vietnam Syndrome," 76–89.

3. Nixon, *No More Vietnams*, 13.

4. Maureen Dowd, "War Introduces a Tougher Bush to Nation," *New York Times*, 2 March 1991; June Jordan quoted in Peter Applebome, "War Heals Wounds at Home, but Not All," *New York Times*, 4 March 1991.

5. Turner, *Echoes of Combat*, 11.

6. See Sturken, *Tangled Memories*; Jeffords, *The Remasculinization of America*; Kinney, *Friendly Fire*.

7. B. Anderson, *Imagined Communities*, 5–6.

8. Norris, "Military Censorship and the Body Count in the Persian Gulf War," 224.

9. Rabinowitz and Jeffords, introduction, 17–18.

10. Baudrillard, *The Gulf War Did Not Take Place*.

11. E. J. Dionne Jr., "Kicking the Vietnam Syndrome," *Washington Post*, 4 March 1991.

12. Michael R. Gordon, "Desert Missions by Commandos Aided in Victory," *New York Times*, 1 March 1991.

13. "Saigon Surrenders," *Chicago Tribune*, 20 April 1975; Hubert Van Es, "Thirty Years at 300 Millimeters," *New York Times*, 29 April 2005.

14. Fox Butterfield with Kari Haskell, "Getting It Wrong in a Photo," *New York Times*, 23 April 2000.

15. Pham Thanh, "My Two Countries, My Flesh and Blood," *New York Times*, 19 April 1991.

16. Lam, "My Vietnam, My America," 94, originally published in *Nation*, 12 October 1990.

17. Benjamin, "The Work of Art in the Age of Mechanical Reproduction," 236. The phrase also appears in his essay "A Short History of Photography," 203, published in 1931.

18. Gunning, "The Exterior as Intérieur," 126. Hal Foster describes a similar fascination with the optical unconscious underlying surrealism, which draws on not only film and photography but other physical objects as indices of the repressed real, which erupts like the uncanny to disturb "unitary identity, aesthetic norms, and social order." Rosalind E. Krauss's work on the optical unconscious in high modernist art also focuses on ways that embodiment, the material world, and nonvisual sensory experience emerge even within seemingly nonreferential, abstract images such as Mondrian's geometrical drawings and Pollack's drip paintings, although she acknowledges that her use of Benjamin's term is "at an angle" to his, situating this unconscious within the entirety of optics and the visual field rather than simply the mechanical productions of commodified culture. See Foster, *Compulsive Beauty*, xv–xix; Krauss, *The Optical Unconscious*, 178–80.

19. Foucault, *The Order of Things*, xi.

20. Beidler, "The Last Huey," 3–16.

21. For this idea I am indebted to the work of Sarah Bishop, who is currently writing a dissertation reevaluating the concept of indexicality and exploring its political deployment by various avant-garde authors and filmmakers of the 1960s and 1970s.

22. See Lott, *Love and Theft*; Deloria, *Playing Indian*.

23. It is difficult to assign dates to the Vietnam War conclusively, as U.S. involvement extended beyond the years that the war was officially waged, and many historians use different events to mark the country's entrance into and exit from the war. For example, George C. Herring starts with Truman's support for the French in Indochina in 1950 and ends with the fall of Saigon in 1975, while Marilyn B. Young begins with the liberation of French Indochina from Japanese occupation in 1945 and continues to 1990 and possibly beyond, with the invocations of Vietnam in the lead-up to the first Persian Gulf War. See Herring, *America's Longest War*; Young, *The Vietnam Wars 1945–1990*. The dates I cite here correspond to the narrowest definition of the Vietnam War, from the 1964 Gulf of Tonkin Resolution, authorizing official U.S. involvement, to the signing of the Paris Peace Accords and the beginning of the withdrawal of U.S. forces in 1973.

24. A classic image of the polis organized as a human body may be found in Plato's *Republic*, but the idea is widespread in political theory, particularly in theories of the monarchy as the head of the body politic. See, for example, Kantorowicz, *The King's Two Bodies*. The Jungian concepts of the collective unconscious and archetypes gained popularity in the humanities in the middle of the twentieth century, manifesting in archetypal analysis and a renewed interest in ritual and comparative religion, all with the aim of understanding the commonality of human experience across history and

cultures. For two very different manifestations of this trend, see Frye, *Anatomy of Criticism*, and Campbell, *The Hero with a Thousand Faces*. The "myth and symbol" school is a related movement within American historical and cultural studies, roughly adapting the concept of myth to the framework of national identity. Two of its main works are H. N. Smith, *Virgin Land*, and Marx, *The Machine in the Garden*.

25. Laplanche, "The Unfinished Copernican Revolution," 82; Butler, *Gender Trouble*, 73–100; Cheng, *The Melancholy of Race*, 103–38.

26. B. Anderson, *Imagined Communities*, 5–6.

27. See, for example, Redfield, "Imagi-Nation," 58–83; Axel, "Poverty of the Imagination," 111–33.

28. See Freud, *The Interpretation of Dreams*, 277–78.

29. Sturken, *Tangled Memories*, 1–7; Berlant, *The Anatomy of National Fantasy*, 4–5.

30. Laplanche, "The Theory of Seduction and the Problem of the Other," 657–58, my emphasis; Laplanche, "The Unfinished Copernican Revolution," 71. Laplanche plays on the difference between the German definite articles *das* (neuter form, suggesting thing-ness) and *der* (masculine form, suggesting subjecthood). At the end of "The Unfinished Copernican Revolution," in reference to Freud's famous phrase from *The Ego and the Id*, "Wo Es war, soll Ich werden," Laplanche challenges the overcoming of the unconscious (the German *Es* or "it," but translated into English as the Latinate "Id") by the conscious self (Ich/I/ego), asserting instead that "Wo Es war, wird (soll? muss?) immer noch Anderes sein": Where it was, there will (should? must?) always be an Other (83).

31. Ultimately I consider Laplanchian and Lacanian psychoanalysis complementary in many respects, especially in their opposition to American ego psychology and their reclamation of a Freudian theory of the drives. However, much psychoanalytic film theory influenced by Lacan has emphasized cinema's compensation for the subject's essential lack or castration in terms of imaginary plentitude and mapping this lack/plentitude binary onto sexual difference, thus leading to a lack of attention to or oversimplification of social phenomena which are difficult to binarize, such as race. Many theorists interested in working against this binary logic while preserving other psychoanalytic insights into the unconscious and desire have in fact turned to Laplanche's theory of fantasy as an alternative to this Lacanian scaffolding. For example, see E. Cowie, "Fantasia"; Friedberg, "The Denial of Difference"; Silverman, *Male Subjectivity at the Margins*; Rodowick, *The Difficulty of Difference*.

32. I am alluding both to works that explicitly evoke the concept of fantasy, such as Franklin, *Vietnam and Other American Fantasies*, and Kolodny, *The Land before Her*, as well as works that speak of an American mythology in explicitly Jungian terms, such as Slotkin, *Gunfighter Nation*. In a separate essay, "Myth and the Production of History," Slotkin aligns his use of "myth" with Roland Barthes's French poststructuralist approach that treats the term along the lines of "ideology" rather than a Jungian collective unconscious, although the sense here is still of a false consciousness which the process of historicization can demystify (70, 90).

33. Laplanche, "Seduction, Persecution, Revelation," 196.

34. Althusser, "Ideology and Ideological State Apparatuses," 127–186; Butler, *Gender Trouble*, 134–49.

35. Steven Shaviro in particular views Deleuze and psychoanalytic film theory as fundamentally in opposition to one another, claiming that psychoanalysis overemphasizes the role of mastery in the cinematic gaze and is ultimately suspicious of all forms of viewing, whereas Deleuze allows for the reinsertion of the body and its unruly pleasures within film theory. I think Shaviro overstates the incommensurability of these two bodies of thought, particularly since one can employ not only Laplanche but also Lacan and Freud in a reading of psychoanalysis that also privileges masochism, the fragmentation of the body-ego, and the instability of specular identification. See Shaviro, *The Cinematic Body*, 1–82.

36. Deleuze and Guattari, *Anti-Oedipus*, 30.

37. Deleuze and Guattari, *Anti-Oedipus*, 61.

38. Bhabha, "The Other Question," 66, original emphasis.

39. Freud, "Mourning and Melancholia," 249. Describing how melancholia differs from mourning, Freud explains that the melancholic ego preserves the lost object by identifying with it, thus absorbing this loss into the conception of the self: "Thus the shadow of the object fell upon the ego."

40. Said, *Orientalism*, 3.

41. See Ahmad, *In Theory*, 159–220; Clifford, *The Predicament of Culture*, 255–76.

42. Said, *Orientalism*, 21.

43. Said, *Orientalism*, 26, 206.

44. Omi and Winant, *Racial Formation in the United States*, 54–76.

45. C. J. Kim, "The Racial Triangulation of Asian Americans," 105–38.

46. Lowe, *Critical Terrains*, 5.

47. Lowe, *Critical Terrains*, 8.

48. Ngai, "American Orientalism," 409.

49. Lowe, *Immigrant Acts*, 5.

50. Yu, *Thinking Orientals*, 83.

51. Palumbo-Liu, *Asian/America*, 19.

52. Said, *Orientalism*, 2.

53. Desser, "The Kung Fu Craze," 38. This quote is analyzed in more depth in chapter 4.

54. The confusion seems to arise from the fact that neither the Korean nor the Vietnam War began with an official declaration of war from the U.S. Instead the Korean War was officially designated as a "police action" under the auspices of the United Nations, and the American involvement in Vietnam was described as "assistance" to an official ally, South Vietnam, in fighting its own civil war. Incidentally Library of Congress subject headings use the term "Korean War" but "Vietnamese Conflict."

55. Wei, *The Asian American Movement*, 11–43; Espiritu, *Asian American Panethnicity*, 19–52.

56. S. Chan, *Asian Americans*, 174.

57. Deleuze, *Cinema 2*, 220.

58. For example, see S. Chan, *Asian Americans*, 145–65; Ng, *The History and Immigration of Asian Americans*; Hing, *Making and Remaking Asian America through Immigration Policy*.

59. Lowe, *Immigrant Acts*, 16–17.

60. Schlesinger, *Violence*, 53.

61. Isserman and Kazin, *America Divided*.

62. R. Williams, *Keywords*, 279.

63. S. Chong, "From 'Blood Auteurism' to the Violence of Pornography," 249–68. In *The Secret Museum* Walter Kendrick provides a historical context for the Anglo-American censorship of sexual obscenity. There is an extensive literature on the legal interpretation of obscenity, often centered on the narrative of a conflict between freedom of speech and moral obligations against harm to others. See, for example, Feinberg, *Offense to Others*; Saunders, *Violence as Obscenity*; Schauer, *Free Speech*. For a history of the various systems of censorship and content control over the American film industry, see Leff and Simmons, *The Dame in the Kimono*; Lewis, *Hollywood v. Hard Core*.

64. The Oxford English Dictionary (draft revision December 2007) tersely declares "obscene" to be a word of "uncertain origin." Its Latin antecedent, *obscēnus*, primarily signifies ill boding, inauspicious, or ominous—meanings echoed in the earliest English usages by Shakespeare and traced by Samuel Johnson in his Dictionary of 1786, yet ignored by most legal scholars who draw upon etymology to buttress their claims. See Saunders, *Violence as Obscenity*, 67–69, and Warren Burger's majority opinion in *Miller v. California*, 413 U.S. 15 (1973). Among those who argue for the connection to the Latin term *caenum* (filth) are Ellis, "The Revaluation of Obscenity," and Clor, *Obscenity and Public Morality*. Those who have theorized the link to the Latin term *scaena* (scene) include Lawrence, "Pornography and Obscenity"; Michelson, *Speaking the Unspeakable*, xi–xii; and L. Williams, *Hard Core*, 280–315. While older discussions of obscenity tend to promote a Foucauldian repressive hypothesis, regarding the taboo against it as an injunction of power that demands a heroic, liberal transgression, more recent scholars such as Williams and Michelson recognize that the injunction against obscenity is itself an incitement to discourse.

65. "'Brutal Films Pale before Televised Vietnam'—Valenti," *Variety*, 21 February 1968.

66. Desser, "The Kung Fu Craze," 38.

Chapter 1. Bringing the War Home

The full source citation of this chapter's epigraph is National Commission on the Causes and Prevention of Violence, *Progress Report of the National Commission on the Causes and Prevention of Violence to President Lyndon B. Johnson* (Washington, D.C.: Government Printing Office, 1969). 1–2. The emphasis is mine.

1. Max Frankel, "Johnson Appoints Panel on Violence," *New York Times*, 6 June 1968. Milton Eisenhower was the younger brother of President Eisenhower. He was also a former director of the War Relocation Authority, the agency responsible for carrying out the internment of Japanese Americans during the Second World War.

2. Sturken, *Tangled Memories*, 9–12.

3. David Morrell, "The Man Who Created Rambo," *Playboy*, August 1988, 89, 134. This essay is reprinted in a shortened form as the preface to *First Blood* (1990 edition), and the anecdote appears in a shortened form in numerous other articles and interviews. See Morrell, preface to *First Blood*, i–iv. Interestingly in the *Playboy* essay this memory is dated 1969, but in the preface, it is traced to 1968.

4. The one exception to this would have been the riots in Miami 8–13 August 1968, roughly the same time as the Republican National Convention there. But this riot was relatively small compared to the ones from the summer of 1967, or even those of April 1968, after the assassination of Martin Luther King Jr., and merited only a single CBS news broadcast on 8 August 1968.

5. "David Morrell: FAQ," www.davidmorrell.net, accessed 1 June 2008.

6. I take my inspiration for calling this year the American 1968 from Michael Rogin. In distinguishing between the American and European versions of another pivotal year, 1848, Rogin points out that the major threat to European nationalisms after the utopianism of the French Revolution was the potential of class war, whereas the main stresses to American nationalism following the Mexican-American War revolved around the question of slavery. See Rogin, *Subversive Genealogy*, 102–3. One could also argue for a global 1968 that encompasses not only the American 1968 but also the Tet Offensive in Vietnam; major student rebellions in New York, Mexico City, Paris, Tokyo, and Berlin; and the Soviet invasion of Czechoslovakia. But the American 1968 was characterized by an emphasis on race and racial strife that was missing in the global 1968, not only in terms of its convergence with the civil rights movement, but also in recognition of the Vietnam War itself as a race war according to black power activists and the growing Asian American, Chicano, and American Indian student movements. For a starting point on the global 1968, see Fink, Gassert, Junker, and Mattern, *1968*.

7. Television news expanded from a fifteen-minute daily broadcast patterned after radio news to a daily half-hour program in 1963, and soon overtook print news as the most widely consumed format within the news media. The technological apparatus of television news also changed in this era, enabling an expanding aura of presence and liveness. Lightweight and compact 16mm cameras and wireless sound recorders and microphones became widespread in television after 1960, enabling cameramen and sound engineers to become more mobile and timely in their newsgathering. Communications satellites, which were first launched in the mid-1960s, also allowed television news to broadcast live footage from around the world, as opposed to waiting for film to be flown in to studios in New York. Narrative accounts of these formative events in the development of television news can be found in Stephens, *A History of News*; Barnouw, *Tube of Plenty*, 265–430; Donovan and Scherer, *Unsilent Revolution*, 3–107.

8. Torres, *Black, White, and in Color*, 6.

9. Hallin, *The "Uncensored War*," 105.

10. *Nineteen Sixty-Eight*, CBS, 5 August 1978; "The Making of the President: 1968," CBS, 9 September 1969.

11. Freud, "From the History of an Infantile Neurosis," 29–47.

12. Laplanche and Pontalis, *The Language of Psycho-Analysis*, 331.

13. Laplanche and Pontalis, *The Language of Psycho-Analysis*, 332.

14. Laplanche and Pontalis, *The Language of Psycho-Analysis*: "It is significant that these inaugural events [primal fantasies] are referred to as *scenes*" (331); "Even where they can be summed up in a single sentence, phantasies are still scripts (*scenarios*) of organized scenes which are capable of dramatization—usually in a visual form" (318).

15. Laplanche has tried to elevate the terms Nachträglichkeit and nachträglich into theoretically important categories that shed light on the status of temporality in the subject's relationship to agency. One difficulty in creating a consistent theory around these terms is their inconsistent translation from the German into other languages. In the official English translation of the *Standard Edition of the Complete Works of Sigmund Freud*, James Strachey translates the German terms as "deferred action" and "deferred," although American scholars have preferred "belatedness" and "belated." The translators of a new French *Standard Edition*, advised by Laplanche, have proposed "effet d'après coup" and "après coup," with the English equivalents "afterwardness" and "afterwards." This struggle over translation suggests the difficulty of defining the exact temporal dimensions of these terms, which originate in Freud's work on the etiology of traumatic neuroses and hysterias. See Laplanche, "Notes on Afterwardness," 263; Thomä and Cheshire, "Freud's Nachträglichkeit and Strachey's 'Deferred Action,'" 407–8, 421–22; Bhabha, "Dissemination," 155; Caruth, *Unclaimed Experience*, 4–18. For instances of the usage of these terms in the Freudian corpus, see Freud, "Project for a Scientific Psychology," 356, and "From the History of an Infantile Neurosis," 44, 45n1, 47.

16. This translation predates Strachey's later revision, when he includes "Project for a Scientific Psychology" in the *Standard Edition* and translates this sentence as "has only become a trauma by deferred action." Both translations are discussed in Thomä and Cheshire, "Freud's Nachträglichkeit and Strachey's 'Deferred Action,'" 410.

17. Laplanche, *Life and Death in Psychoanalysis*, 41.

18. Caruth, *Unclaimed Experience*, 11.

19. Arlen, *The Living-Room War*, 83.

20. Arlen, *The Living-Room War*, 8.

21. See, for example, Hallin, *The "Uncensored War*," 163–68.

22. For a historicized overview of these debates, see Bodroghkozy, *Groove Tube*, 21–60.

23. Laplanche, *Life and Death in Psychoanalysis*, 102.

24. Laplanche, "The Theory of Seduction and the Problem of the Other," 661. Laplanche describes the "making-see" as a form of address, albeit of an enigmatic

signifier that may reside purely on the level of the unconscious for both the sender and the receiver. "If a little brother-or-sister is beaten in the presence of the child, it is not like beating an egg white in the kitchen. Nor is it neutral and innocent (in Grusha's unconscious) to scrub the floor in front of the child with her buttocks projecting." Laplanche, "Interpretation between Determinism and Hermeneutics," 156.

25. Ted Gold helped lead the Columbia University protests in March and April 1968 as a member of the SDS. He was also one of three members of the Weather Underground who were killed when a bomb they were assembling prematurely exploded in their Greenwich Village townhouse.

26. John Skow, "Carnography," *Time*, 29 May 1972, 82.

27. Morrell, *First Blood*, 33.

28. Morrell, "The Man Who Created Rambo," 134.

29. Morrell, *First Blood*, 173.

30. Morrell, *First Blood*, 173.

31. Statistics from "Dementia in the Second City" and "Who Were the Protesters," *Time*, 6 September 1968, 21–25. My account of other details of the protests is taken from DeBenedetti and Chatfield, *An American Ordeal*, 220–30; Farber, *Chicago '68*, 165–207, unless otherwise noted.

32. Sylvan Fox, "Guard Told to Shoot if Defied in Chicago," *New York Times*, 24 August 1968; Harry Golden Jr., "Daley Orders 'Shoot to Kill' for Arson," *Washington Post*, 16 April 1968.

33. Paul Cronin, "Mid-Summer Mavericks," *Sight and Sound* 11.9 (2001), 26. See also Guy Flatley, "Chicago and Other Violences," *New York Times*, 7 September 1969.

34. Donald Jansons, "Police Assaults on 21 Newsmen in Chicago Are Denounced by Officials and Papers," *New York Times*, 28 August 1968; "Police Injure 6 More Newsmen," *Chicago Tribune*, 29 August 1968. In his supplementary report on the Chicago protests to the National Commission on the Causes and Prevention of Violence, Daniel Walker estimates that sixty-three journalists were physically attacked by police during the course of the convention protests. See Walker, *Rights in Conflict*, vii–xiii, 191–220.

35. CBS *Evening News*, 29 August 1968.

36. Jerry Rubin, "I Am the Walrus!," WIN 4 (15 February 1968), 4, quoted in DeBenedetti and Chatfield, *An American Ordeal*, 224.

37. "Cover Story: The Nation: Survival at the Stockyards," *Time*, 6 September 1968, 15–25; Sylvan Fox, "300 Police Use Tear Gas to Breach Young Militants' Barricade in Chicago Park," *New York Times*, 27 August 1968; *Newsweek*, 6 September 1968, 16E.

38. Quoted in Farber, *Chicago '68*, 204.

39. DeBenedetti and Chatfield, *An American Ordeal*, 254–55. The Chicago Eight were the Yippie leaders Jerry Rubin and Abbie Hoffman, the Mobe leaders Tom Hayden, David Dellinger, and Rennie Davis, Black Panther Bobby Seale, and two academics, John Froines and Lee Weiner, who worked as Mobe marshals at the protests. All were eventually acquitted of charges to incite a riot when their cases were dismissed upon appeal.

40. Quoted in Varon, *Bringing the War Home*, 91.

41. Varon, *Bringing the War Home*, 12.

42. DeBenedetti and Charfield, *An American Ordeal*, 219, 230. The most famous of these incidents involved the Catonsville Nine, a group led by the brother priests Daniel and Philip Berrigan, who burned the draft cards from a Catonsville, Maryland, draft board on 17 May 1968.

43. DeBenedetti and Chatfield, *An American Ordeal*, 294–311. For a detailed, first-person account of the VVAW's major protests in the 1970s, see Stacewicz, *Winter Soldiers*, 229–51.

44. DeBenedetti and Chatfield, *An American Ordeal*, 284; see also Wells, *The War Within*, 2–3.

45. Although conventional wisdom would identify the first group as pro-war and the second as antiwar, the ideological struggle over the meaning of these veterans is much more complex. The antiwar VVAW had a more nuanced message than other antiwar groups regarding the meaning of military service, as it simultaneously sought benefits for its members who recognized the patriotic nature of their duty and used their firsthand experiences in Vietnam to condemn the culture of atrocity that the military forced upon its soldiers. In contrast, although the Nixon administration was deeply invested in continuing the Vietnam War, it also contributed to the demonizing of Vietnam veterans as crazy, in part to neutralize critiques such as those of the VVAW. For more on this dynamic, see Lembcke, *The Spitting Image*, 27–70.

46. Morrell, *First Blood*, 245.

47. Ron Miller, "Rambo: A Great Character Who Haunts Morrell Still," *Colum nists.com*, accessed 19 July 2006. Murphy was known as the most decorated veteran of the Second World War, having received thirty-three medals, including the Medal of Honor, and later became a Hollywood star, appearing in forty-nine films, including the dramatization of his war memoir, *To Hell and Back* (book published in 1949, film released in 1955). For more on Murphy's struggles with war trauma, see D. Graham, *No Name on the Bullet*, 184–92, 253–62.

48. Morrell, *First Blood*, 51.

49. Morrell, *First Blood*, 43.

50. It is a point of contention whether to call these events from the 1960s "riots" or "rebellions." While "riot" is preferred by those wishing to cast the violence as purely criminal activity with no political or social meaning, many who were sympathetic to the events were more likely to view them as acts of resistance or rebellion against horrendous conditions within black urban populations. As I explain below, much of this distinction breaks down along racial lines. Although I prefer the term "rebellion" as well, I switch between both terms depending on context, since the term "riot" dominates contemporary news reports on these events.

51. G. L. Carter, "In the Narrows of the 1960s U.S. Black Rioting," 118.

52. Morry Roth, "News Panel Rates Race Crisis More Explosive Story Than Vietnam War," *Variety*, 10 April 1968, 34, 48, my emphasis.

53. The term "ghetto" has a complicated racialized history in the U.S., with connotations not only of racial segregation, but of crime and poverty. Kenneth Kusmer warns against indiscriminate use of the terms "ghetto," "slum," "inner city," and "underclass area," since many racially segregated areas are not always in traditionally urban areas, and because the nature of racial segregation concentrates racial minorities of various social classes into the same residential areas. See Kusmer, "African Americans in the City since World War II," 501n88.

54. Gitlin, The Sixties, 245.

55. Many commentators have pointed out the stark difference in racial violence before and after the 1960s. See, for example, Grimshaw, "Changing Patterns of Racial Violence in the United States," 488–500; Harris, The Logic of Black Urban Rebellions, 37–43. Although many of the incidents discussed in these works are of white-on-black violence, it is important to note that the pattern before 1960 extends to violence against other racial groups, as the Rock Springs massacre and the Zoot Suit riots indicate. In fact these incidents have become important touchstones in Asian American studies and Latino studies. For more on the Rock Springs Chinese massacre, see Saxton, The Indispensable Enemy, 201–12; Choy, Dong, and Hom, The Coming Man, 137–44; Daniels, Anti-Chinese Violence in North America. For more on the Chicago race riots of 1919, see Tuttle, Race Riot. For more on the Zoot Suit riots, see Pagán, Murder at the Sleepy Lagoon; Escobar, Race, Police, and the Making of a Political Identity.

56. For example, Thomas Sugrue details the impact of federal housing policy and banking practices, along with extralegal violence from white homeowners, that steadily isolated Detroit's black community into crowded and deteriorating ghettos. These same factors produced patterns of residential segregation across the nation, leading to a state of crisis Douglas Massey and Nancy Denton have called "American apartheid." See Sugrue, The Origins of the Urban Crisis, 181–208; Massey and Denton, American Apartheid, 1–59.

57. Kusmer writes, "Although it received little attention at the time, the differences between black and white perceptions of the Watts disturbance was so great that many blacks did not even use the word riot to describe it. Many African Americans, whether they took part in the civil disturbance or not, perceived it as a revolt whose purpose was to make whites aware of conditions in the ghetto." See Kusmer, "African Americans in the City since World War II," 469–70.

58. Torres, Black, White, and in Color, 13–35; MacDonald, Television and the Red Menace, 223–24.

59. One Little Rock resident said to a reporter upon learning that he was a northerner, "I see the North got what it wants." Farnsworth Fowle, "Bayonets of Troops Bring School Order," New York Times, 26 September 1957. Although there are no images of the Little Rock Nine being attacked, the photographer Will Counts captured images of white protesters kicking and grabbing at Alex Wilson, a black reporter for the Tri-State Defender. See Hank Klibanoff, "L. Alex Wilson," Media Studies Journal 14.2 (2000), www.freedomforum.org accessed 22 July 2008.

60. Torres, *Black, White, and in Color*, 23–35.

61. Fogelson, *Violence as Protest*, 29.

62. National Advisory Commission on Civil Disorders, *Report of the National Advisory Commission on Civil Disorders* (Washington, D.C.: Government Printing Office, 1968), 204.

63. See Johnson, Sears, and McConahay, "Black Invisibility, the Press, and the Los Angeles Riot," 698–721; Paletz and Dunn, "Press Coverage of Civil Disorders," 328–45.

64. "An American Tragedy—Detroit, 1967," *Newsweek*, 7 August 1967, 22–23.

65. Virilio, *War and Cinema*, 20.

66. The Watts riot in 1965 was the first urban riot to feature extensive use of news helicopters. Elizabeth Wheeler's detailed analysis of local evening news broadcasts during the Watts riot by the CBS affiliate KNXT reveals that such aerial footage replicated the logic of cold war, space-age militarism. In some cases the telecopter even became an extension of the law enforcement apparatus, as telecopter crews directed their voice-over commentary to the police by pointing out suspicious activity for surveillance. See Wheeler, "More Than the Western Sky," 11–26; "Hell in the City of Angels," KTLA, 11–14 August 1965.

67. For instance, a car carrying a local CBS camera crew during the Watts riot in 1965 was overturned and set on fire, and the cameraman and soundman barely escaped injury. Donovan and Scherer, *Unsilent Revolution*, 72.

68. Quoted in Donovan and Scherer, *Unsilent Revolution*, 75.

69. Button, *Black Violence*, 121.

70. It is estimated that only 1 percent of the National Guard during the Vietnam era were black. See Appy, *Working-Class War*, 19, 37; Button, *Black Violence*, 130.

71. Quoted in Fine, *Violence in the Model City*, 225.

72. Thomas A. Johnson, "Negro Veteran Is Confused and Bitter," *New York Times*, 29 July 1968; Fine, *Violence in the Model City*, 196–223.

73. The U.S. military had been integrated by executive order after the Korean War, and previous generations of black activists had advocated military service as a way of furthering black civil rights by performing a symbolically significant national duty. See Westheider, *Fighting on Two Fronts*, 8–17.

74. Fine, *Violence in the Model City*, 214.

75. Fine, *Violence in the Model City*, 156.

76. Thomas A. Johnson, "Negro in Vietnam Uneasy about U.S.," *New York Times*, 1 May 1968.

77. Quoted in "43 Black GIs Refuse Chicago Riot Duty," *The Ally* 9 (1968), reprinted on "Supporting Materials for Sir! No Sir!," www.sirnosir.com, accessed 28 July 2008. The Fort Hood 43, as the protesters who were arrested became known, were in many cases decorated Vietnam veterans from the 1st and 2nd Airborne Divisions. See Cortright, *Soldiers in Revolt*, 56–57; Moser, *The New Winter Soldiers*, 84.

78. In the print media, see Bernard Weinraub, "Detroit Saddens a G.I. in Vietnam,"

New York Times, 30 July 1967; Jesse W. Lewis Jr., "I Think the War Is Here," Washington Post, 25 July 1967.

79. Terry, "Bringing the War Home," 207.

80. M. Davis, City of Quartz, 224.

81. Arlen J. Large, "Riot Repercussions," Wall Street Journal, 27 July 1967.

82. In a more contemporary setting, we can see parallels between the reaction to images of black rioters in the 1960s and the reaction to the video footage of the beating of Rodney King by Los Angeles police in 1992. Whereas many saw in the King video a clear-cut case of police brutality, the manipulation of the video during the trial, including a frame-by-frame analysis, transformed the motions of King's body, thrashing on the ground after being Tasered, into a potentially lurching beast ready to attack the arresting officers. See L. Williams, Playing the Race Card, 252–95.

83. Morrell, First Blood, 29.

84. Morrell, First Blood, 155.

85. For more on the workings of Project 100,000 and its effect on the overall makeup of Vietnam combat troops, see Appy, Working-Class War, 32–33; Helmer, Bringing the War Home, 3–10. Daniel Moynihan praised Project 100,000, comparing the opportunities that the Vietnam War offered to African Americans as analogous to those of the Second World War for Japanese Americans, who were allowed to prove their loyalty and worthiness to the nation by "acquiring a reputation for military valor." See Moynihan, quoted in H. Graham, The Brothers' Vietnam War, 19.

86. According to James Westheider, "Between October 1966 and June 1969, 246,000 men were recruited into the military under Project 100,000, and 41 percent of them were black. Less than half of the project's recruits had high school diplomas, and more than a third could not read at the fifth-grade level. Not surprising, thirty-three percent of them were assigned to combat arms and more than half would eventually end up in Vietnam." See Westheider, Fighting on Two Fronts, 35. Herman Graham calculates that, given the smaller number of black men who were physically and academically qualified for the draft, eligible black were actually drafted at twice the rate of qualified white men. See Graham, The Brothers' Vietnam War, 81.

87. "Clay Plans to Apologize in Chicago for Remarks about Draft Classification," New York Times, 22 February 1966.

88. Quoted in H. Graham, The Brothers' Vietnam War, 73. The latter quote is the ostensible source for the slogan "No Vietnamese Ever Called Me Nigger," although Ali never uttered this exact phrase in public.

89. Quoted in Deutsch, " 'The Asiatic Black Man,' " 194. Deutsch's essay does not focus on Ali, but instead concentrates on the strands of pan-Asiatic influences on the Black Muslim groups Moorish Science Temple and the Nation of Islam, the latter of which Ali belonged to at the time of his draft resistance. For more on Ali's own relationship to the Nation of Islam and the outcome of his draft case, see H. Graham, The Brothers' Vietnam War, 67–89.

90. See H. Graham, The Brothers' Vietnam War, 81.

91. Student Non-Violence Coordinating Committee, "Statement on Vietnam: SNCC Press Release," in Taylor, *Vietnam and Black America*, 258–59.

92. Huey P. Newton, "Letter to the National Liberation Front of South Vietnam (With Reply)," in Taylor, *Vietnam and Black America*, 290–95, reprinted from *To Die for the People: The Writings of Huey P. Newton* (New York: Random House, 1970), 290–93.

93. Eldridge Cleaver, "The Black Man's Stake in Vietnam," in Taylor, *Vietnam and Black America*, 276, reprinted from Cleaver, *Soul on Ice* (New York: Dell, 1968), 121–27.

94. At Bandung representatives of twenty-nine African and Asian nations, including Vietnam, met to discuss their common cause in a postcolonial world. Vijay Prashad describes Bandung as a powerful symbol of Third World solidarity, even though the tensions of the cold war made it difficult for any practical alliance to come out of these aspirations. See Prashad, *Everybody Was Kung Fu Fighting*, 140–45.

95. According to Cynthia Young, Cuba's proximity to the U.S. allowed for direct intellectual exchange with black activists such as Robert Williams, Harold Cruse, and LeRoi Jones, while its own revolutionary and communist history offered direct analogies to the current conflict in Vietnam. See Young, *Soul Power*, 18–53.

96. Mullen, *Afro-Orientalism*, xi–xliv. The intellectual terrain of black internationalism in general is explored more fully in Gilroy, *The Black Atlantic*; Edwards, *The Practice of Diaspora*.

97. The Fort Hood Three announced in June 1966, "We have decided to take a stand against this war, which we consider immoral, illegal, and unjust." They mentioned in particular the impact of the war on their minority communities. For instance, echoing Ali, Johnson exhorted other black soldiers to see "a direct relationship between the peace movement and the civil rights movement": "The South Vietnamese are fighting for representation like we ourselves. . . . Therefore the Negro in Vietnam is just helping to defeat what his black brother is fighting for in the United States." See Moser, *The New Winter Soldiers*, 69–70; Halstead, *Out Now!*, 167–86.

98. Quoted in Moser, *The New Winter Soldiers*, 70.

99. Given the importance of a martial masculinity to the rise of black power, it is no wonder that a unique African American military culture would arise, resignifying the experience of war as racial consciousness raising and producing "the Black Power GI." See H. Graham, *The Brothers' Vietnam War*, 90–119.

100. Westheider, *Fighting on Two Fronts*, 150. Other documentaries that were featured in GI coffeehouses include *Bobby Seale* (Newsreel, 1969), *Yippies* (Newsreel, 1968), *Hey, Stop That!* (Robert Feldman, 1966), and *The Streets Belong to the People* (Sarah Elbert, 1968).

101. DeBenedetti and Chatfield, *An American Ordeal*, 174.

102. Leroy F. Aarons, "125,000 Marchers Protest War," *Washington Post*, 16 April 1967; Wells, *The War Within*, 134.

103. Carmichael, "Berkeley Speech," 59.

104. "Carmichael Urges a 'Vietnam' in U.S.," *New York Times*, 28 July 1967.

105. "Carmichael Is Quoted as Saying Negroes Form Guerilla Bands," *New York*

Times, 26 July 1967; Michael Arkus, "Carmichael Turns Up in Havana, Calls for U.S. Guerrilla Warfare," *Washington Post*, 26 July 1967.

106. Reitan, *The Rise and Decline of an Alliance*, 43–44, 60–63. Clayborne Carson speculates that Carmichael's bravado was directed at his Cuban audience, whom he had to convince that blacks were already engaged in a struggle against American capitalism, rather than to black America itself, especially given that he did not return to the U.S. after these statements for another five months. See Carson, *In Struggle*, 274.

107. See Greenlee, *The Spook Who Sat By the Door*. The novel was made into a film in 1973 by the African American director Ivan Dixon, but was withdrawn from theatrical release by United Artists for its politically controversial viewpoints.

108. H. G. Locke, *The Detroit Riot of 1967*, 111.

109. To give two well-known examples: Fred Hampton was a member of the Illinois chapter of the BPP who was killed under suspicious circumstances during a police raid in Chicago in 1969; George Jackson was serving time in San Quentin State Prison in California when he was shot by prison guards during an alleged escape attempt in 1971. The efforts of COINTELPRO against the BPP are detailed in Churchill and Wall, *Agents of Repression*, 37–102.

Chapter 2. Reporting the War

1. In addition to Kalb, "A View from the Press," see Hammond, *Reporting Vietnam*; Hallin, "The Media, the War in Vietnam, and Political Support"; Mohr, "Once Again."

2. Philip Geyelin, "It's Not Just 'Vietnam Syndrome,'" *Washington Post*, 15 December 1981; John Corry, "TV: The Tet Offensive in Vietnam," *New York Times*, 8 November 1983.

3. David Halberstam, introduction to Faas and Page, *Requiem*, 9.

4. Andy Grundberg, "Eddie Adams, Journalist, 71; Showed Violence of Vietnam," *New York Times*, 20 September 2004.

5. Sturken, *Tangled Memories*, 90.

6. Moeller, *Shooting War*, 402.

7. See, for example, Wexler, *Tender Violence*; L. Williams, *Playing the Race Card*; Berlant, *The Female Complaint*.

8. As Daniel Hallin notes, producers and editors also held back from displaying identifiable American casualties out of deference to both the military and the soldiers' families, but did not use this same discretion in showing Vietnamese losses, either allied or enemy. See Hallin, *The "Uncensored" War*, 129.

9. Throughout this chapter I use the terms "movement-image" and "action-image" interchangeably because they both refer to the dominant form of representation in popular American moving-image culture. However, in Deleuze's taxonomies of the moving image, the movement-image is the larger category within which the action-image is subsumed. There are two other subcategories of movement-images worth noting: the "perception-image," which allows the cinematic apparatus to map its

images to the perceptions of a body-subject within the film, and "affection-images," which lie halfway between the perception-image and action-image and indicate subjective impulses or mental states that mediate between perception and action. Deleuze helpfully maps these image types to grammatical forms: the perception-image relates to nouns, the action-image to verbs, and the affection-image to adjectives. See Deleuze, *Cinema 1*, 64–65.

10. Deleuze, *Cinema 2*, xi.

11. Deleuze, *Cinema 1*, 198–211.

12. Moeller, *Shooting War*, 407.

13. Bailey and Lichty, "Rough Justice on a Saigon Street," 221–38.

14. Tom Buckley, "Portrait of an Aging Despot," *Harper's*, April 1972, 68; Jack Pitman, "TV Newsmen's Viet Heroics: 'Like It Is' vs. Official Image," *Variety*, 7 February 1969, 41.

15. Browne's photo of the burning monk did not even appear in major periodicals such as the *New York Times*, although it was in some regional papers such as the *Philadelphia Inquirer* and was fairly widely seen. See McCutcheon, *Manufacturing Religion*, 170. Images of President Diem's corpse were entirely overshadowed by the Kennedy assassination, as both events occurred in the same month and in some instances were reported side by side. See "Photos Show Bodies of Late Vietnamese Leaders," *New York Times*, 30 November 1963; "The Bodies," *Time*, 6 December 1963, 42. Although many commentators point out that Chapelle's photograph of an executed Viet Cong predated Adams's by several years, it apparently was published in such an obscure publication that even Chapelle's biographer could not locate it. See Ostroff, *Fire in the Wind*, 220–21, 341; "Dead Vietnamese Man" (ca. 1961), Image ID: WHi-32771, at the Wisconsin Historical Society, Dickey Chapelle Image Collection, http://www.wisconsinhistory .org, accessed 4 September 2008. Akimoto's photographs were published in the Japanese magazine *Shukan Asahi* and were even written about at length by the journalist and novelist Kaikō Takeshi (pen name Kaikō Ken), but the event received no news coverage in the U.S., although, notably, film footage of the execution later appeared in Emile de Antonio's antiwar documentary *In the Year of the Pig* (1969), most likely from a European source. See "Betonamu no gyo (or akatsuki) ni shisu" (Killed in the Vietnam dawn), *Shukan Asahi* (Asahi weekly), 12 February 1965, 7–12; Kaiko, *Into a Black Sun*, 130–37; Suttmeier, "Seeing Past Destruction," 457–86; Powell, "Japanese Writer in Vietnam," 219–44; Kellner and Streible, "Introduction," 34–35.

16. Quoted in Braestrup, *Big Story*, 348.

17. Bazin's original quotation is "Now, for the first time, the image of things is likewise the image of their duration, *change mummified* as it were." Bazin, "The Ontology of the Photographic Image," 15, my emphasis.

18. Deleuze, *Cinema 1*, 23.

19. Flaxman, introduction, 5.

20. Deleuze, *Cinema 1*, 65.

21. Rodowick, *Gilles Deleuze's Time Machine*, 68.

22. Deleuze, *Cinema 1*, 155.

23. Deleuze, *Cinema 1*, 210.

24. "Street Clashes Go On in Vietnam, Foe Still Holds Parts of Cities; Johnson Pledges Never to Yield," *New York Times*, 2 February 1968.

25. *Time*, 9 February 1968, 24–25.

26. "Street Clashes Continue in Vietnam, Enemy Still Controls Parts of Cities," *New York Times*, 2 February 1968.

27. Quoted in L. Williams, *Hard Core*, 37.

28. The term "enigmatic signifier" has a specific meaning within Laplanchian psychoanalysis, as a message from the parents' unconscious that helps to constitute the child's own unconscious during the primal scene, but here I am using it in a more general sense, as a message to be translated. See Laplanche, "The Kent Seminar," 21–23.

29. L. Williams, *Hard Core*, 113.

30. The contents of this clip as originally broadcast on the NBC *Huntley-Brinkley Report* are described in detail in Cook, "Over My Dead Body," 203–16. Although this particular broadcast is not available in the Vanderbilt Television News Archive, the footage was rebroadcast, with a few cuts, on NBC *Evening News*, 11 April 1985. Bailey and Lichty describe how NBC producers in New York further edited the already abridged video feed of "Saigon Execution" from their Tokyo bureau, which received the raw footage from Vo Suu and Vo Huynh in Saigon, trimming the portion after the gunshot from twenty-three seconds to six seconds. See Bailey and Lichty, "Rough Justice on a Saigon Street," 226–27. When this footage is repurposed in documentaries such as *Vietnam: A Television History* (1983) or *Hearts and Minds* (1974) it is often further shortened from the version originally broadcast on NBC, in each case cutting away almost immediately after the body has been shot. In *Vietnam: A Television History*, the "Saigon Execution" footage totals thirty seconds, mostly concentrated on the slow walk leading up to the shooting; in *Hearts and Minds*, the footage is a mere four seconds long, entirely centered on the shooting itself.

31. This image can be seen in the rebroadcast of this footage on NBC *Evening News*, 11 April 1985, but is omitted from *Vietnam: A Television History*, from which these frame enlargements are taken. See also Cook, "Over My Dead Body."

32. The Viet Cong killed in "Saigon Execution" has been identified posthumously by several names. Adams calls him Nguyen Tan Dat in Tom Buckley, "Portrait of an Aging Despot," *Harper's*, April 1972, 68. However, the photojournalist Horst Faas identifies him as Nguyen Van Lem, alias Bay Lop, and claims to have visited his widow in a Saigon suburb. Horst Faas, "The Saigon Execution," *The Digital Journalist*, October 2004, http://www.digitaljournalist.org, accessed 5 January 2008. Because of this confusion I choose to leave the suspect unnamed rather than risk misidentifying him.

33. "The Viet Cong," CBS, 20 February 1968.

34. Deleuze, *Cinema 2*, 18, my emphasis.

35. Sobchack, "Inscribing Ethical Space," 252, 253.

36. Bazin, "Death Every Afternoon," 30.

37. Guy Flatley, "Chicago and Other Violences," New York Times, 7 September 1969; Stephen Farber and Estelle Changas, "Putting the Hex on 'R' and 'X,' " New York Times, 9 April 1972.

38. Quoted in Knightley, The First Casualty, 406. For an example of Griffiths's work in an explicitly antiwar context, see Griffiths, Vietnam Inc.

39. Braestrup, Big Story, 351.

40. Deleuze, Cinema 2, 3.

41. Oliver, The My Lai Massacre in American History and Memory, 11–52. Lt. William Calley, the first of several soldiers to stand trial for the massacre, was charged with murder in September 1969, but the case received no attention in the mainstream media until that November, when the first accounts of the massacre began appearing. The journalist Seymour Hersh is often credited with publishing the first written accounts of My Lai through wire services to multiple newspapers on 13 November 1969; see Hersh, "How I Broke the Mylai 4 Story," Saturday Review, 4 July 1970, 46–49. Ronald Haeberle's photographs did not appear until a week later, in the Cleveland Plain Dealer, 20 November 1969. While the Haeberle photographs were distributed widely thereafter, their most infamous manifestation was in a full-page color format accompanying the article by Hal Wingo, "The Massacre at My Lai," Life, 5 December 1969, 36–45.

42. Letters to the editor, Life, 19 December 1969, 46–47. See also Slotkin's discussion of the Life coverage of My Lai in Gunfighter Nation, 581–91.

43. Oliver, The My Lai Massacre in American History and Memory, 59.

44. Franklin, Vietnam and Other American Fantasies, 101. Franklin is referring to a photograph of a female guerrilla that appeared on the front page of the radical newspaper Guardian, 10 February 1968, which was subsequently made into a 29 in. × 17 in. poster for the antiwar movement. Other images and descriptions of armed Vietnamese women appear throughout the Asian American alternative press; see "Vietnamese Sisters," Gidra, March 1970, reprinted from Sisters United 1 (January 1970); "Quotes from the Asian War," Gidra, June–July 1970, 7; Linda Iwataki, "Women's History," Gidra, January 1971, 9, 12; "Victory to the United Peoples of Indochina!," Getting Together 2.3 (1971), cover page; Why An Asian War?, brochure published to advertise a teach-in in San Francisco on 11 April 1970, archived in the Steve Louie Asian American Movement newspapers collection, reel 1, UCLA Asian American Studies Center; Pat Sumi, "Notes from a Meeting with the Central Committee of the Vietnamese Women's Union," Gidra, June 1971, 7–9; Gidra, June 1972, cover page; Liz Nakahara, "Vietnamese Women and Culture," Gidra, September 1973, 18–21.

45. Wingo, "The Massacre at My Lai," 36, 40.

46. Oliver, The My Lai Massacre in American History and Memory, 210.

47. Quoted in Wingo, "The Massacre at My Lai," 39.

48. Quoted in Wingo, "The Massacre at My Lai," 36, 43.

49. Quoted in Wingo, "The Massacre at My Lai," 41.

50. Herr, Dispatches, 20. Significantly this is the same quote that Cathy Caruth uses

to introduce her concept of historical Nachträglichkeit in *Unclaimed Experience*, 10. There is an extended discussion of Nachträglichkeit and the televisual primal scene in chapter 1.

51. Jon Hendricks, Irving Petlin, and Frazier Doherty (Art Workers Coalition), "Q. And Babies? A. And Babies," 1969–70, reproduced in Martin, *Decade of Protest*, 35. Frascina describes the making of this poster in "Meyer Shapiro's Choice," 491–95. A transcript of the Paul Meadlo interview which supplied the poster's caption and title was published in "Transcript of Interview of Vietnam War Veteran on His Role in Alleged Massacre," *New York Times*, 25 November 1969.

52. "A U.S. Infantry Company Just Came Through Here," a leaflet for Operation Rapid American Withdrawal, September 1970, quoted in Huebner, *The Warrior Image*, 221.

53. Oliver, *The My Lai Massacre in American History and Memory*, 59.

54. General Westmoreland, quoted in *Hearts and Minds* (1974). The earliest citation I found for the phrase "gook syndrome" is Polner, *No Victory Parades*, 71. The phrase "The only good gook is a dead gook" has its antecedents in the Indian Wars and the Second World War. Congressman James Michael Cavanaugh said in 1868 during a debate over an Indian appropriations bill, "I have never in my life seen a good Indian (and I have seen thousands) except when I have seen a dead Indian," which is quoted in Mieder, " 'The Only Good Indian Is a Dead Indian,' " 42. President Theodore Roosevelt commented about Native Americans, "I don't go so far as to think that *the only good Indians are dead Indians*, but I believe nine out of every ten are" (quoted in Dower, *War without Mercy*, 151). A similar phrase was commonly used during the Second World War: "GOOD JAPS are dead Japs" (quoted in Dower, *War without Mercy*, 79).

55. Roediger, "Gook," 50–54.

56. Lifton, *Home from the War*, 205. South Korean involvement in the Vietnam War began in 1964, with a deployment of 140 medics and instructors, but rose to 49,000 troops in 1966. By 1970 it is estimated that over 100,000 Korean soldiers had served a tour of duty in Vietnam. See S. J. Kim, "South Korea's Involvement in Vietnam and Its Economic and Political Impact," 519–32.

57. Robert Jay Lifton, "The 'Gook Syndrome' and 'Numbed Warfare,' " *Saturday Review*, December 1972, 66–72; Lifton, *Home from the War*, 200–201.

58. Lifton, *Home from the War*, 204–5.

59. Chaim F. Shatan helped introduce the term "post-Vietnam syndrome" into popular usage, although his work stemmed from his involvement in the VVAW rap groups, group counseling sessions organized and run by the veterans themselves. See Shatan, "Post-Vietnam Syndrome," *New York Times*, 6 May 1972, and "The Grief of Soldiers," 640–53. Interestingly Shatan and Lifton were both initially drawn into the VVAW rap groups not because of direct contact with veterans suffering from these syndromes, but as a result of mainstream media coverage of the war; for Lifton, it was reading about the My Lai massacre in the *New York Times*, while for Shatan, it was the story of a decorated black veteran, Dwight Johnson, who was killed while committing

an armed robbery in his hometown of Detroit. Sarah Haley, a social worker at the Boston Veterans Administration who also worked with Shatan and Lifton on the definition of this syndrome, interviewed veterans who claimed they had participated in the My Lai massacre. See Scott, "PTSD in DSM-III," 294–310.

60. These testimonies are gathered in Vietnam Veterans Against the War, *The Winter Soldier Investigation*.

61. An interesting contrast to the testimonies from the Winter Soldier hearings in Detroit is a similar event sponsored by the California Veterans Movement and hosted by KPFK, the Los Angeles branch of the progressive Pacifica Radio network. These hearings, which because of their location involved a larger number of Asian American veterans, were dominated less by melancholic proclamations of guilt than by accusations of the transference of American racism from Vietnamese to Asian American victims. See Mike Nakayama, "Winter Soldiers," *Gidra*, July 1971, 12.

62. Kerry and Vietnam Veterans Against the War, *The New Soldier*, 1–3.

63. Lembcke, *The Spitting Image*, 49–70. Lembcke credits the birth of the myth of the spat-upon veteran as one consequence of this reversal: the post-Vietnam syndrome "provided a necessary obverse dimension to [the] narrative of the betrayed and abused veteran: just as the image of spitting activists conjured up the image of the good veteran, the image of psychiatrically impaired veterans conjured up the political and cultural forces that caused the hurt," which for Nixon was the antiwar movement (125).

64. Oliver, *The My Lai Massacre in American History and Memory*, 177. The difficulty of correctly identifying the victims and confirming details of the massacre is recounted at length, 175–230.

65. The larger story of how the VVAW's activism translated into the codification of the PTSD diagnosis by the American Psychiatric Association is recounted in A. Young, *The Harmony of Illusions*, 89–117; Scott, *The Politics of Readjustment*.

66. MacPherson, *Long Time Passing*, 59.

67. Scruggs and Swerdlow, *To Heal a Nation*; "To Heal a Nation," NBC, 29 May 1988.

68. Espiritu, *Asian American Panethnicity*, 14–20. As particular Asian ethnic groups were singled out for harassment and surveillance, such as Japanese Americans during the Second World War and Chinese Americans during the 1950s and 1960s, other ethnic groups would attempt to secure social privileges by highlighting their differences from the persecuted group. For instance, during the Second World War some Chinese and Korean Americans wore buttons that read "Not Japanese" or "I am Chinese," both to avoid receiving the rabid racism being directed at Japanese Americans, but also to position themselves as a sort of "model minority" in comparison to the Japanese. See also K. S. Wong, *Americans First*, 74–81.

69. See Althusser, "Ideology and Ideological State Apparatuses," 127–86. My use of the term "racial interpellation" derives from both Althusser's theory of ideology and subject formation and Frantz Fanon's interpretation of psychoanalysis in the French colonial context. For an extended discussion of the genealogy of this concept, see S. Chong, " 'Look, an Asian!,' " 30–37.

70. Laplanche and Pontalis, "Identification," in *The Language of Psycho-Analysis*, 205–8.

71. I am playing here on the Marxian distinction between "class in itself" (the economic conditions under which people live, whether or not they realize it) and "class for itself" (class as a politically aware and actively organized group). See Hall, "Gramsci's Relevance for the Study of Race and Ethnicity," 423.

72. S. Chan, *Asian Americans*, 174.

73. Chris Kando Iijima, Joanne Nobuko Miyamoto, and "Charlie" Chin (Yellow Pearl), "We Are the Children," *Grain of Sand: Music for the Struggle of Asians in America*, Paredon Records, 1973, rereleased by Smithsonian Folkways, 2006.

74. Espiritu, *Asian American Panethnicity*, 134.

75. Obviously I cannot provide a full account of the myriad activities of the Asian American movement, which was not a centralized political development but rather a belated name given to a number of separate events, organized by disparate groups, and taking place throughout the U.S. in the late 1960s through the 1980s. For a more detailed discussion of the events organized under the rubric of the "Asian American movement," see Fujino, "Who Studies the Asian American Movement?," 127–69; Wei, *The Asian American Movement*; Omatsu, *Salute to the 60s and 70s*; Louie and Omatsu, *Asian Americans*; Ho, Antonio, Fujino, and Yip., *Legacy to Liberation*.

76. Figures extrapolated from Rumbaut, "Vietnamese, Laotian, and Cambodian Americans," 267, and Gibson and Jung, *Historical Census Statistics, on Population Totals by Race*, appendix table A-1.

There were a few notable exceptions to the rule, such as Nguyen Thai Binh, a University of Washington student who was eventually deported and murdered for his antiwar activities, and Monique Truong Kim Anh, a UCLA student and the daughter of Truong Dinh Dzu, a failed South Vietnamese politician and rival to Gen. Nguyen Van Thieu. Truong addressed the Democratic National Convention in 1968 on behalf of her father and was a frequent presenter at Asian American peace rallies and antiwar teach-ins in California; she is listed as a speaker for the teach-in in San Francisco on 11 April 1970 and the rally in Los Angeles' Little Tokyo on 17 January 1970. See "Fears for Her Father: Candidate's Daughter Charges Thieu Plot," *Los Angeles Times*, 3 October 1967; Steve Harvey, "Daughter of Jailed Viet Leader Counts on 'Pressure' Campaign," *Los Angeles Times*, 23 September 1968. Binh's activities were mostly in the Seattle area—he turned his graduation ceremony at the University of Washington in 1972 into a one-man protest—but he also took part in a sit-in with nine other Vietnamese students at the South Vietnamese consulate in New York on 10 February 1972. See "Vocal Antiwar Protester: Slain Viet Hijacker Identified as Honor Student in Seattle," *Los Angeles Times*, 3 July 1972; Paul L. Montgomery, "Hijacker Killed in Saigon; Tried to Divert Jet to Hanoi," *New York Times*, 3 July 1972. After his death Binh was memorialized by the Union of Vietnamese in the United States, the only antiwar Vietnamese American group of the era, and the Black Panthers in San Francisco; a group calling itself the Thai Binh Brigade protested the war at the Nisei Week parade in Los Angeles' Little Tokyo in

August 1972. See "Memorial for Binh," *Getting Together* 3.12 (1972), 1; Mike Murase, "Nisei Week," *Gidra*, September 1972, 2–3; T. Q. Nguyen, "Caring for the Soul of Our Community," 285–304.

77. Pham, "Antedating and Anchoring Vietnamese America," 137–52.

78. Deleuze, *Cinema 2*, 216.

79. Deleuze and Guattari, *A Thousand Plateaus*, 291.

80. Deleuze and Guattari, *A Thousand Plateaus*, 291.

81. Rodowick, *Gilles Deleuze's Time Machine*, 152.

82. Deleuze, *Cinema 2*, 217.

83. Wingo, "The Massacre at My Lai," 41.

84. Letter to the editor, *Life*, 19 December 1969, 46–47.

85. According to the U.S. Census in 1970, Asian Americans collectively made up 0.67 percent of the total population (1.4 million out of 177.7 million). In the Vietnam-era military there were approximately 34,600 Asian Americans, making up 0.4 percent of the 8.7 million Americans who served during this conflict. Compare this with African Americans, who made up 11.1 percent of the population in 1970 and 10.6 percent of the armed forces in Vietnam. See Gibson and Jung, *Historical Census Statistics on Population Totals by Race*; table 523, "Armed Forces Personnel—Summary of Major Conflicts"; *Statistical Abstract of the United States: 2003* (Washington, D.C.: U.S. Census Bureau, 2003); Kiang, "About Face," 22–40.

86. For an account of Japanese Americans' military service during the Second World War that does not simply subsume them into a master narrative of American patriotism and exceptionalism, see Commission on Wartime Relocation and Internment of Civilians, *Personal Justice Denied*, 185–212, 253–60.

87. Maehara, "Think on These Things," 124.

88. M. A. Uyematsu, "G.I. Blues: A Short Story," *Gidra*, July 1971, 12.

89. Mike Nakayama, "Nam and U.S.M.C.," *Gidra*, May 1971, 17.

90. Sam Choy, "A Long Way From Home," *Gidra*, May 1970, 10. The original article appeared in I Wor Kuen's newsletter, *Getting Together* 1.2 (1970), 12–13.

91. Afterward Choy was sent to Long Binh Jail, an infamous stockade outside of Saigon nicknamed "LBJ," and eventually court-martialed for aggravated assault and sentenced to eighteen months of hard labor at Fort Leavenworth.

92. Paul Wong, "The Emergence of the Asian-American Movement," *Bridge*, September–October 1972, 35–36. A similar description of the difference between the Asian American and mainstream antiwar movements can be found in Asian Coalition, "On White Antiwar Movement," *Gidra*, March 1973, 20.

93. Mike Murase, "Asians March for Peace," *Gidra*, February 1970, 2, 11; Kashu Mainichi, "300 Asians in SF Peace March," *Gidra*, December 1969, 2; "Asian Contingent," *Getting Together* 2.4 (1971), 4; Steve Tatsukawa, "April March," *Gidra*, May 1972, 12; Mike Murase, "Why an Asian Contingent?," *Gidra*, May 1972, 13.

94. "Agnew Explains 'Polack' and 'Jap,'" *New York Times*, 24 September 1968; "Matsunaga Raps Agnew for 'Fat Jap' Remark," *Washington Post*, 24 September 1968.

95. Wei, *The Asian American Movement*, 38. See also Espiritu, *Asian American Pan-ethnicity*, 42–43.

96. Uyematsu, "The Emergence of Yellow Power in America," 9–13.

97. Advertisement for Asian Americans for Peace, *Gidra* 1.10 (1970), 15; Yuji Ichioka, quoted in Murase, "Asians March for Peace." The short quote in the slogan comes from a longer statement from an anonymous Iowa housewife, who wrote a letter to Ronald Ridenhour, a GI who sparked the investigation of the My Lai massacre, criticizing his efforts to publicize this case: "Bunch of worthless Asians in a part of the world that's already over-populated anyway. It's no real loss." See Kenneth Reich, "My Lai Story Brings Ex-GI Praise, Scorn," *Los Angeles Times*, 11 December 1969.

98. Warren Furutani, "The March," *Gidra*, February 1970, 5, 8.

99. On the cold war origins of the model minority myth, see R. G. Lee, *Orientals*, 145–79; Palumbo-Liu, *Asian/America*, 149–81.

100. Postcard reproduced in Louie and Omatsu, *Asian Americans*, 118.

101. Wei, *The Asian American Movement*, 67.

102. Pisters, *The Matrix of Visual Culture*, 89, 94.

103. The caption "Accidental Napalm Attack" is found in Fox Butterfield, "South Vietnamese Drop Napalm on Own Troops," *New York Times*, 9 June 1972. Kim Phuc is referred to as the "napalm girl" in " 'Napalm Girl' Has Surgery," *Washington Post*, 3 August 1984, and in A. H. Carter and Petro, *Rising from the Flames*, 106.

104. For more on these earlier antinapalm protests, see Franklin, *Vietnam and Other American Fantasies*, 47–88.

105. Donna Hale, "Eyewitness to War," *News Photographer* 54.3 (1999), 20–25; "Obituaries: Alan Downes," *Independent* (London), 11 October 1996.

106. *Los Angeles Times*, 8 June 1972.

107. Quoted in Knightley, *The First Casualty*, 406.

108. " 'Dragon Lady' of S. Viet Nam Defies Critics," *Chicago Tribune*, 19 August 1963. In a discussion of the meaning of obscenity beyond sexuality, Joel Feinberg, a legal scholar, cites Madame Nhu's comments alongside examples from the film *Bonnie and Clyde*, public beheadings, and the racial epithet "nigger." See Feinberg, *Offense to Others*, 115–16.

109. "Viet War Photo Is Challenged," *Washington Post*, 19 January 1986.

110. Silverman, *The Acoustic Mirror*, 39.

111. Hariman and Lucaites, *No Caption Needed*, 137–207.

112. D. Chong, *The Girl in the Picture*, 73–74; Judith Coburn, "The Girl in the Photograph," *Los Angeles Times*, 20 August 1989.

113. Hariman and Lucaites, *No Caption Needed*, 176.

114. Caviness, "Obscenity and Alterity," 174.

115. Sontag, *On Photography*, 18.

116. Quoted in Hale, "Eyewitness to War," 23.

117. Coburn, "The Girl in the Photograph," 8.

118. CBS *Evening News*, 27 June 1972. The connection of Dr. Barsky and the Center

for Plastic and Reconstructive Surgery to the Hiroshima Maidens project is made explicit in the documentary *The Gooks* (1971). For more on the Hiroshima Maidens, see Shibusawa, *America's Geisha Ally*, 213–54; Simpson, *An Absent Presence*, 113–48; Klein, *Cold War Orientalism*, 143–59.

119. "Where We Stand in Indochina," CBS, 30 June 1970.

120. "A Timetable for Vietnam," CBS, 12 December 1969, my emphasis.

121. "Diem's War or Ours?," CBS, 29 December 1961; *The Anderson Platoon*, CBS, 4 July 1967; "Hanoi: A Report by Charles Collingwood," CBS, 16 April 1968. This last report makes a point of contrasting the "Westernized" appearance of Saigon's markets and nightclubs with the austere appearance of communist Hanoi, replete with bicycles and "drab clothes like colorless uniforms."

122. Deleuze, *Cinema 2*, xi. The quote is originally from Marcel Proust's *Remembrance of Things Past* (*À le recherché du temps perdu*, more literally translated as *In Search of Lost Time*).

123. Caruth, *Unclaimed Experience*, 102. The original dream is described in Freud, *The Interpretation of Dreams*, 509–11.

124. Lacan, *The Four Fundamental Concepts of Psychoanalysis*, 53–60.

125. Caruth, *Unclaimed Experience*, 105.

126. "Energetic Vietnam Veteran Exposes a Big War Lie," Opinion, Inc., *Guest Opinion Columns—Accuracy in Media*, 15 January 1998, http://www.opinioninc.com, accessed 13 July 2006; Ronald N. Timberlake, "The Fraud behind the Girl in the Photo: Hijacking the History of the Vietnam Veteran," January 1999, http://www.mystae.com, accessed 13 July 2006; Tom Bowman, "Vietnam Story Was Pastor's Lie; 'Pilot' Had Nothing to Do with Infamous Napalm Bombing," *Toronto Star*, 18 December 1997.

127. Peter Pae and Maria Glod, "Vets Challenge Minister's Account of Napalm Attack; Va. Man Says He Ordered Strike That Led to Photo," *Washington Post*, 19 December 1997.

128. The notion of "care" I am using comes from Martin Heidegger's concept of *Sorgen* (care or solicitude), which reveals human Being (*Dasein*) as also "Being alongside entities within-the-world," or a form of ethical intersubjectivity. Care is linked to Dasein's "thrownness," which is another way of understanding the relationship of human subjects to a world (in Lacanian terms, the Real) which exceeds their grasp and control. See Heidegger, *Being and Time*, 225–73.

Chapter 3. Restaging the War

1. See Doherty, *Projections of War*; Koppes and Black, *Hollywood Goes to War*.

2. Suid, *Guts and Glory*, 352–54; Pat H. Broeske, "The Curious Evolution of John Rambo," *Los Angeles Times*, 27 October 1985.

3. Quoted in J. Smith, *Looking Away*, 10.

4. Quoted in Suid, *Guts and Glory*, 345.

5. Dempsey, "Hellbent for Mystery," 11; Axeen, "Eastern Western," 17; Kinder, "Political Game," 14. All of these essays were published in a special section of *Film Quarterly* titled "Four Shots at *The Deer Hunter*," as evidence of its controversial reception among film scholars.

6. Production notes, *The Deer Hunter*, DVD, Universal Studios.

7. John Kinch, quoted in Hal Wingo, "The Massacre at My Lai," *Life*, 4 December 1969, 44. This same quote is also reproduced in Hersh, *My Lai 4*, 85–86.

8. Cumings, *War and Television*, 95. For more on the CBS broadcast with Morley Safer in August 1965 in which U.S. soldiers lit thatch huts in the village of Cam Ne with their Zippo lighters, see Hallin, *The "Uncensored War,"* 132.

9. Pauline Kael, "The Current Cinema: The God-Bless-America Symphony," *New Yorker*, 18 December 1978, 72.

10. Freud, " 'A Child Is Being Beaten,' " 184–86. Note that this version is derived from four case studies of young girls' fantasies, which leads Freud to conclude that masochism is essentially feminine. He goes on to modify the sequence of phases for young boys to include a complicated relationship to the mother.

11. Freud, "Instincts and Their Vicissitudes," 109–40.

12. Laplanche and Pontalis, "Phantasy," in *The Language of Psycho-analysis*, 318.

13. Laplanche, *Life and Death in Psychoanalysis*, 102.

14. Laplanche, "The Other Within," 34.

15. Clover, *Men, Women, and Chain Saws*, 166–230; Silverman, *Male Subjectivity at the Margins*, 185–213; Rodowick, *The Difficulty of Difference*, 67–100.

16. Janet Maslin, "Screen Violence—How Much Is Too Much?," *New York Times*, 25 February 1979, my emaphsis.

17. Suid, *Guts and Glory*, 352–55.

18. Michael Cimino, "Ordeal by Fire and Ice," *American Cinematographer*, October 1978, 1028.

19. Quoted in Leticia Kent, "Ready for Vietnam? A Talk with Michael Cimino," *New York Times*, 10 December 1978.

20. David Denby, "Nightmare into Epic," *New York*, 18 December 1978, 98.

21. Tom Buckley, "Hollywood's War," *Harper's*, April 1979, 84. See also Gloria Emerson's description of Leticia Kent's experiences interviewing Cimino for the *New York Times* in "Oscars for Our Sins," *Nation*, 12 May 1979, 541. Another critic who used these allegations against Cimino to undermine the film is Richard Grenier, "A New Patriotism?," *Commentary*, April 1979, 78–79.

22. Emerson, "Oscars for Our Sins," 541. The journalists to whom Emerson referred were Tom Buckley, Seymour Hersh, and Peter Arnett.

23. John Pilger, "The Gook-Hunter," *New York Times*, 26 April 1979.

24. Aljean Harmetz, "Oscar-Winning 'Deer Hunter' Is Under Attack as 'Racist' Film," *New York Times*, 26 April 1979.

25. "Playboy Interview: Sam Peckinpah," *Playboy* 19.8 (1972), 70, quoted in Prince, *Savage Cinema*, 49.

26. Devon Scott, "Mailbag: Vietnam and Artistic Integrity," *New York Times*, 17 June 1979.

27. Vincent Canby, "How True to Fact Must Fiction Be?," *New York Times*, 17 December 1978; Barbara Grizzuti Harrison, "A Last Clean Shot at 'The Deer Hunter,'" *Ms.*, June 1979, 32.

28. "U Self-Rates 'Hunter' Stricter Than MPAA, But It's a Mistake," *Variety*, 22 November 1978, 4. Among other places, these ads appeared in the *New York Times*, 19 November 1978. Although the film had already been rated R, which means that those under seventeen would be admitted only if accompanied by a parent or guardian, the ads carried the following warning which corresponded to an X rating: "Due to the nature of this film, no one under the age of 18 will be admitted. (There will be strict adherence to this policy.)" This language was retracted in later ads.

29. Laplanche, *Life and Death in Psychoanalysis*, 88.

30. Laplanche, *Life and Death in Psychoanalysis*, 97.

31. I take up this point on the legal discourse of obscenity in S. Chong, "From 'Blood Auteurism' to the Violence of Pornography," 249–68.

32. See Aristotle, *Nicomachean Ethics*, book 7, section 2. There are numerous commentaries on *akrasia*, but one interesting article is Rorty, "The Social and Political Sources of Akrasia," 644–57. Rorty presents a Vietnam veteran suffering from PTSD as a paradigmatic example of an akrasic subject, given to outbursts of rage that are not fully within his control.

33. Foucault, *The Use of Pleasure*, 31.

34. See J. Locke, *Two Treatises on Government*, in particular book 2, chapter 4, "Of Slavery," and chapter 5, "Of Property."

35. Scarry, "Consent and the Body," 869.

36. Freud, "The Economic Problem of Masochism," 155–70. The complexity of assigning masochism to men is discussed in more detail in Silverman, *Male Subjectivity at the Margins*, 185–213.

37. *Pratt v. Davis*, 118 Ill. App. 161, 166 (1905), affirmed 224 Ill. 30, 79 N.E. 562 (1906), cited in Scarry, "Consent and the Body," 868.

38. Grosz, *Volatile Bodies*; Kristeva, *The Powers of Horror*; Bordo, *Unbearable Weight*.

39. For legal discussions of these racialized violations of bodily sovereignty, see Luna, "Sovereignty and Suspicion," 787–889; Rao, "Property, Privacy, and the Human Body," 359–460.

40. Gootenberg, "Talking about the Flow," 35.

41. Kuzmarov, "From Counter-Insurgency to Narco-Insurgency," 344–78.

42. See Flamm, *Law and Order*, 13–50. The Republican Party's deployment of the phrase "law and order" as a code for race allowed the development of the so-called southern strategy that drew conservative Democrats away from their party's civil rights agenda. The association of African Americans and urban rioting also contributed to the racialization of this discourse.

43. Art Harris, "One of Company C's Troops Takes a Big Step Forward," *Washington Post*, 10 February 1978.

44. See Kuzmarov, "From Counter-Insurgency to Narco-Insurgency," 359; Jack Anderson, "Ex-GIs Operate Asia Heroin Ring," *Washington Post*, 23 May 1971; Philip A. McCombs, "100 Tied to Heroin Ring: War Dead Allegedly Used by Smugglers," *Washington Post*, 5 January 1973.

45. Jenkins, *Decade of Nightmares*, 96–105. Carter's main policy intervention into the Vietnam syndrome was the pardon he issued in 1977 to Vietnam-era draft dodgers, affecting potentially over 120,000 men. See "Pardon for Draft Evaders," *Los Angeles Times*, 21 January 1977; "Texts of Documents on the Pardon," *New York Times*, 22 January 1977.

46. Richard Cuskelly, " 'Coming Home': 'Best Years of Our Lives' for the '70s," *Los Angeles Herald Examiner*, 14 February 1978.

47. Lembcke, "From Oral History to Movie Script," 65–86.

48. Vincent Canby, "Post-Vietnam Romantic Triangle," *New York Times*, 16 February 1978.

49. Richard Turner, "The Worst Years of Our Lives: You Lost the War, Now See the Movie," *New Times*, 20 March 1978, Margaret Herrick Library, clippings file.

50. Hershberger traces Fonda's antiwar activities in *Jane Fonda's War*. She points out that Fonda's gender and sexuality made her the target of particularly virulent attacks by both the Nixon administration (which placed her under FBI surveillance) and present-day POW/MIA activists, who accuse Fonda of causing the torture of American POWs through her visits to North Vietnam. For a sense of the continuing hatred directed toward Fonda, see Holzer and Holzer, "*Aid and Comfort*," which purports to be a legal brief outlining the case for charging Fonda with treason for her antiwar activities.

51. Williams notes that Fonda won the "Battle of Penetration" with director Hal Ashby by refusing to "ride" Voight and simulate vaginal intercourse, which Ashby desired so as to more directly indicate Voight's newfound potency. See L. Williams, *Screening Sex*, 175–76.

52. Quoted in *Hearts of Darkness: A Filmmaker's Apocalypse* (1991, dir. Fax Bahr and George Hickenlooper).

53. Michael Dempsey, "Apocalypse Now," *Sight and Sound* 49.1 (1979–80), 5.

54. Sol Yurick, "Apocalypse Now, Capital Flow," *Cineaste*, Winter 1979–80, 21–23.

55. See Kinder, "The Power of Adaptation in *Apocalypse Now*," 12–20; Norris, "Modernism and Vietnam," 730–66; Hansen, "Traces of Transgression in *Apocalypse Now*," 123–35.

56. Narita, "The Young T. S. Eliot and Alien Cultures," 523–525. See also Torgovnick, *Primitive Passions*, 10; Barkan and Bush, *Prehistories of the Future*.

57. Rydell, *All the World's a Fair*, 154–83.

58. Suid, *Guts and Glory*, 332–35; P. Cowie, *The Apocalypse Now Book*, 14–16.

59. Sussman, "Bulls in the (Indo)China Shop," 26; P. Cowie, *The Apocalypse Now Book*, 49.

60. B. Anderson, "Cacique Democracy," 21.

61. See Blackburn, *Mercenaries and Lyndon Johnson's "More Flags"*; Lockwood, "The Philippines."

62. Sussman, "Bulls in the (Indo)China Shop," 26.

63. Bernard Wideman, "A Vietnam Epic: Coppola's Gamble," *Washington Post*, 14 October 1976.

64. P. Cowie, *The Apocalypse Now Book*, 57.

65. Ward Just, "Vietnam: The Camera Lies," *Atlantic Monthly*, December 1979, 64.

66. P. Cowie, *The Apocalypse Now Book*, 30, 68.

67. P. Cowie, *The Apocalypse Now Book*, 30.

68. In reality this paternalistic benevolence was also enforced by coercion from both sides, as American and North Vietnamese forces fought each other and the Montagnards for their loyalty. See McLeod, "Indigenous Peoples and the Vietnamese Revolution," 353–89.

69. McKay and Perez, " 'Apocalypse Yesterday Already!' "

70. Rafael, *White Love and Other Events in Filipino History*, 33, 79; Finin, *The Making of the Igorot*, 25, 39.

71. The term "Igorot" was used by both the Spanish and the Americans to refer to a variety of tribes and linguistic subgroups, including the Ifugao, the Bontoc Igorot, and the Kalinga people, who occupied the Cordillera mountain area in northern Luzon. Eventually a pan-Cordillera identity emerged out of this originally colonial designation, and members still employ the collective term "Igorot," even if they are from a different tribe. See Finin, *The Making of the Igorot*, 8–36.

72. Deloria, *Playing Indian*, 73–74. Finin points out that American administrators in colonial Philippines often referred to the natives as "indios," thus likening them, as well as the policies directed toward them, to the Indian problem in the American West. See Finin, *The Making of the Igorot*, 25.

73. Yengoyan, "Shaping and Reshaping the Tasaday," 565–73.

74. Slotkin, *Regeneration through Violence*, 473–563.

75. John Simon, "$30 Million in Search of an Author," *National Review*, 29 September 1979, 1247.

76. McKay and Perez, " 'Apocalypse Yesterday Already!' "; P. Cowie, *The Apocalypse Now Book*, 86–88. Eleanor Coppola's film footage of the original sacrifice is shown in *Hearts of Darkness: A Filmmaker's Apocalypse*.

77. Finin, *The Making of the Igorot*, 51–57.

78. For example, see Ngai, *Impossible Subjects*, 225–70; S. Chan, *Asian Americans*, 145–65.

79. Lowe, *Immigrant Acts*, 16–17.

80. Figures from 1964 are from Takaki, *Strangers from a Different Shore*, 448; later figures are from the census of 1990.

81. U.S. Bureau of the Census, *We the Americans*. Numbers are rounded to the nearest thousand. On the legislation that pertained to refugees from the Vietnam War, includ-

ing those from Laos and Cambodia, see S. Chan, *The Vietnamese American 1.5 Generation*, 78–96; Rutledge, *The Vietnamese Experience in America*, 1–14, 35–57.

82. Desbarats, "Indochinese Resettlement in the United States," 184–200. Desbarats describes three distinct phases of immigration from Southeast Asia after 1975: the first consisted of those South Vietnamese able to be evacuated soon after the fall of Saigon, predominantly government officials and their families; the second phase were the so-called boat people from Vietnam and Cambodia, arriving in the U.S. in 1979–81 after first fleeing to refugee camps in Thailand; the third phase, beginning in 1982, was smaller due to changes in the number of refugees allowed, and contained a larger number of Cambodians and Laotians.

83. M. G. Wong, "Post-1965 Asian Immigrants," 202–20; Takaki, *Strangers from a Different Shore*, 451.

84. Suid, *Guts and Glory*, 350.

85. Jennifer Kerr, "Playing Vietnamese in Movie Being Filmed in Valencia," *Los Angeles Times*, 27 September 1977.

86. Robert Lindsey, "Viet Nam Refugees Find Work Restaging the War," *Chicago Tribune*, 1 November 1977.

87. "The Haunted General," *Newsweek*, 3 May 1976, 11.

88. Tom Buckley, "The Villain of Vietnam," *Esquire*, 5 June 1979, 61–64.

89. Palumbo-Liu, *Asian/America*, 240.

90. R. G. Lee, *Orientals*, 190.

91. "Charlie Company at Home: The Veterans of Vietnam," CBS, 17 January 1978.

92. "The Vietnam War: The Executioner," *Newsweek*, 13 November 1978, 70.

93. "The Case of Nguyen Ngoc Loan," *New York Times*, 13 November 1978.

94. William Buckley Jr., "Deport General Loan?," *National Review*, 8 December 1978, 1526; Murray Kempton, "Finding a Fall-Guy," *Progressive*, January 1979, 10–11.

95. Frank Baxter, "Of War, Extermination, and Guilt," letter to the editor, *New York Times*, 27 November 1978; W. A. Fultz, "Of Nguyen Ngoc Loan and 'Tender Concern,' " letter to the editor, *New York Times*, 30 November 1978.

96. Martin Tolchin, "Carter Will Not Seek to Deport Former Vietnam General, Aide Says," *New York Times*, 2 December 1978.

97. Quoted in Harms, "Redefining 'Crimes of Moral Turpitude,' " 262.

98. Pilcher, "Justice without a Blindfold," 311.

99. "Interrogation," *Washington Post*, 21 January 1968; Tom Harkin, "The Tiger Cages of Con Son," *Life*, 17 July 1970, 26–29.

100. Michael Sragow, "Anything but Like Spartans," *Los Angeles Herald Examiner*, 6 September 1978.

101. Geoffrey Gorer, *Japanese Character Structure and Propaganda* (New Haven: Committee on National Morale and the Council on Intercultural Relations, 1942), quoted in Dower, *War without Mercy*, 127.

102. Cheng, *The Melancholy of Race*, 10.

103. Adams, "The Tet Photo," 182–85.

104. Robert McG. Thomas Jr., "Nguyen Ngoc Loan, 67, Dies; Executed Viet Cong Prisoner," *New York Times*, 16 July 1998.

Chapter 4. Kung Fu Fighting

1. "The Kung Fu Craze," *Newsweek*, 7 May 1973, 76; "Bruce Lee, Hong Kong Film Star, Dies at 32," *Los Angeles Times*, 21 July 1973; "Germany Reaps 'Wild East' Bonanza as Chinese Actioners Fill Sexpo Gap," *Variety*, 2 May 1973, 4; "Hong Kong Chop-Socky Pix and Cannes," *Variety*, 30 May 1973, 20.

2. Diana Benzaia, "The Orient Express to Good Health: The Martial Arts Quick Way to a Better Body," *Harper's Bazaar*, June 1981, 126–27, 157; Lee Gutkind, "Striking a Blow for Christ," *Sports Illustrated*, 30 July 1973, 32–34; " 'Kung Fu' and 'Sanford' Praised as Aids in Teaching of Reading," *New York Times*, 24 June 1973.

3. Desser, "The Kung Fu Craze," 38.

4. See "TV Syndication: AP's Primetime 'China' Docu in Feb.," *Variety*, 19 January 1972, 42; "Television Reviews: Michelangelo Antonioni's Chung Kuo (China)," *Variety*, 24 January 1973, 40; Benjamin J. Stein, "Television: Kung Fu," *National Review*, 1 March 1974, 265, 273; Howard Thompson, "Wushu Troupe Dazzles," *New York Times*, 5 July 1974.

5. Block, *The Legend of Bruce Lee*, 13.

6. Desser, "The Kung Fu Craze," 39.

7. Teo, *Hong Kong Cinema*; Bordwell, *Planet Hong Kong*; Hunt, *Kung Fu Cult Masters*.

8. Brown, "Global Bodies/Postnationalities," 24–48.

9. David Freeman, "Karate Flicks: What it All Means," *Village Voice*, 17 May 1973, 92.

10. Bud Buonocore, "The GI Budoka," *Black Belt*, February 1974, 47.

11. See Shun, "The Invention of the Martial Arts," 163–73; John Corcoran, "The Untold Story of American Karate's History (Part I)," *Black Belt*, May 1977, 49–53. According to Corcoran, Kano introduced judo to foreign dignitaries as early as 1889. At the Olympic Games in Los Angeles in 1932 Kano organized a demonstration of judo with about two hundred students, although the sport did not become an official Olympic event until 1964.

12. Numerous articles in *Black Belt* feature various American martial arts instructors who first learned the sport while serving in the military in Okinawa, Japan, South Korea, the Philippines, and later Vietnam. See Bob MacLaughlin, "Champions Are People, Too," *Black Belt*, May 1974, 14–19; Sergio Ortiz, "Robert Trias: Pioneer of U.S. Karate," *Black Belt*, April 1976, 36–39; "The Untold Story of American Karate's History (Part II)," *Black Belt*, June 1977, 47–53; "The Untold Story of American Karate's History (Part III)," *Black Belt*, July 1977, 56–63; Michael L. Turner, "G.I.s in Gi: The Military's Contribution to the Martial Arts," *Black Belt 1984 Yearbook*, 12th ed., 54–59, 84.

13. Y.-J. Chang, "The Rise of Martial Arts in China and America," 155–257. Chang, a Taiwanese student who came to the U.S. after the immigration reforms of 1965 to study sociology at the New School for Social Research, based his research in part on

ethnographic work in Chinese American ethnic enclaves. See Lyman, "Introduction to the Article," 449–51.

14. Massad F. Ayoob, "A Bridge between Two Worlds," *Black Belt*, March 1974, 22.

15. Asian American Cultural Society, "The Exploitation of Chinatown (Letter to the Editor)," *Black Belt*, September 1974, 4.

16. Letters to the editor, *Black Belt*, November 1974, 4–8, 78.

17. For an early instance of media activism, see Steve Tatsukawa, "Charlie Chan—Take Two," *Gidra* 3.4 (1971), 12.

18. Hong Kong kung fu films were directly influenced by the "spaghetti western" genre, explicitly linking the mythologies of violence in premodern China with those of the American West. However, this cycle of influence also works the other way around, as several American westerns were modeled directly on earlier Japanese samurai films, for example, *The Magnificent Seven* (1960) on *The Seven Samurai* (1954) and *A Fistful of Dollars* (1964) on *Yojimbo* (1961).

19. DeKoven, *Utopia Limited*, 226.

20. J. Chan, *Chinese American Masculinities*, 87.

21. Heidegger, "The Question Concerning Technology," 34.

22. Foucault, "Technologies of the Self," 18, my emphasis.

23. The other films in this mini-genre are *Angels from Hell* (1968), *The Losers* (1970), and *The Hard Ride* (1971). See J. Smith, *Looking Away*.

24. Shari Greenbaum, "Violence Is Obscene," *Los Angeles Times*, 30 March 1975.

25. John R. Corbett, "Bong Soo Han: Multi-Faceted Martial Artist," *Black Belt*, September 1979, 22–29.

26. Peter Koenig, "America's Secret Military Forces Learn Ancient Guerilla Tactics," *Black Belt*, January 1977, 20.

27. Rex Reed, " 'Billy Jack's' Message: Peace through Sacrifice," *Daily News* (Los Angeles), 30 July 1971, Margaret Herrick Library, clippings file.

28. "Complete Honesty: New Film Technique in 'Billy Jack,' " *Billy Jack* press book, 3, original emphasis, Margaret Herrick Library, clippings file.

29. David Bain, "How to Dub 'Aaaargh!' Into English," *New York Times*, 2 July 1978.

30. The original Chinese title of *Five Fingers of Death*, transliterated in Mandarin, was *Tian Xia Di Yi Quan*, roughly translated as "Number One Fist under the Sun." Although the word *quan* (fist) is common in Hong Kong martial arts film titles, this particular title may have been designed to play on the English title for the Bruce Lee film *Fists of Fury* (1971), which had been circulating in Asia and Europe before it was released in the U.S. a few weeks after *Five Fingers of Death*. The original Chinese title of *Deep Thrust* was *Tie Zhang Xuan Feng Tui*, which translates literally as "Iron Palms and Swirling Wind Legs," emphasizing both the weapon-like hardness of Angela Mao's hands and the quick kicking of her hapkido training.

31. "Review: Deep Thrust—The Hand of Death," *Variety*, 23 May 1973, 28.

32. "Catholics Find MPAA Over-Permissive on Violence; Condemn Hong Kong Pix," *Variety*, 13 June 1973, 7.

33. See "Review: Fists of Fury (The Big Boss)," *Variety*, 27 June 1973, 34. Glaessner also develops the idea of "balletic violence" in *Kung Fu*, 7–14.

34. Commentaries on Foucault's *History of Sexuality* are numerous, but some I found particularly helpful are McWhorter, *Bodies and Pleasures*; Stoler, *Race and the Education of Desire*; Dreyfus and Rabinow, *Michel Foucault*, 126–42. On pornography and Foucault, see L. Williams, *Hard Core*, 1–5, 34–57.

35. Freud, *Beyond the Pleasure Principle*, 18–23.

36. Laplanche, *Life and Death in Psychoanalysis*, 114.

37. Freud, *Beyond the Pleasure Principle*, 76; Laplanche, *Life and Death in Psychoanalysis*, 124.

38. Foucault, *History of Sexuality*, 57.

39. Palmer, Palmer, and Meyers, *The Encyclopedia of Martial Arts Movies*, vii. Although MPAA ratings are rarely explained by the ratings board, the treatment of another film from the early 1970s, Stanley Kubrick's *A Clockwork Orange* (1971), helps to illuminate just how anomalous *The Street Fighter* was. *A Clockwork Orange* was also rated X upon its original release, but this rating was attributed to the film's excessive violence. It was only after Kubrick cut thirty seconds of footage related to sexual activity, and then resubmitted the film for an R rating, that critics realized the original object of the X rating. See "Facesaver: Dr. Stern or Dr. Kubrick?," *Variety*, 30 August 1972, 4.

40. A. H. Weiler, " 'Street Fighter,' Karate Film, Full of Inane Violence," *New York Times*, 30 January 1975.

41. Chow and Spangler, *Kung Fu*, 144.

42. Al Harvin, " 'Martial Artists' Hold Exhibition Today," *New York Times*, 2 June 1974. For more on Aaron Banks, a very visible figure in the martial arts culture of the 1970s, see Jeannette Bruce, "Aaron Banks, New York's Martial Artist," *Sports Illustrated*, 15 April 1974, 36–45.

43. "Focus," *New Yorker*, 23 June 1975, 32–33.

44. Terry Dobson and Brooke Miller, "How to Avoid Being Mugged: An Ounce of Prevention Is Worth a Pound of Bruce Lee," *Esquire*, March 1976, 84–89; Michael S. Feld, Ronald E. McNair, and Stephen R. Wilk, "The Physics of Karate," *Scientific American*, April 1979, 150–58.

45. There is an apocryphal story in which Bruce Lee was originally considered for the leading role in *Kung Fu*, but was dropped in favor of David Carradine because Lee was "too short and too Chinese." Although Lee's friends and biographers and Lee's own papers support this story, it was denied or deflected by the production staff of *Kung Fu*. For instance, David Chow, who served as the martial arts choreographer and technical advisor to the show, wrote that Lee himself "decided not to pursue the starring role in *Kung Fu*," but Lee's biographer Bruce Thomas wrote that Lee was disappointed by the rejection and threw himself into directing and starring in *Way of the Dragon* (1972), his third film, as a result. See Chow and Spangler, *Kung Fu*, 193; Thomas, *Bruce Lee*, 143–45. Ultimately Lee would prove to be the more lasting icon of Asian martial arts in the U.S. For more on Lee's influence on American audiences, see chapter 5.

46. Michael D. Guinan, "Kung Fu: Violence and the Stranger in Our Midst," *Christian Century*, 19 September 1973, 919.

47. "Television Reviews: Kung Fu (Movie of the Week)," *Variety*, 1 March 1972, 44. Keye Luke and Benson Fong appeared in many of the Charlie Chan films of the 1930s and 1940s, with Luke repeatedly featured as Chan's "Number One Son" alongside Warner Oland's yellowface Chan. Notably, although in the Charlie Chan films Luke spoke with a hyper-American accent, in *Kung Fu* Luke employs the same stilted "yellowface" voice which Oland popularized. Richard Loo and Philip Ahn were best known for their roles as evil Japanese soldiers in films set in the Second World War both during and after the war, most notably Loo in *The Purple Heart* (1944) and Ahn in *Betrayal from the East* (1945).

48. Because early Chinese Americans were often branded as immoral pagans, many were receptive to the proselytizing of Protestant missionaries, both in China and in the U.S. Missionaries often took the effort to learn Chinese and become familiar with the culture, a rarity in the early days of Chinese exclusion. For more on the missionary influence in these communities, see Yu, *Thinking Orientals*, 19–92.

49. See Larry Michie, "Surgeon General's TViolence Report Seen Reheating Debate on Kid Angle," *Variety*, 19 January 1972, 34; Larry Michie, "TV Skeds Sweat Out Pastore: Held Off by D.C. Violence Quiz," *Variety*, 22 March 1972, 3.

50. "Television Reviews: Kung Fu," *Variety*, 18 October 1972, 42.

51. Joyce Haber, "David Carradine: The Antihero's Antihero," *Los Angeles Times*, 3 February 1974; Tom Burke, "David Carradine, King of 'Kung Fu,'" *New York Times*, 29 April 1973.

52. For an analysis of how Carradine's persona was constructed with regard to the figure of the Buddhist monk, see Iwamura, "The Oriental Monk in American Popular Culture," 25–43.

53. Cyclops, "Kung Foolishness," *Newsweek*, 12 February 1973, 51.

54. Stephen J. Sansweet, "The Rock 'Em, Sock 'Em World of Kung Fu," *Wall Street Journal*, 4 October 1973.

55. Frank Chin, "Kung Fu Is Unfair to Chinese," *New York Times*, 24 March 1974.

56. Chin et al., "Introduction," xxi–xlviii.

57. Ed Spielman, "I'm Proud to Have Created 'Kung Fu,'" letter to the editor, *New York Times*, 14 April 1974. Spielman is writing in response to Frank Chin's earlier piece decrying the show's inherent racism and disregard for Asian American history.

58. Eng, *Racial Castration*, 35–103.

59. R. G. Lee, *Orientals*, 64–67.

60. D. Keith Mano, "Kung Phooey," *National Review*, 2 May 1980, 546–47.

61. Prashad, *Everybody Was Kung Fu Fighting*, 126–49.

62. Ho, "Kickin' the White Man's Ass," 296.

63. See, for example, Bordwell, *Planet Hong Kong*, 50; Desser, "The Kung Fu Craze," 38.

64. R. F. Williams, *Negroes with Guns*, 76, 82.

65. "NAACP Leader Urges 'Violence,'" *New York Times*, 7 May 1959. Williams made this statement in response to the trial of Lewis Medlin, a white man who had raped and beat a pregnant black woman and was acquitted of all charges despite eyewitness testimony from the victim and other black community members. Williams later clarified his argument, saying that he was not calling for retaliatory violence, but that blacks had to defend themselves from violent attack because they could not count on the courts to defend them. His full statement was, "This demonstration today shows that the Negro in the South cannot expect justice in the courts. He must convict his attackers on the spot. He must meet violence with violence, lynching with lynching." See Tyson, *Radio Free Dixie*, 127–65.

66. Hill, *The Deacons for Defense*, 258–73.

67. Matlin, "'Lift Up Yr Self!,'" 91–116.

68. McCaughey, *Real Knockouts*, 50–57.

69. Grace Lichtenstein, "Feminists Hold Rape-Defense Workshop," *New York Times*, 18 April 1971.

70. Susan Pascalé, Rachel Moon, and Leslie Tanner, "Karate as Self-Defense for Women," *Women: A Journal of Liberation*, Winter 1970, reprinted in Baxandall and Gordon, *Dear Sisters*, 207–8.

71. Brownmiller, *Against Our Will*, 403.

72. Victoria Pellegrino, "A Beginner's Guide to the Martial Arts," *Ms.*, December 1974, 14–15.

73. Richard W. Johnston, "Dangerous Delusion," *Sports Illustrated*, 18 October 1976, 88–92.

74. Brownmiller, *Against Our Will*, 427. Brownmiller's disturbing conclusion is also discussed in Bevacqua, *Rape on the Public Agenda*.

75. A. Y. Davis, "Rape, Racism and the Myth of the Black Rapist," 172–201.

76. Review of *Cleopatra Jones*, *Product Digest*, 8 August 1973, Margaret Herrick Library, clippings file.

77. Foucault, *History of Sexuality*, 25.

78. See Lewis, *Hollywood v. Hard Core*, 11–49; Skinner, *The Cross and the Cinema*; Wertham, *Seduction of the Innocent*.

79. "A Public Health Problem," *Variety*, 24 May 1972, 35, 49.

80. Christopher Lydons, "Hearings to Weigh TV Violence Study," *New York Times*, 18 January 1972.

81. See Joseph B. Treaster, "Youthful Violence Grows and Accused Are Younger," *New York Times*, 4 November 1974. Among the reasons for this growth of violence among youth that Treaster cites is "the influence of movies and television with their violence and their two-fisted hero-policemen and Kung Fu fighters." Although race is not the primary topic of his article, Treaster also notes a study of juvenile delinquency in New York City that found that 80 percent of these youth were black or Puerto Rican.

82. "Sees 'Manuals of Crime' Lurking in Black Hoodlums of Screen," *Variety*, 8 May 1974, 66.

83. "Metropolitan Brief: Melee in Beacon after Kung Fu Movie," *New York Times*, 17 November 1974.

84. Don A. Schanche, "Commonsense Rules You'd Better Follow If You're into Karate," *Today's Health*, July 1974, 33; "Killer Sticks," *Newsweek*, 15 October 1973, 67.

85. Ad in *Variety*, 16 February 1972, 44–45.

86. Dr. George Gerbner, professor of communications at University of Pennsylvania, quoted in Jane E. Brody, "TV Violence Cited as Bad Influence," *New York Times*, 17 December 1975.

87. Linda Charlton, "F.C.C.'s Johnson Accuses TV of Molesting Children's Minds," *New York Times*, 23 March 1972. Nicholas Johnson, a member of the Federal Communications Commission, was himself denounced by a Senate subcommittee member as violent for making such inflammatory remarks.

88. Marilyn Wellemeyer, "The Fun of Fighting—Oriental Style," *Fortune*, 16 January 1978, 37–46; Robert Levy, "The Black Belts of Business," *Dun's*, November 1973, 92–96. One of Wellemeyer's interviewees states, "As powerful as I felt in my business and my intellectual life, I felt so inadequate as a physical person" (37).

89. See the entire issue of *New York*, 8 February 1982, whose cover is "Protecting Yourself against Crime."

90. Ongiri, "Bruce Lee in the Ghetto Connection," 254.

91. Ongiri, "Bruce Lee in the Ghetto Connection," 254.

Chapter 5. Being Bruce Lee

1. Chu, *Hong Kong Cinema*, 38. Many Chinese martial arts films focus on the transition from the Ming Dynasty (1368–1644) to the Ch'ing dynasty (1644–1911) because they are derived from popular histories and folktales surrounding the Shaolin temple, such as in the mid-twentieth-century *wuxia* novels of Jin Yong, but knowledge of this historical context is often missing in the Western reception of Chinese martial arts films, resulting in a perception of their settings as simultaneously archaic and yet representative of modern China—the quintessential orientalist history of Asia.

2. Because of the confusion between different translations and release names of Hong Kong film titles, for consistency I refer to Lee's films by their American release titles, noting their alternate titles in notes. Lee's first martial arts film was *Fists of Fury* (*Tang Shan Da Xiong* in Mandarin Chinese, roughly translated as "The big brother/ boss of Tangshan"), also known in the U.S. as *The Big Boss*. His second film, *The Chinese Connection* (*Jing Wu Men* in Mandarin, referring to the historical Jin Wu athletic school in Shanghai), was also known as *Fist of Fury*. *Return of the Dragon* (*Meng Long Guo Jiang* in Mandarin, translated as "The fierce dragon crosses the river"), the fourth of Lee's films to be released in the U.S., was actually his third film. Lee directed this film himself, and it was released in Asia in 1972 under the title *The Way of the Dragon*. After his death the film was retitled *Return of the Dragon* and was rereleased in the U.S. in August 1974 as if it were a sequel to *Enter the Dragon*.

3. Deleuze, *Cinema 2*, xi.

4. E. F. Wong, *On Visual Media Racism*, 34.

5. A. Anderson, "Action in Motion," 1, my emphasis.

6. Tasker, *Spectacular Bodies*, 3.

7. Lott, "All the King's Men," 198.

8. A. Anderson, "Action in Motion," 1.

9. Michael Seiler, "Kung Fu Talent Search: Kicking Up Their Heels for Role," *Los Angeles Times*, 17 April 1973; Charles Lucas, "They All Had Faces Like Bruce," *Black Belt Magazine's Best of Bruce Lee 2* (Los Angeles: Rainbow, 1974), 72–79.

10. Dana Harris, " 'Dragon' Resurrects Lee," *Daily Variety*, 15 November 2001.

11. Mark Tetreau, review of "Bruce Lee: Quest of the Dragon," 17 December 2003, (http://www.kungfucinema.com). *Bruce Lee: Quest of the Dragon* was released in 2002 for the Xbox gaming platform by Universal Interactive.

12. Kei, "The Development of 'Martial Arts' in Hong Kong Cinema," 31.

13. Chiao, "Bruce Lee," 33.

14. This fight also highlights Lee's preference for casting trained martial artists as his sparring partners, since an untrained actor would not have the necessary control and technique to engage in such sparring and to actually make contact with Lee without injuring himself or Lee. Sammo Hung was one of the Seven Little Fortunes who later choreographed the fight scenes in Clouse's *Game of Death*, and also directed and starred in his own Bruce Lee homage, *Enter the Fat Dragon* (1978).

15. Kaminsky, "Kung Fu Film as Ghetto Myth," 129–38.

16. "Review: Fists of Fury (The Big Boss)," *Variety*, 27 June 1973, 34; Vincent Canby, "Violence and Beauty Mesh in 'Wild Bunch,' " *New York Times*, 26 June 1969. The adjective "balletic" is also applied to Lee's *The Chinese Connection* in Fredric Milstein, "Cream of Karate Chop," *Los Angeles Times*, 5 July 1973; and to *Game of Death* in Linda Gross, "Movie Review: Bruce Lee, Double in 'Game of Death,' " *Los Angeles Times*, 9 June 1979.

17. Quoted in Block, *The Legend of Bruce Lee*, 90–91.

18. Rayns, "Bruce Lee," 110–12.

19. M. T. Nguyen, "Bruce Lee I Love You," 271–304; H. T. Nguyen, "The Resurrection of Brandon Lee," 223–70. Brandon Lee was the name of Bruce Lee's son, whose ill-fated death during the production of the film *The Crow* (1994) uncannily recalled Lee's own death; the Brandon Lee that H. T. Nguyen refers to is the stage name of an Asian American porn star with no relation to Lee.

20. See, for example, Heidegger discussing the problem of *Dasein* (roughly translated as "human Being"), temporality, and historicality in *Being and Time*, 424–55. Heidegger's concept of history, or what he calls "historicality," is tied up with the "specific movement in which Dasein is *stretched along and stretches itself along*," here referring to the interval between birth and death that "*already lies in the Being of Dasein*" (427, 426, original emphases).

21. L. Lee, *Bruce Lee*, 77. Flipbook images are on 78–131.

22. Deleuze, *Cinema 1*, 1, 4.

23. B. Lee, *Chinese Gung Fu*.

24. Lacan, "Desire and the Interpretation of Desire in Hamlet," 36.

25. Lo, "Muscles and Subjectivity," 109.

26. Hunt, *Kung Fu Cult Masters*, 76–98. See also websites such as "Bruceploitation Is a Crime," 17 December 2003, a filmography of Bruce Le and Bruce Li films complete with reviews (http://www.geocities.com/many_bruces), and Bruceploitation Pictures, 17 December 2003, with a list of Bruceploitation films available on DVD (http://www .geocities.com/udar552003/main.html). For more on the exploitation tradition in American cinema, see E. Schaefer, *"Bold! Daring! Shocking! True!."* For more on blaxploitation films, see Guerrero, *Framing Blackness*, 69–112.

27. Hu, " 'Bruce Lee' after Bruce Lee," 124.

28. Bruce Li is the stage name of Tao Ho Chung, a Taiwanese martial artist and actor and one of the more prominent of the Lee clones. Li starred in *Goodbye Bruce Lee: His Last Game of Death* (1975) and *Exit the Dragon, Enter the Tiger* (1976). Bruce Le, whose real name was Wong Kin Lung, was sometimes credited as Bruce Ly; he was a contract actor for the Shaw Brothers before branching out to other Bruceploitation films such as *My Name Called Bruce* (1978) and *Enter the Game of Death* (1980). Li, Le, and Dragon Lee were the most prolific Bruce Lee clones; the others starred in only a handful of Lee-themed films. Bruce Lea (Jun Chong) played the lead in the South Korean production *Bruce Lee Fights Back from the Grave* (1976); Bruce Leong (Leung Siu-Lung) had an uncredited appearance in *The Clones of Bruce Lee* (1977) and starred in *The Dragon Lives Again* (1977); Bruce Rhee starred alongside Dragon Lee in his only film, *Kung Fu Fever* (1979). For an extended discussion of these and other Bruce Lee clones, see "Bruceploitation," November 2002, http://www.geocities.com/many_bruces/, accessed 20 January 2004.

29. Laplanche, "Time and the Other," 255.

30. Laplanche, "Time and the Other," 255.

31. Thomas, *Bruce Lee*, 204.

32. Advertisement, *Los Angeles Times*, 10 June 1979.

33. Deleuze, *Cinema 2*, 36, 37.

34. Deleuze, *Cinema 2*, xi.

35. Deleuze, *Cinema 2*, 36.

36. Thomas, *Bruce Lee*, 158.

37. Hunt, *Kung Fu Cult Masters*, 94. Only Kim Tai Chong (alternately spelled Kim Tai Chung and Kim Tai Jong) is listed in the end credits as portraying Billy Lo, three screens after Bruce Lee is listed as doing the same. The other two body doubles are not listed at all. Yuen Biao, who was another of the Seven Little Fortunes along with Jackie Chan and Sammo Hung, features more prominently in Ng See-Yuen's *Game of Death II* (1981), which was seen mainly in Asia. Chen Yao-Po was a nonprofessional actor producer Raymond Chow discovered in a Hong Kong disco and wanted only to be referred to as "Herbert X." See Jim Harwood, "Finally Completed Bruce Lee Pic Bows O'Seas; U.S. Not Set," *Daily Variety*, 29 March 1978.

38. Block, *The Legend of Bruce Lee*, 15, 132–34.

39. Linda Gross, "Movie Review: Bruce Lee, Double in 'Game of Death,'" *Los Angeles Times*, 9 June 1979.

40. Deleuze, *Cinema 2*, 131, original emphases.

41. Deleuze, *Cinema 2*, 126–55.

42. Deleuze, *Cinema 2*, 133. Deleuze is citing one of Arthur Rimbaud's famous letters, where he describes his revelation of what it means to be a poet: "I'm working to turn myself into a seer. . . . It has to do with making your way toward the unknown by a derangement of all the senses. The suffering is tremendous, but one must bear up against it, to be born a poet, and I know that's what I am. It's not at all my fault. It's wrong to say I think: one should say I am thought. Forgive the pun. I is another." See Rimbaud, letter to Georges Izambard, 13 May 1871, in *Rimbaud: Complete Works, Selected Letters*, 302–4. Deleuze finds resonance between Rimbaud's self-othering claim and the work of the French documentarian and ethnographer Jean Rouch, in particular his *Moi un Noir* (1958).

43. Deleuze, *Cinema 2*, 36, 129.

44. Deleuze, *Cinema 2*, 155.

45. Stephen Teo describes Lee's cultural nationalism as "an emotional wish among Chinese people living outside China to identify with China and things Chinese, even though they may not have been born there or speak its national language or dialects." Teo, *Hong Kong Cinema*, 111. As its Chinese title, *Jing Wu Men*, suggests, *The Chinese Connection* is loosely based on the establishment of the Shanghai Pure Martial Calisthenics (*Jing Wu Ti Cao*) School in 1910, during the occupation of Shanghai by Japanese and Western colonial powers. Two of Lee's actions in this film are particularly laden with nationalistic significance: the first is when he kicks down a sign at a public park that reads "No Dogs and Chinese," and the second is when he destroys a banner presented to his Chinese martial arts school that reads "Sick Men of East Asia" (*Dong Ya Bing Fu*). For details on this folklore surrounding the *Jing Wu Men*, see A. D. Morris, *Marrow of the Nation*, 183–95.

46. It was reported that over two hundred policemen were employed to restrain a crowd of ten to twenty thousand mourners in Hong Kong on 25 July 1973. See "200 Police Restrain Crowd at Service for Bruce Lee," *New York Times*, 26 July 1973; Block, *The Legend of Bruce Lee*, 123. Even if American audiences had no visual knowledge of this media event from contemporary news reports, they would have seen this same footage used in the documentary *Bruce Lee, The Legend* (1977).

47. Deleuze, *Cinema 2*, 127.

48. Introduction, *Game of Death* press kit, Margaret Herrick Library.

49. Deleuze, *Cinema 2*, 128, 142.

50. Fred Wei-han Houn, "In Memory of Bruce Lee (a poem)," *Bridge*, May 1975, 26–27.

51. Demetrius Cope, "Anatomy of a Blaxploitation Theater," *Jump Cut* 9 (1975), 22–23.

52. Darius James, *That's Blaxploitation: Roots of the Baadasssss 'Tude*, quoted in Amy

Abugo Ongiri, " 'He Wanted to Be Just Like Bruce Lee,' " 31. See also Cha-Jua, "Black Audiences, Blaxploitation and Kung Fu Films," 199–223.

53. "We Are All Bruce Lee," *Feral Tribune* (Croatia), reposted on TOL Wire, 4 September 2003, http://www.tol.cz, accessed 15 July 2009.

54. Nino Raspudic, "Bruce Lee Monument in Mostar," presentation delivered at Relations Workshop, Halle, Germany, 5 November 2004, available at http://public.city mined.org/KRAX_CARGO/red_krax/mostar/urban_movement_mostar/, accessed 16 July 2009.

55. Teo, *Hong Kong Cinema*, 110–11; Lo, "Muscles and Subjectivity," 109–11.

56. Fu and Desser, introduction, 5. For more on the nature of Hong Kong's unique colonial identity compared to other colonial and postcolonial sites, see Abbas, *Hong Kong*, 1–15.

57. Prashad, *Everybody Was Kung Fu Fighting*, 140.

58. Originally published as Shanlon Wu, "About Men: In Search of Bruce Lee's Grave," *New York Times*, 15 April 1990, this piece has since been anthologized in R. T. Schaefer, *Racial and Ethnic Groups*, and Lieberman and Lester, *Social Work*. In both books the piece appears in a section on the intersections of race and gender.

59. J. Chan, *Chinese American Masculinities*, 77–78.

60. Berry, "Stellar Transit," 219.

61. Interestingly Yune also conflates Bruce Lee with Sylvester Stallone in *Rocky*, referring to the narratives of self-discipline and training that these two film stars invoke through their work. I draw out the explicit connections between martial arts and Vietnam in the conclusion, using Stallone's *Rambo* films to make explicit the return of the oriental body to the scene of the Vietnam War through the stylization of the white ethnic body.

62. Kao was intoxicated after having suffered racist taunts at a local bar, and his neighbors called the police after he started screaming and crying in front of his house. The officer who killed Kao, Jack Shields, shot him only thirty seconds after arriving on the scene and claimed he did so in self-defense because he feared Kao would hurt him with his martial arts skills. Shields was cleared of wrongdoing by his police department, and the U.S. Department of Justice refused to file federal civil rights charges in the case, contrary to the Kao family's wishes. See M. Chang, "Bridging the Gap," 139–60; Chen, "Hate Violence as Border Patrol," 69–101.

63. Quoted in Al Harvin, " 'Martial Artists' Hold Exhibition Today," *New York Times*, 2 June 1974.

64. Thomas, *Bruce Lee*, 222.

65. Miller, *The Tao of Bruce Lee*, 175.

66. I borrow this terminology from Tuan, *Forever Foreigners or Honorary Whites?*

67. M. Morris, "Learning from Bruce Lee," 178.

68. Brown, "Global Bodies/Postnationalities," 33.

69. During the Second World War some black nationalists openly supported or sympathized with the Japanese against the U.S., viewing the Japanese as allies in a

larger war against white supremacy. See Horne, *Race War!*; Dower, *War without Mercy*, 147–80.

70. Paul Attanasio, "Rooting for the 'Dragon,' " *Washington Post*, 25 March 1985.

Conclusion

1. Thomas, *Bruce Lee*, 146.

2. Lee Grant, "Film Clips: Trek from TV to Movie to TV," *Los Angeles Times*, 25 May 1977.

3. Savran, *Taking It Like a Man*, 197–206; Jeffords, *The Remasculinization of America*, 1–22, 48–53, 127–34.

4. Desser, " 'Charlie Don't Surf,' " 96.

5. Mailer, "The White Negro," 340; Lott, *Love and Theft*, 54–55.

6. Mailer, "The White Negro," 341.

7. Unlike many of the other Asian actors who play martial arts villains, Oh was well connected to the Asian American theater scene and was a cofounder of the East-West Players, a troupe based in Los Angeles that commissioned many of the early works of Frank Chin and David Henry Hwang. See Kurahashi, *Asian American Culture on Stage*; E. K. Lee, "Transnational Legitimization of an Actor."

8. Jeffords, *Hard Bodies*, 6–15.

9. Jacobson, *Roots Too*, 100–108.

10. Faust, " 'Numbers on Top of Numbers.' " The Civil War is largely acknowledged as the most brutal war in U.S. history, both in the scale of the casualties and its effect on American society and culture. The total number of Civil War dead is approximately 620,000, based on extensive postwar reconstructions rather than records kept during the war. Faust extrapolates that the "equivalent proportion of today's population would mean 5,500,000 dead" (997).

11. Sledge, *Soldier Dead*, 268.

12. Franklin, *M.I.A.*., 74–75; Lembcke, *The Spitting Image*, 94–100.

13. Hawley, *The Remains of War*, 4.

14. For example, in 1995 the U.S. spent $100 million on the recovery of MIA remains, while pledging only $1 million for prosthetic devices, $1.5 million for assistance to displaced and orphaned children, and $245,000 for disaster relief from typhoon flooding. See Hawley, *The Remains of War*, 232.

15. Hawley, *The Remains of War*, 45.

16. Franklin, *M.I.A.*, 108–17.

17. Hawley, *The Remains of War*, 215.

18. Hawley, *The Remains of War*, 79.

19. Deleuze, *Cinema 1*, 211.

20. Freud, "From the History of an Infantile Neurosis," 33, 35.

21. "The people are missing" is a phrase from Deleuze, *Cinema 2*, 216, and is discussed at length in chapter 2.

22. Alvarez and Pitch, *Chained Eagle*, 2, 234, 278–83; see also Oropeza, *¡Raza Sí!*, 1–10, 142–43.

23. Freud and Breuer, *Studies on Hysteria*, 32–33.

24. The reappearance of imagery from the Second World War was not lost on contemporary reviewers. See review of "Missing in Action," *Daily Variety*, 19 November 1984, Margaret Herrick Library, clippings file.

25. Paul Solotaroff, quoted in Hawley, *The Remains of War*, 119.

26. Pat H. Broeske, "The Curious Evolution of John Rambo," *Los Angeles Times*, 27 October 1985.

27. Broeske, "The Curious Evolution of John Rambo."

28. L. Williams, "Melodrama Revised," 61.

29. Broeske, "The Curious Evolution of John Rambo."

30. Quoted in Vincent Canby, "Revenge Fuels Cold War Movies of the 80s," *New York Times*, 8 December 1985.

31. Espiritu, *Asian American Panethnicity*, 53–133.

32. Omi and Winant, *Racial Formation in the U.S.*, 113–36.

33. Chin, *The Year of the Dragon*, 86; see also S. C. Wong, *Reading Asian American Literature*, 55–76.

34. Wang, *Chan Is Missing*, 11; Chin, *The Year of the Dragon*, 71.

35. Trinh, *Woman Native Other*, 98.

36. Quoted in McDonald, introduction, xxii.

37. Chin, "Frank Chin: An Interview," 86.

38. Chin, *The Year of the Dragon*, 110.

39. Chin, *The Year of the Dragon*, 141.

40. Feng, *Identities in Motion*, 155.

41. Wang, *Chan Is Missing*, 74.

42. This battle is famously chronicled in another well-known early Asian American film, Curtis Choy's documentary *The Fall of the I-Hotel* (1983). For a detailed study of the activism that arose around the demolition of this hotel, see Habal, *San Francisco's International Hotel*.

43. Andy Klein, "Bull in a China Shop," *Reader*, 23 August 1985, Margaret Herrick Library, clippings file; Peter Rainer, "There's a Nasty Twist in Cimino's 'Dragon' Tale," *Los Angeles Herald Examiner*, 16 August 1985.

44. R. G. Lee, *Orientals*, 196–203; Marchetti, *Romance and the "Yellow Peril,"* 202–21.

45. Dino de Laurentiis Corp. and MGM/UA Entertainment, *Year of the Dragon* press book, 16 July 1985, 3–5, Margaret Herrick Library, clippings file.

46. David Hwang, "Are Movies Ready for Real Orientals?," *New York Times*, 11 August 1985.

47. Zia, *Asian American Dreams*, 43. For a discussion of the photograph's role in Kingston's and Chin's novels, see Eng, *Racial Castration*, 35–103.

48. See Chin et al., "Introduction," xxi–xlvii; Chin, "Come All Ye Asian American Writers of the Real and the Fake," 1–91. However, Chin's fiction does not always fulfill

the machismo of his manifestoes, showing characters with a much more ambivalent relationship to hegemonic masculinity. For a larger analysis of Chin's gender politics, see D. Y. Kim, *Writing Manhood in Black and Yellow*, especially 160–202.

49. For a more detailed description of Asian Americans' role in affirmative action debates, see Wu, *Yellow*, 131–72; R. G. Lee, *Orientals*, 180–91.

50. Jon Funabiki, "Asian Actors Aim to Curb Stereotypes," *San Diego Union-Tribune*, 1 August 1985. The conference was organized by the National Asian American Telecommunications Association (recently renamed the Center for Asian American Media), which suspended its organization of the San Francisco Asian American Film Festival that year to devote itself to this conference. See Center for Asian American Media, "Film Festival: History," http://festival.asianamericanmedia.org, accessed 15 February 2010.

51. Mark Pinsky, "Extra-ordinary Problem in Casting of 'Dragon,'" *Los Angeles Times*, 18 November 1984; John Horn, "Battle over 'Dragon' Continues," *Los Angeles Times*, 7 September 1985; Lyons, "The Paradox of Protest," 277–318.

52. John Horn, " 'Dragon' to Get a Disclaimer," *Los Angeles Times*, 30 August 1985; Wei, *The Asian American Movement*, 258–60.

53. Columbia Pictures, "The Karate Kid: Preliminary Production Information," 4, Margaret Herrick Library, clippings file.

54. Hwang, "Are Movies Ready for Real Orientals?"

55. William Petersen, "Success Story, Japanese-American Style," *New York Times Magazine*, 9 January 1966.

56. Shibusawa, *America's Geisha Ally*, 4–5.

57. R. G. Lee, *Orientals*, 190.

58. Ronald J. Hall, letter to the editor, *Los Angeles Times*, 7 April 1985; Paul Conrad, "Hirohito's Revenge," *Los Angeles Times*, 31 March 1985.

59. *Who Killed Vincent Chin?* (1987); Wei, *The Asian American Movement*, 193–96; Zia, *Asian American Dreams*, 55–81.

.

Archival Sources

MH: Margaret Herrick Library, Academy of Motion Picture Arts and Sciences, Los Angeles.
MTR: Museum of Television and Radio (now The Paley Center for Media), Los Angeles and New York.
UCLA-AA: UCLA Asian American Studies Center Reading Room/Library, Los Angeles.
UCLA-FTA: UCLA Film and Television Archive, Los Angeles.
VTA: Vanderbilt Television Archive, Nashville.

Films and Television Shows, by year

1961
   "Diem's War or Ours?" CBS Eyewitness News. CBS. 29 December. MTR.

1963
   "Nineteen Sixty-Three: A Television Album, Part 1 of 2." CBS. 22 February. MTR.

1964
   "Vietnam: It's a Mad War." NBC News Special. NBC. 1 December. MTR.

1965
   "Hell in the City of Angels, Parts I and II." KTLA-TV. 11–14 August. MTR.
   "The Battle of Ia Drang Valley." CBS News Special Report. CBS. 11 November 1965. MTR.

1966
   "Saga of a Western Man: I Am a Soldier." ABC News. ABC. 8 May. MTR.
   "Vietnam Perspective: Eric Sevareid's Personal Report." CBS News Special Report. CBS. 21 June. MTR.
   The Anderson Platoon. Dir. Pierre Schoendoerffer. Prod. French Broadcasting System. Rebroadcast on CBS News Special Report. CBS. 4 July 1967. MTR. Videocassette. International Historic Films, 1986.

1968

"The Viet Cong." CBS *Reports*. CBS. 20 February. MTR.

"Hanoi: A Report by Charles Collingwood." CBS *News Special*. CBS. 16 April. MTR.

CBS *Evening News*. 27 August. VTA.

CBS *Evening News*. 29 August. VTA.

No Vietnamese Ever Called Me Nigger. Dir. David Loeb Weiss. Videocassette. Paradigm Films/The Cinema Guild.

1969

"The Making of the President: 1968." CBS *News Special*. 9 September. MTR.

"A Timetable for Vietnam." CBS *Reports*. 12 December. MTR.

Medium Cool. Dir., prod., and writ. Haskell Wexler. Perfs. Robert Forster, Verna Bloom, Harold Blankenship, Marianna Hill. Paramount Pictures. DVD. Paramount Home Video, 2004.

1970

"Where We Stand in Indochina." CBS *News Special Report*. CBS. 30 June. MTR.

"The World of Charlie Company." CBS *News Special Report*. CBS. 14 July. MTR.

Watermelon Man. Dir. and writ. Melvin Van Peebles. Prod. Leon Mirell. Perfs. Godfrey Cambridge, Estelle Parsons. Columbia Pictures. DVD. Sony Pictures, 2004.

1971

The Gooks. Dir. Pierre D. Gaisseau. Canadian Broadcasting Corporation. UCLA-FTA.

Billy Jack. Dir. Tom Laughlin (as T. C. Frank). Prod. Tom Laughlin (as Mary Rose Solti). Perfs. Tom Laughlin, Delores Taylor, Bong Soo Han. Warner Brothers. DVD. Warner Home Video, 2004.

Fists of Fury (The Big Boss). Chinese title: *Tang Shan Da Xiong*. Dir. Lo Wei. Prod. Raymond Chow. Perfs. Bruce Lee, Ying-Chieh Han, Nora Miao. Golden Harvest. U.S. dist. National General Pictures, 1972. DVD. 20th Century-Fox Home Entertainment, 2005.

1972

"The Way of the Tiger, the Sign of the Dragon." *Kung Fu*. Pilot episode. Dir. and prod. Jerry Thorpe. Perfs. David Carradine, Philip Ahn, Keye Luke, Benson Fong, James Hong. Warner Brothers Television/ABC Movie of the Week. ABC. 22 February. DVD. Warner Home Video, 2004.

NBC *Nightly News*. 8 June. VTA.

CBS *Evening News*. 27 June. VTA.

"The Siege of Kontum." *World in Action*. Prod. Michael Beckham and Brian Moser. ITV. UCLA-FTA.

Winter Soldier. Feat. John Kerry, Rusty Sachs, Carl Rippberger, Mark Lenix. Winterfilm Collective. DVD. Milliarium Zero, 2005.

The Chinese Connection (Fist of Fury). Chinese title: *Jing Wu Men*. Dir. Lo Wei. Prod. Raymond Chow. Perfs. Bruce Lee, Nora Miao, James Tien, Robert Baker. Golden

Harvest. U.S. dist. National General Pictures, 1973. DVD. 20th Century-Fox Home Entertainment, 2005.

Five Fingers of Death (King Boxer). Chinese title: *Tian Xia Di Yi Quan*. Dir. Cheng Chang Ho. Prod. Run Run Shaw. Perfs. Lo Lieh, Ping Wang, Hsiung Chao. Shaw Brothers. U.S. dist. Warner Brothers, 1973. DVD. Weinstein Company Home Entertainment, 2007.

Return of the Dragon (The Way of the Dragon). Chinese title: *Meng Long Guo Jiang*. Dir. and writ. Bruce Lee. Prod. Raymond Chow. Perfs. Bruce Lee, Nora Miao, Chuck Norris, Robert Wall. Golden Harvest. U.S. dist. Bryanston, 1974. DVD. 20th Century-Fox Home Entertainment, 2005.

Deep Thrust—Hand of Death (Lady Whirlwind). Chinese title: *Tie Zhang Xuan Feng Tui*. Dir. Huang Feng. Prod. Raymond Chow. Perfs. Angela Mao, Chang Yi, Pai Ying. Golden Harvest. U.S. dist. American International Pictures, 1973. DVD. Joy Star Films and Video, 1993.

1973

Enter the Dragon. Dir. Robert Clouse. Prod. Fred Weintraub, Paul Heller, Raymond Chow. Perfs. Bruce Lee, Jim Kelly, John Saxon, Shih Kien, Angela Mao, Bolo Yeung, Robert Wall. Warner Brothers. DVD. Warner Home Video, 1998.

Cleopatra Jones. Dir. Jack Starrett. Prod. William Tennant. Perfs. Tamara Dobson, Shelley Winters. Warner Brothers. DVD. Warner Home Video, 1999.

1974

The Street Fighter. Japanese title: *Gekitotsu! Satsujin ken*. Dir. Ozawa Shigehiro. Perf. Sonny Chiba. Toei Pictures. U.S. dist. New Line Cinema, 1974. DVD. Madacy Entertainment Group, 2004.

The Trial of Billy Jack. Dir. Tom Laughlin. Prod. Joe Cramer. Perfs. Tom Laughlin, Delores Taylor. Taylor-Laughlin. DVD. Ventura Distribution, 2000.

Black Belt Jones. Dir. Robert Clouse. Prod. Fred Weintraub, Paul Heller. Perfs. Jim Kelly, Gloria Hendry, Scatman Crothers. Warner Brothers. DVD. Blax Films, 2009.

Hearts and Minds. Dir. Peter Davis. Prod. Bert Schneider. Dist. Warner Brothers. DVD. Criterion Collection, 2004.

1976

Rocky. Dir. John Avildsen. Prod. Gene Kirkwood. Writ. Sylvester Stallone. Perfs. Sylvester Stallone, Talia Shire, Carl Weathers. United Artists. DVD. MGM Home Entertainment, 2001.

Bruce Lee Fights Back from the Grave. Dir. Doo-yong Lee. Perfs. Bruce K. L. Lea, Deborah Chaplin. Habdong Films. U.S. dist. Aquarius Releasing, 1978. DVD. American Home Treasures, 2001.

1977

Bruce Lee, the Legend. Dir. Leonard Ho. Prod. Raymond Chow. Golden Harvest. DVD. 20th Century-Fox Home Entertainment, 2002.

The Clones of Bruce Lee. Dir. Joseph Kong. Perfs. Bruce Le, Dragon Lee, Bruce Lai, Bruce Thai. Film Line Enterprises. U.S. dist. Newport Releasing, 1980. DVD. Video Asia, 2004.

Kentucky Fried Movie. Dir. John Landis. Writ. David Zucker, Jerry Zucker, Jim Abrahams. Prod. Kim Jorgensen. Perfs. Evan Kim, Bong Soo Han. United Film Distribution Company. DVD. Anchor Bay Entertainment, 2000.

1978

"Charlie Company at Home: The Veterans of Vietnam." *CBS News Special.* CBS. 17 January. MTR.

Boys in Company C. Dir. Sidney Furie. Prod. Raymond Chow. Perfs. Stan Shaw, Lee Ermey, Andrew Stevens, Craig Wasson, Vic Diaz. Columbia Pictures. DVD. Henstooth Video, 2008.

Coming Home. Dir. Hal Ashby. Prod. Jerome Hellman. Perfs. Jane Fonda, Jon Voight, Bruce Dern. United Artists. DVD. MGM Home Entertainment, 2002.

Good Guys Wear Black. Dir. Ted Post. Prod. Michael Leone. Perfs. Chuck Norris, Ann Archer, James Franciscus, Soon-Tek Oh. American Cinema Releasing. HBO Home Video, 2000.

Go Tell the Spartans. Dir. Ted Post. Prod. Michael Leone. Perfs. Burt Lancaster, Evan Kim, Craig Wasson, Joe Unger. AVCO Embassy Pictures. DVD. HBO Home Video, 2005.

Nineteen Sixty-Eight: A Look for New Meanings. Correspondent Harry Reasoner. CBS. 25 August. Videocassette. Princeton, NJ: Films for the Humanities, 1978.

The Deer Hunter. Dir. and prod. Michael Cimino. Perfs. Robert De Niro, Christopher Walken, John Savage, Meryl Streep. Universal Pictures. DVD. Universal Studios Home Entertainment, 2005.

CBS Evening News. 2 November. VTA.

Game of Death. Dir. Robert Clouse. Prod. Raymond Chow. Perfs. Bruce Lee, Kim Tai Chong, Dean Jagger, Hugh O'Brian, Gig Young, Colleen Camp, Kareem Abdul-Jabbar, Dan Insanto, Chi Hon Joi. Golden Harvest. U.S. dist. Columbia Pictures, 1979. DVD. 20th Century-Fox Home Entertainment, 2005.

1979

Apocalypse Now. Dir. and prod. Francis Ford Coppola. Perfs. Martin Sheen, Marlon Brando, Robert Duvall. United Artists. DVD. Paramount, 1999.

1982

They Call Me Bruce? Dir. Elliott Hong. Prod. Johnny Yune. Perfs. Johnny Yune, Margaux Hemingway. Artists Releasing Corporation. DVD. Madacy Records, 2003.

First Blood. Dir. Ted Kotcheff. Prod. Andrew Vajna, Mario Kassar. Perfs. Sylvester Stallone, Richard Crenna, Brian Dennehy, David Caruso. Orion Pictures. DVD. Artisan Entertainment, 1998.

Chan Is Missing. Dir., prod., and writ. Wayne Wang. Perfs. Wood Moy, Marc Hayashi. New Yorker Films. DVD. Koch Lorber Films, 2006.

1983

"Tet (1968)." *Vietnam: A Television History*. Episode 6. Writ. and prod. Austin Hoyt. WGBH Boston. DVD. WGBH Boston Video, 2004.

1984

Missing in Action. Dir. Joseph Zito. Prod. Yoram Globus, Menahem Golan, Lance Hool. Perfs. Chuck Norris, M. Emmet Walsh, James Hong. Cannon Film Distributors. DVD. MGM, 2000.

The Karate Kid. Dir. John Avildsen. Prod. Jerry Weintraub. Perfs. Ralph Macchio, Pat Morita, Martin Kove, William Zabka. Columbia Pictures. DVD. Sony Pictures Home Entertainment, 2005.

1985

NBC *Evening News*. 11 April. VTA.

Rambo: First Blood Part II. Dir. George Cosmatos. Prod. Andrew Vajna, Mario Kassar. Perfs. Sylvester Stallone, Richard Crenna, Steven Berkoff, Julia Nickson, Charles Napier, Martin Kove. TriStar Pictures. DVD. Artisan Entertainment, 1998.

Missing in Action 2: The Beginning. Dir. Lance Hool. Prod. Yoram Globus, Menahem Golan. Perfs. Chuck Norris, Soon-Tek Oh. Cannon Film Distributors. DVD. MGM, 2002.

Year of the Dragon. Dir. Michael Cimino. Prod. Dino de Laurentiis. Perfs. Mickey Rourke, Ariane Koizumi, John Lone, Dennis Dun. MGM/UA Entertainment. DVD. Warner Home Video, 2005.

The Last Dragon. Dir. Michael Schultz. Prod. Berry Gordy. Perfs. Taimak, Julius Carry, Jim Moody, Glen Eaton, Vanity. TriStar Pictures. DVD. Sony Pictures, 2001.

1986

No Retreat, No Surrender. Dir. Corey Yuen. Prod. Ng See-Yuen. Perfs. Kurt McKinney, Kim Tai Chong, Jean-Claude Van Damme. New World Pictures. Videocassette. Starmaker Entertainment, 1990.

1987

NBC *Evening News*. 23 July. VTA.

Who Killed Vincent Chin? Dir. Christine Choy, Renee Tajima-Pena. Videocassette. Filmmakers Library.

Full Metal Jacket. Dir. Stanley Kubrick. Prod. Jan Harlan. Perfs. Matthew Modine, Vincent D'Onofrio, Lee Ermey. Warner Brothers Pictures. DVD. Warner Home Video, 1999.

"Fighting Back, 1957–1962." *Eyes on the Prize I: America's Civil Rights Years (1954–1965)*. Episode 2. Dir. Judith Vecchione. WGBH Boston. DVD. PBS Video, 2006.

"Bridge to Freedom, 1965." *Eyes on the Prize I: America's Civil Rights Years (1954–1965)*. Episode 6. Dir. Callie Crossley and James A. DeVinney. WGBH Boston. DVD. PBS Video, 2006.

1988

"To Heal a Nation." Dir. Michael Pressman. Prod. General Electric Theater. NBC. 29 May. MTR.

Rambo III. Dir. Peter MacDonald. Prod. Andrew Vajna, Mario Kassar. Perfs. Sylvester Stallone, Richard Crenna. TriStar Pictures. DVD. Artisan Entertainment, 1998.

Braddock: Missing in Action III. Dir. Aaron Norris. Prod. Yoram Globus, Menahem Golan. Perfs. Chuck Norris, Aki Aleong. The Cannon Group. DVD. MGM, 2002.

1990

"Two Societies, 1965–1968." *Eyes on the Prize II: America at the Racial Crossroads (1965–1985)*. Episode 2. Dir. Sheila Bernard and Sam Pollard. WGBH Boston. DVD. PBS Video, 2006.

1991

Hearts of Darkness: A Filmmaker's Apocalypse. Dir. Fax Bahr, George Hickenlooper. Triton Pictures. DVD. Paramount Home Entertainment, 2007.

Game of Death. Dir. Kip Fulbeck. Videocassette. National Asian American Telecommunications Association. DVD. Video Data Bank, 2005.

1993

Dragon: The Bruce Lee Story. Dir. Rob Cohen. Perfs. Jason Scott Lee, Lauren Holly. Universal Pictures. DVD. Universal Home Video, 1998.

1995

Bontoc Eulogy. Dir. Marlon Fuentes. Independent Television Services/National Asian American Telecommunications Association. Videocassette. Cinema Guild, 2003.

Looking Like the Enemy. Dir. Robert Nakamura. Videocassette. Japanese American National Museum, 1995.

1997

Kim's Story: The Road from Vietnam. Dir. Shelley Saywell. CBC/Telefilm Canada. Videocassette. First Run/Icarus Films.

1998

No Hop Sing, No Bruce Lee: What Do You Do When None of Your Heroes Look Like You? Dir. Janice Tanaka. DVD. Video Data Bank, 2000.

2003

1967 Detroit Riots: A Community Speaks. Dir. Sedric Sawyer. DVD. Carousel Film and Video.

2006

The Slanted Screen: Asian Men in Film and Television. Dir. Jeff Adachi. DVD. Asian American Media Mafia. DVD.

2007

Finishing the Game: The Search for a New Bruce Lee. Dir. Justin Lin. Prod. Joan Huang, Jeff Gou. Perfs. Jake Sandvig, Roger Fan. IFC Films. DVD. IFC Films, 2008.

Works Cited

Abbas, Ackbar. Hong Kong: Culture and the Politics of Disappearance. Minneapolis: University of Minnesota Press, 1997.

Adams, Eddie. "The Tet Photo." To Bear Any Burden, ed. Al Santoli. New York: E. P. Dutton, 1985. 182–85.

Ahmad, Aijaz. In Theory: Classes, Nations, Literature. London: Verso, 1992.

Althusser, Louis. "Ideology and Ideological State Apparatuses." Lenin and Philosophy and Other Essays. New York: Monthly Review Press, 1971. 127–86.

Alvarez, Everett, Jr., and Anthony S. Pitch. Chained Eagle: The Heroic Story of the First American Shot Down over North Vietnam. New York: Donald J. Fine, 1989.

Anderson, Aaron. "Action in Motion: Kinesthesia in Martial Arts Films." Jump Cut 42 (1998), 1–11, 83.

Anderson, Benedict. "Cacique Democracy in the Philippines: Origins and Dreams." Discrepant Histories: Translocal Essays on Filipino Cultures, ed. Vicente Rafael. Philadelphia: Temple University Press, 1995. 3–47.

——. Imagined Communities: Reflections on the Origin and Spread of Nationalism. Revised ed. London: Verso, 1991.

Appy, Christian. Working-Class War: American Combat Soldiers and Vietnam. Chapel Hill: University of North Carolina Press, 1993.

Aristotle. Nicomachean Ethics. 2nd ed. Trans. Terence Irwin. Indianapolis: Hackett, 1999.

Arlen, Michael J. Living-Room War. 1966; reprint Syracuse: Syracuse University Press, 1997.

Axeen, David. "Eastern Western." Film Quarterly 32.4 (1979), 17–18.

Axel, Brian Keith. "Poverty of the Imagination." Anthropology Quarterly 76.1 (2003), 111–33.

Bailey, George A., and Lawrence W. Lichty. "Rough Justice on a Saigon Street: A Gatekeeper Study of NBC's Tet Execution Film." Journalism Quarterly 49 (Summer 1972), 221–38.

Barkan, Elazar, and Ronald Bush, eds. Prehistories of the Future: The Primitivist Project and the Culture of Modernism. Stanford: Stanford University Press, 1995.

Barnouw, Erik. Tube of Plenty: The Evolution of American Television. New York: Oxford University Press, 1975.

Baudrillard, Jean. *The Gulf War Did Not Take Place.* Trans. Paul Patton. Bloomington: Indiana University Press, 1995.

——. *Simulacra and Simulation.* Trans. Sheila Faria Glaser. Ann Arbor: University of Michigan Press, 1994.

Baxandall, Rosalyn, and Linda Gordon. *Dear Sisters: Dispatches from the Women's Liberation Movement.* New York: Basic Books, 2000.

Bazin, André. "Death Every Afternoon." Trans. Mark A. Cohen. *Rites of Realism: Essays on Corporal Cinema,* ed. Ivone Margulies. Durham: Duke University Press, 2002. 27–31.

——. "The Ontology of the Photographic Image." *What Is Cinema?* Vol. 1. Trans. Hugh Gray. Berkeley: University of California Press, 1967. 9–16.

Beidler, Philip D. "The Last Huey." *The Vietnam War and Postmodernity,* ed. Michael Bibby. Amherst: University of Massachusetts Press, 1999. 3–16.

Benjamin, Walter. "A Short History of Photography." *Classic Essays in Photography,* ed. Alan Trachtenberg, trans. P. Patton. New Haven: Leetes Island Books, 1981. 199–216.

——. "The Work of Art in the Age of Mechanical Reproduction." *Illuminations,* ed. Hannah Arendt. New York: Schocken Books, 1968. 217–52.

Berlant, Lauren. *The Anatomy of National Fantasy: Hawthorne, Utopia, and Everyday Life.* Chicago: University of Chicago Press, 1991.

——. *The Female Complaint: The Unfinished Business of Sentimentality in American Culture.* Durham: Duke University Press, 2008.

Berry, Chris. "Stellar Transit: Bruce Lee's Body, or Chinese Masculinity in a Transnational Frame." *Embodied Modernities: Corporeality, Representation, and Chinese Cultures,* ed. Fran Martin and Larissa Heinrich. Honolulu: University of Hawaii Press, 2006. 218–34.

Bevacqua, Maria. *Rape on the Public Agenda: Feminism and the Politics of Sexual Assault.* Boston: Northeastern University Press, 2000.

Bhabha, Homi K. "Dissemination: Time, Narrative, and the Margins of the Modern Nation." *The Location of Culture.* New York: Routledge, 1994. 139–70.

——. "The Other Question: Stereotype, Discrimination and the Discourse of Colonialism." *The Location of Culture.* New York: Routledge, 1994. 66–84.

Blackburn, Robert M. *Mercenaries and Lyndon Johnson's "More Flags": The Hiring of Korean, Filipino, and Thai Soldiers in the Vietnam War.* Jefferson, N.C.: McFarland, 1994.

Block, Alex Ben. *The Legend of Bruce Lee.* New York: Dell, 1974.

Bodroghkozy, Aniko. *Groove Tube: Sixties Television and the Youth Rebellion.* Durham: Duke University Press, 2001.

Bordo, Susan. *Unbearable Weight: Feminism, Western Culture, and the Body.* Berkeley: University of California Press, 1993.

Bordwell, David. *Planet Hong Kong: Popular Cinema and the Art of Entertainment.* Cambridge: Harvard University Press, 2000.

Braestrup, Peter. *Big Story: How the American Press and Television Reported and Interpreted the*

Crisis of Tet 1968 in Vietnam and Washington. Abridged ed. Novato, Calif.: Presidio Press, 1994.

Brown, Bill. "Global Bodies/Postnationalities: Charles Johnson's Consumer Culture." *Representations* 58 (Spring 1997), 24–48.

Brownmiller, Susan. *Against Our Will: Men, Women, and Rape.* 1975; reprint New York: Simon and Schuster, 1978.

Butler, Judith. *Gender Trouble: Feminism and the Subversion of Identity.* New York: Routledge, 1990.

Button, James W. *Black Violence: Political Impact of the 1960s Riots.* Princeton: Princeton University Press, 1978.

Campbell, Joseph. *The Hero with a Thousand Faces.* 1949; reprint Princeton: Princeton University Press, 1968.

Carmichael, Stokely. "Berkeley Speech." 1971. *Stokely Speaks: From Black Power to Pan-Africanism.* Chicago: Lawrence Hill Books, 2007. 45–60.

Carson, Clayborne. *In Struggle: SNCC and the Black Awakening of the 1960s.* Cambridge: Harvard University Press, 1995.

Carter, Albert Howard, III, and Jane Arbuckle Petro. *Rising from the Flames: The Experience of the Severely Burned.* Philadelphia: University of Pennsylvania Press, 1998.

Carter, Gregg Lee. "In the Narrows of the 1960s U.S. Black Rioting." *Journal of Conflict Resolution* 30.1 (1986), 115–27.

Caruth, Cathy. *Unclaimed Experience: Trauma, Narrative, and History.* Baltimore: Johns Hopkins University Press, 1996.

Caviness, Madeline H. "Obscenity and Alterity: Images That Shock and Offend Us/Them, Now/Then?" *Obscenity: Social Control and Artistic Creation in the European Middle Ages,* ed. Jan M. Ziolkowski. Leiden, Netherlands: Brill, 1998. 155–75.

Cha-Jua, Sundiata Keita. "Black Audiences, Blaxploitation and Kung Fu Films, and Challenges to White Celluloid Masculinity." *China Forever: The Shaw Brothers and Diasporic Cinema,* ed. Poshek Fu. Urbana: University of Illinois Press, 2008. 199–223.

Chan, Jachinson. *Chinese American Masculinities: From Fu Manchu to Bruce Lee.* New York: Routledge, 2001.

Chan, Sucheng. *Asian Americans: An Interpretive History.* New York: Twayne, 1991.

——. *The Vietnamese American 1.5 Generation: Stories of War, Revolution, Flight, and New Beginnings.* Philadelphia: Temple University Press, 2006.

Chang, Michael. "Bridging the Gap: The Role of Asian American Public Interest Organizations in the Pursuit of Legal and Social Remedies to Anti-Asian Hate Crimes." *Asian Law Journal* 7 (December 2000), 139–60.

Chang, Ying-Jen. "The Rise of Martial Arts in China and America." PhD diss., New School for Social Research, 1978.

Chen, Terri Yuh-lin. "Hate Violence as Border Patrol: An Asian American Theory of Hate Violence." *Asian Law Journal* 7 (December 2000), 69–101.

Cheng, Anne Anlin. *The Melancholy of Race: Psychoanalysis, Assimilation and Hidden Grief.* Oxford: Oxford University Press, 2001.

Chiao, Hsiung-Ping. "Bruce Lee: His Influence on the Evolution of the Kung Fu Genre." *Journal of Popular Film and Television* 9.1 (1981), 30–42.

Chin, Frank. "Frank Chin: An Interview with Robert Murray Davis." *Amerasia Journal* 14.2 (1988), 81–95.

———. "Come All Ye Asian American Writers of the Real and the Fake." *The Big Aiiieeeee! An Anthology of Chinese and Japanese American Literature*, ed. Jeffrey Paul Chan, Frank Chin, Lawson Fusao Inada, and Shawn Wong. New York: Meridian Books, 1991. 1–91.

———. *The Year of the Dragon. The Chickencoop Chinaman and The Year of the Dragon: Two Plays.* Seattle: University of Washington Press, 1981. 67–142.

Chin, Frank, et al. "Introduction to Chinese- and Japanese-American Literature." *Aiiieeeee! an Anthology of Asian American Writers*, ed. Jeffrey Paul Chan, Frank Chin, Lawson Fusao Inada, and Shawn Wong. Washington, D.C.: Howard University Press, 1974. xxi–xlviii.

Chong, Denise. *The Girl in the Picture: The Story of Kim Phuc, the Photograph, and the Vietnam War.* New York: Viking, 2000.

Chong, Sylvia Shin Huey. "From 'Blood Auteurism' to the Violence of Pornography: Sam Peckinpah and Oliver Stone." *New Hollywood Violence*, ed. Stephen Jay Schneider. Manchester, England: Manchester University Press, 2005. 249–68.

———. "'Look, an Asian!' The Politics of Racial Interpellation in the Wake of the Virginia Tech Shootings." *Journal of Asian American Studies* 11.1 (2008), 27–60.

Chow, David, and Richard Spangler. *Kung Fu: History, Philosophy and Technique.* Hollywood: Unique Publications, 1980.

Choy, Philip P., Lorraine Dong, and Marlon K. Hom, eds. *The Coming Man: 19th Century American Perceptions of the Chinese.* Seattle: University of Washington Press, 1995.

Chu, Yingchi. *Hong Kong Cinema: Coloniser, Motherland, and Self.* London: Routledge Curzon, 2003.

Churchill, Ward, and Jim Vander Wall. *Agents of Repression: The FBI's Secret Wars against the Black Panther Party and the American Indian Movement.* Boston: South End Press, 1990.

Clark, Michael. "Remembering Vietnam." *The Vietnam War and American Culture*, ed. John Carlos Rowe and Rick Berg. New York: Columbia University Press, 1991. 177–207.

Clifford, James. *The Predicament of Culture: Twentieth-Century Ethnography, Literature, and Art.* Cambridge: Harvard University Press, 1988.

Clor, Henry M. *Obscenity and Public Morality: Censorship in a Liberal Society.* Chicago: University of Chicago Press, 1969.

Clover, Carol. *Men, Women and Chain Saws: Gender in the Modern Horror Film.* Princeton: Princeton University Press, 1992.

Commission on Wartime Relocation and Internment of Civilians. *Personal Justice Denied: Report of the Commission on Wartime Relocation and Internment of Civilians.* Seattle: University of Washington Press, 1997.

Cook, Bernard. "Over My Dead Body: The Ideological Use of Dead Bodies in Network News Coverage of Vietnam." *Quarterly Review of Film and Video* 18.2 (2001), 203–16.

Cope, Demetrius. "Anatomy of a Blaxploitation Theater." *Jump Cut* 9 (1975), 22–23.

Cortright, David. *Soldiers in Revolt: The American Military Today*. Garden City, N.Y.: Anchor Press, 1975.

Cowie, Elizabeth. "Fantasia." *The Woman in Question: M/f*, ed. Parveen Adams and Elizabeth Cowie. Cambridge: MIT Press, 1990. 149–96.

Cowie, Peter. *The Apocalypse Now Book*. London: Faber and Faber, 2000.

Cumings, Bruce. *War and Television*. London: Verso, 1992.

Daniels, Roger, ed. *Anti-Chinese Violence in North America*. New York: Arno Press, 1978.

Davis, Angela Y. "Rape, Racism and the Myth of the Black Rapist." *Women, Race, and Class*, ed. Angela Y. Davis. New York: Random House, 1981. 172–201.

Davis, Mike. *City of Quartz: Excavating the Future in Los Angeles*. New York: Vintage, 1990.

DeBenedetti, Charles, and Charles Chatfield. *An American Ordeal: The Antiwar Movement of the Vietnam Era*. Syracuse: Syracuse University Press, 1990.

DeKoven, Marianne. *Utopia Limited: The Sixties and the Emergence of the Postmodern*. Durham: Duke University Press, 2004.

Deleuze, Gilles. *Cinema 1: The Movement-Image*. Trans. Hugh Tomlinson and Barbara Habberjam. Minneapolis: University of Minnesota Press, 1986.

———. *Cinema 2: The Time-Image*. Trans. Hugh Tomlinson and Robert Galeta. Minneapolis: University of Minnesota Press, 1989.

Deleuze, Gilles, and Félix Guattari. *Anti-Oedipus: Capitalism and Schizophrenia*. Trans. Robert Hurley, Mark Seem, and Helen R. Lane. Minneapolis: University of Minnesota Press, 1983.

———. *A Thousand Plateaus: Capitalism and Schizophrenia*. Trans. Brian Massumi. Minneapolis: University of Minnesota Press, 1987.

Deloria, Philip J. *Playing Indian*. New Haven: Yale University Press, 1998.

Dempsey, Michael. "Hellbent for Mystery." *Film Quarterly* 32.4 (1979), 10–13.

Desbarats, Jacqueline. "Indochinese Resettlement in the United States." *The History and Immigration of Asian Americans*, ed. Franklin Ng. New York: Garland, 1998. 184–200.

Desser, David. " 'Charlie Don't Surf': Race and Culture in the Vietnam War Films." *Inventing Vietnam: The War in Film and Television*, ed. Michael Anderegg. Philadelphia: Temple University Press, 1991. 81–102.

———. "The Kung Fu Craze: Hong Kong Cinema's First American Reception." *The Cinema of Hong Kong: History, Arts, Identity*, ed. Poshek Fu and David Desser. Cambridge: Cambridge University Press, 2000. 19–43.

Deutsch, Nathaniel. " 'The Asiatic Black Man': An African American Orientalism?" *Journal of Asian American Studies* 4.3 (2001), 193–208.

Doherty, Thomas. *Projections of War: Hollywood, American Culture, and World War II*. New York: Columbia University Press, 1993.

Donovan, Robert J., and Ray Scherer. *Unsilent Revolution: Television News and American Public Life, 1948–1991*. New York: Cambridge University Press, 1992.

Dower, John. *War without Mercy: Race and Power in the Pacific War*. New York: Pantheon Books, 1986.

Dreyfus, Hubert L., and Paul Rabinow. *Michel Foucault: Beyond Structuralism and Hermeneutics*. Chicago: University of Chicago Press, 1983.

Edwards, Brent Hayes. *The Practice of Diaspora: Literature, Translation, and the Rise of Black Internationalism*. Cambridge: Harvard University Press, 2003.

Elegant, Robert. "How to Lose a War: The Press and Viet Nam." *Encounter* 57.2 (1981), 73–90.

Ellis, Havelock. "The Revaluation of Obscenity." *On Life and Sex*. New York: Signet Books, 1922.

Eng, David. *Racial Castration: Managing Masculinity in Asian America*. Durham: Duke University Press, 2001.

Escobar, Edward J. *Race, Police, and the Making of a Political Identity: Mexican Americans and the Los Angeles Police Department, 1990–1945*. Berkeley: University of California Press, 1999.

Espiritu, Yen Le. *Asian American Panethnicity: Bridging Institutions and Identities*. Philadelphia: Temple University Press, 1992.

Faas, Horst, and Tim Page, eds. *Requiem: By the Photographers Who Died in Vietnam and Indochina*. New York: Random House, 1997.

Farber, David. *Chicago '68*. Chicago: University of Chicago Press, 1988.

Faust, Drew Gilpin. " 'Numbers on Top of Numbers': Counting the Civil War Dead." *Journal of Military History* 70.3 (2006), 995–1009.

Feinberg, Joel. *Offense to Others: The Moral Limits of the Criminal Law*. Oxford: Oxford University Press, 1985.

Feng, Peter X. *Identities in Motion: Asian American Film and Video*. Durham: Duke University Press, 2002.

Fine, Sidney. *Violence in the Model City: The Cavanagh Administration, Race Relations, and the Detroit Riot of 1967*. Ann Arbor: University of Michigan Press, 1989.

Finin, Gerard A. *The Making of the Igorot: Contours of Cordillera Consciousness*. Quezon City, Philippines: Ateneo de Manila University Press, 2005.

Fink, Carole, Philipp Gassert, Detlef Junker, and Daniel S. Mattern, eds. *1968: The World Transformed*. New York: Cambridge University Press, 1998.

Flamm, Michael W. *Law and Order: Street Crime, Civil Unrest, and the Crisis of Liberalism in the 1960s*. New York: Columbia University Press, 2005.

Flaxman, Gregory. Introduction to *The Brain Is the Screen: Deleuze and the Philosophy of Cinema*, ed. Gregory Flaxman. Minneapolis: University of Minnesota Press, 2000. 1–57.

Fogelson, Robert M. *Violence as Protest: A Study of Riots and Ghettos*. Westport, Conn.: Greenwood Press, 1971.

Foster, Hal. *Compulsive Beauty*. Cambridge: MIT Press, 1993.

Foucault, Michel. *The History of Sexuality: An Introduction*. Trans. Robert Hurley. New York: Vintage Books, 1978.

——. *The Order of Things: An Archaeology of the Human Sciences*. New York: Vintage Books, 1970.

——. "Technologies of the Self." *Technologies of the Self: A Seminar with Michel Foucault*, ed. Luther H. Martin, Huck Gutman, and Patrick H. Hutton. Amherst: University of Massachusetts Press, 1988. 16–48.

——. *The Use of Pleasure*. Vol. 2 of *The History of Sexuality*. Trans. Robert Hurley. New York: Vintage, 1985.

Franklin, H. Bruce. M.I.A. *or Mythmaking in America*. Chicago: Lawrence Hill Books, 1992.

——. *Vietnam and Other American Fantasies*. Amherst: University of Massachusetts Press, 2000.

Frascina, Francis. "Meyer Shapiro's Choice: My Lai, Guernica, MOMA and the Art Left, 1969–70." *Journal of Contemporary History* 30 (1995), 481–511.

Freud, Sigmund. *Beyond the Pleasure Principle* [1920]. *The Standard Edition of the Complete Psychological Works of Sigmund Freud*. Vol. 18. Trans. and ed. James Strachey. London: Hogarth Press and the Institute of Psychoanalysis, 1955.

——. " 'A Child Is Being Beaten': A Contribution to the Study of the Origin of Sexual Perversions [1919]." *The Standard Edition of the Complete Psychological Works of Sigmund Freud*. Vol. 17. Trans. and ed. James Strachey. London: Hogarth Press and the Institute of Psychoanalysis, 1955. 175–204.

——. "The Economic Problem of Masochism [1924]." *The Standard Edition of the Complete Psychological Works of Sigmund Freud*. Vol. 19. Trans. and ed. James Strachey. London: Hogarth Press and the Institute of Psychoanalysis, 1961. 155–70.

——. "From the History of an Infantile Neurosis [1914]." *The Standard Edition of the Complete Psychological Works of Sigmund Freud*. Vol. 17. Trans. and ed. James Strachey. London: Hogarth Press and the Institute of Psychoanalysis, 1955. 1–122.

——. "Instincts and Their Vicissitudes [1915]." *The Standard Edition of the Complete Psychological Works of Sigmund Freud*. Vol. 14. Trans. and ed. James Strachey. London: Hogarth Press and the Institute of Psychoanalysis, 1957. 109–40.

——. *The Interpretation of Dreams* [1900]. *The Standard Edition of the Complete Psychological Works of Sigmund Freud*. Vols. 4 and 5. Trans. and ed. James Strachey. London: Hogarth Press and the Institute of Psychoanalysis, 1953.

——. "Mourning and Melancholia [1917]." *The Standard Edition of the Complete Psychological Works of Sigmund Freud*. Vol. 17. Trans. and ed. James Strachey. London: Hogarth Press and the Institute of Psychoanalysis, 1955. 237–58.

——. "Project for a Scientific Psychology [1895]." *The Standard Edition of the Complete Psychological Works of Sigmund Freud*. Vol. 1. Trans. and ed. James Strachey. London: Hogarth Press and the Institute of Psychoanalysis, 1966. 281–397.

Freud, Sigmund, and Joseph Breuer. *Studies on Hysteria* [1893–1895]. *The Standard Edition of the Complete Psychological Works of Sigmund Freud*, Vol. 2. Trans. and ed. James Strachey. London: Hogarth Press and the Institute of Psychoanalysis, 1966.

Friedberg, Anne. "The Denial of Difference: Theories of Cinematic Identification." *Psychoanalysis and Cinema*, ed. E. Ann Kaplan. New York: Routledge, 1990. 36–45.

Frye, Northrop. *Anatomy of Criticism: Four Essays.* 1957; reprint Princeton: Princeton University Press, 2000.

Fu, Poshek, and David Desser. Introduction to *The Cinema of Hong Kong: History, Arts, Identity.* Cambridge: Cambridge University Press, 2000. 1–12.

Fujino, Diane C. "Who Studies the Asian American Movement? A Historiographic Analysis." *Journal of Asian American Studies* 11.2 (2008), 127–69.

Geyelin, Philip L. "The Vietnam Syndrome." *Vietnam in Remission,* ed. James F. Veninga and Harry A. Wilmer. College Station: Texas A&M University Press, 1985. 76–89.

Gibson, Campbell, and Kay Jung. *Historical Census Statistics on Population Totals by Race, 1790 to 1990, and by Hispanic Origin, 1970 to 1990, for Large Cities and Other Urban Places in the United States.* Ed. U.S. Census Bureau, Population Division. Working Paper No. 76, 2005, www.census.gov, accessed 9 July 2008.

Gilroy, Paul. *The Black Atlantic: Modernity and Double Consciousness.* Cambridge: Harvard University Press, 1993.

Gitlin, Todd. *The Sixties: Years of Hope, Days of Rage.* New York: Bantam Books, 1987.

Glaessner, Verina. *Kung Fu: Cinema of Vengeance.* New York: Bounty Books, 1974.

Gootenberg, Paul. "Talking about the Flow: Drugs, Borders, and the Discourse of Drug Control." *Cultural Critique* 71 (Winter 2009), 13–46.

Gorer, Geoffrey. *Japanese Character Structure and Propaganda.* New Haven: Committee on National Morale and the Council on Intercultural Relations, 1942.

Graham, Don. *No Name on the Bullet: A Biography of Audie Murphy.* New York: Viking, 1989.

Graham, Herman, III. *The Brothers' Vietnam War: Black Power, Manhood, and the Military Experience.* Gainesville: University Press of Florida, 2003.

Greenlee, Sam. *The Spook Who Sat by the Door.* Detroit: Wayne State University Press, 1990.

Griffiths, Philip Jones. *Vietnam Inc.* 1971; reprint New York: Phaidon Press, 2001.

Grimshaw, Allen D. "Changing Patterns of Racial Violence in the United States." *Racial Violence in the United States,* ed. Allen D. Grimshaw. Chicago: Aldine, 1969. 488–500.

Grosz, Elizabeth A. *Volatile Bodies: Toward a Corporeal Feminism.* Bloomington: Indiana University Press, 1994.

Guerrero, Ed. *Framing Blackness: The African American Image in Film.* Philadelphia: Temple University Press, 1993.

Gunning, Tom. "The Exterior as Intérieur: Benjamin's Optical Detective." *boundary 2* 30.1 (2003), 105–30.

Habal, Estella. *San Francisco's International Hotel: Mobilizing the Filipino American Community in the Anti-Eviction Movement.* Philadelphia: Temple University Press, 2007.

Hall, Stuart. "Gramsci's Relevance for the Study of Race and Ethnicity." *Stuart Hall: Critical Dialogues in Cultural Studies,* ed. David Morley and Kuan-Hsing Chen. London: Routledge, 1996. 411–40.

Hallin, Daniel C. "The Media, the War in Vietnam, and Political Support: A Critique of the Thesis of an Oppositional Media." *Journal of Politics* 46.1 (1984), 2–24.

——. The "Uncensored War": The Media and Vietnam. New York: Oxford University Press, 1986.

Halstead, Fred. Out Now! A Participant's Account of the American Movement against the Vietnam War. New York: Monad Press, 1978.

Hammond, William M. Reporting Vietnam: Media and Military at War. Lawrence: University of Kansas Press, 1998.

Hansen, Miriam. "Traces of Transgression in Apocalypse Now." Social Text 3 (Autumn 1980), 123–35.

Hariman, Robert, and John Louis Lucaites. No Caption Needed: Iconic Photographs, Public Culture, and Liberal Democracy. Chicago: University of Chicago Press, 2007.

Harms, Brian C. "Redefining 'Crimes of Moral Turpitude': A Proposal to Congress." Georgetown Immigration Law Journal 15 (2001), 259–88.

Harris, Daryl B. The Logic of Black Urban Rebellions: Challenging the Dynamics of White Domination in Miami. Westport, Conn.: Praeger, 1999.

Hawley, Thomas M. The Remains of War: Bodies, Politics, and the Search for American Soldiers Unaccounted for in Southeast Asia. Durham: Duke University Press, 2005.

Heidegger, Martin. Being and Time. Trans. John MacQuarrie and Edward Robinson. New York: Harper, 1962.

——. "The Question Concerning Technology." The Question Concerning Technology and Other Essays. New York: Harper and Row, 1977. 3–35.

Helmer, John. Bringing the War Home: The American Soldier in Vietnam and After. New York: Free Press, 1974.

Herr, Michael. Dispatches. New York: Vintage, 1991.

Herring, George C. America's Longest War: The United States and Vietnam 1950–1975. 2nd ed. New York: Alfred A. Knopf, 1986.

Hersh, Seymour M. My Lai 4: A Report on the Massacre and Its Aftermath. New York: Vintage, 1970.

Hershberger, Mary. Jane Fonda's War: A Political Biography of an Antiwar Icon. New York: New Press, 2005.

Hill, Lance. The Deacons for Defense: Armed Resistance and the Civil Rights Movement. Chapel Hill: University of North Carolina Press, 2004.

Hing, Bill Ong. Making and Remaking Asian America through Immigration Policy, 1850–1990. Stanford: Stanford University Press, 1993.

Ho, Fred. "Kickin' the White Man's Ass: Black Power, Aesthetics, and the Asian Martial Arts." Afroasian Encounters: Culture, History, Politics, ed. Heike Raphael-Hernandez and Shannon Steen. New York: New York University Press, 2006. 295–312.

Ho, Fred, Carolyn Antonio, Diane Fujino, and Steve Yip, eds. Legacy to Liberation: Politics and Culture of Revolutionary Asian Pacific America. San Francisco: Big Red Media, 2000.

Holzer, Henry Mark, and Erika Holzer. "Aid and Comfort": Jane Fonda in North Vietnam. Jefferson, N.C.: McFarland, 2002.

Horne, Gerald. Race War! White Supremacy and the Japanese Attack on the British Empire. New York: New York University Press, 2003.

Hu, Brian. " 'Bruce Lee' after Bruce Lee: A Life in Conjectures." *Journal of Chinese Cinemas* 2.2 (2008), 123–35.

Huebner, Andrew J. *The Warrior Image: Soldiers in American Culture from the Second World War to the Vietnam Era.* Chapel Hill: University of North Carolina Press, 2007.

Hunt, Leon. *Kung Fu Cult Masters: From Bruce Lee to Crouching Tiger.* London: Wallflower Press, 2003.

Isaacs, Susan. "The Nature and Function of Phantasy." *International Journal of Psycho-analysis* 29 (1948), 73–97.

Issacs, Arnold R. *Vietnam Shadows: The War, Its Ghosts, and Its Legacy.* Baltimore: Johns Hopkins Press, 1997.

Isserman, Maurice, and Michael Kazin. *America Divided: The Civil War of the 1960s.* 3rd ed. New York: Oxford University Press, 2008.

Iwamura, Jane Naomi. "The Oriental Monk in American Popular Culture." *Religion and Popular Culture in America*, ed. Bruce David Forbes and Jeffrey H. Mahan. Berkeley: University of California Press, 2000. 25–43.

Jacobson, Matthew Frye. *Roots Too: White Ethnic Revival in Post–Civil Rights America.* Cambridge: Harvard University Press, 2006.

Jeffords, Susan. *Hard Bodies: Hollywood Masculinity in the Reagan Era.* New Brunswick, N.J.: Rutgers University Press, 1994.

——. *The Remasculinization of America: Gender and the Vietnam War.* Bloomington: Indiana University Press, 1989.

Jenkins, Philip. *Decade of Nightmares: The End of the Sixties and the Making of Eighties America.* New York: Oxford University Press, 2006.

Johnson, Paula B., David O. Sears, and John B. McConahay. "Black Invisibility, the Press, and the Los Angeles Riot." *American Journal of Sociology* 76.4 (1971), 698–721.

Kaikō Takeshi. *Into a Black Sun.* Trans. Cecilia Segawa Seigle. Tokyo: Kodansha International, 1980.

Kalb, Marvin. "A View from the Press." *Taken by Storm: The Media, Public Opinion, and U.S. Foreign Policy in the Gulf War*, ed. W. Lance Bennett and David L. Paletz. Chicago: University of Chicago Press, 1994. 3–7.

Kaminsky, Stuart M. "Kung Fu Film as Ghetto Myth." *Journal of Popular Film* 3.2 (1974), 129–38.

Kantorowicz, E. H. *The King's Two Bodies: A Study in Mediaeval Political Theology.* Princeton: Princeton University Press, 1957.

Kei, Sek. "The Development of 'Martial Arts' in Hong Kong Cinema." *A Study of the Hong Kong Martial Arts Film.* Hong Kong: Urban Council, 1980. 27–38.

Kellner, Douglas, and Dan Streible. "Introduction: Emile de Antonio: Documenting the Life of a Radical Filmmaker." *Emile de Antonio: A Reader*, ed. Douglas Kellner and Dan Streible. Minneapolis: University of Minnesota Press, 2000. 1–84.

Kendrick, Walter. *The Secret Museum: Pornography in Modern Culture.* Berkeley: University of California Press, 1987.

Kerry, John, and Vietnam Veterans Against the War. *The New Soldier*. New York: Macmillan, 1971.

Kiang, Peter Nien-Chu. "About Face: Recognizing Asian and Pacific American Vietnam Veterans in Asian American Studies." *Amerasia Journal* 17.3 (1991), 22–40.

Kim, Claire Jean. "The Racial Triangulation of Asian Americans." *Politics and Society* 27.1 (1999), 105–38.

Kim, Daniel Y. *Writing Manhood in Black and Yellow: Ralph Ellison, Frank Chin, and the Literary Politics of Identity*. Stanford: Stanford University Press, 2005.

Kim, Se Jin. "South Korea's Involvement in Vietnam and Its Economic and Political Impact." *Asian Survey* 10.6 (1970), 519–32.

Kinder, Marsha. "Political Game." Film Quarterly 32.4 (1979), 13–17.

———. "The Power of Adaptation in Apocalypse Now." Film Quarterly 33.2 (1979–80), 12–20.

Kinney, Katherine. *Friendly Fire: American Images of the Vietnam War*. New York: Oxford University Press, 2000.

Klein, Christina. *Cold War Orientalism: Asia in the Middlebrow Imagination, 1945–1961*. Berkeley: University of California Press, 2003.

Knightley, Phillip. *The First Casualty: From the Crimea to Vietnam: The War Correspondent as Hero, Propagandist, and Myth Maker*. New York: Harcourt Brace Jovanovich, 1975.

Kolodny, Annette. *The Land before Her: Fantasy and Experience of the American Frontiers, 1630–1860*. Chapel Hill: University of North Carolina Press, 1984.

Koppes, Clayton R., and Gregory D. Black. *Hollywood Goes to War: How Politics, Profits and Propaganda Shapes World War II*. Berkeley: University of California Press, 1987.

Krauss, Rosalind E. *The Optical Unconscious*. Cambridge: MIT Press, 1993.

Kristeva, Julia. *The Powers of Horror: An Essay on Abjection*. Trans. Leon S. Roudiez. New York: Columbia University Press, 1982.

Kurahashi, Yuko. *Asian American Culture on Stage: The History of the East West Players*. New York: Garland, 1999.

Kusmer, Kenneth L. "African Americans in the City since World War II: From the Industrial to the Post-Industrial Era." *Journal of Urban History* 21.4 (1995), 458–504.

Kuzmarov, Jeremy. "From Counter-Insurgency to Narco-Insurgency: Vietnam and the International War on Drugs." *Journal of Policy History* 20.3 (2008), 344–78.

Lacan, Jacques. "Desire and the Interpretation of Desire in Hamlet." *Yale French Studies* 55/56 (1977), 11–52.

———. *The Four Fundamental Concepts of Psychoanalysis*. Trans. Alan Sheridan. New York: W. W. Norton, 1977.

Lam, Andrew. "My Vietnam, My America." *Perfume Dreams: Reflections on the Vietnamese Diaspora*. Berkeley: Heyday Books, 2005. 93–98.

Laplanche, Jean. "The Freud Museum Seminar: 3 May 1990." *Jean Laplanche: Seduction, Translation, and the Drives*, ed. John Fletcher and Martin Stanton. Trans. Martin Stanton. London: Institute of Contemporary Arts, 1992. 41–63.

———. "Interpretation between Determinism and Hermeneutics." *Essays on Otherness*, ed. John Fletcher. New York: Routledge, 1998. 138–65.

———. "The Kent Seminar, 1 May 1990." *Jean Laplanche: Seduction, Translation, and the Drives*, ed. John Fletcher and Martin Stanton. Trans. Martin Stanton. London: Institute of Contemporary Arts, 1992. 21–40.

———. *Life and Death in Psychoanalysis*. Trans. Jeffrey Mehlman. Baltimore: Johns Hopkins University Press, 1976.

———. "Notes on Afterwardness." *Essays on Otherness*, ed. John Fletcher. New York: Routledge, 1998. 264–69.

———. "The Other Within: Rethinking Psychoanalysis." *Radical Philosophy* 102 (July–August 2000), 31–41.

———. "Seduction, Persecution, Revelation." Trans. Philip Slotkin. *Essays on Otherness*, ed. John Fletcher. London: Routledge, 1999. 166–96.

———. "The Theory of Seduction and the Problem of the Other." Trans. Luke Thurston. *Journal of Psycho-Analysis* 78 (1997), 653–66.

———. "Time and the Other." *Essays on Otherness*, ed. John Fletcher. London: Routledge, 1999. 238–63.

———. "The Unfinished Copernican Revolution." Trans. Luke Thurston. *Essays on Otherness*, ed. John Fletcher. London: Routledge, 1999. 52–83.

Laplanche, Jean, and J.-B. Pontalis. "Fantasy and the Origins of Sexuality." *Formations of Fantasy*, ed. Victor Burgin, James Donald, and Cora Kaplan. London: Routledge, 1989. 5–34.

———. *The Language of Psycho-Analysis*. Trans. Donald Nicholson-Smith. New York: W. W. Norton, 1973.

Lawrence, D. H. "Pornography and Obscenity." *Sex, Literature, and Censorship*, ed. Harry T. Moore. New York: Twayne, 1959. 69–88.

Lee, Bruce. *Chinese Gung Fu: The Philosophical Art of Self Defense*. 1963; reprint Santa Clarita, Calif.: Ohara Publications, 1987.

Lee, Esther Kim. "Transnational Legitimization of an Actor: The Life and Career of Soon-Tek Oh." *Modern Drama* 48.2 (2005): 372–406.

Lee, Linda. *Bruce Lee: The Man Only I Knew*. New York: Warner Paperback Library, 1975.

Lee, Robert G. *Orientals: Asian Americans in Popular Culture*. Philadelphia: Temple University Press, 1999.

Leff, Leonard, and Jerold L. Simmons. *The Dame in the Kimono: Hollywood, Censorship, and the Production Code from the 1920s to the 1960s*. New York: Grove and Weidenfeld, 1990.

Lembcke, Jerry. "From Oral History to Movie Script: The Vietnam Veteran Interviews for 'Coming Home.'" *Oral History Review* 26.2 (1999), 65–86.

———. *The Spitting Image: Myth, Memory, and the Legacy of Vietnam*. New York: New York University Press, 1998.

Lewis, Jon. *Hollywood v. Hard Core: How the Struggle over Censorship Saved the Modern Film Industry*. New York: New York University Press, 2000.

Lieberman, Alice, and Cheryl Lester, eds. *Social Work: Practice with a Difference*. New York: McGraw Hill, 2003.

Lifton, Robert Jay. *Home from the War: Vietnam Veterans: Neither Victims nor Executioners*. New York: Simon and Schuster, 1973.

Lo, Kwai-Cheung. "Muscles and Subjectivity: A Short History of the Masculine Body in Hong Kong Popular Culture." *Camera Obscura* 37 (January 1996), 105–25.

Locke, Hubert G. *The Detroit Riot of 1967*. Detroit: Wayne State University Press, 1969.

Locke, John. *Two Treatises of Government and a Letter Concerning Toleration*. Ed. Ian Shapiro. New Haven: Yale University Press, 2003.

Lockwood, Kathleen. "The Philippines: Allies During the Vietnam War." *Vietnam Magazine*, June 1999, n.p. Republished at www.historynet.com, accessed 23 March 2009.

Loo, Chalsa M. "Race-Related PTSD: The Asian American Veteran." *Journal of Traumatic Stress* 7.4 (1994), 637–56.

Lott, Eric. "All the King's Men: Elvis Impersonators and White Working-Class Masculinity." *Race and the Subject of Masculinities*, ed. Harry Stecopoulos and Michael Uebel. Durham: Duke University Press, 1997. 192–227.

———. *Love and Theft: Blackface Minstrelsy and the American Working Class*. Oxford: Oxford University Press, 1993.

Louie, Steve, and Glenn Omatsu, eds. *Asian Americans: The Movement and the Moment*. Los Angeles: UCLA Asian American Studies Center Press, 2001.

Lowe, Lisa. *Critical Terrains: French and British Orientalisms*. Ithaca: Cornell University Press, 1991.

———. *Immigrant Acts: On Asian American Cultural Politics*. Durham: Duke University Press, 1996.

Luna, Eric G. "Sovereignty and Suspicion." *Duke Law Journal* 48 (February 1999), 787–889.

Lyman, Stanford. "Introduction to the Article by Ying-Jen Chang." *Urban Life* 4.4 (1976), 449–51.

Lyons, Charles. "The Paradox of Protest: American Film, 1980–1992." *Movie Censorship and American Culture*, ed. Francis G. Couvares. Washington, D.C.: Smithsonian Institution, 1996. 277–318.

MacDonald, J. Fred. *Television and the Red Menace: The Video Road to Vietnam*. New York: Praeger, 1985.

MacPherson, Myra. *Long Time Passing: Vietnam and the Haunted Generation*. Garden City, N.Y.: Doubleday, 1984.

Maehara, G. Akito. "Think on These Things: A Perspective from a Vietnam Era Veteran." *Amerasia Journal* 17.1 (1991), 123–27.

Mailer, Norman. "The White Negro." *Advertisements for Myself*. New York: G. P. Putnam's Sons, 1959. 337–58.

Marchetti, Gina. *Romance and the "Yellow Peril": Race, Sex, and Discursive Strategies in Hollywood Fiction*. Berkeley: University of California Press, 1993.

Martin, Susan, ed. *Decade of Protest: Political Posters from the United States, Viet Nam, Cuba, 1965–1975*. Santa Monica, Calif.: Smart Art Press, 1996.

Marx, Leo. *The Machine in the Garden: Technology and the Pastoral Ideal in America*. New York: Oxford University Press, 1964.

Massey, Douglas, and Nancy Denton. *American Apartheid: Segregation and the Making of the Underclass*. Cambridge: Harvard University Press, 1993.

Matlin, Daniel. " 'Lift Up Yr Self!' Reinterpreting Amiri Baraka (LeRoi Jones), Black Power, and the Uplift Tradition." *Journal of American History* 93.1 (2006), 91–116.

McCaughey, Martha. *Real Knockouts: The Physical Feminism of Women's Self-Defense*. New York: New York University Press, 1997.

McCutcheon, Russell T. *Manufacturing Religion: The Discourse on Sui Generis Religion and the Politics of Nostalgia*. Oxford: Oxford University Press, 1997.

McDonald, Dorothy Ritsuko. Introduction to *The Chickencoop Chinaman and The Year of the Dragon: Two Plays*, by Frank Chin. Seattle: University of Washington Press, 1981. ix–xxix.

McKay, Deirdre, and Padmapani L. Perez. " 'Apocalypse Yesterday Already!' Ifugao Extras and the Making of Apocalypse Now." *Our Own Voice*, March 2004, www .oovrag.com, accessed 12 February 2009.

McLeod, Mark W. "Indigenous Peoples and the Vietnamese Revolution, 1930–1975." *Journal of World History* 10.2 (1999), 353–89.

McWhorter, Ladelle. *Bodies and Pleasures: Foucault and the Politics of Sexual Normalization*. Bloomington: Indiana University Press, 1999.

Michelson, Peter. *Speaking the Unspeakable: A Poetics of Obscenity*. Albany: State University of New York Press, 1993.

Mieder, Wolfgang. " 'The Only Good Indian Is a Dead Indian': History and Meaning of a Proverbial Stereotype." *Journal of American Folklore* 106.419 (1993), 38–60.

Miller, Davis. *The Tao of Bruce Lee: A Martial Arts Memoir*. New York: Harmony Books, 2000.

Moeller, Susan D. *Shooting War: Photography and the American Experience of Combat*. New York: Basic Books, 1989.

Mohr, Charles. "Once Again—Did the Press Lose Vietnam?" *Columbia Journalism Review* 22.4 (1983), 51–56.

Morrell, David. *First Blood*. New York: Armchair Detective Library, 1990.

Morris, Andrew D. *Marrow of the Nation: A History of Sport and Physical Culture in Republican China*. Berkeley: University of California Press, 2004.

Morris, Meaghan. "Learning from Bruce Lee: Pedagogy and Political Correctness in Martial Arts Cinema." *Keyframes: Popular Cinema and Cultural Studies*. New York: Routledge, 2001. 171–86.

Moser, Richard. *The New Winter Soldiers: GI and Veteran Dissent during the Vietnam Era*. New Brunswick, N.J.: Rutgers University Press, 1996.

Mullen, Bill. *Afro-Orientalism*. Minneapolis: University of Minnesota Press, 2004.

Mulvey, Laura. "Visual Pleasure and Narrative Cinema." *Visual and Other Pleasures*. Bloomington: Indiana University Press, 1989. 15–25.

Narita, Tatsushi. "The Young T. S. Eliot and Alien Cultures: His Philippine Interactions." *Review of English Studies* 45.180 (1994), 523–25.

National Commission on the Causes and Prevention of Violence. *Progress Report of the National Commission on the Causes and Prevention of Violence to President Lyndon B. Johnson.* Washington, D.C.: Government Printing Office, 1969.

Ng, Franklin, ed. *The History and Immigration of Asian Americans.* New York: Garland, 1998.

Ngai, Mae M. "American Orientalism." *Reviews in American History* 28 (2000), 408–15.

——. *Impossible Subjects: Illegal Aliens and the Making of Modern America.* Princeton: Princeton University Press, 2004.

Nguyen, Hoang Tan. "The Resurrection of Brandon Lee: The Making of a Gay Asian American Porn Star." *Porn Studies,* ed. Linda Williams. Durham: Duke University Press, 2004. 223–70.

Nguyen, Mimi Thi. "Bruce Lee I Love You: Discourses of Race and Masculinity in the Queer Superstardom of JJ Chinois." *Alien Encounters: Popular Culture in Asian America,* ed. Mimi Thi Nguyen and Thuy Linh Nguyen Tu. Durham: Duke University Press, 2007. 271–304.

Nguyen, Tram Quang. "Caring for the Soul of our Community: Vietnamese Youth Activism in the 1960s and Today." *Asian Americans: The Movement and the Moment,* ed. Steve Louie and Glenn Omatsu. Los Angeles: UCLA Asian American Studies Center Press, 2001. 285–304.

Nixon, Richard. *No More Vietnams.* New York: Arbor House, 1985.

Norris, Margot. "Military Censorship and the Body Count in the Persian Gulf War." *Cultural Critique* 19 (Fall 1991), 223–45.

——. "Modernism and Vietnam: Francis Ford Coppola's *Apocalypse Now.*" *Modern Fiction Studies* 44.3 (1998), 730–66.

Oliver, Kendrick. *The My Lai Massacre in American History and Memory.* Manchester: Manchester University Press, 2006.

Omatsu, Glenn, ed. *Salute to the 60s and 70s: The Legacy of the San Francisco State Strike.* Special issue of *Amerasia Journal* 15.1 (1989).

Omi, Michael, and Howard Winant. *Racial Formation in the United States from the 1960s to the 1990s.* 2nd ed. New York: Routledge, 1994.

Ongiri, Amy Abugo. "Bruce Lee in the Ghetto Connection: Kung Fu Theater and African Americans Reinventing Culture at the Margins." *East Main Street: Asian American Popular Culture,* ed. Shilva Davé, LeiLani Nishime, and Tasha G. Oren. New York: New York University Press, 2005. 249–61.

——. " 'He Wanted to Be Just Like Bruce Lee': African Americans, Kung Fu Theater and Cultural Exchange at the Margins." *Journal of Asian American Studies* 5.1 (2002), 31–40.

Oropeza, Lorena. *¡Raza Sí! ¡Guerra No! Chicano Protest and Patriotism during the Viet Nam War Era.* Berkeley: University of California Press, 2005.

Ostroff, Roberta. *Fire in the Wind: The Life of Dickey Chapelle*. New York: Ballantine Books, 1992.

Pagán, Eduardo Obregón. *Murder at the Sleepy Lagoon: Zoot Suits, Race, and Riot in Wartime L.A.* Chapel Hill: University of North Carolina Press, 2003.

Paletz, David L., and Robert Dunn. "Press Coverage of Civil Disorders: A Case Study of Winston-Salem, 1967." *Public Opinion Quarterly* 33.3 (1969), 328–45.

Palmer, Bill, Karen Palmer, and Ric Meyers, eds. *The Encyclopedia of Martial Arts Movies*. Metuchen, N.J.: Scarecrow Press, 1995.

Palumbo-Liu, David. *Asian/America: Historical Crossings of a Racial Frontier*. Stanford: Stanford University Press, 1999.

Pham, Vu. "Antedating and Anchoring Vietnamese America: Toward a Vietnamese American Historiography." *Amerasia Journal* 29.1 (2003), 137–52.

Pilcher, Susan L. "Justice without a Blindfold: Criminal Proceedings and the Alien Defendant." *Arkansas Law Review* 50 (1997), 269–333.

Pisters, Patricia. *The Matrix of Visual Culture: Working with Deleuze in Film Theory*. Stanford: Stanford University Press, 2003.

Polner, Murray. *No Victory Parades: The Return of the Vietnam Veteran*. New York: Holt, Rinehart and Winston, 1971.

Powell, Irina. "Japanese Writer in Vietnam: The Two Wars of Kaikō Ken." *Modern Asian Studies* 32.1 (1998): 219–44.

Prashad, Vijay. *Everybody Was Kung Fu Fighting: Afro-Asian Connections and the Myth of Cultural Purity*. Boston: Beacon Press, 2001.

Prince, Stephen. *Savage Cinema: Sam Peckinpah and the Rise of Ultraviolent Movies*. Austin: University of Texas Press, 1998.

Rabinowitz, Lauren, and Susan Jeffords. Introduction to *Seeing through the Media: The Persian Gulf War*, ed. Susan Jeffords and Lauren Rabinowitz. New Brunswick, N.J.: Rutgers University Press, 1994. 1–18.

Rafael, Vicente L. *White Love and Other Events in Filipino History*. Durham: Duke University Press, 2000.

Rao, Radhika. "Property, Privacy, and the Human Body." *Boston University Law Review* 80 (April 2000), 359–460.

Rayns, Tony. "Bruce Lee: Narcissism and Nationalism." *A Study of the Hong Kong Martial Arts Film, Catalog of the Fourth Hong Kong International Film Festival*. Hong Kong: Urban Council, 1980. 110–12.

Redfield, Marc. "Imagi-Nation: The Imagined Community and the Aesthetics of Mourning." *Diacritics* 29.4 (1999), 58–83.

Reitan, Ruth. *The Rise and Decline of an Alliance: Cuba and African American Leaders in the 1960s*. East Lansing: Michigan State University Press, 1999.

Rimbaud, Arthur. *Rimbaud: Complete Works, Selected Letters*. Trans. Wallace Fowlie. Chicago: University of Chicago Press, 1966.

Rodowick, D. N. *The Difficulty of Difference: Psychoanalysis, Sexual Difference, and Film Theory*. New York: Routledge, 1991.

——. *Gilles Deleuze's Time Machine*. Durham: Duke University Press, 1997.

Roediger, David. "Gook: The Short History of an Americanism." *Monthly Review* 43.10 (1992), 50–54.

Rogin, Michael Paul. *Subversive Genealogy: The Politics and Art of Herman Melville*. New York: Alfred A. Knopf, 1983.

Rorty, Amélie Oksenberg. "The Social and Political Sources of Akrasia." *Ethics* 107.4 (1997), 644–57.

Rumbaut, Ruben G. "Vietnamese, Laotian, and Cambodian Americans." *Asian Americans: Contemporary Trends and Issues*, ed. Pyong Gap Min. 2nd ed. Thousand Oaks, Calif.: Pine Forge Press, 2006. 262–89.

Rutledge, Paul James. *The Vietnamese Experience in America*. Bloomington: Indiana University Press, 1992.

Rydell, Robert. *All the World's a Fair: Visions of Empire at American International Expositions, 1879–1916*. Chicago: University of Chicago Press, 1984.

Said, Edward. *Orientalism*. New York: Vintage Books, 1978.

Saunders, Kevin W. *Violence as Obscenity: Limiting the Media's First Amendment Protection*. Durham: Duke University Press, 1996.

Savran, David. *Taking It Like a Man: White Masculinity, Masochism, and Contemporary American Culture*. Princeton: Princeton University Press, 1998.

Saxton, Alexander. *The Indispensable Enemy: Labor and the Anti-Chinese Movement in California*. Berkeley: University of California Press, 1971.

Scarry, Elaine. "Consent and the Body: Injury, Departure, and Desire." *New Literary History* 21.4 (1990), 867–96.

Schaefer, Eric. "*Bold! Daring! Shocking! True!*" *A History of Exploitation Films, 1919–1959*. Durham: Duke University Press, 1999.

Schaefer, Richard T., ed. *Racial and Ethnic Groups*. New York: Prentice Hall, 2002.

Schauer, Fredrick. *Free Speech: A Philosophical Inquiry*. Cambridge: Cambridge University Press, 1982.

Schlesinger, Arthur, Jr. *Violence: America in the Sixties*. New York: Signet Books, 1968.

Scott, Wilbur J. *The Politics of Readjustment: Vietnam Veterans since the War*. New York: Aldine de Gruyter, 1993.

——. "PTSD in DSM-III: A Case in the Politics of Diagnosis and Disease." *Social Problems* 37.3 (1990), 294–310.

Scruggs, Jan C., and Joel L. Swerdlow. *To Heal a Nation: The Vietnam Veterans Memorial*. New York: Harper and Row, 1985.

Shatan, Chaim F. "The Grief of Soldiers: Vietnam Combat Veterans' Self-Help Movement." *American Journal of Orthopsychiatry* 43.4 (1973), 640–53.

Shaviro, Steven. *The Cinematic Body*. Minneapolis: University of Minnesota Press, 1993.

Shibusawa, Naoko. *America's Geisha Ally: Reimagining the Japanese Enemy*. Cambridge: Harvard University Press, 2006.

Shun, Inoue. "The Invention of the Martial Arts: Kano Jigoro and Kodokan Judo." *The*

Mirror of Modernity: Invented Traditions of Modern Japan, ed. Stephen Vlastos. Berkeley: University of California Press, 1998. 163–73.

Silverman, Kaja. *The Acoustic Mirror: The Female Voice in Psychoanalysis and Cinema*. Bloomington: University of Indiana Press, 1988.

———. *Male Subjectivity at the Margins*. New York: Routledge, 1992.

Simpson, Caroline Chung. *An Absent Presence: Japanese Americans in Postwar American Culture, 1945–1960*. Durham: Duke University Press, 2001.

Skinner, James. *The Cross and the Cinema: The Legion of Decency and the National Catholic Office for Motion Pictures, 1933–1970*. Westport, Conn.: Praeger, 1993.

Sledge, Michael. *Soldier Dead: How We Recover, Identify, Bury, and Honor Our Military Fallen*. New York: Columbia University Press, 2005.

Slotkin, Richard. *Gunfighter Nation: The Myth of the Frontier in Twentieth-Century America*. New York: Atheneum, 1992.

———. "Myth and the Production of History." *Ideology and Classic American Literature*, ed. Sacvan Bercovitch and Myra Jehlen. New York: Cambridge University Press, 1986. 70–90.

———. *Regeneration through Violence: The Mythology of the American Frontier, 1600–1860*. Middletown, Conn.: Wesleyan University Press, 1973.

Smith, Henry Nash. *Virgin Land: The American West as Symbol and Myth*. 1950; reprint Cambridge: Harvard University Press, 1970.

Smith, Julian. *Looking Away: Hollywood and Vietnam*. New York: Charles Scribner's Sons, 1975.

Sobchack, Vivian. "Inscribing Ethical Space: Ten Propositions on Death, Representation, and Documentary." *Carnal Thoughts: Embodiment and Moving Image Culture*. Berkeley: University of California Press, 2004. 226–57.

Stacewicz, Richard. *Winter Soldiers: An Oral History of the Vietnam Veterans Against the War*. New York: Twayne, 1997.

Stephens, Mitchell. *A History of News: From the Drum to the Satellite*. New York: Viking, 1988.

Stoler, Ann Laura. *Race and the Education of Desire: Foucault's History of Sexuality and the Colonial Order of Things*. Durham: Duke University Press, 1995.

Sturken, Marita. *Tangled Memories: The Vietnam War, the AIDS Epidemic, and the Politics of Remembering*. Berkeley: University of California Press, 1997.

Sugrue, Thomas. *The Origins of the Urban Crisis: Race and Inequality in Postwar Detroit*. Princeton: Princeton University Press, 1996.

Suid, Lawrence H. *Guts and Glory: The Making of the American Military Image in Film*. Revised ed. Lexington: University Press of Kentucky, 2002.

Sussman, Gerald. "Bulls in the (Indo)China Shop: Coppola's 'Vietnam' Revisited." *Journal of Popular Film and Television* 20.1 (1992), 24–28.

Suttmeier, Bruce. "Seeing Past Destruction: Trauma and History in Kaikō Takeshi." *Positions* 15.3 (2007), 457–86.

Takaki, Ronald. *Strangers from a Different Shore: A History of Asian Americans*. New York: Penguin, 1989.

Tasker, Yvonne. *Spectacular Bodies: Gender, Genre and the Action Cinema*. London: Routledge, 1993.

Taylor, Clyde., ed. *Vietnam and Black America: An Anthology of Protest and Resistance*. Garden City, N.Y.: Anchor Press, 1973.

Teo, Stephen. *Hong Kong Cinema: The Extra Dimensions*. London: British Film Institute, 1997.

Terry, Wallace, II. "Bringing the War Home." *Vietnam and Black America: An Anthology of Protest and Resistance*, ed. Clyde Taylor. Garden City, N.Y.: Anchor Press, 1973. 200–219.

Thomä, Helmut, and Neil Cheshire. "Freud's Nachträglichkeit and Strachey's 'Deferred Action': Trauma, Constructions and the Direction of Causality." *International Review of Psycho-analysis* 18 (1991), 407–27.

Thomas, Bruce. *Bruce Lee: Fighting Spirit*. Berkeley: Frog, 1994.

Torgovnick, Marianna. *Primitive Passions: Men, Women, and the Quest for Ecstasy*. Chicago: University of Chicago Press, 1998.

Torres, Sasha. *Black, White, and in Color: Television and Black Civil Rights*. Princeton: Princeton University Press, 2003.

Trinh, Minh-ha T. *Woman Native Other*. Bloomington: Indiana University Press, 1989.

Tuan, Mia. *Forever Foreigners or Honorary Whites? The Asian Ethnic Experience Today*. New Brunswick, N.J.: Rutgers University Press, 1998.

Turner, Fred. *Echoes of Combat: The Vietnam War in American Memory*. New York: Anchor Books, 1996.

Tuttle, William. *Race Riot: Chicago in the Red Summer of 1919*. Urbana: University of Illinois Press, 1970.

Tyson, Timothy B. *Radio Free Dixie: Robert F. Williams and the Roots of Black Power*. Chapel Hill: University of North Carolina Press, 1999.

U.S. Bureau of the Census. *We the Americans: Asians*. Washington, D.C.: Government Printing Office, 1993.

Uyematsu, Amy. "The Emergence of Yellow Power in America." *Roots: An Asian American Reader*, ed. Amy Tachiki, Eddie Wong, Franklin Odo, and Buck Wong. Los Angeles: UCLA Asian American Studies Center, 1971. 9–13.

Varon, Jeremy. *Bringing the War Home: The Weather Underground, the Red Army Faction, and Revolutionary Violence in the Sixties and Seventies*. Berkeley: University of California Press, 2004.

Vietnam Veterans Against the War. *The Winter Soldier Investigation: An Inquiry into American War Crimes*. Boston: Beacon Press, 1972.

Virilio, Paul. *War and Cinema: The Logistics of Perception*. Trans. Patrick Camiller. London: Verso, 1989.

Walker, Daniel. *Rights in Conflict: The Violent Confrontation of Demonstrators and Police in the*

Parks and Streets of Chicago during the Week of the Democratic National Convention of 1968. New York: Bantam Books, 1968.

Wang, Wayne. *Chan Is Missing: A Film.* Honolulu: Bamboo Ridge Press, 1984.

Wei, William. *The Asian American Movement.* Philadelphia: Temple University Press, 1993.

Wells, Tom. *The War Within: America's Battle over Vietnam.* Berkeley: University of California Press, 1994.

Wertham, Fredric. *Seduction of the Innocent.* New York: Rinehart, 1954.

Westheider, James. *Fighting on Two Fronts: African Americans and the Vietnam War.* New York: New York University Press, 1997.

Wexler, Laura. *Tender Violence: Domestic Visions in an Age of U.S. Imperialism.* Chapel Hill: University of North Carolina Press, 2000.

Wheeler, Elizabeth A. "More Than the Western Sky: Watts on Television, August 1965." *Journal of Film and Video* 54.2–3 (2002): 11–26.

Williams, Linda. *Hard Core: Power, Pleasure, and the "Frenzy of the Visible."* Revised ed. Berkeley: University of California Press, 1999.

——. "Melodrama Revised." *Refiguring American Film Genres*, ed. Nick Browne. Berkeley: University of California Press, 1998. 42–88.

——. *Playing the Race Card: Melodramas of Black and White from Uncle Tom to O. J. Simpson.* Princeton: Princeton University Press, 2001.

——. *Screening Sex.* Durham: Duke University Press, 2008.

Williams, Raymond. *Keywords: A Vocabulary of Culture and Politics.* New York: Oxford University Press, 1976.

Williams, Robert F. *Negroes with Guns.* 1962; reprint Detroit: Wayne State University, 1998.

Wong, Eugene Franklin. *On Visual Media Racism: Asians in the American Motion Pictures.* New York: Arno Press, 1978.

Wong, K. Scott. *Americans First: Chinese Americans and the Second World War.* Cambridge: Harvard University Press, 2005.

Wong, Morrison G. "Post-1965 Asian Immigrants: Where Do They Come from, Where Are They Now, and Where Are They Going?" *The History and Immigration of Asian Americans*, ed. Franklin Ng. New York: Garland, 1998. 202–20.

Wong, Sau-ling Cynthia. *Reading Asian American Literature: From Necessity to Extravagance.* Princeton: Princeton University Press, 1993.

Wu, Frank H. *Yellow: Race in America beyond Black and White.* New York: Basic Books, 2002.

Yengoyan, Aram A. "Shaping and Reshaping the Tasaday: A Question of Cultural Identity." *Journal of Asian Studies* 50.3 (1991), 565–73.

Young, Allan. *The Harmony of Illusions: Inventing Post-Traumatic Stress Disorder.* Princeton: Princeton University Press, 1995.

Young, Cynthia. *Soul Power: Culture, Radicalism, and the Making of a U.S. Third World Left.* Durham: Duke University Press, 2006.

Young, Marilyn B. *The Vietnam Wars 1945–1990*. New York: Harper Collins, 1991.

Yu, Henry. *Thinking Orientals: Migration, Contact and Exoticism in Modern America*. Oxford: Oxford University Press, 2001.

Zhou, Min. "Are Asian Americans Becoming White?" *Contexts* 3.1 (2004), 29–37.

Zia, Helen. *Asian American Dreams: The Emergence of an American People*. New York: Farrar, Straus, and Giroux, 2000.

belatedness. See *Nachträglichkeit*

Benjamin, Walter, 7, 284 n. 18

Bergson, Henri-Louis, 89

Berlant, Lauren, 12

Berry, Chris, 237

Bhabha, Homi, 16

Big Boss, The. See Fists of Fury (aka The Big Boss) (1971)

Billy Jack (1971), 30, 181–84, 186, 240, 252

Black Belt Jones (1974), 203

Black Belt magazine, 178–80, 182, 250

blackface, 10, 71, 251

Black Panther Party (BPP), 49, 105, 201, 245; opposition to Vietnam War and, 64, 66, 68, 70–72, 302 n. 76

blaxploitation films, 26, 199, 203, 220, 232–33

Block, Alex Ben, 175, 225

"Blood Sunday" (Selma), 55

Bloom, Verna, 47

Bonanza, 236–37

Bontoc Eulogy (1995), 159

Boys in Company C, The (1978), 29, 129, 141, 143–48, 163, 169

Braddock: Missing in Action III (1988), 265

Breakfast at Tiffany's, 235–36

Bronson, Charles, 236, 250–51

Brown, Bill, 178, 244

Browne, Malcolm, 81, 297 n. 15

Brownmiller, Susan, *Against Our Will: Men, Women, and Rape*, 202–3

Bruce Lee Fights Back from the Grave (1976), 221, 318 n. 28

Bruce Lee: The Legend (1977), 220, 319 n. 46

Buddhism, 26, 81, 114, 190, 206, 265, 314 n. 52

Bush, George H. W., 1–2, 11

Butler, Judith, 12, 14

Calley, William, 93, 98–100, 126, 166, 182, 299 n. 41. *See also* My Lai massacre

Cambodia, 1, 3, 21, 113, 115, 157–59, 162, 266, 268, 310 n. 82

Carmichael, Stokeley, 66, 68, 70–71

Carradine, David, 192, 194, 313 n. 45, 314 n. 51

Carter, Jimmy, 148, 166

Caruth, Cathy, 42, 121, 299 n. 50

Catonsville Nine, 49

censorship, 4, 7, 23–24, 145, 287 n. 63

Chan, Charlie, 107, 175, 193–94, 236–37, 272, 276, 312 n. 17, 314 n. 47

Chan, Jackie, 221, 243, 319 n. 37

Chan, Sucheng, 20, 104

Chan Is Missing (1982), 31, 268, 270–72, 275

Chapelle, Dickey, 81, 297 n. 15

Cheng, Anne, 12, 170

Chiao, Hsiung-Ping, 215

Chiba, Sonny, 183, 189, 207

Chicago, as film setting, 144

Chicago Eight, trial of, 49

Chicago Race Riots (1919), 53, 292 n. 55

Chin, Frank, 194–95, 197–98, 250, 274, 321 n. 7. *See also Year of the Dragon, The* (1974 play)

Chin, Vincent, 112, 280. *See also Who Killed Vincent Chin?*

China, 10, 19, 66, 107, 174, 179, 234, 276; diaspora and, 210, 232, 249; martial arts and, 175, 178, 191, 193–94, 206, 210–11, 243, 316 n. 1, 319 n. 45. *See also* Hong Kong

Chinese Americans, 19, 109, 144, 178–80, 193, 232–33, 235, 239, 244–47, 250, 301 n. 68, 314 n. 48; Chinatown and, 25, 110, 179, 210, 266–73, 276; in nineteenth century, 18, 53, 194–98, 274, 292 n. 55

Chinese Connection, The (aka *Fist of Fury*) (1972), 211, 224–25, 229–30, 232, 234, 244, 246, 317 n. 16

Chow, David, 191, 313 n. 45

Chow, Raymond. *See* Golden Harvest
Choy, Sam, 107–8, 303 n. 91
Cimino, Michael, 131–32, 135, 137–38,
   154, 267, 272–73, 275–76
civil rights movement, 20, 22–28, 33–
   38, 53–68, 196, 200–203, 252, 262,
   267
Civil War, 23, 48, 54, 60, 257
Clark, Jim, 56, 63
Cleaver, Eldridge, 66
Cleopatra Jones (1973), 26, 203
Clones of Bruce Lee, The (1977), 221, 318
   n. 28
Clouse, Robert, 214, 222, 224–26
Clover, Carol, 134
cold war, 19, 45, 67, 78, 103, 156, 279,
   304 n. 99
colonialism, 10, 16, 18–21, 29, 154–62,
   235, 244
Coming Home (1978), 29, 129, 141, 143,
   148–54, 167, 252
Connor, Bull, 63
Conrad, Joseph, 155
continuity, 211–12, 216, 223–24, 226–33
Cooper, James Fenimore, 160
Coppola, Francis Ford, 154–62
Cosmatos, George, 265
Counter Intelligence Program (COIN-
   TELPRO), 72, 296 n. 109
Cronkite, Walter, 81
Cuba, 66, 71, 295 n. 95, 296 n. 106
Cumings, Bruce, 133

Daley, Richard, 47
Davis, Peter, 118, 123
Davis, Rennie, 48–49
Days of Rage, 28, 49
Deacons for Defense, 200
de Antonio, Emile, 297 n. 15
death drive, 46, 186–87, 262
DeKoven, Marianne, 180
Deep Thrust—Hand of Death (aka Lady

Whirlwind) (1972), 30, 184–86, 187–
   90, 192–93, 195, 217
Deer Hunter, The (1978), 8, 27, 127, 129–
   41, 148; *Apocalypse Now* and, 154–55,
   160; *Billy Jack* and, 181, 184; *Coming
   Home* and, 151–52; *Good Guys Wear
   Black* and, 252, 254; *Go Tell the Spartans*
   and, 162–63, 166–67; *Rambo: First
   Blood Part II* and, 256, 265; *Year of the
   Dragon* and, 272, 275
Desser, David, 19, 25, 175–76, 234, 251
Deleuze, Gilles, 14–16, 20, 78, 105–6,
   230, 286 n. 35, 319 n. 42. *See also* con-
   tinuity; movement-image; sensory-
   motor schema; time-image
Deloria, Philip, 159
Democratic National Convention (1968),
   36, 39, 46–47, 49, 51, 61, 302 n. 76
Desser, David, 175–76, 251
Detroit, 99, 103, 204, 280, 300 n. 59; as
   film setting, 240; 1967 riots in, 28, 48,
   57, 59–61, 67, 71, 292 n. 56
Diem, Ngo Diem. *See* Ngo Dinh Diem
Dinh Phuc Le, 113
disability, 22, 149–54
Downes, Alan, 113, 118–19
Dragon: The Bruce Lee Story (1993), 228,
   235
Du Bois, W. E. B., 66

Eastwood, Clint, 236, 250–51
Eisenhower, Dwight D., 54, 288 n. 1
Eisenhower, Milton, 34, 288 n. 1
Eisenhower Commission. *See* National
   Commission on the Causes and Pre-
   vention of Violence
Eisenstein, Sergei, 222, 223
Elegant, Robert, 75–76
Eliot, T. S., 155
El Salvador, U.S. military involvement in,
   76
Eng, David, 195

Enter the Dragon (1973), 30, 184, 203, 210–22, 224, 236, 252, 255; non-Asian identifications with, 232, 234, 245, 247; as parodied in Kentucky Fried Movie, 239–40

Espiritu, Yen Le, 104, 267

Eyes on the Prize II: America at the Racial Crossroads (1990), 57, 60–61

Federal Communications Commission, 205, 316 n. 87

Faas, Horst, 115, 298 n. 32

feminism, 10, 23–24, 141, 148, 151–54, 174, 198–203, 279

Feng, Peter, 270

Finishing the Game: The Search for a New Bruce Lee (2007), 223

First Blood (1982 film), 254–56, 262–64

First Blood (1972 novel), 28, 35–38, 44–46, 50–51, 53, 63, 252; as transformed in Kotcheff's film, 73, 127, 262

Fist of Fury. See Chinese Connection, The

Fists of Fury (aka The Big Boss) (1971), 211, 214, 216, 234, 237, 312 n. 30, 316 n. 2

FitzGerald, Frances, 180

Five Fingers of Death (aka King Boxer) (1972), 26, 177, 184, 193, 209

Floyd, Randy, 118–22

Fogelson, Robert, 56

Fonda, Jane, 150–53, 166, 308 n. 50

Fong, Benson, 193

Fort Hood Forty-Three, 61, 293 n. 77

Fort Hood Three, 67, 295 n. 97

Foster, Hal, 284 n. 18

Foucault, Michel, 7, 142, 180, 185, 187

442nd Regimental Combat Team, 107, 236–37, 277, 303 n. 86

Franklin, H. Bruce, 94, 257, 285 n. 32, 299 n. 44

Freeman, David, 177–78

Freud, Sigmund, 8, 12–16, 44, 103, 121,

170, 176, 188, 259. See also beating fantasy; primal scene; trauma

Fu, Poshek, 234

Fuentes, Marlon, 159

Fulbeck, Kip, 239–40

Full Metal Jacket (1987), 118, 144, 254

Fu Manchu, 146, 194, 237, 269, 273

Furie, Sidney. See Boys in Company C, The

Furutani, Warren, 110–12

Game of Death (1978 film), 30, 212–13, 222–31, 233, 242, 247, 317 n. 14, 317 n. 16; Return of the Dragon and, 250

Game of Death (1991 film), 239

Garwood, Robert, 258

GI resistance movement, 67

Gitlin, Todd, 44, 53

going native, 50, 154–62, 173, 181, 264

Gold, Ted, 290 n. 25

Golden Harvest, 128–29, 184, 224, 252

Good Guys Wear Black (1978), 250–54, 263

gook: as economic threat, 164; as syndrome, 98–100, 103, 110, 264, 280

Gordy, Berry, 244

Go Tell the Spartans (1978), 29, 129, 141, 162–63, 167–70, 239

Green Berets, 45, 51, 127, 132, 137, 157, 181–82

Greenlee, Sam, The Spook Who Sat by the Door, 71

Guattari, Félix, 14–15, 105

Guevara, Che, 71

Gulf of Tonkin Resolution, 38, 284 n. 23

Gunning, Tom, 7

Haeberle, Ronald, 76, 92–97, 299 n. 41. See also My Lai massacre

Halberstam, David, 76

Hall, Delos, 47–48

Hallin, Daniel, 38, 296 n. 8

Han, Bong Soo, 181, 240

hapkido, 175, 181, 183, 184, 224

National Advisory Commission on Civil Disorders (Kerner Commission), 57

National Commission on the Causes and Prevention of Violence, 33–35, 44, 54

National Guard, 35, 46–47, 54, 59, 63, 70, 115, 293 n. 70

National Liberation Front (NLF), 62–63, 66, 160

National Mobilization to End the War in Vietnam (Mobe), 46, 64

Native Americans, 9–10, 14, 98–99, 128, 181–82, 262, 265, 300 n. 54; American Indian Movement and, 20, 23; Filipinos compared with, 159–61, 309 n. 72

Newark riots (1967), 36, 48, 57

New York City, 44, 67, 71, 107–8, 110, 166, 183, 191, 201, 204; as film setting, 244, 272

Ngai, Mae, 18

Ngo Dinh Diem, 81, 114–15

Ngo Dinh Nhu (Madame Nhu), 115, 304 n. 108

Ng See-Yuen, 243

Nguyen Ngoc Loan: 81, 84–85, 88–89, 91; effort to deport, 130, 162, 164–67, 170–71, 253. See also "Saigon Execution"

Nguyen Tan Hoang, 217, 317 n. 19

Nguyen Thi Xi, 117

1967 Detroit Riots: A Community Speaks (2003), 61

Nineteen Sixty-Eight: A Look for New Meanings (1978), 39–40, 44

Nixon, Richard, 2, 257, 308 n. 50; Vietnam veterans and, 102, 291 n. 45, 301 n. 63; visit to China of, 175, 179; "War on Drugs" and, 144–45

No Hop Sing, No Bruce Lee: What Do You Do When None of Your Heroes Look Like You? (1998), 236, 238

No Retreat, No Surrender (1986), 241–45, 278

Norris, Chuck, 26, 31, 178, 225, 249–55, 259–60, 262, 264–65

No Vietnamese Ever Called Me Nigger (1968), 67–68

obscenity, 22–24, 90–92, 115–16, 287 n. 64; as pornography of violence, 23, 45, 85, 185–89. See also oriental obscene

Oh, Soon-Tek, 253, 321 n. 7

Okamoto, Vincent, 107

Oliver, Kendrick, 93, 94, 102

Omi, Michael, 17

Ongiri, Amy Abugo, 205

Ono, Shin'ya, 49

orientalism, 21, 26, 49, 63, 156, 177–80, 190, 193–95, 198, 206–7, 240–41, 244–45, 256, 316 n. 1; American, 16–19, 162, 167; African American, 64–66

oriental obscene, 10–22, 25–31, 37–38, 51, 77–78, 171, 174, 177, 184, 210, 212–13, 233, 241, 251–54, 264, 266–68, 276, 279–81

Palumbo-Liu, David, 18, 164

Paris Peace Accords, 174, 252, 258, 284 n. 23

Pastore, John, 193

Peckinpah, Sam, 138, 216

Persian Gulf War, 1–7, 11, 284 n. 23

Petersen, William, 277–78

Pham, Vu, 105

Phan Can Cuong, 117

phantasmatic, 13–14; racial, 9–11, 15–17, 27, 78, 103, 121, 134, 280–81. See also beating fantasy; oriental obscene; primal scene

Phan Thanh Tam, 116, 119

Phan Thi Kim Phuc, 76, 113, 115–16, 119, 122–23. See also "Napalm Girl"

phenomenology, 15, 78–79, 83, 89, 184, 218

Philippines, 10, 21, 29, 104, 234, 266, 268, 309 n. 72, 311 n. 12; actors from, 145, 224; as filming location, 155–61; immigrants from, 3, 19, 268, 270–71
Phuc, Kim. *See* Phan Thi Kim Phuc
Plummer, John, 122–25
Post, Ted. See *Good Guys Wear Black*; *Go Tell the Spartans*
post-traumatic stress disorder (PTSD). *See* trauma
post-Vietnam syndrome, 93, 99, 102, 176, 300 n. 59, 301 n. 63
Prashad, Vijay, 199, 235
Presley, Elvis, 213–14, 251
primal scene, 13, 16, 28, 35–45, 51–52, 72–73, 79–80, 91–92, 135, 259, 289 n. 14
prisoners of war (POWs), 51, 81–92, 131–41, 257–66, 308 n. 50
projection, 9, 15, 45, 64, 108, 131
Project 100,000, 65

Rambo: First Blood Part II (1985), 1, 10, 73, 254–56, 260, 264–66, 277
Rambo III (1988), 265
Rayns, Tony, 217
Reagan, Ronald, 2, 255
realism, 24–27, 38, 138–39, 159, 215–16, 223–31, 276
Reasoner, Harry, 39
repetition compulsion, 8, 34, 73, 184, 186–89, 256
Republican National Convention (1968), 39, 288 n. 4
Return of the Dragon (aka *The Way of the Dragon*) (1972), 211, 218, 222, 224, 234, 245, 249–50, 252–53
Rhee, Bruce, 221, 318 n. 28
Rhee, Phillip, 236
Rheinstein, Fred, 58–59
Rippberger, Carl, 99–101
Rock Springs massacre (1885), 53, 292 n. 55

Rocky (1976), 241–42, 255, 320 n. 61
Rodowick, D. N., 106, 134
Roediger, David, 98
Rogin, Michael, 288 n. 4
Rubin, Jerry, 48–49. *See also* Yippies

Safer, Morley, 76, 306 n. 8
Said, Edward, 16–19, 63
Saigon, "fall of," 8, 128–29, 131, 139, 157, 163, 284 n. 23, 310 n. 82; Van Es's photograph of, 4–8, 22, 24
"Saigon Execution" (Adams photograph), 27, 29, 76, 80–93, 96, 113, 115, 125, 143, 184, 218, 227–28, 258, 298 n. 30, 298 n. 32; Asian American identity and, 103, 105; Nguyen Ngoc Loan and, 162, 166, 170; as reimagined in *The Deer Hunter*, 129–33, 135–40
San Francisco, 67, 210, 302 n. 76, 322 n. 42, 323 n. 50; as film setting; 252–53, 269–71
San Francisco State University, 20
Savran, David, 251
Saxon, John, 211, 234
Saywell, Shelley, 122
Scarry, Elaine, 142
Schlesinger, Arthur, Jr., 23
Schrader, Paul, 128
Schwarzenegger, Arnold, 255, 266
scientia aggressionis, 193, 203–4
screen memory, 35–38
Scruggs, Jan, *To Heal a Nation*, 102
Second World War, 18–19, 50, 167, 169, 193, 241, 252, 280, 291 n. 47, 300 n. 54, 301 n. 68, 321 n. 69; Deleuze and European cinema and, 15, 28, 79; effects of, in Asia, 30, 157, 178; film and, 127–28, 193, 261–62, 266, 314 n. 47; Japanese American internment in, 104, 106, 277–79, 288 n. 1, 300 n. 68; nonwhite soldiers in, 107, 201,

Sylvia Shin Huey Chong is associate professor
of film and Asian American studies in the English
Department and the Program in American Studies
at the University of Virginia.

Library of Congress Cataloging-in-Publication Data
Chong, Sylvia Shin Huey
The Oriental obscene : violence and racial fantasies in
the Vietnam era / Sylvia Shin Huey Chong.
   p. cm.
Includes bibliographical references and index.
ISBN 978-0-8223-4840-5 (cloth : alk. paper)
ISBN 978-0-8223-4854-2 (pbk. : alk. paper)
1. Vietnam War, 1961–1975—Motion pictures and the war.
2. Vietnam War, 1961–1975—Television and the war.
3. Vietnam War, 1961–1975—United States.
4. United States—Race relations—History—20th century.
5. Violence—United States—History—20th century.
I. Title.
DS557.73.C46 2012
791.43'658597043—dc23   2011021932